Red Hot Lies

Red Hot Lies

How Global Warming Alarmists Use Threats, Fraud, and Deception to Keep You Misinformed

Christopher C. Horner

Since 1947
REGNERY
PUBLISHING, INC.
An Eagle Publishing Company • Washington, DC

Cataloging-in-Publication data on file with the Library of
Congress

ISBN 978-1-59698-538-4

Published in the United States by
Regnery Publishing, Inc.
One Massachusetts Avenue, NW
Washington, DC 20001
www.regnery.com

Manufactured in the United States of America

10 9 8 7 6 5 4 3 2 1

Books are available in quantity for promotional or premium
use. Write to Director of Special Sales, Regnery Publishing,
Inc., One Massachusetts Avenue NW, Washington, DC 20001,
for information on discounts and terms or call (202) 216-0600.

CONTENTS

Greenpeace Steals My Trash

It was spring. Young men's hearts turned to fancy. And Greenpeace started stealing my trash.

I noticed that my garbage was getting collected much more efficiently than normal—and late the night before it was scheduled to go. I also noticed that soon, the media revealed a secret cabal I orchestrated from my basement. At least, that's how London's left-wing *Guardian* wrote the story, cobbled together from unrelated, offal-smeared pages plucked from my refuse. If I ever questioned the hippies' dedication to their cause, no more: in those steamy summer months of mystery trash abductions, I rededicated myself to strict obeisance of local requirements to collect the weekly output of my two large breed dogs.

"You too!?" howled the amused wife of a White House aide when we realized we both enjoyed the same, selectively hyper-efficient, midnight garbage service. Apparently Greenpeace was just certain that her husband, who in fact hardly spoke to me, was part of my cabal.

Soon, European Greenpeace franchises were issuing press releases in German about who had lunch with me in Brussels, and spinning phony tales to Spanish newspapers of secret meetings I supposedly had with pretty much anyone they found problematic.

I had arrived. If they would spend so much energy to, well, trash *me*, I must be important, right?

But I soon learned from others that this is standard operating procedure for the global warming industry—which regularly does much worse things. They have tried to ruin careers, blacklisted scientists, knowingly spread lies about dissenters, called for the imprisonment of skeptics, and used government pressure to cut off rivals' funding. One scientist has had the lug nuts on his wheels secretly loosened when publicly voicing his rejection of climate orthodoxy. Threats now regularly issue against individuals, and the broader idea of free thought and expression.

Which got me thinking: shouldn't the public know about this? Are these tactics consistent with the environmentalists' image as philanthropic, self-sacrificing, earth-lovers? Doesn't their desperation reflect a fundamental weakness in the truth of their arguments and the soundness of their proposals? Wouldn't the media expose such tactics by the other side?

Isn't it relevant to the debate about global warming that the alarmist side engages in this systematic campaign consisting of intimidation and threats, wheels falling off cars, abuses being inflicted on schoolchildren, demands of censorship, revising history, and telling flat-out lies?

Well, yes. People should know. And now they will.

CHAPTER 1

Media on a Mission

Lies, Distortions, Cover-Ups, and the Reporters Who Push Them

"I believe it is appropriate to have an over-representation of factual presentations on how dangerous it is."

Al Gore

A STRANGE THING HAPPENED RECENTLY. A shark ate a kangaroo. Here's the odd part: the media didn't blame "global warming."[1]

Today's press breathlessly touts any occurrence—no matter how tenuously connected to the weather—as the result of Man-made global warming. A 2007 Reason Foundation paper aptly summarized the media coverage:

> Global warming causes everything. A brief perusal of stories from the last several years reveals that warming has been blamed for a huge array of problems, including increased teenage drinking, stray cats, poison ivy, and sharks. More seriously, global warming has also been blamed for widespread malnutrition and outbreaks of disease, Hurricane Katrina, and the crisis in Darfur.[2]

Don't forget impoverished fashion houses,[3] hard times for Bulgarian brothels,[4] and attacks by big cats.[5] It causes summer frost in Africa[6] and freezing penguin chicks,[7] poorly rising bread dough,[8] "makes island kids bony, stunted,"[9] contaminates transfusion blood,[10] and causes more landslides,[11] and stronger earthquakes.[12] It caused the 2008 salmonella outbreak,[13] and an increase in kidney stones.[14] Blogger William Briggs compiled media assertions of other global warming horrors: "Lizards will undergo sex changes,[15] there will be 'waves of rape,'[16] a rash of camel deaths will occur,[17] the Earth will spin faster[18] (hold on!), and, worst and most frightening of all, there will be an increase in lawyers[19] (to handle all the 'who's fault is it?' litigation)."[20] Oh yeah, it will also cause giant Burmese pythons to colonize one-third of the United States.[21]

Why, they have even blamed the sacking of English football coaches on global warming,[22] though sometimes the mainstream media leave it to the popular scientific outlets to warn us of outcomes like "Global warming poses deaf threat to tropical fish."[23] After all, they don't want to look foolish.

INSTITUTIONALIZED HYSTERIA

The establishment media organs go to mind-bending lengths to carry water for the alarmist industry of which they clearly are now part. They regularly hype, and even repeat as gospel, claims that are unsubstantiated or simply unsupportable were they to ask around, while refusing to respect or acknowledge the preponderance of recent studies contradicting the cries of alarm. They refuse to correct mistakes—when these errors are on the side of alarmism—or report on alarmist scientists being forced to correct themselves, even when scandalous. But when exposure of these scandals requires rehabilitation of their allies, stories pour forth minimizing the revelations.

Everyone down to *Sports Illustrated* and *Golf Digest* weighs in, while a still-skeptical public leaves the industry bible, *Columbia Journalism Review*, to navel-gaze about "why the media have failed to explain climate change in a way the public 'gets.'"[24] Conclusion? One Max Boycoff pleads that "it's not that balanced reporting needs to be shunned when addressing climate-change issues . . . . It just needs to be used much more carefully." He even laments, "To make matters worse, the global-warming stories that do make it onto the front page tend to concern the most contentious aspects of climate science." That is, the front page of news sections should be reserved, or at least have substantial portions set aside, for non-news scare stories. Actual discourse, if one must allow it, should be shuffled off to less prominent placement.

Sure enough, in the ultimate act of desperation, they ban the opposing viewpoint from their outlets.[25] Consider *Time* magazine, which has over the past few years run a series of increasingly frantic alarmist cover stories which detail impending doom but without the slightest trace of an effort at balance.[26] When MSNBC interviewed Managing Editor Richard Stengel, he was at least honest about *Time*'s mission.

"One of the things that's needed in journalism," Stengel said, "is that you have to have a point of view about things. . . . You can't always just say 'on the one hand, on the other and you decide.' People trust us to make decisions. We're experts in what we do. So I thought, you know what, if we really feel strongly about something let's just say so."[27] So, *Time* editors "feel strongly" about new taxes in the name of the environment and expensive, climatically meaningless regimes in order to show the rest of the world the seriousness of our purpose. It's still a mystery what Stengel was talking about when he said "we're experts in what we do."

The flagship alarmist outlet, the *New York Times*, perfectly demonstrated its zealotry with its coverage of "dead zones" in the ocean. An editorial in March 2008 titled "Oceans at Risk" blamed "global warming" for these patches of low oxygen.[28] The *Seattle Post-Intelligencer*, located nearer the problem at issue although as a rule nearly as alarmist as the *Times*, revealed that such dead zones had appeared before—*forty years ago*, during the three-decades long cooling.[29]

Less alarming (or at least less useful) claims typically are of no interest. Little ink is spilled explaining how birds, fleas, and trees produce more CO_2 than humans,[30] or that cows' CO_2 and methane emissions dwarf those from autos.[31] *Well, silly, we aren't looking to regulate birds, trees, or fleas!*

The media have no use for realities such as how deaths and death rates from all extreme weather events have been dropping for decades in the U.S. as well as globally.[32] Further out of character would be discussing how society's wealth (precisely what their favored regulations threatens) empowers people to adapt if climate—as it constantly has for recorded history—changes.[33]

> "There is a clear attempt to establish truth not by scientific methods but by perpetual repetition."
>
> *Richard S. Lindzen, PhD*
> *Professor of Meteorology, MIT*

Although even the less ridiculous-sounding claims of global warming impacts, such as disappearing honeybees[34] and increased heart attacks[35] were soberly debunked, the debunking was largely ignored.[36] Similarly, the establishment press showed zero interest in covering a compendium of work by skeptical scientists undermining the "consensus" premise upon which Congress is seeking to make trillion-dollar decisions.[37]

When Republican U.S. senator James Inhofe produced a list of peer-reviewed work by more than 400 scientists countering the "consensus," the *Times* mentioned it only in a blog, where it was dismissed as "a distraction." But when forty-four Baptists, led by a 25-year-old seminarian, got really worried about Man-made climate change, it was a newsworthy development.[38]

The *Washington Post* gave page-16 treatment to a meeting of hundreds of "skeptics" in a piece offering alarmists plenty of space to criticize it—with name-calling only, and not one substantive remark[39]—but gave front-page, uncritical treatment the very next week to another in a series of claims by well-known alarmists that they've got a computer model saying that things will be much worse than previously thought.[40] So the media have an agenda, which justifies disparate treatment based upon what is said or who says it. Shocking, no?

GOOD, OLD FASHIONED WEATHER

These double-standards are legion: unseasonably warm weather is clear evidence of global warming, while exceptional cold is merely an anomaly. Warm weather and retreating glaciers are signs of warming; cool weather and advancing glaciers are signs of nothing. Oh, sure, occasionally cooling is proof of warming, such as when the *Washington Post* hilariously spun the *Old Farmers Almanac* projection of a cold 2008–2009 winter—the cooling to possibly continue to for decades.[41] It seems that this shows how warming has now made climate modeling very difficult, as shown by the fact that they keep modeling warming only to actually get cooling.

And, of course, it is crucial to unearth who funds the groups that dispute alarmism, or whose profits depend on resisting regulation; but who's funding the alarmists (say, for a $300 million campaign), and who would profit from a slew of new regulation or climate-directed subsidies—that's not news. Three years is a pattern...unless it is three years of cooling. Ten years of something is conclusive, unless during that period—such as is the case with the past decade—there has been no warming.

In early 2008, when confronted with more than three years of cooling, the media felt the need to discuss this "cold spell." *It's just a meaningless aberration in the face of a bigger picture—and any fool knows we are warming,* we were told. The *New York Times* suddenly found discrete weather events and temperatures not indicative of things to come. *Times* reporters located the phone numbers of some scientists who felt that weather was, well, weather, and not every blip of the thermometer foretells some irrevocable trend. These same sober scientists who were so "distracting" when they denied that past warming was part of an irreversible march, were now worth quoting. The cold trend, we learned, was "just good old fashioned weather."[42] This is the very same thing that they would have said about warm weather and storms had the *Times* sought to ask them during those episodes—which, of course, they didn't.

In an amazing fit of sobriety which was not to last, the *Times* decided that "if anything else is afoot—like some cooling related to sunspot cycles or slow shifts in ocean or atmospheric patterns that can influence temperatures—an array of scientists who have staked out differing positions on the overall threat of global warming agree that there is no way to pinpoint whether such a new force is at work." This paragraph belongs in every climate story but appears in almost none. This is the same line that "skeptics" rightly tout in the face of any such period of weather or discrete event; it is the alarmists who will admit it only in this very inconvenient situation. It was useful here because observations were contrary to the *Times'* agenda.

The media are clearly undone by such things. *Times* columnist Thomas Friedman, ABC's reliably absurd Bill Blakemore, the *Las Vegas Sun*, and *Times* editorialists, among others, immediately followed suit in one fashion or another, generally berating climate realists for seizing on the cooling for their cynical purposes as the warming industry and establishment media do every week. In the meantime, the calmer voices were then ignored until the next time they could be trotted out to assure the public that calamitous warming still awaited them.

EDITING THE RECORD

When the media forget their lines, they readily revert to form when slapped with a reminder by their green colleagues. For example, "Global Temperatures 'to decrease,'" read the April 4, 2008 head-line. Which lying shill for the oil industry was publishing this clap-trap? The British Broadcasting Corporation. BBC News environmental analyst Roger Harrabin was the author, and the quotation in the headline came from the head of the World Mete-orological Organization.[43]

Such outrageous lack of catastrophism by the BBC raised the ire of the pressure group "Campaign Against Climate Change." One of its activists, Jo Abess, wrote e-mails complaining to Harrabin, objecting to his article as a "piece of media that seems like it's been subject to spin or skepticism." God forbid a journalist apply an ounce of *skepticism*! Actually, she meant that by reporting unalarming news he was parroting climate skepticism and, in her complaint, she specifically instructed him to never quote skeptics. This non-scientist, with no apparent qualifications other than being a green pressure group agitator, railed to him about how non-scientists were distorting the debate. Yet the offensive quote in Harrabin's piece came neither from a skeptic nor a non-scientist, but the head of the WMO—parent of the IPCC—who happened to say something insufficiently gussied up with alarmist bells and whistles.

Abbess soon crowed about her dominance and released the communications which showed that Harrabin stood his ground for all of two e-mails, noting that to do what was rather menacingly demanded of him would make "people feel like debate is being censored which makes them v [sic] suspicious." He then caved, compliantly and radically altering the story and shooting a note to Abbess, that she should "have a look in 10 minutes and tell me you are happier. We have changed the headline and more."

And how. Activist Abbess had assailed Harrabin specifically for his accurate headline because some people only read headlines, so Harrabin changed the headline *several times*. The ever-dangerous "cooling" became "a dip in global warming" when Harrabin eliminated his third paragraph originally noting how there had been no increase in temperatures since 1998. That was intolerable to the censoring greens even though Harrabin still included misleading, alarmist boilerplate about the horrid future we nonetheless face. He recast it upon demand, dropping the reference to recent history except to note that 1998 was a record and that 2008 temps—predicted and on its way by that time to being a fourth straight year of cooling—"would still be way above average," followed by a prediction of future warming. As Tim Worstall of the Adam Smith Institute mocked in the aftermath, if the BBC had left the story as written, it "might make people think that the world has, umm, not been warming and might even have been cooling since 1998. Can't let the proles know the truth now, can we?"[44]

If you weren't checking on the piece every five minutes, though, you wouldn't have even suspected this extraordinary influence of a green pressure group in this article. Its time-stamp online never reflected that this was anything but the original piece. As the revision changed the import of the story it was not merely a "minor" edit, which is the only situation for which the BBC's internal rules allow that practice, and as the BBC insisted to *Nature* magazine.[45] This failure to acknowledge the edit with a new timestamp was indeed a "stealth edit" in violation of BBC policy expressly designed to avoid the "impli[cation]" that we are actively trying to hide what we are doing."[46] As discussed elsewhere in these pages this was by no means the only example of the BBC going back into its articles on global warming to change the substance in a way that flagrantly exposed their bias. Fortunately, Harrabin's entire pathetic exchange with CACC was obtained and posted in full by Australian Jennifer Marohasy on her wonderful blog, prompting the closest thing to an examination of the media's wretched dishonesty in its advocacy of the alarmist agenda.[47]

RUNNING FROM THE SUN

While Harrabin danced to the "Campaign Against Climate Change" tune, his BBC colleague Richard Black was having his own efforts on behalf of the warming industry exposed. Black informed BBC's readers about research he claimed "at the very least puts the cosmic ray theory, developed by Danish scientist Henrik Svensmark at the Danish National Space Center (DNSC), under very heavy pressure."[48]

Svensmark's idea was that—brace yourself for this—the sun has a major impact on global temperatures. He has revealed an amplification several times over of solar forcing of global temperatures, bringing the relationship between the sun's activity and temperatures into strong correlation. Specifically, increased solar activity (solar wind) strongly suppresses the intensity of cosmic rays. Given that cosmic rays increase cloud coverage, a more active sun means fewer clouds are formed and temperatures are warmer, and a less active sun allows more cloud formation leading to cooler temps.

Black's headline, "'No sun link' to climate change," was at least a good example of recycling—it was precisely what Black titled his attempt to discredit the same menace just a few months prior. Conserving electricity as well, on neither occasion is there any evidence that Black bothered writing or calling Svensmark, the scientist whose work he claimed was being debunked. Don't try to follow the logic; it takes years of journalism school to grasp. Had Black contacted Svensmark he would have been informed, among other things, that the work Black championed as debunking Svensmark actually did not claim "no sun link to climate change," but instead claimed that the process that Svensmark identified contributes perhaps as much as 25 percent of the warming.

Got that? Man contributes at the margins of an already marginal GHG and somehow drives climate; the sun, in an apparent least-case scenario, contributes 25 percent and is meaningless. Richard Black, desperate warrior in the fight against heliocentrism.

This obvious corruption of journalistic standards led to a minor uproar among the relevant parties, apparently prompting Black to go back into his article, well after he had gotten the mileage out of claiming to have shown Svensmark to be debunked, to then insert a comment by Svensmark. Keeping with apparent BBC standards if still in violation of their written code, he didn't append the piece to indicate the change but stuffed it in between two pre-existing comments by people hostile to Svensmark, while also beefing up other parts of his article, again after the fact.[49]

> **RIDDLE ME THIS**
>
> "The next time somebody in the media denies that there is media bias, ask how they explain the fact that there are at least a hundred stories about the shrinking arctic ice cap for every one about the expanding Antarctic ice cap, which has now grown to record size."
>
> *Columnist Thomas Sowell*

Clearly there is little the media won't do to earn the labels given its coverage as "climate porn"[50] and "storm porn,"[51] and otherwise affirm its key role in the alarmist industry.

When people like me point out this bias, our objections are decried as "menacing."[52] This comes from the same people who dismiss actual professional threats experienced by skeptics as the exaggerated product of loopy contrarians. But if you ask James Hansen to stick to science and not pretend he's a policy official, you're intimidating him. As such, none of the following should come as a surprise.

COOL TO THE FACTS

In December 2005, media outlets ran screaming with news that the Atlantic Ocean's winds would stop blowing, killing the Gulf Stream and the Jet Stream—a phenomenon called "thermohaline shutdown," the scenario at the heart of the movie *The Day After Tomorrow*.[53]

The Tyndall Centre's Mike Hulme (not a journalist) was about the only one who continued to follow the claims once contrary research shot the claim down. He wrote in the *Times of London*: "Eighteen months later, however, and unremarked by the media, two studies in equally reputable journals pointed out that such [the trend prompting that paper] was within the range of natural variability and may signify nothing at all."[54]

The double standard is everywhere. Federal courts ruled on two different climate-change-related cases in the same week, in early September 2007, both filed by alarmist plaintiffs, but with different results—and thus very different media coverage. When a circuit court judge in Vermont ruled against the Bush administration, finding that states can regulate GHG emissions, this ruling naturally landed on page A-1 of the *New York Times* among other generous coverage throughout the media.[55]

When a federal judge in California, however, dismissed outright the alarmists' case in *California v. General Motors*—the case argued that automakers owe damages for the climate change induced by the emissions from their tailpipes[56]—it was noted by one paper in Detroit and some smaller local papers in California.

A report on "record" ice melt in the Arctic gets prime play in the *Washington Post*.[57] The fact that the Antarctic ice sheet is getting thicker, well, that's not news.[58]

The media audaciously ignore accepted opinion when that opinion is depressingly non-catastrophic, but then run a *shocked* story that the boring accepted wisdom it hasn't wanted to tell you about *might not be true*. Again regarding Antarctica, the *Washington Post* spent years ignoring the fact that the ice down south was growing, but then professed alarm that possibly Antarctica actually *was* melting (fittingly shocked, it seems, to find they'd accidentally been right).[59] However, scrutiny revealed that the claimed melting wasn't occurring compared to reality so much as compared against someone's computer model.[60] Worse, the real threat was that this "rais[ed] the prospect of faster sea-level rise than current estimates," even though the day before the very same newspaper had let slip an item (by other than their environment beat reporters) on research showing sea levels were actually lower during a previous, greater warming when there was much *less* Antarctic ice.[61]

When research concluded that the hyped, 2002 break-offs from the Larsen ice shelves were the product of long-term, natural activities, only the lead-author's local paper in Wales bothered to note the work. This is of little wonder considering his unfashionable statements such as: "But our new study shows that ice-shelf break-up is not controlled simply by climate. A number of other atmospheric, oceanic and glaciological factors are involved."[62]

Up at the top of the planet, the *Post* warned us, "The relentless grip of the Arctic Ocean that defied man for centuries is melting away. The sea ice reaches only half as far as it did 50 years ago. In the summer of 2006, it shrank to a record low. This summer, the ice pulled back even more, by an area nearly the size of Alaska."[63] The *Post* makes no mention that the "record" it cites is actually the satellite record, which is only about thirty years long, and that before those readings began, ships navigated the Northwest Passage with some frequency in the first half of the century until the planetary cooling.

When research assessing a more historically relevant period (1,500 years) found, inconveniently, Arctic *cooling* over that time,[64] the far North was of no more interest to the press than when NASA research "suggest[ed] not all the large changes seen in Arctic climate in recent years are a result of long-term trends associated with global warming."[65]

When NASA then issued a release noting that the northern melt was due to unusual winds[66]—attributable to the Arctic and North Atlantic Oscillations, not us nasty human beings[67]—the media again sat this one out. Reporting on it might have raised other questions, leading folks to learn about the well-established pattern of regional climatic shifts called the Pacific Decadal Oscillation, which happens to correlate nicely with global temperature patterns. The PDO shifted to warming in 1978, the summer of which also saw the warming of North Pacific water which makes its way into the Arctic through the Bering Straits begin, coinciding with the diminution in Arctic ice thickness and extent. NASA's Jet Propulsion Laboratory announced that it seems to have shifted back in 2008, promising an end to the supposed "Baked Alaska," a warming that actually occurred largely in that one year but is touted as proof of a global warming trend.[68]

There's just something about the upper northern latitudes that causes reporters and editors to completely abandon perspective. One factor could be that the predicted global warming is largely limited to the northern hemisphere. In fact, despite the radio silence in the face of inconvenient research, the Arctic gets disproportionate attention from the media given that it contains less than 3 percent of the world's ice compared to the cooling Antarctic whose growing ice mass represents approximately 90 percent. But consider how they loved spouting claims of Greenland purportedly

melting away and at a record pace,[69] but proved utterly uninter-
ested in Greenland's history if it meant going further back than *18
years.*[70] The alarmists selling them the story didn't find it relevant,
why should they? It wouldn't have taken much effort to learn the
rather non-alarming truth from the Goddard Institute of Space
Studies. After all, it's run by that "muzzled" man they can't stop
themselves from quoting, James Hansen, so, it isn't like they did-
n't have his number. On speed dial.

How do the media react when we get Greenland temperatures
below those of the 1930s and 1940s, together with ice melt slower
than the 1990s, 1930s, 1940s, 1950s, and 1960s?[71] Reuters blares
the headline, "Greenland thaw biggest in 50 years."[72] When
research reveals "a return to near-normal conditions around
Greenland after several years of low ice concentrations," even
viewed from the modern lens,[73] there's silence. Not that those several years of low ice concentrations hadn't been a favorite topic of
hand-wringing. When someone claims that global warming is
causing more earthquakes in Greenland, the media love the
(absurd) story line,[74] and even though actual experts on glacial
quakes exist,[75] they are not cited in the widespread coverage of this
supposedly ominous claim.

Even climate researchers[76] have criticized the press's sensationalism and habitual use of apocalyptic imagery. The desperation is
certainly on display when hyping stories about polar bear populations being threatened. The media love little more than touting
claims by (heavily vested) bureaucrats that we are chasing that
ultimate in charismatic mega-fauna, the polar bear, from the
world's frozen stage, but leave it to the *Nunatsiaq News*—published in the bear's backyard—to give space to actual expert-in-
the-field opinion, which is that the bear is thriving and will in all
likelihood continue to do so.[77] Either that, or else has apparently
gone extinct several times before,[78] given that the Arctic during the

early Holocene was warmer and had less ice cover than the present. More telling, Arctic summer temperatures during the Last Interglacial Period (LIG) were 4–8°C warmer than the present.[79]

Topping *Time* magazine's silly "Be Very Worried" polar bear cover story, Reuters' Alister Doyle used a small and unscientific study to bolster the alarmism. Senator James Inhofe told the story: Doyle "quoted a visitor to the Arctic who claims he saw two distressed polar bears. According to the Reuters article, the man noted that 'one of [the polar bears] looked to be dead and the other one looked to be exhausted.' The article did not state the bears were actually dead or exhausted, rather that they 'looked' that way."[80] Although people who live to tell about how polar bears *looked*, generally looked at them from a distance, Doyle wrote a story saying the bears were fatigued and that this surely must be due to global warming.[81]

Of course it is. *Everything* is.

The press breathes heavily over too-good-to-be-true shrieks about any sort of devastation, for example the serial obituaries-in-waiting for coral reefs.[82] Research revealing that coral reefs actually appear to be protected by a natural thermostat[83]—explaining how they, like polar bears, have not gone extinct during the numerous prior warmings greater than those experienced in the early and late twentieth century—is not deemed newsworthy.

The same holds true for their promotion of another Hollywood scenario, massive future sea-level rise.[84] When a peer-reviewed article in the journal *Global and Planetary Change* concluded that sea-level rise would be about 27 percent lower than the UN was predicting,[85] it never got popular press coverage. Nor did the evidence that the UN's information was actually falsified.[86] There is doubtless a very simple explanation, going something like this: surely you are already aware that, for whatever reason, the IPCC's sea-level assessment is *not* generally produced by sea-level experts,[87] so there's no need to waste space on it when debunked ("*everyone already knows that*" being a favorite line of biased journalists when challenged in person on their sins of omission).

Apparently it is enough to simply pass along to readers the *scary* stuff.

PEOPLE WHO KILL TREES BY THE ACRE

The media shares something else with CO_2-spewing warmists like Al Gore, which is a need to take a long look in the mirror (knowing a few journalists, I'm confident they won't object), and ask whether their own lifestyles match their alarmism. Possibly, as seems to be the case with Gore, such conflicts are pushed to the side by a belief that their own enormous carbon footprints are simply a necessary cost of saving the world, far outweighing the damage that they implicitly accept they inflict upon it.

For example, the *Chicago Tribune* was keen enough to note the dissonance between NBC's hysteria and sending its stars traveling around the world to reveal how, well, traveling around the world threatens to destroy it. Anne Curry was off to nearby Antarctica and Al Roker halfway around the world to Ecuador, expanding the already enormous carbon footprint of a television network's massive energy requirements and dependence upon every viewer plugging in and turning on an appliance. When called on it, they offered the expected response of the elites that *their* emissions are necessary in order to educate others on the horrors of their own:

> It's [host Matt] Lauer's hope that if the special, far-flung *Today* broadcasts do what they're supposed to do, whatever the cost to the environment will be repaid many times over. "If we do our job well at these three locations, and in our programming, not just in that week but from now on, then I think we should get credit if we can motivate people...to improve their lives and

reduce their carbon footprint in very little ways," he said. "Measure this trip [by] the impact it will have on the people." That includes some introspection for a father of three with an SUV. "Is there a way that I can get around that? These are the questions we're going to try to ask during this week," Lauer said. Said Vieira: "The bar is very high, and I can tell you every one on the team wants to reach it." Even if it means taking the subway?[88]

Of course NBC just happens to be owned by General Electric, a manufacturer of electricity-gulping appliances and incandescent light bulbs, but also of the more profitable (if less effective or adaptable) compact fluorescent light bulb that Congress just made you buy in the 2007 "energy" bill. It also owns the same windmill company that prompted its previous owner, that icon of corporate responsibility Enron, to push the Kyoto agenda and seek "to monitize [sic] our relationship with the green groups."[89] Oh yeah, they've also invested in greenhouse gas credits,[90] a Pet Rock-style novelty which is worthless until Congress regulates greenhouse gas emissions.

Not content to stop there, as the Democratic presidential candidates prepared for an "environmentally themed debate" in November 2007, NBC helped soften up the audience by mainstreaming the moonbattery, with an entire "Green Week" heavily pushed with breathless spots on television and radio and of course redoing their website and adding a dedicated section.[91] They followed this with an Earth Week in April 2008. At least it wasn't entirely nuts; there was a segment on "Green Astrology." I did my part by turning off NBC. Only *legitimate* emissions for me.

A SCARE IS BORN

CBS News perfectly encapsulated the state of environmental journalism in a job-listing seeking an environmental reporter. The network made clear that a sense of humor was more important than knowledge of the issues, which CBS went so far as to downplay as not necessary.[92] Apparently, they'll tell you what you need to know. Or those nice groups who send the useful press releases you'll be transcribing. The funny bone, however, is required largely for the running joke the press is pulling on the public when it comes to presenting tales about the environment and especially the greatest threat since the last greatest threat.

In fact, for over a century the print and electronic media have made clear to today's global warming industry that they'd be there for them, promiscuously feeding the public never-ending tales of projected horrors in hopes of selling copy or drawing viewers. As such, they were among the first to cash in on the notion that contemporary weather events—and even, for example, the *Titanic* hitting an iceberg—were omens of future climate catastrophe.

Whether it was cooling, warming, cooling, or now warming again, the media ritually followed the weather with confident predictions, always grounded in expert opinion. At some point this becomes self-parody, particularly as the Information Age leaves them occasionally squirming out from under past gasbaggery, leaving bits and bytes to forever mock their current panic.

From one perspective, it is completely understandable how the media strive to ignore the previous, entirely contrary predictions and their own participation in the hype. The same resistance to come clean likely also contributes to their reticence to report evidence of scientific professional misconduct and even fraud in the world of climate-related research.

But-for the media's exploitation of public trust, and shameless trumpeting as *settled truth* every conceivable angle of the Man-as-agent-of-doom theory, today's global warming alarmism would not be what it is among thousands of increasingly edgy activists spewing hate, making threats and chaining themselves to industrial facilities and construction sites.

The media contort even the most mundane reportage to invoke an angle of climate change intrigue. For example, a recent BBC headline blared "Autumn 'one of driest on record.'"[93] As an attention grabber, I've seen better, but consider the alternative: no story. My British colleague Iain Murray reminds me that a wet and cool summer, turned dry and warm autumn, is a well-known weather pattern in Old Blighty. But it needn't be merely that. Instead, it is *one of the driest on record.* At least this particular story was honest enough to reveal that "on record" means since 1972.

Think about how tired the phrase has become, "one of the (fill in the blank) on record." It is an indispensable tool of today's reporter, adding just enough zest to keep you awake for a story on how wet or dry the autumn has or hasn't been, preparing us all for that moment in line at the post office when forced to make conversation. *Thank you, BBC!*

Yet such meaningless reportage is also now a staple in itself even if, as I understand statistics, the odds are about fifty-fifty that any one year will be above average of whatever it is we are measuring, and equally likely to be below (averages themselves being mere artifacts of data). If your threshold for newsworthiness is fitting into the top or bottom quartile, "one of the [blank]est [blank]s on record" is a fair assessment of one out of every two years for any given indicator.

Although banal, these endless efforts to make average weather newsworthy are a gateway drug for an alarmist press eager to assist the global warming industry, of which it is a part.

TRICKS OF THE TRADE

Now when the press does deal with skeptics, it is with noses firmly held, knowing full well it is unnecessary and even inappropriate. The *Financial Times*'s Fiona Harvey, whose reportage is actually less hysterical than that of many American reporters, candidly admitted as much to über-alarmist Mark Hertsgaard of that self-parody of righteous green indignation *Vanity Fair* (which, for some reason, refuses to publish even its hyped "green issue" on recycled paper[94]). Said Harvey, European-based reporters refuse to provide even the American level of "giv[ing] equal credence to the skeptics...not because we're not balanced but because we think it's unbalanced to give equal validity to a fringe view with no science behind them."[95] Such blindness led to, for example, Ms. Harvey penning a story with the lead "Scientists have been able to say with virtual certainty for the first time that the climate change observed over the past four decades is man made and not the result of natural phenomena." In truth, this was absurd because the cited study "found" no such thing, but instead expressly *assumed* it, then gamed out scenarios which were then styled with the risible "consistent with warming" and, therefore, caused by man. That episode reflected neither science nor journalism.

The press also adopts the greens' rhetoric. Remember the day you noticed how "global warming" had suddenly become "climate change," with no questions asked? Remember when George W. Bush suddenly both "refused to sign" and "withdrew from" the Kyoto Protocol, a metaphysically impossible combination that also managed to leave unmentioned that Bush *couldn't* sign Kyoto—Clinton already had—and he couldn't withdraw from it, because we had never ratified it. We then read that Bush "refused to ratify" Kyoto, in the strange phraseology of the *Washington Post* among others, revealing a certain lack of familiarity with our constitutional separation of powers.

We read that he "squandered post-9/11 goodwill," by refusing to push for ratification of any agreement that exempted China and India—though this was the Clinton-Gore position. We were told that Bush must match Europe's success (as Europe's emissions and energy prices skyrocket), and must stop being a rogue actor (as the U.S. leads the world in terms of growing its economy while reducing the rate of growth of CO_2 emissions, which apparently do not really matter). They parrot environmentalist talking points about how the U.S. is "being left behind"—by actually having better emission performance than others, which they don't tell you—and "going it alone"—with 155 other nations.

We are to assume that such coordinated, incomprehensible breathlessness originated with reporters. An entire industry somehow gets the same things wrong in the same couple of ways, if consistent with the language of green groups who happen to require the same particular, misstated dynamic for their fundraising and political ends.

COULDA, SHOULDA, WOULDA

The environmental press, including editors, management, and ownership, are addicted to substantively useless verbal auxiliaries such as "could," "may," and "might." As Australian professor Robert Carter notes, "Since the early 1990s, the columns of many leading newspapers, worldwide, have carried an increasing stream of alarmist letters and articles on hypothetical, human-caused climate change.... Each such alarmist article is liberally larded with words such as—if, may, might, could, probably, perhaps, likely, expected, projected or modelled [sic]—and many involve such deep dreaming, or ignorance of scientific facts and principles, that they are akin to nonsense."[96] Add to this an infatuation with "perhaps."[97]

Amy Kaleita and Gregory Forbes of the Pacific Research Institute explained the phenomenon: "Apocalyptic stories about the irreparable, catastrophic damage that humans are doing to the natural environment have been around for a long time. These hysterics often have some basis in reality, but are blown up to illogical and ridiculous proportions. Part of the reason they're so appealing is that they have the ring of plausibility along with the intrigue of a horror flick. In many cases, the alarmists identify a legitimate issue, take the possible consequences to an extreme, and advocate action on the basis of these extreme projections."[98]

A classic example of the media's transparent alarmism occurred in the aforementioned honeybee crisis, just after research was published in September 2007 in a journal prone to alarmism and at the altar of which, therefore, the media pray. Yet the findings weren't actually alarmist, but pointed a finger elsewhere than "climate change." No such research can be allowed to stand, however, and the *Washington Post* dutifully ran a full page, A-Section story, buzzing with a border-to-border headline, "Weather may account for reduced honey crop."[99]

Once you've learned alarm-ese, you realize what this really means: weather may not account for a reduced honey crop. In fact, here we see how "may" generally is code for "likely doesn't" (or "won't"). The *Post* admits in the third paragraph that the conclusion was that a virus is responsible, not "global warming." "[L]ast week, the journal *Science* published a report that found a new virus, Israeli acute paralysis virus, appeared to be associated with [colony collapse disorder]."

So of course the headline said the opposite.

This is merely one more example of non-alarmist research being the kind that the *Post* and *New York Times* generally do not cover, unless and until they can turn it on its head or fill space with critics dismissing it. The *Post* also arranged to further promote the countervailing, alarmist claims by making the story's author available on-line that day "to discuss this year's disappointing honey crop and how extreme weather is affecting honeybees." What he didn't have time for is to read his own story, apparently, and anyone else who would tell you about how a virus is affecting honeybees was also busy.

That very same day the *Post* also ran a scary piece about the number of "gray whales [which] roamed the Pacific before humans decimated [sic] the population through hunting, and human-induced climate change may now be depriving those that remain of the food they need. . . . The research, based on a detailed analysis of DNA taken from gray whales living in the eastern Pacific, highlights how human behavior has transformed the oceans, the scientists said."[100]

For purposes of context, now compare this Man-as-agent-of-doom stuff to the can't-really-be-good-news headline reporting *precisely the opposite* the year before, "PACIFIC COAST: Gray whales thrive in the Arctic, for now. More calves being born, but effects of warming not clear." Actually, far from being unclear as to why the whales were prospering, this article's opening paragraph confirmed the reason as being quite clear: slightly warmer waters. "The number of baby gray whales born along the Pacific Coast has increased over the last five years, leading scientists to believe that for now the pregnant females are doing all right feeding in a warming Arctic environment."[101] It seems that clarity only strikes headline writers when the indicator favors their doomsaying.

Also note the irresistible *For now.* As in, *bad news about the planet is always around the corner.*

MOTIVES MATTER, MAYBE

It is standard media practice to label contrary voices as possibly "industry supported" (as are most greens, of course). Likewise, the media demean opinions of businesses who *aren't* selling global warming get-rich-quick schemes. Firms who are interested parties facing serious consequences from the global warming agenda are simply not credible as they are tainted by possible profit motives. Yet the press regularly touts companies that are heavily vested in ensuring the agenda come to fruition as *responsible* actors willing to place right and good above mere commercial concerns.

So what if GE ended up with the big windmill concern that Enron had purchased as part of its making money off of lobbyists?

The fact is that GE (like Enron) is pushing for media-approved, massive governmental interventions in the economy in the name of saving the planet. They are therefore *responsible*. Like Al Gore. And those unnamed interests giving him $300 million to advance the agenda. And so on.

And to the extent the media allows contrary opinion to infect their pieces, they typically assign it possible financial motives, ties or interests, sometimes even just calling it "for hire." It seems this widespread practice is driven by the belief that anyone who dares challenge their view must be on the take to do so. *Newsweek* surely subscribes to this philosophy, as most grossly revealed in its "well-funded denial machine" cover story bemoaning the daunting challenge confronting our poor planet and its doughty defenders.[102]

This is neither fair nor balanced. Environmental groups are massively funded and not merely from the super-wealthy and left-wing charitable foundations. They closely coordinate the warming agenda with "big business" seeking to cash in on any such cow ever since Enron got the ball rolling on this more than a decade ago. Yet the media harp only on the few corporate supports of those who oppose the alarmist agenda. Yet even the promiscuous use of ExxonMobil as the poster child is absurd not only given their actual stance on the matter but that the

> "Back in 2001, I wondered out loud—and in print—if it would take 'an environmental 9/11' to finally break the corporate brake that is holding up all action on global warming in America. Since then, New Orleans has drowned, the South-east has dried up so severely the city of Atlanta is nearly out of water, and the skies over California have been turned red by the worst wildfires since records began....Yet still the political debate in the US remains stuck far short of the drastic cuts in carbon emissions we need now if we are to stop this Weather of Mass Destruction."
>
> *Johann Hari of* The Independent *(UK)*

company donates millions of dollars to environmentalist causes and pressure groups, a fact you likely have never heard.[103]

The media elect not to report how the environmentalist groups, which they cite for unbiased and expert opinion on these matters, also have cleverly used the Kyoto process to nicely feather their own nests with lucrative consultancies, roles as assessors of emissions, reductions and greenhouse gas "credit" veracity, and otherwise as paid supporters of the same carbon rationing or "cap-and-trade" scheme that for-profit industry is trying to milk.

A similar error of omission is media's refusal to provide readers with the broader ideological stances and very specific rantings of the greens. Stories regularly set context by noting that business groups which are quoted want to make profits and/or avoid regulatory costs; groups such as the Competitive Enterprise Institute supporting free-market environmentalism and classical liberalism instead simply are "industry-supported." This is not a new practice for the media, who acknowledge to it on occasion, for example with their erstwhile favorite global warming iconoclast, Senator John McCain,[104] going so far as to "admit that reporters sometimes cover for him by not reporting controversial things he tells them on the record 'because they don't want to see him flame out and burn up a great story.'"[105] That is, until McCain ran against their candidate for president, at which point he became just another Republican pretender.

The press similarly cover for the rest of the global warming or broader "green" movement, not finding it worthwhile to report the more revealing comments from this movement's leaders—comments such as pining for massive depopulation including through painful malaria deaths, placing the value of a forest over stopping child sex slavery, and generally admitting that it is the imposition of values and lifestyle controls through the acquisition of power that they crave.[106] Environmentalists "aspire to a cultural model in which killing a forest will be considered more contemptible and more criminal than the sale of 6-year-old children" (German Green party official Carl Amery) and believe that "To feed a starving child is to exacerbate the world population problem" (now-infamous activist Lamont Cole).

The truth behind the movement is breathtaking, and if widely known, it would doom much of the massive fundraising appeal the greens have from elites, suburbia, and corporate America. It therefore is never mentioned when noting the greens as policy experts and prognosticators. Should a "skeptic" be caught expressing a view about abortion, affirmative action, or the Second Amendment that the press views as flat-out nuts (that is, the non-Left-wing perspective), then any mention of his work is deemed naked without it.

All of the above, if taken in isolation or if only engaged in on occasion, might arguably be no more than sloppiness or ignorance. But these are not merely instances; they are practices, applied unilaterally and with impressive discipline. The media cannot credibly deny their obvious, institutional decision to be active combatants in an ideological struggle no matter how much they protest or alternately insist that they must as an industry now commence these practices. Instead, they flaunt their commitment, admitting its equivalent—"balance is bias!"—as if it were the most natural thing in the world.

JUST DOIN' OUR JOB

It is true that the Fourth Estate cannot dictate events; it can merely influence them. The money and foot soldiers driving the agenda forward remain the ideologues, meaning-seekers, anti-Americans, pandering politicians, cynical Third World rent-seekers and, most important, the industries shamelessly seeking money for nothing that they could sell on its merits. It is the media campaign, however, without which the current dynamic would not exist of Americans facing policymakers actually considering wildly expensive, sovereignty-eroding, energy-insecure, and (under any scenario or set of assumptions) climatically meaningless regimes to redistribute your wealth.

The media hardly operate in a vacuum, but have instead joined in a cooperative effort with particular climate scientists, in violation of journalism's basic tenets which are not permitted to intrude on the alarmists' march. As Christopher Shea noted in the *Boston Globe*, "More and more environmentalists and climate scientists have been making the point that 'objective' journalists are doing as much as anyone (except maybe Hummer enthusiasts) to forestall action on global warming."[107] If people hear both sides, the alarmists lose.

It was only logical for the alarmist industry to target and indeed recruit the press for the struggle. Even the slightest doubt, if permitted to go unpunished, is fatal when the claims are so outlandish and the demanded response so expensive. Shea also cites how Michael Mann (more on him later) has warned science writers that to even quote a skeptic is akin to granting "the Flat Earth Society an equal say with NASA in the design of a new space satellite." Mann ignores that the notion of a flat Earth came from the "consensus" of elites who insisted that the science had been decided and that dissent was intolerable.

The alarmist science writers take their campaign beyond the popular press and printed page, where they clearly consider the battle as won, toward seizing the reins of policy, which they caution will be an even greater challenge.

We are entering a period when careful interpretation and communication of the economic, political and social dimensions of climate change will be vital. Failure to tell these aspects of the story could be of even greater significance than the painfully slow arrival at the basics of the science. The media will offer the context within which we decide the If, How and When of transforming energy-hungry lifestyles and economies.... The open terrain of these questions presents media decision-makers with a new set of challenges, and the way they handle scepticism will again be central to their performance.[108]

This is the counsel of environmental media researchers Eleni Andreadis and Joe Smith, in the *British Journalism Review*, reminding environmental journalists of their crucial role in herding policymakers toward desired ends: "Their principal question should be: Will this help to reduce emissions dramatically, or is it a way of only denting the status quo?" They exhorted their peers with advice, that "the media will also need to marry their critical faculties to a commitment to enable debate about action and change." Also, "most [politicians] are frightened of sticking their necks out. They need to be given the space to think and experiment and lead public debate on action." In short, we're all in this movement together, so help the pols out by providing cover because, given the costs involved, those unpopular policies won't simply enact themselves.

SOCIETY AFFAIR

The sorry state of environmental journalism as a harbor and front for global warming activists is exemplified by the organization and membership of the Society of Environmental Journalists (SEJ), the self-selecting if recognized and establishment peer group of those wooly left-wingers who have chosen to "report" on the issues as their contribution to the cause.

SEJ's website offers a view into the group's purpose and self-image. "The mission of the Society of Environmental Journalists is to advance public understanding of environmental issues by improving the quality, accuracy, and visibility of environmental reporting."[109] Such a vague description could easily apply to an organization of objective writers or an activist group. By now, however, you should spot the balancing test or tension inherent in a journalist seeking to improve one's accuracy *and* visibility, particularly when it comes to the environment.

In this case, the statement applies to a group that is both scribbler and activist. Gauzy mission statements by no means dictate a group's actions, but it is "visibility" that tips the SEJ's hand. Nothing elevates a longtime backwater group such as theirs like promotion of "global warming." No longer are they mere environmental scribes dealing with turgid regulatory policy, but warriors neckdeep in international negotiations, high finance, and now *saving the planet.*

SEJ's "objectives" include two red flags, "to stimulate more and better coverage of a range of critically important environmental issues," and "to encourage addition or expansion of environmental reporting positions within broadcast, print, and internet news organizations." If the atmosphere isn't warming, as ours hasn't for a decade,[110] there certainly would not be "more" coverage of the issue, leaving "environmental journalism" less well-off. Therefore "better" coverage, by the emerging, express industry standard, means abandoning any pretense to balance. So write that things are warming, dangerously.

Consider the comment of *NYT* environment guru Andy Revkin in a 2008 interview, relating the mood of the October 2006 SEJ conference. "I heard a lot of reporters doing public soul searching about climate change, saying that they were failing in their professional duty to calibrate the importance of the climate story to the amount of coverage."[111] He acknowledged, "We've certainly had a big up-tick in journalism coverage of climate change," only to despair that Matthew Nesbit, communications professor at American University, researched the recent burst of coverage and his polling "show[ed] that it hasn't really mattered, that opinions haven't really changed; they've become more polarized." As noted, the *CJR* weighed in to suggest the tool of censorship.

These SEJ gatherings to which Revkin alluded include prominent roles for such doomsayers as Paul Ehrlich,[112] who predicted that that in the 1970s and 1980s, "hundreds of millions of people will starve to death." At these confabs SEJ members swoon over boys-made-good like ABC's Bill Blakemore opining that "I don't like the word 'balance' much at all" when it comes to producing global warming pieces, which he at least admits is an "existential" dilemma.[113] But apparently people like yours truly are confronting "psychological obstacles" in our resistance to dire predictions of a climate crisis. This is of course a professional opinion because, "After extensive searches, ABC News has found no such [scientific] debate on global warming."[114]

Despite implicitly admitting to having done not a moment of research, "Blakemore, who has covered numerous wars over the years, said global warming is the most challenging story he's worked on. 'It's surreal to have pre-eminent scientists tell us very seriously that civilization as we know it is over,' Blakemore said. 'The scale is unprecedented. It touches every aspect of life.'"[115]

Remember, this is a reporter we're talking about.

We also see such shining examples of professionalism as CBS's Scott Pelley, whose promotion of global warming alarmism is so ham-fisted that when he seeks to explain away his bias he merely adds to the evidence. To wit, Pelley says his professional standards don't require inclusion of opinions counter to the alarmists' because: "If I do an interview with Elie Wiesel, am I required as a journalist to find a Holocaust denier?"[116] (Of course, after making this claim he flew halfway around the world to actually interview the Holocaust denier Mahmoud Ahmadinejad, only further confusing his analogy.) Like Blakemore, Pelley also claimed he couldn't find any "respected" skeptics anyway.[117]

As Pacific Research Institute's Kaleita and Forbes noted about SEJ's bias, particularly when it comes to "global warming" alarmism:

Disturbingly, alarmist reporting on the science of climate change is now considered by many to be the most appropriate way to communicate this complicated issue to the public...[T]he Spring 2006 *SEJournal*, published by the Society of Environmental Journalists (SEJ), argued *against* balance in the discussion. Arguments such as these send the dangerous message that it's acceptable to present extreme viewpoints without providing either the larger context or an assessment of the likelihood of extreme outcomes.[118]

The *American Thinker's* Christopher Alleva noted a typically hoary SEJ publication cleverly titled "Climate Change: A guide to the information and disinformation":[119]

Except for the seventh chapter titled with the freighted descriptive: "Deniers, Dissenters and Skeptics," the guide is a one sided presentation that resoundingly affirms global warming and puts down anyone with a different point of view. The site is a virtual digest of the global warming industry. If you're looking for a road map to the special interest groups behind the hysteria, this is the place to go. The journalist members of this association have obviously abandoned all pretense of objectivity.

The site is largely a compendium of links to global warming promoters. Many of the links use adjectives like prestigious, best respected, and reputation unrivaled to burnish their credibility. The so-called deniers on the other hand are described with adjectives like, highly polemical, outright false, and deceptive partisan attack dogs. The description of the Competitive

Enterprise Institute is especially derisive, citing the often leveled false accusation that they are the tool of Exxon Mobil.[120]

I am affiliated with CEI, and although I make a point of not seeking to know where support comes from, it is unavoidable to have learned that ExxonMobil provides CEI no support, which was also the case when this report was issued. Such advocacy and sloth prompted Alleva to ask, "And this is journalism at its finest?" noting also that "[t]he SEJ is supported mainly by foundation grants from many of the places that fund Bill Moyers and PBS." With SEJ members committed to the idea that funding dictates the mission, surely they'll agree that this is all you need to know.

WHO'S THE ONE IN DENIAL?

USA Today worked overtime to actually *deny* the past cooling panic. In a February 2008 article the paper trumpeted a claim that "[t]he supposed 'global cooling' consensus among scientists in the 1970s—frequently offered by global-warming skeptics as proof that climatologists can't make up their minds—is a myth."[121] Clearly the past is (again) proving inconvenient to alarmists. The problem with this as with all such revisionism is that it is phony.

It is undeniable that global cooling was officially on the international scientific agenda as early as October 1963, when the United Nations Food & Agriculture Organization convened a conference in Rome on the threat that global cooling posed to world food supplies. Eminent British climatologist Hubert Lamb led the discussions, and after that the cooling story ran through the late 1970s.[122] Documentaries then also seized the cooling angle, for example the *The Weather Machine* (1974), a two-hour production for the BBC, WNET, and four other national broadcasters in which leading experts detailed their great concerns about what the global cooling portended.

Popular books included both *Hot House Earth* and *The Cooling*, but also *The Weather Conspiracy—The Coming of the New Ice Age* written with the assistance of reporters and which derided zeitgeist-heretics as "hot-earth men."[123]

It is also true that the media did run with a minority shrieking about cooling when it appears a majority among the very-divided scientific community were gunning the warming bandwagon's engine. But this claim proves too much: back then as in recent years, what was in the literature was not what was driving the debate, which was instead driven by a filtered view of it; but the gatekeepers then are the same as today.

To now claim that the cooling assertions came from fringe elements is to deny the record, including debates by the American Association for the Advancement of Science.[124] In short, the media listen to whom they wish to listen, and write what they wish to write, but it rarely reflects the true nature of the literature.

Sociologist Dr. Benny Peiser, who publishes the CCNet summary of climate literature and media coverage, has detailed how "many environmental writers and editors have all but abandoned traditional forms of journalistic balance over the issue of global warming."[125] Consider the following example of collective guilt. Amid the Bali negotiations to draft a successor to the doomed Kyoto Protocol in December 2007, climate scientist Roger Pielke Jr. focused on the media's systematic exclusion of "skeptic" voices and inconvenient research. He cited a study (Vecchi and Soden 2007) revealing no link between hurricanes and "global warming" that actually made its way past the censors at *Nature* magazine—a source to which environmental journalists turn almost daily for heated stories—but which fell on deaf ears while the press love-bombed Webster and Holland (*Philosophical Transactions of the Royal Society of London* 2007), a study appearing in a less-prominent journal claiming the opposite. Pielke Jr. pointed out that the media covered the Webster and Holland study in seventy-nine stories. Vecchi and Soden made it only into three. "What accounts for the 26 to 1 ratio in news stories?" Pielke asked.[126]

This bias was affirmed when NOAA pronounced what experts had been saying to an unitered media for years: the increase in storms' destruction was not from angrier or more frequent hurricanes but people putting more and more things in the storms' paths.[127] That's not exactly the media's story line, so it was largely ignored.

Although the media love promoting scary stores out of *Nature*, *National Review* blogger and *Detroit News* cartoonist Henry Payne chronicled a complete lack of interest in Pielke's eye-opening revelation.[128] Payne examined the excuse offered by the *Times'* Andy Revkin: that it simply springs from the media's preference for reporting on conflict.[129]

While a revealing attempt at admission, would that it were in fact even remotely plausible. As Payne notes, that very same week the press managed to ignore numerous conflicts at the Bali conference which they also saturated with coverage, touting the U.S.-bad-Europe-good line. These included the UN's denying press credentials to non-conforming journalists, denying access to non-conforming scientists, and even threatening to have them removed by force, signatures by more than one hundred scientists (including pioneers like Freeman Dyson) on a letter to Ban Ki-moon calling for a halt to the UN's alarmist push temperature data released revealing no warming trend, and open discussion about the fact that the bogeyman U.S. had superior CO_2 emission performance to Europe.[130]

Peiser, Pielke Jr., and Payne are certainly not alone in noticing this unbalanced reporting, which includes risible hype of even the silliest assertions, like Reuters' uncritical promotion of a claim that Mammoth dung exposed in melting permafrost "will lead to a type of global warming which will be impossible to stop."[131] It seems more like "global warming" is leading to unstoppable quantities of dung, as a New York television station took this "story" one step further, casually describing permafrost melting as "releasing more deadly greenhouse gas."[132] *Deadly?* That's simply a manifestation of the deadly combination of conditioning and ignorance.

MAKING A DIFFERENCE

Some media players embody the environmental advocate using journalism as their vehicle. For example, at a "communications workshop" hosted for alarmist and media elites in 2005, *San Diego Union Tribune* science writer Bruce Lieberman said editors need to recognize that while weather and climate are not synonymous, particular weather patterns can provide "teachable moments" if put "in the proper context."[133] Just what that context might be is hinted at by his further complaint that the notion of the "settled science" of climate change was insufficiently ingrained in the broader public.

Seattle Post-Intelligencer editorial page editor Mark Trahant declared near the end of the previous year's session, "Fairness, or journalistic balance, is the obstacle. . . . It's time for journalists . . . to declare outright that truth is a higher calling than fairness."[134] When Michael Mann's hockey-stick-shaped graph of historical temperatures was debunked, Trahant called it "quibbling."[135] Revkin is actually more thoughtful if quite obviously a convicted alarmist. Despite being among the greens' more sophisticated advocates, even he brings their calumny down upon himself[136] with the occasional fit of balance.[137] Unfortunately, those fits are too few and too far between.

Andy wrote a book called *The North Pole Was Here* (okay, so the North Pole actually can't really melt as implied, because it is the point in the northern hemisphere where the Earth's axis of rotation meets the Earth's surface; what's pushing a little ignorance on kids if it's in the name of scaring them?). This book targeting children takes only the alarmist side; nowhere does Andy acknowledge that the computer models might be wrong, are being proven wrong, or that natural climate variability could be dominant.

Mr. Revkin has also created a story[138] and slide show[139] for the AARP called "global meltdown." He molds young journo-activist minds teaching "environmental journalism" at Columbia University. He also tours other classrooms to reveal that he is no unifaceted journalist but also an environmental musician and songwriter, with one ditty in his repertoire title "Liberated Carbon":

Then Satan came along and said,
'Hey, try lighting this.'
He opened up the ground and showed us coal and oil.
He said, 'Come liberate some carbon. It'll make your blood
    boil.'
Liberated carbon, it'll spin your wheels.
Liberated carbon it'll nuke your meals.
Liberated carbon, it'll turn your night to day.
Come on and liberate some carbon, babe, it's the American way.

Ah, that old device of objectivity, analogizing your subject to the Devil's Plaything.

The point here is that Andy has a definite perspective. Political journalists vote Democrat 90 percent of the time and insist that their perspective doesn't infect their coverage. That is as demonstrably untrue with them as such a claim would be in this case.

Andy coined a new term on his blog: The "Anthrocene" era—indicating his belief that the present is the era of a human-shaped Earth. With that premise securely stowed in his bandolier, and following publication of the Fourth IPCC report in 2007, Andy rather typically wrote, "In a bleak and powerful assessment of the future of the planet..."[140] This assessment disguised an inconvenient truth, that the document at issue actually *reduced* its projection since the last time around of Man's total impact on the climate and cut its sea level rise, and so on.

In a highly compensated speech in Washington State, Andy did not disappoint. As the *Olympian* reported, in a piece whose headline fittingly noted his activism, "Speakers exhort crowd to act on Earth's behalf":

> Revkin emphasized that carbon emissions will remain in the atmosphere for decades, and younger generations will be stuck with their effects. "This is their climate more than our climate," he said. . . . He added that developing countries would be disproportionately affected by growing gas emissions from industrialized countries such as the United States, because 70 percent of emissions come from them. Some rich people in the Netherlands are building floating houses that can withstand sea-level rise, but the coastal poor in Bangladesh will be swamped, he said. "There's a growing realization that a kid in Bangladesh is your neighbor," he said.[141]

Even drained of its emotional attachment to the issue (and the scare tactics intimating some high level of confidence that massive sea level rise is in the near or even foreseeable future), this is not a newsman reporting, this is the purest expression that even possibly the best environment reporter in the game is an advocate, an activist.

CASE STUDY IN INSTITUTIONAL MEDIA ALARMISM AND BIAS: THE *WASHINGTON POST*

All of our national newspapers are deeply vested players in the global warming industry. The *Washington Post, New York Times, Los Angeles Times,* and *USA Today* all regularly weigh in with editorials, in-house columnists, "news" items and human interest stories declaring certain catastrophe, and irresponsibility of those whose politics they do not like.

The *Post's* assault is typical in its disregard for facts and reason. Its heated issuances are merely more frequent, given its proximity to that source of all the world's problems—the Bush White House.

If nothing else, the *Post* is good at volume control—getting loud when the news is "good" (bad), and quieting down otherwise. It hurled a three-pronged assault of brow-furrowing at the Supreme Court in the days before argument in the important *Massachusetts v. EPA* case, including heart-wrenching tales of ski resorts in peril. Yet within months, when the ski slopes confronted a record season, the *Post* was no longer interested in the fate of that industry. Who cares about Switzerland having its strongest early winter accumulation in fifty-five years, or early snow in the ski-dependent Wyoming Tetons, Oregon Cascades, New Hampshire, and Idaho, as well as China, Hungary, Serbia, and England. The *Post* was too busy that very week running a series of end-of-days, full-page stories on the IPCC's tales of catastrophic warming.

Had it been late warming instead of early winter, or were we back in the cooling panic of the '70s, or were treaties in the mix declaring war on planetary freezing, you can bet the *WaPo* coverage would've made Revelation look like a child's bedtime story.

When the series of scandals exposing the flimsy nature of the alarmists' case emerged in 2007, the national papers including the *Post* proved completely unwilling to directly report on facts. Substantiated claims that are inconsistent with the prevailing media template of *warming-bad–U.S.-worse* are typically revealed only well after the fact, for purposes of giving the alarmists a platform to diminish its significance.[142]

Finally, consider the *Post's* sister publication, *Newsweek*, which boasts a decades-long track record of climate hysteria and presently employs one of the sillier scribblers on the topic. Sharon Begley, co-author of *Newsweek's* bizarre "how not to report on 'global warming'" cover story, "The Truth about Denial"[143]—a piece so bad that one of the magazine's editors immediately published a sharp rebuke/*apologia*—has long been peddling one version or another of doomsday, consistent with the prevailing wisdom.

As Pat Michaels noted in his 2004 book *Meltdown*, "For years, science reporter Sharon Begley has been chasing a peculiar twist on global warming hysteria: that heating the planet will cause an ice age."[144] Begley's "Truth about Denial" piece was a conspiracy script: "Since the late 1980s, this well-coordinated, well-funded campaign by contrarian scientists, free-market think tanks and industry has created a paralyzing fog of doubt around climate change."

The website for the GOP side of the Senate's Environment and Public Works Committee saw a problem here: "The only problem is—*Newsweek* knew better. Reporter Eve Conant, who interviewed Senator James Inhofe (R-Okla.), the Ranking Member of the Environment & Public Works Committee, was given all the latest data proving conclusively that it is the proponents of man-made global warming fears that enjoy a monumental funding advantage over the skeptics. (A whopping $50 BILLION to a paltry $19 MILLION and some change for skeptics—Yes, that is BILLION to MILLION)."[145]

Begley's sins of commission and omission were too much for *Newsweek* Contributing Editor Robert Samuelson who posted a response in the magazine's next issue, calling it a "highly contrived story" relying upon "discredited" allegations and that in essence it was "fundamentally misleading."[146] Wrote Samuelson, "We in the news business often enlist in moral crusades. Global warming is among the latest. Unfortunately, self-righteous indignation can undermine good journalism. Last week's *Newsweek* cover story on global warming is a sobering reminder." Ouch. And that's from her own team.

Eyes wide shut, Begley was soon right back at it, hysterically if without justification blaming the 2008 U.S. Midwest floods on Man-made global warming.[147]

As blowback against the odious "Holocaust denier" tag grew, and despite being called out by a highly respected colleague for her name-calling, Begley sought to cleverly change the vernacular to allow the practice to continue. In another forum at about the same time, she opted instead for analogizing those who deny future climate horrors to those "who think the moon landings took place on a stage in Arizona."[148] Begley's persistence is certainly endearing, in an embarrassing way.

BLOWIN' WITH THE WIND—THE WEATHER CHANNEL

The media's tone seems to be exemplified if not actually *set* by The Weather Channel, an outlet whose entire existence is dedicated to putting fannies on the sofa to stare at programs about weather. Guess which kind of weather they prefer? TWC has gone beyond forecasting and has delved into full-blown global warming alarmism, even bringing some climate activists on staff.

TWC's financial interest in promoting scary stories and even outright alarm is axiomatic. Programs about pleasant days and waves calmly lapping at the shores do not draw good ratings. Pushing scary weather is not, however, the same thing as promoting the green agenda by slinging alarmist invective against heretical climate rationalists and pushing governmental policies designed to make energy more expensive and therefore more scarce. Yet both activities are now TWC hallmarks.

In a broadside aimed at alarmism, generally, but drawn in great part from disillusionment over how far his project has strayed from its original vision, Weather Channel founder John Coleman wrote scathingly of how a handful of "dastardly scientists with environmental and political motives manipulated long term scientific data to create an illusion of rapid global warming."[149] He railed against the artifice of the "consensus" they then created, and how "friends in government steered huge research grants their way to keep the movement going."

> I am incensed by the incredible media glamour, the politically correct silliness and rude dismissal of counter arguments by the high priest of Global Warming. In time, a decade or two, the outrageous scam will be obvious. As the temperature rises, polar ice cap melting, coastal flooding and super storm pattern all fail to occur as predicted everyone will come to realize we have been duped.[150]

Coleman's statement drew attention from big-audience voices like Rush Limbaugh and Glenn Beck. With its franchise under attack before an audience of millions a clearly chagrined TWC rushed out a statement to distance themselves from Coleman and deflect his message. In its entirety, the statement by Ray Ban (seriously) read:

> We have received several media inquiries regarding a recent statement by John Coleman. While we do not plan to comment on his statement, we would like share the following information.
>
> John Coleman was a founder of The Weather Channel; however, he is no longer affiliated with the company, having left the network in 1983.
>
> The Weather Channel is an advocate for environmental efforts and has adopted a broader initiative called Forecast

Earth, which focuses on educating the public about climate change and empowering people to make a difference. The Weather Channel has issued an official statement representing the company's position on climate change, which can be found here [link omitted].[151]

So, unlike so many others, The Weather Channel at least admits its activism.

CNN—JOURNALISM IN PERIL

CNN's chief technology and environment correspondent Miles O'Brien has a lack of seriousness that knows little shame or boundaries. O'Brien has gone from staking out alarmist positions (only to later deny that he said any such thing),[152] to calling those who doubt the media's line about catastrophic Man-made global warming "dead-enders," a "tiny fraction of a minority," and a "very small fringe."[153] Meanwhile it is they, he insists, who are "in the dark."[154] O'Brien is so big on doing his homework that he routinely insists to interviewees that they are wrong, he is right, the science is *too* settled and alarmingly so. He even lapsed into warning that the fictional Hollywood scenario in *The Day After Tomorrow* was a real-life threat.

Maybe O'Brien could sleep through the night—and therefore stay awake during the day when covering the issue[155]—if he knew that, so long as the Earth turns and the wind blows, the Gulf Stream and the Jet Stream shutting down entirely is not going to happen.[156]

It might not matter, as invention seems to be CNN's standard approach to the issue. Possibly because O'Brien actually showed a short-lived spasm of balance after so many embarrassments—dedicating an entire (and surprisingly evenhanded) hour to the UK High Court's ruling against Gore's alarmism—CNN passed on

O'Brien in favor of a triumvirate of hysterics, Anderson Cooper, Jeff Corwin, and Dr. Sanjay Gupta, to craft a two-part special titled "Planet in Peril" (who would watch "Planet OK"?).

When promoting the special, network talent brazenly touted the annual Southern California wildfires as possibly the "result of global warming in some way."[157] Of course an increase in the global mean surface temperature of about one degree over 150 years would be hard pressed to start fires. What hasn't changed is that Southern California has been warm and dry for a very long time. Indeed, the U.S. was warmer in the 1930s than today, and that was a quiet decade for wildfires.

The 1970s in contrast were so cool that they saw a "global cooling" panic begin, and that was a busy time for fires, which tend not to correlate with temperatures but with wet seasons producing greater growth of the plants that serve as fuel.[158] All of which was far too inconvenient for the media, which rushed headlong into a week of breathless coverage suggesting and sometimes expressly stating the contrary. Things were so bad that the *Los Angeles Times* proved the adult in the room—its physical proximity to the fire yielding sobriety while far-flung hysterics apparently viewed the fire as an ideological matter—implicitly chastising the jackals for capitalizing on genuine human tragedies which ought not to be the subject of such ghoulish scribbling.

With a requisite "no one really knows for sure" to qualify the alarmism it telegraphed, CNN's Tom Foreman warned viewers of a horrific future, a possible "century of fires, just like what we're seeing now" as a result of global warming. Just like what we're seeing now. But due to warming. With the network having "warned reporters not to 'irresponsibly link' the fires to 'Global Warming,'"[159] this raises the question what sort of coverage *would* constitute the verboten linkage.

Cooper assured us that the purpose of "Peril" was simply to provide an honest, objective assessment of the evidence. "We set out to report, not be advocates, no agenda." But he couldn't keep a straight face, collapsing into "You've seen the front lines [NB: *It's a war*!], the facts on the ground. Overpopulation, deforestation, species lost, climate change. Nothing happens in a vacuum. What happens in one place now affects us all." For example, alarmist hype on CNN causes viewers to switch to FOX News.

So, when setting out to produce this special we are to accept that CNN actually thought it might air two nights of "Everything's A-OK!" but was swamped instead by evidence of calamity. For example, an Anderson Cooper voice-over: "Greenland's ice sheet, 40 percent of it gone in the past forty years." This is pure, unadul-terated fiction, if seemingly sup-ported by a guest who claimed, "We have never seen a temperature rise in Greenland that drastic over a short period. It's only about eight years."

Well, actually that's true only for people who haven't *looked*. Greenland has cooled since several previous (stronger) warming peri-ods in the early and mid–twentieth century—which were well before Man could have conceivably had even the remotest CO_2-driven influence—all of which failed to aggressively melt its ice mass as CNN warns might now happen.[160] As Petr Chylek of Los Alamos National Laboratory noted in the peer-reviewed *Journal of Geo-physical Research Letters*, the rate of warming in 1920–1930 was

> "No ice chip of skepticism threatened CNN's scary story line. Cooper—who made a major gaffe when he said 40 percent of Greenland's ice sheet had gone away in the last 40 years—did manage to admit it was not likely the island's 630,000 cubic miles of ice were going to melt anytime soon. But for perspective's sake, he might have noted how Greenland got its name— because it was hotter—and greener—900 years ago than it is today."
>
> *Bill Steigerwald*, Pittsburgh Tribune-Review, *on CNN's "Planet in Peril"*

about 50 percent higher than that in 1995–2005. "We find that the current Greenland warming is not unprecedented in recent Greenland history."[161] This guy obviously doesn't watch Miles O'Brien.

The reliance upon scary, computer-generated future scenarios reached its nadir when CNN discussed everyone's favorite, the polar bear. Basic facts somehow ended up on the cutting room floor, such as the numbers showing polar bear populations booming, and Canadian arctic biologist Mitch Taylor reporting that in warmer southern areas of their range in Canada, bear populations are exploding with some of the biggest cubs born on record.[162] It does seem to be the case that the greatest threat to polar bears is computer models. Maybe we should ration them, too.

No Earth-on-Fire report is complete without the irrepressible James Hansen, resident NASA alarmist and longtime Al Gore advisor, whom CNN positioned as offering the final word in waiving away scientific challenge and pushing his own imaginings (the oil industry is propping up the "skeptics"). In selecting Hansen of all people to dismiss the well-substantiated reality that the warming alarmists are well-funded, CNN simply outdid itself.

The very same Hansen has been documented receiving an unrestricted grant of $250,000 from the activist Heinz Foundation in 2001,[163] then subsequently endorsing John Kerry for president in 2004, who is married to Teresa Heinz, who runs the Heinz Foundation. This was followed by a $1 million "prize" for his work ringing the alarm bell,[164] and possibly up to hundreds of thousands of dollars more in legal and PR support from a George Soros-funded group to assist with promoting Hansen's claims of "censorship" by the George W. Bush administration (despite the fact Hansen did over 1,400 on-the-job media interviews, and that he also said this about the George H. W. Bush administration).[165] No questions about this fortune and related political advocacy made it into the final program, if they were ever asked.

CNN's crown jewel of global warming advocacy proved to be nothing more than doctrinaire advocacy packaged in several hours over two nights and breaking no new ground. It prattled on about rising sea levels and the shrinking Lake Chad being driven by "global warming," even though that very myth was deconstructed and debunked during the three days of evidence—not a sixty-minute special—by the UK High Court just two weeks prior to the special being aired. CNN's team further set out to press all the usual levers aimed at frightening with segments dedicated to reaching those most useful advocates of the alarmist industry, "the children," preparing special classroom materials.

CASE STUDY IN MEDIA ADVOCACY: GUILT BY ASSOCIATED PRESS

With stories distributed worldwide in papers large and small, the Associated Press is a leading beacon in the global warming movement. This is exemplified almost daily, for example in the October 22, 2007, story by AP's Randolph E. Schmid.[166]

In it Schmid uses "carbon dioxide emissions" to mean *Manmade* CO_2 emissions betraying—and conveying—his mistaken belief that all CO_2 emissions come from human activity (he's off by about 96 percent). Typical journalist. But, confusing things even further, he seems to also conflate CO_2 emissions with CO_2 *concentrations*—which is like confusing the number of births in a year with the entire population.

When a paper was published revealing that the Earth's surface had warmed up not "faster than thought," but only half as much, the AP, like the rest of the media, had no interest.[167]

Such examples are child's play compared to the prose regularly churned out by the AP's Seth Borenstein, whose theatrics are exemplified by the breathless item, "Scientists beg for climate action" filed as the December 2007 post-Kyoto negotiations in Bali ginned up.[168] This story cheered the alarmists having finally rounded up a list of signatories to *something*—a letter signed by 215 of them demanding "action" in Bali. It opened with, "For the first time, more than 200 of the world's leading climate scientists, losing their patience, urged government leaders to take radical action to slow global warming because 'there is no time to lose.'" This may sound familiar, because for years a leading meme in Borenstein's work has been the false notion that "thousands of scientists" collectively beg for urgent action because there is no time to lose.

Two weeks later, Borenstein saw no news value in a listing of more than 400 scientists, including many who participate in the IPCC process, whose work specifically belies the IPCC's alarmism and the sham claim of "consensus."[169] This was unavoidable enough to get picked up by major papers from the UK to Australia, even Croatia, but was too dangerous for the AP's "warming" guru (or ABC, NBC, CBS, or CNN) to touch.

Borenstein is, however, exercised by energy industry support for skeptics, if not so much over their support for alarmists. For example, to date he has found no interest in the aforementioned funding streams given to Gore advisor and activist scientist James Hansen.

So it isn't Borenstein's cup of tea to upset the Left by asking questions, particularly those which might prove uncomfortable to *both* sides—non-activists might call this showing journalistic "balance." But Borenstein showed great interest in

NEW YORK (AP)—It's a tough world, all right. Too bad it's not tougher. Right now Earth is looking pretty fragile as it suffers from increasing human punishment. This isn't really news, of course. But CNN has packed the two-night, four-hour "Planet in Peril" with information and images that give a familiar story new urgency. Here is an eye-opening, often heart-wrenching exploration.

Associated Press story announcing "CNN Takes stock of a 'Planet in Peril'," October 21, 2007

$100,000 of support provided to underwrite work by Professor Patrick Michaels. Michaels claims that Man has a meaningful role in recent planetary warming while also noting that observations and sober modeling indicate that such warming—whatever the cause and assuming it resumes—clearly will be below even the lowest UN model projection. By daring to explain how data points to a one hundred-year increase of a mere 1.5 °C or so, however, Michaels draws media attacks on his credibility. While he'll never earn the paeans the alarmists get, he can hope for "even Patrick Michaels [insert "industry-funded" line here] agrees that" Man is doing something that they implicitly equate with calamity.

Borenstein rushed to cover this particular grant to Michaels and portray him as a global warming "critic for hire," in the words of LiveScience's headline running above Borenstein's piece[170] which offered no evidence that Michaels' opinions are influenced by financial support. *Michaels receives underwriting from energy companies, and he disagrees with us. QED.*

It seems impossible to believe that Borenstein is unaware of the relative sums bestowed upon alarmists and skeptics, yet he clearly implied the amount of this grant as being a significant sum worthy of indignation. Because he never covers the other side, his readers have no way of comparing.

Doing his best George Costanza—who famously counseled, "Jerry, just remember, it's not a lie if *you* believe it"—he opened his piece with what would be a lie in any world other than *Seinfeld*: Michaels is "one of the few remaining scientists skeptical of the global warming harm caused by industries that burn fossil fuels." Instead of acquiescing to the facts, Borenstein merrily piles on with evidence that either he lives under a rock in the AP newsroom, or is as much a dishonest shill for his pals in the alarmist industry as he claims Michaels is for others. The flood of science and scientists against climate alarmism is actually so great that even *Washington Post* beat writer Juliet Eilperin acknowledged the obvious, sustained trend that the numbers of climate rationalists "appear to be expanding rather than shrinking"[171]—though she had to step outside of the *Post's* pages to write that.

Borenstein knew or should have known of the recent flow of non-alarmist literature and that thousands of scientists actually are on record as proof positive against his statement.[172] Add to this his inability to mention, let alone *write about*, the lucrative trade being waged by global warming alarmists for hire. He has taken sides, has an agenda and is an advocate posing as a reporter.

PROTECTING HIS OWN

In what may be the most spectacular advertisement of his partisanship on the issue, Borenstein and the Associated Press scrambled to provide some flank support for Gore when his movie *An Inconvenient Truth* first began taking fire for presenting non-truths as gospel.

The initial offering designed to shield Gore, "Scientists OK Gore's Movie for Accuracy,"[173] either escaped editorial review or else reveals lengths to which the establishment will go to protect its own and their shared agenda. Consider Borenstein's remarkably subjective opening line, "The nation's top climate scientists are giving *An Inconvenient Truth*, Al Gore's documentary on global warming, five stars for accuracy." Whoever constitutes this list of greats and on what basis, readers are not told, but Seth Borenstein thinks they're the nation's leading scientists. For all we know their greatness is attained by simple virtue of this belief, sort of like the UN IPCC's "world's leading scientists" attaining such honorific simply by agreeing to participate.

Borenstein's third paragraph provided evidence for the intrepid to follow: "The AP contacted more than 100 top climate researchers by e-mail and phone for their opinion. Among those contacted were vocal skeptics of climate change theory. Most scientists had not seen the movie, which is in limited release, or read the book." (While the novice reader would assume that the "most scientists" referred at least to that universe of 100 scientists contacted, it was actually only "most" of the forty who returned their call.)

So AP actually reports that more than half of those who got back to them had chosen not to see the film. From Borenstein's rhetorical gymnastics, let's conclude that nineteen scientists on AP's call or email lists who did get back to them *had* seen it. AP explains away this disinterest among relevant practitioners by noting that Gore's movie is in "limited release." Of course, film-goers are a self-selecting universe, and we have evidence there is a less flattering reason most "leading scientists" didn't go see this bit of Hollywood: KBJR-TV Meteorologist Carl Spring explained that he, as one expert, "wouldn't pay a dime to see [*AIT*]" because the pre-release publicity made clear to the expert's eye that Gore "takes facts and extrapolates them to such extremes" so that they don't make any sense but to project "a doomsday scenario."

Also discouraging scientists from seeing this ballyhooed production, the movie's flaws were well known fairly soon after its release. The George Marshall Institute revealed what the AP sought to mask with its reportage:

Mr Gore's movie and book contain numerous assertions that are inconsistent with our state of knowledge: A few of these differences include:

- The National Academy of Science's recent repudiation of the so-called hockey stick temperature history;
- The National Academy of Science's 2001 statement on the nearly impossible task of determining the degree of causality that can be assigned to human factors when the extent of natural variability in the climate is unknown;
- The fact that the Arctic was just as warm in 1940 as it is today;

- The fact that the Greenland ice sheet is growing when global mean temperature is increasing; and the [sic]
- The debate over the relationship between climate change and hurricanes.

This is just a short list of errors cited by Mr. Gore. There are many more, demonstrating that his movie and book are advocacy, not factual information.

It is just a short list, indeed. My colleague Marlo Lewis was well ahead of the UK court system in detailing hundreds of misstatements, distortions, half-truths and outright falsehoods in *AIT*.[174] Christopher Lord Monckton, a former advisor to Margaret Thatcher, has also inveighed in detail against Gore's untruthfulness with "35 Inconvenient Truths: the errors in Gore's movie."[175]

Such troubles never occurred to Borenstein, who waived off the incuriosity of people who are sufficiently driven as to attain advanced degrees in technical fields, but didn't see a movie dealing with their field with which he was quite taken. Yet even further down in the piece and despite the obvious travails placed in these scientists' paths, AP informs us that, somehow, "more than 1 million people have seen the movie since it opened." So, unlike most of the general population, most climate scientists live in theater-deprived, out of the way places? Humorously, this course correction was in service the breathless disbelief AP then unleashed, that *"Washington's top science decision makers" have not managed to go see this film!* To recap, scientists who actually work on the issue are to be forgiven for not going to see *AIT*, but can *you believe the nerve of Bush and the heads of EPA and NASA not hearing Gore's case? Don't they know that lots of* other *people have?* This is simply schizophrenic advocacy.

Borenstein cited a total of five people, omitting mention that some of them had ties to the Clinton-Gore administration and environmentalist pressure groups. The two critical opinions of Gore's flick: one individual thought Gore distracted from the alarmist case by focusing on Hurricane Katrina, and another thought Gore *understated* the nature of challenge. Hard-hitting, to be sure.

Meanwhile plenty of contrary opinion existed and was already out in the ether, in the unlikely event that Borenstein actually wanted to find it. Timothy Ball, the first Canadian PhD in Climatology, asserted "I branded Gore's 100-minute documentary an error-filled propaganda piece. I'm not alone. James Hansen, Gore's own science adviser and political supporter conceded, with huge understatement, the movie has imperfections and technical flaws. The flaws are large enough to fail a term paper from any student in attendance."[176]

University of Pennsylvania Professor Robert Giegengack claimed he voted for Gore and would again, as appears to be the case with most academics and, although he shares Gore's (other) politics, unlike the cheerleaders rounded up by Borenstein he pulls no punches or detail when discrediting Gore's claims and lack of understanding about the principles and specifics underlying his own claims.[177]

In truth, the movie had been exposed prior to this apparent effort to rehabilitate it. Further, the consensus (there's that word!) about Gore's claims has since clearly emerged, and Borenstein's five sources are not part of it. So one must ask, could Borenstein actually be saying, as it seems, that those five individuals are the nation's top scientists? Is it really so simple as returning a call from the AP to gain such distinction?

The minority spokesman for the Senate Environment and Public Works Committee had no trouble immediately tracking down substantive criticism by sources ranging from award-winning scientists to chaired Ivy League professors of relevant disciplines. Underlining the ease with which anyone who was sincerely interested could gauge expert opinion of Gore's claims, that office issued a challenge that the AP bring its piece up to reasonable jour-

nalistic standards, or at minimum provide the information necessary for readers to evaluate its facially absurd thesis:

> AP chose to ignore the scores of scientists who have harshly crit-
> icized the science presented in former Vice President Al Gore's
> movie *An Inconvenient Truth*. In the interest of full disclosure,
> the AP should release the names of the "more than 100 top cli-
> mate researchers" they attempted to contact to review "An
> Inconvenient Truth." AP should also name all 19 scientists who
> gave Gore "five stars for accuracy." AP claims 19 scientists
> viewed Gore's movie, but it only quotes five of them in its arti-
> cle. AP should also release the names of the so-called scientific
> 'skeptics' they claim to have contacted.[178]

Responding to Sen. Inhofe's criticism of this particularly shameless
advocacy, the AP released a statement vowing that the Borenstein
story was "completely accurate" and said it "met AP's high standards in every way." Seriously.

COURTING RIDICULE

Borenstein was no one-hit wonder when it came to covering for
Gore's embarrassments. The withering criticism of *AIT* that even
prompted judicial scrutiny of Gore's claims couldn't find its way
into Borenstein's reportage. It isn't precisely true to say he was
silent when that UK court bounced Gore's money claims. Days
later he did note the decision—in paragraph sixteen of a story
touting Gore's receipt of a Nobel Peace Prize.

This treatment of the court's decision was straight from a
bizarre "guidance" memo sent by Roger Harrabin to his BBC
colleagues actually styling the verdict as a *victory* for the film
even though the defendant UK government was unable to support even *one* of the litany of specific claims on which the Court

sought evidence, all of which were rejected as unfounded. Wrote Borenstein:

> The film won praise but also generated controversy. On Wednesday, a British judge ruled in a lawsuit that it was OK to show the movie to students in school. High Court Judge Michael Burton said it was "substantially founded upon scientific research and fact" but presented in a "context of alarmism and exaggeration." He said teachers must be given a written document explaining that.[179]

That's it. No mention of any among the laundry list of laughable lies, except to falsely claim that only "a couple" of them were rejected. Borenstein went on in the next paragraph to wax nostalgic about that time when he wrote a story about scientists who support the movie's claims, this time vaguely diluting the fawning praise. Only now he muttered that back then, "some were bothered by what they thought were a couple of exaggerations."

CHAPTER 2

Fear and Loathing

Alarmist Scare Tactics, Demonization, and Threats

"Those of us who dare to question the dogma of the global-warming doomsters who claim that C not only stands for carbon but also for climate catastrophe are vilified as heretics or worse as deniers. I am happy to be branded a heretic because throughout history heretics have stood up against dogma based on the bigotry of vested interests. But I don't like being smeared as a denier because deniers don't believe in facts. The truth is that there are no facts that link the concentration of atmospheric carbon dioxide with imminent catastrophic global warming."

UK Botanist and famed environmental campaigner David Bellamy, *The Times* (London), October 2007

THE STRANGE PARADOX OF THE ALARM over "global warming" is that its adherents find it a worthy enough cause to justify the incivility (and worse) described in these pages but not a big enough deal to accept, say, nuclear power (no CO_2) replacing coal-fired electricity. It's important enough that debate on it must be silenced, but not important enough to demand a tax on greenhouse gas emissions, instead favoring convoluted and climatically useless schemes that pay off political constituencies (and act as a hidden tax, costlier than an honest tax). It is also clearly far too important to hold the "good guys" to the standards of honesty, consistency, or proof. In short, the global warming agenda and rhetoric may be a lot of things, but rational is not among them.

Also consider how the most breathless politicians join in the name-calling and persecution, mouthing the most alarmist stance possible; but when it comes to talking to actual voters—say, when running for the White House—they set nearly every other matter as a higher priority. I'm speaking of Al Gore's 2000 presidential run, which almost completely ignored the issue at a time when warming actually appeared to be on the rise; but it also fairly describes John McCain and Barack Obama, who both uttered every platitude of alarm and concern imaginable—in the appropriate setting—only to all but ignore the issue in their announced priorities and when they knew large numbers were paying attention.

The same phenomenon occurred when the Democrats ran a nationalized campaign to regain Congress in 2006. Although the candidates demurred when asked publicly if granting the Democrats a majority would yield the immediate climate action that they demanded of the Republican majority, once the votes were counted, "global warming" suddenly resumed its perch as the ultimate threat. Rhetorically, that is—it was little more than a great topic for hearings, hardly the subject of sincere efforts to enact their rhetoric into law.

So despite having made little mention of it when applying for the job, upon gaveling itself into existence the leadership of the 110th Congress established a select committee on the weather, enabling a globetrotting road show mostly about how mean Republicans are for not agreeing with them. The specifics—and costs—of legislation were best put off until later. Say, after another election.

The excuse for inaction was that President Bush would probably just veto anything they might pass—thus affirming why America needed a bigger Democrat majority and president, too. This excuse is beyond silly. First, Bush never threatened such a veto. Second, on legislative issues the Democrats thought were political winners, the congressional majority repeatedly ignored Bush's actual veto threats and magnified their differences with the GOP. On the issue of saving the world from global warming, though, they cowered before veto non-threats.

After the Democrats explained to the faithful that their inaction proved the need to elect more Democrats, the party's candidates proceeded in the 2008 election to once again barely mention the issue.

All of which is to say that global warming remained just as much a political and fundraising issue and excuse for alarmist finger-pointing no matter who had the votes. It is still largely a vessel into which its adherents' pour their own virtue and, even more frequently, for demonizing opponents.

NOTHING TO OFFER BUT FEAR ITSELF

For example, among the new Congress's early acts was to summon former Vice President Al Gore to "testify" before the House Committee on Government Reform, chaired by Democrat Henry Waxman from Hollywood—under rules of Gore's own insistence and design, meaning he was to give a speech (thankfully, not a slide show). Later that day, Gore reprised his *State of the Climate* address for the Senate Environment and Public Works Committee.

These events and the attendant rhetoric merit a case study in their own right, if only for Gore's memorable intonation (as well as typical display of awareness and proportion), "I've *been* to Chernobyl. I've *been* to Three Mile Island." Not the most apt pairing, unless, unbeknownst to the world, the U.S government had covered up an actual "catastrophe" befalling Pennsylvanians. Somewhere, a particular lawmaker squirmed over the inevitable revival of maudlin jokes about more people dying in his back seat than at the site of "our own Chernobyl."

Also worth cherishing was Gore's invocation of planet-as-infant, the ultimate overreach in the greens' tiresome ritual of claiming that they do *whatever-it-is* for the kids (whom, the greens will often tell you, you should stop having). Gore envisioned a crib which, in his narrative, was alternately on fire or merely holding a child with a fever. Apparently, "If the crib's on fire, you do not speculate that the baby is flame retardant. You take action." In the multiple Gore households this apparently means wrapping your child in a copy of the Kyoto Protocol and calling the UN, *stat*.

With his internal governor having apparently stirred from its slumber, Gore then offered more temperate, but equally incoherent imagery; this time, the child-planet was only a little flush in the cheeks. "The planet has a fever. If your baby has a fever, you go to the doctor. If the doctor says you need to intervene here, you don't say 'I read a science fiction novel that says it's not a problem.'... You take action."

Taking action, in Gore's case, might have meant pushing the Senate to ratify the Kyoto Protocol—something Gore never did while in the White House.

The odd thing is that, while infants have normal temperatures, none of Gore's interlocutors were compelled to ask *what is the planet's*? Is it 98.6° Fahrenheit, too? And, where do you put the thermometer? With the U.S. National Climatic Data Center in charge, as you will read, your planet's fever might just mean that you accidentally placed the thermometer over a barbeque grill or in an asphalt parking lot.

Waxman and Gore delighted in endlessly congratulating one another for brave leadership on the issue. It is certainly true that Gore deserves mention for getting very exercised about the matter *after* he left office, and Waxman a medal for holding lots of hearings to talk about how awful some people are for hating science and generally not agreeing that the world is about to end (as for actually legislating, well, not so much). Becoming chairman required modification of his routine of the previous six years, which amounted to condemning Republicans for holding hearings on the science while not legislating.

Chairman Waxman did find time to thank Gore for educating Congress and the American people "about the gravest threat" in the world, which—judging by the priorities of Mr. Waxman's team upon gaining the majority—means somewhere behind an increase in the federal minimum wage, cutting the interest rate on student loans, peeking at emails about U.S. Attorneys, and other critical issues confronting humanity on which they found time to focus their laser beam.[1] Among Gore's most educational messages was the reminder that "[global warming] is not partisan; this is not political; this is a moral issue." Waxman agreed, dismissing the *criticism* of the global warming agenda as "smack[ing] of fear, and fear can be paralyzing."

Because, you know, Gore's video about twenty-foot sea-level rises in New York, or that Environmental Defense ad depicting global warming as a train about to kill an eight-year-old girl, those weren't about *fear*. Those were science, and people who don't agree hate science.

DEMONIZATION

Gore's Capitol Hill histrionics were actually an entertaining, harmless respite from the day-to-day nastiness of the global warming campaign. British journalist Brendan O'Neill writes of how "climate-change sceptics have been steadily demonised as a public enemy, even a threat to security and prosperity."[2] The alarmists' gateway slur is the slightly less hysterical if equally nonsensical dismissal "as deniers" those who disagree. They rarely bother to set forth what it is that the "denial machine" spends its time denying.

I suppose the alarmists are just too busy denying that climate has *always* changed.

Gore asserts that those who disagree with him also believe the moon landings were faked and belong to a flat Earth society, while his allies among the environmental pressure groups repeat the charge and argue that there are only "about half a dozen" skeptical scientists left in the world (which, if true, would mean the death of science as we've known it). This is to be expected from advocates who have shown no compunction about measuring the words they use. But the increasingly shrill and *ad hominem* head of the UN's Intergovernmental Panel on Climate Change, Chairman Rajendra Pachauri, spouts the same talking point, in addition to his *argumentum ad Hitlerum* noted elsewhere.[3] Meanwhile he is held out as a "world's leading climate scientist" when in fact he is no such thing: he is trained as an economist and engineer, credentials which the alarmists sneer at as irrelevant when worn by critics—*who are they to challenge Mr. Gore, holder of a bachelor's degree in government?*

Bob Ferguson, who runs the Science and Public Policy Institute, notes that "the compulsion to hide uncertainties and silence 'critics' has been a loud whisper in the [global warming]/political community for an overly long time.... The fear of threat to the political orthodoxy of AGW [anthropogenic global warming] policy-science has spun up such a fury that we are witnessing brazen calls for legal prosecution and personal destruction of scientists (or any organization presenting their research and views), who are labeled as comparable to 'Holocaust Deniers' and tobacco-industry-like 'hired guns.'"[4]

At various Kyoto Protocol negotiations that I have attended, Greenpeace posted around the convention hall a "Field Guide to Climate Criminals" with photographs of me and a few others on the enemies list, so that the unwashed children of privilege flocking to these meetings couldn't miss us. Here's a tip: we're the hygienic ones unburdened by the telltale split ends or, to borrow a phrase from P. J. O'Rourke, the kind of ugliness that is the result of years of ill temper, pique, and petty malice.

The point of the greens' rhetoric and tactics of course isn't a logical one but a sign of desperation. Writing in the *Guardian*, Brendan O'Neill aptly described the usage and purpose of the label "climate-change denier," pointing out that it "is used to describe a mixed bag of people—from those who think the planet is getting hotter but argue that we will be able to deal with it, to those who deny outright that any warming is taking place (who are in a tiny minority). The term 'denier' is powerfully pejorative. As Charles Jones, an emeritus Professor of English at Edinburgh University, has argued, the denier label is intended to assign any 'doubters' with 'the same moral repugnance one associates with Holocaust denial.' In short, they are wicked people with base motives."[5]

Confirming such dark fears, one writer in a journal called *Climatic Change* informs us about climate skepticism's nature in a piece titled, "Parallels in reactionary argumentation in the US congressional debates on the abolition of slavery and the Kyoto Protocol."[6]

One prominent alarmist was apparently unsatisfied by the juvenile nature of things as they stand and furious that climate realists get away with only being called skeptics or deniers, so he promoted substitution of these labels with "climate destroyer."[7] This is a grown man, by the way, named Joe Romm. He is a former Clinton administration official now with the George Soros-funded "ClimateProgress" blog. Despite seeming to be an adult in possession of his faculties he attributes nearly every occurrence imaginable to global warming, including the 2007 Minnesota bridge collapse. As fate would have it, he is also a solar panel salesman.

It goes beyond such silliness, however. As Bonner Cohen discusses in his indispensable book *The Green Wave: Environmentalism and Its Consequences*, the alarmist movement's icons such as James Hansen of NASA and Robert F. Kennedy Jr. routinely and promiscuously slur anyone crossing their path as being the sort of folk who ran Nazi Germany or the Soviet Union. Kennedy also slothfully exposes his ignorance on several levels. For example, he charged the Bush administration with oppressing government-employed alarmists by means which are "arguably unmatched in the Western world since the Inquisition."[8] He might want to avoid that particular comparison; it turns out that the Europeans actually burned more than three times as many "witches" in their hysteria over the most recent climate change of significance, the Little Ice Age, than fell victim to the Spanish Inquisition.[9]

The global warming industry leans quite heavily on the Nazi analogy. In addition to the call for "Nuremburg-style trials" for skeptics, they've claimed that putting together an inventory of recent peer-reviewed research that runs counter to the supposed consensus is "something the German Parliament would issue during WW2 to tell the people that the Holocaust is not happening, and if it is the Nazis are not responsible for it."[10] Of course.

Environmentalists have a repellent history for nigh on two decades of diminishing the Holocaust as a way to hype their panic. It is a staple of blogs and e-mails among climate realists, for the simple reason of the anonymity the Internet provides, which does not lessen its importance any more than it does the typically anonymous physical threats made against skeptics. But the *you're-like-Hitler* approach is also a regular tactic of widely read on-line and print magazines.

WHAT TO CALL A NAME-CALLER

Remember, *it's the seriousness of the charge that matters*, so the alarmist world's Internet rantings deserve attention. Of course, this sort of rhetoric began before the Web's invention. As Marc Sheppard of the *American Thinker* details, "In truth, environmentalists' deplorable trivialization of Hitler's genocide can be traced as far

back as the late 1980's (by an ambitious senator from Ten-
nessee)."[11] It wasn't long before one Albert Gore Jr. would be
described by a Democratic operative as comparing a failure to
recycle aluminum cans with the Holocaust and otherwise trivially
invoking that tragedy.[12]

Though equating dissenters from alarmism specifically with
Holocaust deniers became quite fashionable in 2006,[13] Gore
telegraphed his own trajectory with slight tweak on this meme, a
1989 column in the *New York Times* comparing global warming
to the Holocaust.[14] We have seen a similar evolution in recent
years of the notion that for the media to quote skeptics in a story
is proof of the media going too far in the name of unwarranted
even-handedness; the logical next step of this was to call for an end
to "balance" (where none actually exists). Until such final corruption of discourse occurs, it seems that the resort to "denier" is due
to the difficulties of capturing in a single term the arguments of
tens of thousands of scientists among many other policy-relevant
experts. Upon review, "rationalist" does the trick.

Marc Sheppard compiled some of the looniest quotations. Take
this one from "environmental author" Mark Lynas who describes
his blog as "something of a debating hall about climate change."

> I wonder what sentences judges might hand down at future
> international criminal tribunals on those who will be partially
> but directly responsible for millions of deaths from starvation,
> famine and disease in decades ahead. I put this in a similar moral
> category to Holocaust denial—except that this time the Holo-
> caust is yet to come, and we still have time to avoid it. Those
> who try to ensure we don't will one day have to answer for their
> crimes.[15]

David Roberts, writing for the popular green website *Grist* went
into more detail:

When we've finally gotten serious about global warming, when the impacts are really hitting us and we're in a full worldwide scramble to minimize the damage, we should have war crimes trials for these bastards—some sort of climate Nuremberg.[16]

It's not just the unhinged bloggers, though. The World's Greatest Deliberative Body, the United States Senate, is led by Democrat Harry Reid who analogizes coal companies defending themselves to using "the old Hitler lie."[17] Not that there was any shortage of evidence that the alarmists lack proportion, but their belabored analogies of skeptics to mass murderers abandon all sense of reality and perspective.

Academic and activist Ross Gelbspan (who for a long time portrayed himself as a Pulitzer Prize winner, which he isn't) has attacked scientists (which he also is not) as "criminals against humanity" for questioning his apocalyptic future scenarios.[18] One cowardly green-activist website calls a Harvard astrophysicist an attempted mass murderer for discussing the Sun's role in the earth's historical temperature record, and labels other dissenters "felons."[19]

It seems pointless to bother avoiding judgmental terms for people who insist that, if you do not do what they want or otherwise doubt them, quite possibly every person on Earth will be wiped out.[20] *Warmist* is absurdly tame; *alarmist* seems a bare minimum for those who alternately premise rants on delirious global warming being here already, or arriving any day now, despite the rather poor track record over recent decades of similar predictions. *Hysteric* certainly applies; *eco-fundamentalist* seems fitting for those who call anyone daring to disagree with their prophesying as akin to a Holocaust denier.

Sheppard notes that the alarmists rabidly push the dogma "that human salvation demands a coerced return to a less modern, less industrialized society and blind acceptance of fanatical dogma which can currently be neither proved nor disproved," leaving them akin to "an analogous group with similar traits that calls its heretical enemies 'infidels' rather than 'deniers.'"[21]

Dennis Avery, co-author of the book *Unstoppable Global Warming: Every 1,500 Years,* notes that "When global warming alarmists condemn skeptics as 'deniers,' that is an unscientific and socially dangerous characterization. Skeptics are not the enemy. On the contrary, they are crucial to science because they help us search for truth."[22]

So, do the celebrated "deniers" deny that the Earth has warmed? No, the rationalist position agrees that there has been a warming since the end of the Little Ice Age, about 150 years ago, just as the Earth had warmed prior to that, and so on. In fact, we are presently experiencing a cooling trend if you, like the alarmists, want to conveniently select baseline years helpful to your position (the Medieval Warming would be one such baseline, or the Roman Warming, or 1998).

The "deniers" *do* reject the notion that a change of one degree Fahrenheit over the course of a century-plus is unprecedented or calamitous, while some also argue that cooling of any magnitude has always been a very bad thing. The historical record strongly supports both points. Deniers do not deny that our understanding of physics holds that some portion of that warming should be attributable to Man, either. They do note, however, the admission that alarmist computer models do not properly account for the sun's influence (or clouds), and how this ought to dial down promises of impending Man-made doom. After all, the cooling of recent years coincides with a quiet sun, while the CO_2-obsessed models continue to "show" warming.

What "deniers" do reject is that this portends some future delirious warming. For one thing, science informs us that each subsequent carbon dioxide molecule has half of the warming potential of the one before it; that is, that even if one accepts greenhouse warming theory (not the safest of bets) it is clear that we are nearing the end of any possible human CO_2 influence under every feasible emissions scenario.

Therefore, the "deniers" generally are *denying* that it is responsible behavior to rush towards sweeping government-mandated transformation of society in the name of battling climate change.

ON THE TAKE

Possibly confronting the illogic of "denier," a new tack in alarmist name-calling is the recent practice of calling climate rationalists "tobacco scientists." The implication is yet again that anyone who dares dispute their vision of a horrible future world must be on the take, paid to say so. When I have appeared on television jointly with the president of Greenpeace USA, he has more than once struggled to yelp a "last word" that's some variant of the shrill "tobacco scientist!" slur.

Ironically, it is the greens themselves who have adopted the tobacco industry's tactics.[23] This should be no surprise, as John Atkinson points out in the UK newspaper, the *Register*: "The climate science bandwagon has come about solely because of supposed anthropogenic climate change, which means that their funding is intrinsically tied to climate change happening and being man-made. A more self-interested group I could not find anywhere, even looking at the researchers who were paid by big tobacco companies to tell us cigarettes are safe."[24]

Further, the premise behind most alarmist slurs of the "tobacco scientist" variety and the ritual claims of "ties" to "big oil" or "industry," is that a scientist's convictions and the convictions of other dissenters, can be bought. It's illogical to assume that dissenters can be bought but alarmists cannot. Looking at the balance sheets on both sides, their logic would conclude that the greatest amount of corruption occurs on the alarmist side. After all, James

Hansen and Michael Oppenheimer are paid enormous sums of money for their alarmist activities, sums that no "skeptic" has ever been accused of receiving. Those same alarmists also ardently support Al Gore's message and mission even while Gore—the king of claiming that those who disagree are merely in it for the money—makes millions annually from all manner of enterprises premised upon the "climate crisis," and his lucre will increase several fold upon passing the laws his alarmism demands.[25]

The difficult truth is that the alarmists cannot logically fault the skeptics' credibility without also faulting Gore's credibility and that of their heavily compensated rock star alarmists. Yet no "skeptic" receives as much as Gore or even Hansen off of the issue. Think about it.

This blind insistence that whoever disagrees with the alarmist thesis has simply sold their views is most deeply held among college students or professors, self-styled "environmentalists." That is, they reflect the dogma typical to their movement or demographic as opposed to some well-reasoned or at least substantive reasons for their passion. Add to this, however, some adults who ought to be above such nonsense. For example, longtime alarmist and scientist Michael Schlesinger of the University of Illinois casually sends out e-mails to a broad distribution libelously suggesting that esteemed intellects such as former Chancellor of the Exchequer for Margaret Thatcher, Lord Nigel Lawson, "receives a sweetener from big energy" to write his detailed analyses of how alarmist policy is disastrously flawed. By such actions it seems that alarmists are not only terrified of the weather, but of the threat of challenge.

One need not be Lord Lawson to incur such allegations, of course. In addition to constant allusions to my likely having sold my advocacy to the highest bidder, I receive lovely e-mails after television appearances. Environmentalists have written me to wish a slow death from cancer while others rather ignorantly confuse carbon dioxide with carbon monoxide to suggest that, if I like CO_2 so much why don't I go asphyxiate myself in my garage? Generally, those alarmists who elect to reach out are nasty and resort to name calling, somehow aware that this is how alarmists are to confront unsanctioned opinion.

One thoughtful correspondent calling himself "Jimmy R. Nunley jr" was representative of those who found themselves upset with CNN for having used the likes of me for their "but, not *everyone* agrees..." line in a story for which they flew their anchor to Oslo to cover Al Gore's receipt of the Nobel Peace Prize (they do that every year, right?).

To wit:

> You bastards will do anything for money won't you? The sad truth is that it's effective because Americans are ignorant and they don't think for themselves. I've started 42 blogs, to date [NB: being mere hours after CNN aired a comment from me, this is either impressive or delusional], to protest CNN for airing interviewing of Chris Horner because it's noting [sic] but propaganda. It has no basis in fact and it's a shame that a bloodsucking lawyer for a company controlled by the oil industry is able to to [sic] stand up on a national television and make such ridiculous claims. I don't believe in heaven or hell but, if it was real, thats [sic] exactly where Mr. Horner and the rest of your staff need to go. You all need to burn in hell for what your [sic] doing. It's a disgrace!!!!

This gentleman, quite typically, forgot to note which claims of mine he disputes to the tune of four exclamation points. Though the alarmist foot-soldier generally declines to offer actual refutation or challenge amid the invective, they certainly know what they know.

Journalist Lorne Gunter of Canada's *National Post* wrote of the following experience:

> Two weeks ago, I wrote a column that was provocatively titled, "Forget global warming: Welcome to the New Ice Age." In it, I explained that, far from being warming activists, some solar scientists see the recent downturn in solar activity as harbinger of a coming Ice Age.
>
> I wondered how come we don't hear about that in equal measure with the claims of an impending meltdown?
>
> I received over 1,800 e-mails, most of them complimentary. A large number, though, were as hysterical and vicious as any I have received on any subject in almost two decades in journalism.
>
> How could I not believe? Was I being dishonest or just stupid? How much had EXXON paid me? Until I could write in favour of the warming theorists, I should "go back into your oil company-funded bubble. You @*!/x-ing hack."
>
> And that was from a climate scientist at a major university.

Such venom isn't unique to the Great White North, but noteworthy given the otherwise remarkably polite nature of their society and its inhabitants. Canada's first PhD in climatology, Dr. Tim Ball, relates that he's received death threats for his apostasy. Yet the threats of an early grave (when not acted upon) have big shoes to fill living up to the rhetoric of the premier darlings of the alarmist industry. Consider the comments from George Monbiot, star columnist for *The Guardian*, that "every time someone dies as a result of floods in Bangladesh, an airline executive should be dragged out of his office and drowned,"[26] and Gore advisor James Hansen, that "a certain shock treatment is needed, but it would best be delivered with a two-by-four as a solid whack to the head of politicians who remain oblivious to fundamental physical facts."[27] Referring to these gems, climate scientist Roger Pielke Jr. opined:

Allusions to murder and beatings kind of puts a chill on discussing options for climate policy, doesn't it? Maybe that is the point. It certainly makes me think.

In my view people who fashion themselves as public intellectuals have an even greater obligation than everyone else to encourage civil debate and discussion. This applies to people on all sides of political debates. It is all too easy for leaders to incite people to actual violence on issues that they are passionate about. Mr. Monbiot and Dr. Hansen (and others, again on all sides) may not have that outcome in mind as they write such statements, but if they don't watch out, that may be what they get.[28]

THE WHEELS COME OFF

Pielke is right. Noted skeptic, physics professor, and former head of the Geological Museum at the University of Oslo Tom Segalstad related to me an annoying series of pizzas delivered to his home which, although he did not order them, did ensue once he came out in criticism of the environmental alarmists. Oh, those clever greens. Or, maybe not so clever. It seems that, subsequently, the wheels of Segalstad's automobile up and fell off on two separate occasions, including once while his young daughter was in the car. Apparently the lug nuts had been loosened. Of course, his claim is anecdotal. Sort of like the global warmists' purported harbingers of catastrophic climate change.

TRUTH AND ITS CONSEQUENCES

Short of physical attack, science writers Stuart Blackman and Ben Pile document how the alarmists cannot limit themselves to asserting that dissenters are "just corrupt, or disrespectful of the facts, or plain old-fashioned wrong—they are [instead] deluded or ill.... German psychologist Andreas Ernst has developed a theory that people who fail to act to reduce their CO_2 emissions are similar psychologically to rats. And in an editorial earlier this year [2008] in the journal *Medscape General Medicine*, Professor of Psychiatry Steven Moffic proposed the use of aversion therapy involving 'distressing images of the projected ravages of global warming' to encourage responsible environmental behaviour among sceptics. This is less *A Clockwork Orange* and more Clockwork Green."[29]

This only makes more strange the American Psychological Association's campaign to cure the public of skepticism over global warming alarmism. "'We know how to change behavior and attitudes. That is what we do,' says Yale University psychologist Alan Kazdin, association president," deliciously commenting on this classic example of grandiosity and self-absorption.[30] So, maybe he can help Gore change his CO_2-spewing ways? Or as one colleague noted, the APA could examine the compulsion of some people to control the lives of others, be they acquaintance or complete stranger.

Former Weather Channel meteorologist Joe D'Aleo cited colleagues who informed him they would not attend a convention of climate realists "because they 'feared their attendance might affect their employment.'"[31] Is this really just more of the old someone-who-knows-someone-told-me type of mythology, or is the retaliation against skeptics real? *Skepticism* (to coin a phrase) of such claims is warranted, but those of us who have heard it first hand cannot help but be impressed by the preponderance of seemingly upright professionals making such claims.

I have been given names and anecdotes in the course of writing this book, and can attest the individuals in question affirm the incidents and choose not to speak for the record. Also, when preparing the "skeptic" scientists' brief for the Supreme Court case in *Massachusetts v. EPA*, my colleagues and other petitioners asked a particular assistant professor whether he would sign on to the brief, who responded incredulously and in the negative, "Hey, I'm up for promotion!" Tenure was understandably more important to him than joining in what appears to many to be a quixotic effort to fight a formidable machine.

So when alarmists note that some cooler-headed statisticians enter the online debate only anonymously, Steven McIntyre replies that "several of the more serious statisticians have written to me offline and identified themselves. The reasons that they don't identify themselves is that they are afraid of employment repercussions for daring to challenge any statistical aspect connected with climate science."[32] Similarly, atmospheric scientist Dr. Nathan Paldor, Professor of Dynamical Meteorology and Physical Oceanography at the Hebrew University of Jerusalem, author of almost seventy peer-reviewed studies and winner of several awards, explains how many of his fellow scientists have been intimidated, claiming, "Many of my colleagues with whom I spoke share these views and report on their inability to publish their skepticism in the scientific or public media."[33]

It is surely not coincidence that prominent researchers such as NASA's JoAnne Simpson and Portuguese environment scientist Professor Delgado Domingos only began speaking out against alarmism *after* retiring from their positions. Simpson (whom scientist Roger Pielke Sr. says was "among the most preeminent scientists of the last 100 years"[34]) specifically opened her announcement with the illuminating, "Since I am no longer affiliated with any organization nor receive any funding, I can speak quite frankly."[35]

Imagine the ritual keening and invocation of the following example if only the shoe had been on the other foot: Reginald E. Newell, Jane Hsiung, and Wu Zhongxiang of MIT, with scientists from the British Meteorological Office, dared to publish a piece titled "Possible factors controlling global marine temperature variations over the past century" in the *Journal of Geophysical Research*. They concluded, "When the residuals are examined after account is taken of these factors, the global [marine air temperature] trend for 1888–1988 is reduced to 0.24°C. With the present approach the apparent twentieth century temperature increases can be viewed as partly due to a recovery from cooling at the turn of the century, probably associated with volcanic activity."[36]

In other words: *no big deal*.

That, of course, was not going to help keep the gravy train rolling, and given that things were just then picking up steam, such cool thinking actually threatened to help derail it. Newell planned to publish this and another piece in a *Global Ocean Surface Temperature Atlas*, but it turned out that MIT Press couldn't scrape together the funding to publish it. A quick perusal of MIT's catalogue reveals it to be anything but a cash-strapped outfit, one which at the same time approved production of Stephen Schneider's "Scientists in Gaia." For his part, Newell states, "I was warned when I wrote my first paper (which discussed the difference between the climate models and some figures I was looking at for the tropics) that it would be very difficult, and my funding would probably be cut. In fact, it has been cut."[37]

Sherwood Idso and William Happer are among the better-known examples of scientists who found themselves under the gun once Al Gore took office and received the relevant portfolio from Bill Clinton. Bill Gray, the father of storm forecasting and outspoken critic of global warming doomsaying, also suddenly found his proposals serially rejected. Three of these, "Further Development of Quantitative Seasonal Prediction of Atlantic Basin Hurricane Activity and Sahel Rainfall," "Development of Quantitative Seasonal Prediction Schemes for Atlantic Basin Hurricane Activity and African Sahel Rainfall," and "A Global Synthesis of Climate Trends Associated with Atlantic Multi-decadal Variability" were all spurned by NOAA Atlantic Climate Change Program manager David Goodrich for reasons that seem particularly remarkable in hindsight, given subsequent storm activity. These included the claim that "hurricane prediction research is not presently a central focus within ACCP." He needs to read the papers more often. When Gray submitted a proposal to examine "Extended Range Prediction of ENSO [el Niño]," Kenneth A. Mooney, program officer of NOAA Office of Global Programs rejected him with a rote note. Similar rejections of his proposals by UCAR and FEMA and NOAA continued for years.

During the same span, Roger Pielke Sr. resigned as lead author of a chapter for an report of the U.S. Climate Change Science Program (which program had become a taxpayer-funded political hobbyhorse for Al Gore), "Temperature Trends in the Lower Atmosphere: Steps for Understanding and Reconciling Differences." He later noted in a January 2006 public comment on the CCSP report that report editor, Gore-favorite Tom Karl, "systematically excluded a range of views on the issue," "taking the lead in suppressing my perspectives," including "the last minute substitution of a new Chapter 6 for the one I had carefully led preparation of and on which I was close to reaching a final consensus."[38] Karl's editing gave the appearance of a larger greenhouse gas fingerprint—CCSP later buried an admission in a subsequent report that the human fingerprint is actually not found at all (discussed elsewhere). That alarmists sex up these reports is of no interest to the press as revealing it neither fits the template nor advances the agenda.

Chasing scientists out of taxpayer-funded programs, dumpster diving, and rhetorical tantrums, even the call for "war crimes trials for these bastards—some sort of climate Nuremburg,"[39] are weak beer compared to the fire that alarmists already aim at dissenting scientists, academics, and anyone else the alarmist industry sees as a threat.

As skeptical scientist Chris de Freitas of the University of Auckland (New Zealand) puts it, relatively "few scientists are willing to put their head above the parapet, for a variety of reasons, not the least of which is that, to paraphrase Voltaire, it is dangerous to be right when the authorities are wrong."[40]

SKEPTICS IN "HELL"

More bizarre is the case of climate scientist Robert F. Balling, who headed Arizona State University's climate research unit for sixteen years. He has worked with the IPCC-parent World Meteorological Organization, helped author IPCC reports, is a committed Democrat, and wishes Al Gore had won the White House. He lives the life of the green activist, with one small point of disagreement: he does not support catastrophic projections of delirious, Man-made climate.[41] This has earned him the opprobrium not just of environmental activists. Incredibly, "His outspoken views and the criticism they get have put ASU in an awkward position as it tries to shape itself as a leader in climate-change studies, ASU officials said." Isn't that something? A scientist who insists on science as opposed to parroting "the science is settled" threatens an academic institution's efforts to position itself as a leader in scientific research.

It is to prop up such academic philosophy that the taxpayer now spends billions annually, advancing the argument that actual science not be pursued and ignoring the increasingly obvious case that Man might *not* have suddenly become the principal driver of climate over "previously" dominant influences like the Sun. That is the most expensive groupthink in history. Balling dares call for a cut in federal spending as a test of our policymakers' commitment to reducing emissions to 1990 levels; he suggests the government try reducing spending to those levels, too. As you might expect, this is not well received among his peers who don't get the joke.

Balling says of his experience, "Somehow I've been branded this horrible person who belongs in the depths of hell. There's just no tolerance right now." He is publicly booed, is called the equivalent of a believer in a flat Earth, and *Vanity Fair* placed him in its special edition on global warming's "Eighth Circle of Hell." Even an academic colleague of his complains about how the school doesn't also employ a high-profiled alarmist, for the sake of—wait for it— *balance*.

Naturally, the fact that Balling has received private-sector support to help continue his (peer-reviewed) work leads to calls that he is shilling for supporters, offering dishonest claims, even though his own university exemplifies how Big Science has driven non-alarmists to find support elsewhere. Research is fine, as long as it goes with the flow.

Yet another IPCC "expert reviewer" and now outspoken critic of climate alarmism, economist Hans LaBohm of the Netherlands, detailed in a November 2007 e-mail to me a looming climate change conference held by the Royal Netherlands Academy of Science to which, as per usual, none of the prominent climate optimists from that country were invited to speak. He described a previous Academy conference at which two invited speakers—a top scientific journalist for a leading Dutch newspaper, and a director of a scientific institution—independently from one another castigated dissenters as "screamers." The institutional pressures had been mounting:

> One director of the Dutch Royal Meteorological Institute [Tennekes] was sacked, partly because of the fact that he was a nonbeliever. My own departure at the Netherlands Institute of International Relations was also connected with my high public profile as a climate sceptic. Young researchers keep their mouth shut, because of the fear for repercussions for their careers if they come out in favour of climate scepticism. So far climate sceptics have not been able to get one single piece published in the meteorological journal of this country.

There are silver linings, if ever so few, to the experiences of those who are sanctioned for remaining true to science in the face of academic, financial, and political pressures to advance an agenda. For example, as a result of the mob's treatment of then-Oregon State Climatologist George Taylor, Bay Area meteorologist Bob Cohen took to the editorial pages to come out of the skeptic closet, an act of defiance against the corruption of his discipline by politics and a willing establishment.[42]

O BROTHER, WHEREFORE ART THOU?

This reminds us of the religious and indeed cult-like zeal of the warming alarmists, who amusingly bandy about the word "heretic." Leon Festinger's work in *When Prophecy Fails* has never been so appropriate. In that book the father of "cognitive dissonance" theory detailed how the failure of a prophecy to come about can often yield the opposite effect of what the rational person would expect: the cult following gets stronger and its adherents ever more convinced of their truth. Someone phone the American Psychological Association.

It was Greenpeace's Stephen Guilbeault who famously affirmed the movement's faith-based nature, confessing that "global warming can mean colder, it can mean drier, it can mean wetter, that's what we're dealing with."[43] Amen. And the World Wildlife Fund choir sang that record-cold temperatures are entirely consistent with their global warming predictions.[44]

I have a lovely note written to one of the more rational Members of the European Parliament, passed along for my enjoyment. One "Martin Mitchell Assessor for Churches together in England Eco Congregation awards" excoriated said lawmaker for his "disgraceful position" of not accepting the new creed's determination that Man is a weather-maker. This, come to think of it, was also the old creed in the same neighborhood around the sixteenth and seventeenth centuries, when all of those "witches" were burned because their neighbors' crops failed. Today they're torching only SUVs. For now.

Consider Professor David Bellamy, "Great Britain's best-known environmentalist...for most of the last four decades." This upstart apparently has a flair for the written and spoken word, hosting over four hundred television shows on all things green to go along with forty-five books and eighty papers while teaching botany at university. But that's just pedestrian ivory-towerism; how would a green know if Bellamy were truly *one of them*?

He founded or led prominent groups such as The Conservation Foundation, The Royal Society of Wildlife Trusts, Population Concern, Plantlife International, British Naturalists' Association, and Galapagos Conservation Trust, in addition to numerous grassroots bodies operating at the local level. Even the United Nations Environment Program bestowed its Global 500 Award to go along with the Duke of Edinburgh's Award for Underwater Research, Diver of the Year Award, and the Order of the British Empire. Further, "No mere academic and establishment man, this larger-than-life figure also has a striking record as an activist campaigner for green causes, starting with the 1967 Torrey Canyon supertanker disaster off the coast of England. He has led high-profile protests against needless [sic] road building and the loss of moors, and has been jailed for blockading the construction of a hydro dam that would have destroyed a Tasmanian rainforest."[45]

But, so what? After all that it turns out that he also wrote an article titled "What a load of poppycock!" plainly stating, "Whatever the experts say about the howling gales, thunder and lightning we've had over the past two days, of one thing we can be certain. Someone, somewhere—and there is every chance it will be a politician or an environmentalist—will blame the weather on global warming. But they will be 100% wrong. Global warming—at least the modern nightmare version—is a myth."[46]

After that, the above-described résumé might as well simply read "CEO of ExxonMobil."

In his break with the High Church of Climate Alarmism, Bellamy went on to detail the weaknesses of a creed insisting that industrially produced carbon dioxide—produced in massively greater quantities by Mother Nature—is the primary driver of climate. He thereby committed the ultimate sin and the greens labeled him, of course, a "heretic."

As one U.S. activist admitted at an American Bar Association conference priming that industry for its next asbestos or tobacco litigation boondoggle, "We've put so much pressure on the media that they don't dare contact anyone for an opposing view on global warming."[47]

More humorously, in return for his transgressions extending all the way to the depravity of calling carbon dioxide "the most important airborne fertilizer in the world, and without it there would be no green plants at all," his own alma mater Plantlife International harrumphed in outrage that it "would be wrong to ask him to continue" his fifteen-year long term as president. Further:

> The Royal Society of Wildlife Trusts, which manages 2,500 nature reserves across the United Kingdom, likewise announced it would not renew his presidency.... Individual environmentalists were often less respectful in abandoning him, suggesting he had become mentally incompetent, or in the pay of the oil industry. The derision from the environmental camp has not ended with the passage of time. "Looney IPCC debunker," "climate-change denying shill" and "the very sad and deluded David Bellamy," is how the Carbon Trust referred to him earlier (in 2007).[48]

This will ring familiar to students of the global warming issue, redolent of posthumous revision of skeptics' records and particularly the treatment by Al Gore and his colleagues assigned to posthumously smear his old professor, Revelle. When Revelle's last article before he died, "What To Do about Greenhouse Warming: Look before You Leap" emerged during the 1992 campaign, Team Gore portrayed him as a mental incompetent duped into taking a co-authorship credit. This led to litigation against Gore's foot-soldiers, an apology, and the truth emerging which remains to this date not of interest to the establishment press, possibly because it so perfectly captures how Big Green operates.

Rarely discussed is what this tendency illustrates about the alarmists' character and, like the reversion to crying "consensus," the weakness of their position. As University of Auckland's Chris de Freitas notes:

> Rather than debate the issues, they attack those who disagree, using defamatory labels.... The fanatical name calling and personal attacks expose the strong ideological elements that drive global warming alarmist thinking. It's as if the depth of passion is overcompensation for doubt and uncertainty. Why else would environmentalists squander so much effort trying to discredit individuals and organisations who disagree?[49]

SPPI's Bob Ferguson cites Harvard University's Daniel Schrag, whose poisonous op-ed in the *Boston Globe* publicly characterized dissenting witnesses at a Senate hearing—including Professor Bob Carter, who holds a PhD in Paleontology from the University of Cambridge[50]—as a "gathering of liars and charlatans" spouting "outrageous claims intended to deceive and distort."[51] In rather anti-intellectual fashion, Schrag concluded with the *de rigueur* attribution of motive, that they are "sponsored by those industries who want to protect their profits."

On the presumption that this is a legitimate criticism, let's explore it.

SAUCE FOR THE GANDER

Many large companies stand to get rich from the green agenda, and those companies are using their money and their reach to advance this agenda. Alarmists, like the media, pretend to not have noticed this, except to sometimes note they've found that rare "responsible" actor proving the greens' virtue. To do otherwise, of course, would run counter to the template and necessary talking point that it is "Big Business," not a lack of justification, impeding the agenda. In fact but for Big Business this campaign would have died on the vine years ago for lack of political support.

The companies pimping for a rent-seeking agenda coercing people to buy their products or otherwise land themselves "global warming" empires are a *Who's Who* of American and multinational giants, from General Electric to British Petroleum (USA), to many major utilities like Duke Energy along with the natural gas industry and the odd, pure nuclear play weighing in. In the 2008 Democratic primary campaign, nuclear-heavy, Chicago-based utility Exelon found itself the target of claims by Senator Hillary Clinton that it was sweating the policy sheets in a back room with Barack Obama. Obama, by chance, was also the first to distinguish himself among the three leading presidential contenders in early 2008 in support of Exelon's preferred version of a global warming rationing scheme[52] (when it turned out that Clinton's campaign chief Mark Penn had close Exelon ties, the dispute faded). That is, Obama at least called for *selling* the ration coupons to industry rather than give them away. Either way, the consumer finds the bill passed to him, with the only difference being that some players—like nukes—find themselves happily free from having to buy their quotas, unlike their competitors.

The question remains, how many of these Beltway Bandits are following the advice given by Ken Lay's Kyoto aide after the pact was agreed, "we need to monitize [sic] our relationship with the green groups"?

Given the standard now set by the global warming industry, is it not appropriate to ponder aloud why the skeptic-smearing, *ad hominem* DeSmogBlog received "a huge donation" of as much as $300,000[53] "to start and operate"[54] the website and public relations operation? This came from the past-president of and presumably still significant stake-holder in NETeller, "a firm that desperately needs more climate scare for their waning trade of hot air (CO_2 emission allowances)," as one critic has noted.[55] This benevolent donor, one John Lefebvre, is also currently a guest of the federal government's correctional officers as a consequence of certain business transactions, a fact that certainly would be of great interest had he instead cast his lot with the climate optimists.

Of course, revealing that the greens' agenda is some big business's agenda simply prompts name calling of a different sort by the greens: "responsible." Besides, isn't it far nobler to be motivated by the belief that people are pollution in addition to mere money than to be seemingly driven by financial interests alone?[56]

DeSmogBlog, which is dedicated to claiming that climate skeptics are paid shills, happens to be run by James Hoggan and Associates, a PR agency that actually received the $300-large from the NETeller executive. His PR firm represents "alternative energy" companies, as well. Adding to the conflicts, Hoggan is also chair of the board of directors for the David Suzuki Foundation, a radical environmental activist group run by a man who—ironically—calls for climate skeptics to join Lefebvre in jail. This spin machine is aimed at discrediting skeptics.

Further confusing matters, it seems that whenever those who disagree with DeSmogBlog received corporate support, it proves that their opinions are bought, as part of an industry campaign to delude you. Terence Corcoran captured their argument in the *Financial Post*, "It's all a corporate scam, they claim [of the enormous 'skeptical' community of scientists]. 'There are people,' says Mr. Hoggan, a veteran self-promoting pro in the PR business, 'mainly people who are getting paid by oil and coal interests, and [some] who are just basically ideologues, who are trying to confuse the public about climate change.' Says Mr. Suzuki: 'The skeptics are a small group known for their support of corporations like the fossil fuel industry. In fact, many are receiving money directly from the industry.'"[57]

So, one's supporters dictate one's opinions. Funny, I was thinking the same thing.

Corcoran describes Suzuki's and Hoggan's "slanderous campaign" as designed "to portray all who raise doubts about climate change theory—so-called skeptics—as pawns of corporate PR thugs manipulating opinion." One of the scientists targeted by Suzuki and Hoggan writes in an e-mail that "in a further apparent further conflict of interest Hoggan's other clients are mostly alternate energy companies who stand to gain from proving CO_2 is a problem. . . . Somehow this kind of funding and duplicity is acceptable for one side but not the other—we live in an age of hypocrisy."[58]

Further, as Corcoran wrote in a separate piece exposing Hoggan's racket in detail, "As an aside, the fact that BP, Shell, the nuclear industry, giant ethanol firms and others all support climate theory for their own self-interested purposes seems not to bother environmental activists. . . . How does all that work in the conflict arena?"[59]

That's simple. It doesn't.

RENEWABLE FOOLS

Alarmist sanctimony, hypocrisy, illogic, threat-making, and petulance were on wonderful display in a particular episode involving the president of a global warming advocacy group called the American Council on Renewable Energy (ACORE). This individual, who

by all other indications is a fully grown, middle-aged man named
Michael T. Eckhart,[60] wrote to a colleague of mine at the Competitive Enterprise Institute, Dr. Marlo Lewis who, as I enjoy noting, is
living proof that one can indeed overcome a PhD from Harvard.
After seeing Harvard MBA Eckhart in action, however, *that* training seems a more difficult hurdle to surmount.

Lewis wrote an article in the *American Spectator* assessing the
economic impact and lack of climatic impact of the various
"global warming" bills introduced in the 110th Congress.[61]

In response, Eckhart volunteered a thoughtful e-mail:

FROM: Michael Eckhart
SENT: Fri 7/13/2007 1:50 AM
TO: Marlo Lewis
SUBJECT: RE: CEI commentary on cart-before-the-horse climate
          policy. FYI.

Marlo—

You are so full of crap.

You have been proven wrong. The entire world has proven
you wrong. You are the last guy on Earth to get it. Take this
warning from me, Marlo. It is my intention to destroy your
career as a liar. If you produce one more editorial against climate
change, I will launch a campaign against your professional
integrity. I will call you a liar and charlatan to the Harvard community of which you and I are members. I will call you out as a
man who has been bought by Corporate America. Go ahead,
guy. Take me on.

Well. Not that the global warming industry is prone to hyperbole,
but one certainly could better assess this rant if informed precisely
how Lewis had been proven wrong, by the entire world no less. At
least it is useful should one seek refund of your share of that more

than $5 billion that the U.S. taxpayer throws down this particular rat hole *every year*, much to the benefit of Eckhart's group.

Of course, if Lewis insisted on continuing to express his views, boy, watch out. His no doubt lucrative "career as a liar" would come to an end and he would have the crusading Mr. Eckhart to thank for having been set on the straight and narrow. Some kinds of speech just can't be tolerated. Not when billions in subsidies are at stake.

You see, ACORE's membership includes not just green groups and old-line lefty advocates such as Union of Concerned Scientists and old-line lefty deep pockets like the Rockefeller Brothers Fund, but the usual (and some not so usual) suspects like American Ethanol, American Solar Energy Society, and numerous of their member companies, Solar Electric Power Association, Solar Energy Industries Association, American Wind Energy Association and member companies, BioEnergy Producers Association, Renewable Fuels Association, Biofuels America—see any pattern here?—plus Center for Carbon Trading, Chicago Climate Exchange, select utilities, white-shoe law firms representing rent-seekers, National VegOil Board (how else would they become the next "Big Oil"?), National Venture Capital Association, Goldman Sachs, and other venture magnates waiting on the government-mandated windfall, government contractors and other parties revealing from where Mr. Eckhart's passion derives.

There's a lot of money at stake.

Questioning the financial motives of any and all who disagree with them is the global warming industry's rather ironic stock in trade. As Upton Sinclair noted and the greens never tire of parroting, "It is difficult to get a man to understand something when his salary depends upon his not understanding it." Apparently they're on to something.

Less amusing is that numerous agencies of state and the federal government pour taxpayer dollars in the form of dues into such a group, including the U.S. Department of Agriculture, U.S. Department of Commerce, and U.S. Environmental Protection Agency.

Just to confirm how in character this episode of threatening people who disagree with him is, it is worth noting that Eckhart also threatened CEI's Fred Smith with an IRS audit and rescission of Smith's Phi Beta Kappa key, signifying election to the honor society. In September 2006 Eckhart wrote to Smith in outrage over the fact that, at a retreat to which Smith was invited along with Al Gore to debate the issue, Smith actually dared debate it.

Eckhart's sputtering to Smith deserves significant excerpting:

You are clearly a highly trained scientist, and yet you are making a living refuting what is irrefutably the truth....The only explanation that I can see is that you are doing this because you are paid by Exxon Mobil and other clients to do so. I find this outrageous, that my children will have a lesser life because you are being paid by oil companies to spread a false story.

As I said to you at the time, I would give you 90 days to show that CEI is reversing its position on this, or I will take every action I can think of to shut you down.

The 90 days has just passed, and...I am writing to demand that you and CEI reverse course on this, and do so loudly and publicly, within 30 days, or I will personally file on October 25, 2006, two complaints:

1. A complaint with the IRS to have CEI's tax exemption revoked, on the basis that CEI is really a lobbyist for the energy industry;
2. A complaint with Phi Beta Kappa that your key should be withdrawn for using your mathematical skills to do the world harm.

The fact that you are a lobbyist for the oil industry is suggested by Marlo Lewis' opening complaint written below about Al

Gore's movie, that it "[n]ever acknowledges the indispensable role of fossil fuels in ending serfdom and slavery, alleviating hunger and poverty, extending human life spans, and democratizing consumer goods, literacy, leisure, and personal mobility." We are going to see if there is any email traffic between Exxon-Mobil and CEI about the crafting of those words.

You have 30 days to speak the truth, or face the IRS and PBK.

I hope you choose to do the right thing.

Lovely man, that Eckhart. Lovely man. And possessed of such impeccable, Harvard logic: you disagree with me, so it must be because Big Oil pays you to. Meanwhile, it's pretty clear whose tab he's working off of. Guilty conscience, perhaps?

Eckhart's vowed vendetta promises to prove entertaining, given that PBK boasts that "for over two and a quarter centuries, the Society has embraced the principles of freedom of inquiry and liberty of thought and expression,"[62] and that "The ideal Phi Beta Kappa has demonstrated intellectual integrity, tolerance for other views, and a broad range of academic interests."[63] But, then again, we *are* talking about global warming.

After fellow CEI employee's Iain Murray posted Eckhart's first missive to Lewis, without commentary, on *National Review*'s "Planet Gore" site,[64] Eckhart came even further unglued. His next correspondence to Lewis substituted disingenuousness for the bile. Apparently by revealing this threat, Lewis was in "breach of confidentiality, as my email was to your [sic] and in the context of our professional confrontation which began three years ago at [an *Energy and Environment* webcast the two did together]. But that's water under the bridge."

Of course, a plain reading of Eckhart's threat indicated absolutely no intention to keep his tantrum private, but instead a promise to turn wherever he might possibly find assistance with retribution. But, follow the logic. When your tantrum-throwing and threat-making is exposed, indignantly say, *Uh, don't you remember that time we met once a few years ago? Well, I just thought of a good comeback, if completely unrelated to that but driven by an uncontrollable impulse because of something else I saw you do. Here it is...OK. Now, I'm sure you'll agree we should move on.*

Eckhart quickly sought to cover his tracks elsewhere as well, publicly offering the disingenuous claim that his words "intended as a 'private communication' [were] merely 'in the context of personal combat and jousting.'"[65] Surely this has nothing to do with his eclectic, rent-seeking membership smarting from the humiliation of their representative's behavior, but nonetheless Mr. Eckhart wanted to make clear that, all signs to the contrary, he wasn't speaking for the well-heeled industry pouring millions into his group trying to impose "global warming" mandates on the American people after all. He speaks instead for the voiceless billions who have no such pressure groups to do their bidding.

"I apologize to all in the public who were offended...because it was not intended for public display. In my opinion, CEI, and especially Dr. Lewis, has been presenting a false prosecution—a knowingly false prosecution—of the global-warming issue, to the detriment of society and the billions of people who will be affected by climate change."

That's actually what the courts are for and, come to think of it, landing dissenters in the dock is what the warming industry seeks. Such nice people, these alarmists. They really *should* be in charge, you know.

CHAPTER 3

The Establishment Attacks

Woe to Dissenters

"A lot of people are getting very famous and very well-known and very well-funded as a result of promoting the disastrous scenario of greenhouse warming."

Dr. Sherwood Idso, "The Greenhouse Conspiracy," Channel 4 (UK)

WHEN ABC NEWS SOUGHT in March 2008 to discredit a prominent climate scientist who refused to toe the global warming industry's line, they knew where to turn for anonymous slurs: Stanford, Princeton, and NASA.[1] The three bravely anonymous commentators whom ABC rounded up were almost surely Stephen Schneider of "global cooling" and later "we need to tell scary stories" infamy, but who has not published significant research in years; Michael Oppenheimer who would be better identified as a pressure group activist, which he remains to this day; and Gore advisor James Hansen, a man prospering from global warming alarmism possibly better than anyone but the Gore-acle himself.

Pressure group activists hired by Ivy League institutions offering academic prestige to continue this activism under the cloak thereof? Taxpayer-funded NASA staff engaging in personal attacks on the public's dime? Actually, none of this is unusual anymore, and indeed this episode merely reminds us of the interrelationships between the environmental pressure groups, activist academia, professional associations, and governmental institutions. All of these groups collectively push to expand the multi-billion dollar global warming industry in a collaborative way that makes certain incestuous tribes appear chaste in comparison. With their sharing of staff, information, and agendas they also put to shame history's most extravagant conflicts of interest.

There are many examples of seemingly academic or otherwise authoritative bodies, including elite schools with booming tax-payer-financed research practices: laboratories like NASA's Goddard Institute for Space Studies (GISS) where Hansen and his alarmist colleague Gavin Schmidt toil; NOAA's Geophysical Fluid Dynamics Laboratory (GFDL); and the National Center for Atmospheric Research (NCAR). All of these intertwine their environmental activism (in political or organizational form) with groups such as Environmental Defense, Natural Resources Defense Council, and the Sierra Club.

This co-mingling is a major tool in advancing their agenda, enhancing their finances, and attacking opposing views with an eye toward suppressing dissent.

THEY'D ALL LIKE TO THANK THE ACADEMY

The alarmist industry relies heavily on the association of many of its adherents with the prestigious National Academy of Sciences (NAS), which the alarmists have for all intents and purposes captured. This is certainly their greatest coup, the importance of which feat cannot be overstated. NAS is the official conduit between science and government. When the president of the United States wants advice on global warming or whom to award the National Medals of Science, he turns to the president of the NAS. His own White House science advisor, in any administration, would most likely not dare to cross the NAS, or would do so only at his or her professional peril.

Now the NAS has become an activist organ, even making long-time Malthusian, and Club of Rome and UN Earth Summit organizer Maurice Strong the first non-citizen winner of its Public Welfare Medal, for his tireless support of "multilateral approaches to sustainable and equitable development and international peace."[2] Strong of course is most well known for being a little too loose with his lips about the horrors of modern civilization and, particularly, economic growth.

The politicization of the NAS—while it preserves its reputation as unimpeachable, disinterested, and impartial—is a crucial tool in the alarmist agenda.

Like most select clubs, the Academy is rather secretive about its procedures, which is particularly unfortunate given that election to its ranks offers immediate scientific credibility and prestige to the person elected, no matter how their elevation came about. For years there has been a back door for environmentalists to gain membership, and they have proceeded to establish a veto power over all new selections who might challenge the alarmist position.

A first step in this came over two decades ago with the election to the NAS of zoologist, butterfly expert, and longtime doomsayer Paul Ehrlich. This came after nomination by a special Temporary Nominating Committee for the Global Environment, bypassing normal election procedures. This Temporary Nominating Group had been created on the argument of a few particularly enviro-conscious NAS members that there was insufficient membership of people concerned with the global environment. This was untrue and clearly referred to a particular, politically active type of "interest in the global environment" that was increasingly fashionable at the time.

As with most bad ideas, particularly those swaddled in the soothing gauze of being "temporary", this one soon became *de facto* permanent if with a name that varies with the times, as another among the NAS's official "Sections." So, to the ranks of geophysics, geology, physics, mathematics, etc., was added the slightly more agenda-driven and doomsayer-heavy "global environment" (occasionally, "global change").

Each section prepares the nominations for membership in the Academy. Before the aforementioned development, the practice of ecologically activist types elected to the Academy was to join various other sections with a goal of attaining around a 10 percent membership of their ilk therein, because if a nominee's support falls below about 90 percent his or her chances of election to the Academy are very dim. Therefore, if there are a few dozen members in the physical sciences section, a very small handful can keep the unsympathetic types out. Illustrating the mindset behind these machinations, a scientist, who was eventually elected, had previously written a paper suggesting natural variability lay behind some climate change. Supporters urged that this paper not be mentioned in the process, apparently expecting that knowledge of this paper would blacklist him.

In addition to Ehrlich there are many notable global warming enthusiasts who entered the NAS that way, such as Susan Solomon, William Chameides, current NAS president Ralph Cicerone—who in 2006 testified before a U.S. House committee that the mechanics of CO_2 and climate are more understood than causes of lung cancer[3]—and others who were distinguished by their association with the environmental movement. Another person elected via the Temporary Nominating Group for the Global Environment was Judith Lean. Described to me by one meteorologist as "a good solider for the AGW movement," Lean was a minor solar physicist who then worked closely with the environmentalists to produce a speculative (unmeasured) history of solar output from earlier in the twentieth century, in which the sun heated the planet quite a bit during the 1920s through the 1930s only to fade out in the 1970s. This then allowed climate modelers to say that they could account for the earlier warming on the basis of solar activity, but that the warming of the last thirty years had to be due to man (yes, environmentalist science also permits one to argue that the only possible temperature drivers are solar and human influences).

Others entering through this route include Gore advisor and the world's most renowned global warming alarmist, the astronomer Jim Hansen, and Jane Loubchenco—a key driver in the regulate-in-the-name-of-climate-change effort by Oregon Governor Ted Kulongoski, discussed below. Loubchenco's activism is the subject of fawning profiles by the likes of the left-wing *Mother Jones* magazine.[4]

Not long after Cicerone was elected to the academy, he was on the nominating committee that chose Bruce Albert as the NAS president, then followed Albert in the position. Vocal alarmists Stephen Schneider and John Holdren, a professor at Harvard who is primarily employed by the Woods Hole Research Center (an environmental advocacy group, not to be confused with the Woods Hole Oceanographic Institution which is a research organization—both discussed below) were also elected from the temporary nominating group, so we see the cadre of global warming alarmists elected to the NAS actually came in through other than the regular channels. And the process self-perpetuates.

This green revolution soon bore fruit in work bearing the NAS's prestigious imprimatur. In 1999 the National Academies' contract arm, the National Research Council, issued a transparently ideological report, "Our Common Journey: A Transition Toward Sustainability."[5] This was done under the aegis of its sustainability board that included, among others, global warming activists such as Cicerone, Jerry Mahlman of GFDL, Warren Washington of NCAR, as well as John Bongaarts of the Population Council (one of those trotted out by *Scientific American* to assail Bjørn Lomborg). This report urged decarbonization and, of course, acceleration in fertility reduction through contraception and birth postponement to reduce family size so as to achieve 10 percent reduction in the projected nine billion population by 2050.[6] It was funded in part by Mitchell Energy and Development Corp.—a natural gas company that prospered wildly with the increased (and dangerous, according to Alan Greenspan among others) reliance upon natural gas resulting from the environmentalist assault on coal—and the Cynthia and George Mitchell Foundation. The various Mitchell arms repeatedly pop up as having underwritten numerous endeavors promoting the "global warming" agenda and others advanced by this interlocking group of academics, bureaucrats, and activists sharing the broader "limits to growth" and Malthusian agenda.[7]

In 2003 the NAS accepted a $20 million matching grant from the George and Cynthia Mitchell Endowment for Sustainability Science,[8] which amounted to 6 percent of its total endowment. This was initiated by Peter Raven, Academy member and frequent collaborator with warming activists, including Holdren. A similar grant from a foundation associated with coal would, no doubt, pass without comment from the environmentalist and media establishments.

THE BIG GREEN MACHINE

As further evidence of the interrelationships, consider Michael Oppenheimer of the activist group Environmental Defense. Despite having had less than a handful of minor publications on climate to his credit, and usually as a secondary author, he was made a professor at Princeton University—the Albert G. Milbank Professor of Geosciences and International Affairs in the Woodrow Wilson School and the Department of Geosciences, an odd hybrid of a position that seems to have been created specifically for him, among other baubles.[9] His publication list, which obviously grew after this appointment, therefore appears to be a product of his gaining an Ivy League academic position as opposed to the typical pathway of publishing one's way onto such a platform. That's quite a leap from serving as the "Barbra Streisand" scientist at an alarmist pressure group. This chaired professorship in geosciences and . . . *international affairs* (*of course!*) . . . is also a wonderfully contrived combination of precisely what the pressure groups practice: politics and scientific claims.

To grasp the relevance of this one example, imagine such coincidences among climate realists; one particularly effective climate realist, Ivy League researcher and professor, Richard Lindzen, is still styled as an industry shill for having more than fifteen years ago once served as a consultant, and taking an honorarium—as do most academics, including alarmists, if far more frequently and lucratively.

Such hypocritical claims are part of a smokescreen of claiming scientific bias arising from one's funding. *New York Times* resident contrarian John Tierney reveals about this inanity, "One of the researchers who'd supposedly been bought off [to challenge the now debunked 'consensus' on dietary fats] noted that he'd received $250,000 from the food industry in his career versus $10 million from government agencies—and wondered why this didn't make him a 'tool of government.'"[10]

Government funding is right and good. So long as it funds the alarmists, that is, as it usually does. Just in case, the alarmists have installed themselves in positions to help perpetuate this practice, which doesn't need that much help given that nothing boosts an agency's annual appropriation like being indispensable in the fight to rescue humanity.

Add to this the vocal Holdren, who predicted in the mid-1980s that climate-related catastrophes might kill as many as one billion people before the year 2020[11] but now brushes away such failed catastrophism with: "That the impacts of global climate disruption may not become the dominant sources of environmental harm to humans for yet a few more decades cannot be a great consolation."[12] Despite his outside affiliations and activism he typically instead carries the Harvard tag, lending the institution's academic prestige to his environmentalist advocacy. He also happens to be a longtime collaborator with none other than failed prognosticator of doom Paul Ehrlich. Typical of their doomsaying they collaborated to hold a "Cassandra Conference" in 1988 (Cassandra is the lass from Greek mythology whose prophecies were always true and always ignored).

It is no surprise that it was at the urging of the Sierra Club that Ehrlich produced his seminal work of alarmism, *The Population Bomb*—in which, as with today's alarmism, the enemy was "Western society" engaging in "the rape and murder of the planet for economic gain"[13] (recall how Sierra Club executive director Carl Pope cut his teeth at Zero Population Growth). Holdren's name also pops up in various, largely successful efforts to elevate taxpayer funding of the global warming industry.[14]

The self-referential and self-affirming nature of these groups is well illustrated by their coalescing to celebrate the sixtieth birthday of Stephen Schneider. In February 2005 this historic event was marked by a Whole Earth System Symposium,[15] sponsored by Stanford's Center for Environmental Studies and Policy, the Energy Modeling Forum, the Stanford Institute for the Environment, the New-Land Foundation,[16] the Ju Tang Chu and Wu Ping Chu Foundation, the Climate, Community and Biodiversity Alliance,[17] and anonymous donors. Attendees for the three-day event included Teresa Heinz-Kerry, Ben Santer (of IPCC-scandal fame, discussed below), Gore confidant Tom Wigley, Rick Piltz of "Climate Science Watch"[18] (discussed later), the *New York Times*'s Andrew Revkin, Anthony Socci (see below), Gore's movie collaborator Lonnie G. Thompson, the aforementioned Mahlman, Oppenheimer, Hansen, Lubchenco, Ehrlich, Holdren, Michael Mann, and Kurt Cuffey of the disgraced "Hockey Stick" fame, as well as prominent alarmists Michael MacCracken, who ran Gore's U.S. National Assessment on Climate Change, Peter Gleick, Syukuro Manabe, William Easterling, Curt Covey, Robert Chen, former Gore White House aide and current University of Michigan instructor/activist Rosina Bierbaum, Joan Abrahamson, Jonathan Aronson, Jean-Pascal van Ypersele, James Sweeney, Allen M. Solomon, Lee Schipper, Sherwood Rowland, and Donald Kennedy.[19] This remarkable circle of friends happened to also constitute a *Who's Who* of the alarmist world.

Kennedy, editor of *Science*, the journal of the American Association for the Advancement of Science, in a presentation at the symposium talks about Schneider being a model for "letting real needs drive his science."[20] He says scientists need to "take a different and more purposeful approach to how they choose their work; accepting a different relationship to the polity and the media."

SKY IS FORECAST TO FALL

The American Meteorological Society, which has aggressively placed its bets with the alarmist industry, hired the climate activist and former Al Gore staffer Tony Socci as its spokesman. Among his career's highlights is having overseen grants for Gore's pet project, the U.S. Global Change Research Program, and a 1998 paper in the Aspen Global Change Institute's Elements of Change 1998, "Communicating Climate Science to Decision-Makers, with Special Reference to the Policy Community."[21] In it he admonishes scientists not to use statistical levels of uncertainty when touting global warming, as it just confuses the poor dears into thinking uncertainty exists. Similarly, he counseled against engaging in debate, as "Debate is a Loaded Word," "hard-wired" to imply "two sides to an issue, and that the sides are divided equally, and the issue is therefore, very much undecided."

To hammer the approved beliefs home, AMS brought in leading alarmist Kevin Trenberth to lecture attendees of its 2008 broadcast meteorologist conference in Denver that any skeptics in the audience were really "pseudo-scientists." This was despite promising a "balanced" panel discussion. Unfortunately, award-winning scientist Dr. Roy Spencer found himself barred from the panel not only because of his skepticism but, as a nationally known broadcast meteorologist who attended informed me, because he believed in creationism/intelligent design. The point is clear if ham-fisted: if you value your AMS broadcast seal of approval, get in line with the program.

Socci has also coordinated a series of communications workshops boasting luminaries from the alarmist and media establishments as participants, arguing that "when the scientific community is mostly in consensus, the focus of a story should not be solely on a few dissenters but include and be focused on the implications of the scientific consensus for policy considerations."[22] He queried journalists, "Does balance distort?" Subsequent workshops concluded that, *yes, balanced reporting on climate change is biased reporting*, and encouraged reporters to avoid reporting contrarian and skeptical views on climate science, or at least labeling them as the denialists they are when doing so.[23] These gatherings proceeded apace, churning out such nonsense twice a year for four years, with scientists chosen by Socci presenting the evidence for global warming to journalists from major U.S. media outlets around the nation.[24]

Joining AMS is the American Association for the Advancement of Science, which publishes *Science* Magazine, the organ that stooped to running the phony "consensus" essay[25] and, back as far as 1979 when the UN made its first run at seizing the cooling/

warming opportunity, wrote the absurd headline "CO_2 in Climate: Gloomsday Predictions Have No Faults."[26] Avert thy gaze.

This breathless "gloomsday" reportage was based on a report produced by none other than the National Academies. In 1980, current NAS head and longtime climate alarmist Cicerone was appointed senior scientist and director of the Atmospheric Chemistry Division at the National Center for Atmospheric Research in Boulder, Colorado. To illustrate how institutionalized the alarmist bullying tactics are, note that in May of that same year NCAR Director Walter Orr Roberts proposed, and GFDL Director Joe Smagorinsky seconded, a motion to censure scientist Sherwood Idso for "publishing articles containing opinions contrary to results from models of CO_2 effects on climate developed by the climate research community."[27]

Outside of private pressure groups and professional associations, the scientific picture has been distorted by a variety of means including the creation of nominal research centers, like the Tyndall Centre (UK) and Potsdam Institute (Germany), which involved and associated with pressure groups like Greenpeace and World Wildlife Fund (WWF). Indeed, a lead IPCC co-author is the career activist Bill Hare, listed by the IPCC as affiliated with Potsdam even though he is paid by Greenpeace International and also is an advisor at Tyndall.[28] Potsdam's description of Hare's scientific specialty, among its practitioners of "Global biosphere dynamics and feedbacks between the biosphere" and "Conceptual modeling of the stability of the oceanic pycnocline," is, in its entirety, "explaining environmental issues to policy makers, IPCC negotiator."[29] Otherwise known as "lobbyist."

Similarly, one of Tyndall's explicit aims is to "exert a seminal influence on the design and achievability of the long-term strategic objectives of UK and international climate policy." This hardly reveals a focus on basic research designed to resolve climate uncertainty. Rather, it is pure advocacy, apparently commited to a particular answer—however unlikely that answer may be.

Tyndall and Potsdam both have representatives of Greenpeace or WWF on their boards. The Tyndall Centre is also, by chance, the largest contributor of participants to the IPCC process. Tyndall was heavily involved in writing the contemptible Stern Review[30]—which is to the economics of climate alarmism what the "Hockey Stick" was to the science, and which has been similarly debunked[31]—release of which was timed to coincide with the U.S. mid-term elections. Tyndall's "strategic director" is Al Gore's old friend Bob Watson, formerly of the IPCC. Tyndall is part of University of East Anglia, which is the home of the Climatic Research Centre, headed by Phil Jones, notorious for refusing access to his data, and whose activities are discussed elsewhere in these pages.[32]

Potsdam is part of the Global Governance Project,[33] along with other EU institutions, notably the London School of Economics and Political Science, which has as a fellow none other than Nicholas Stern—for whom the Stern Review was named (it seems impossible to fathom that he actually authored such readily dissected advocacy and questionable professional practices).

The scientific service unit which runs the IPCC scientific assessment (called "Working Group 1") is in the Hadley Centre of the UK Meteorological Office, the latter's new chairman of the board being Robert Napier, who is also the chief executive of WWF-UK. WWF also has links with the UK government and the Royal Society, and it is from these three institutions that some of the world's most officious and bombastic pronouncements of doom issue, as well as urgent calls for a particular agenda.[34]

In the U.S., John Firor, who was for many years the administrative director of the National Center for Atmospheric Research, was also the chairman of the board of the Environmental Defense

Fund. University and governmental administrations get in on the act with their own efforts at imposing a scientific speech code ensuring that this unprecedented gravy train runs on time. Tom Karl, regularly seen by then-Vice President Al Gore's side during alarmist press availabilities, found himself running the National Climatic Data Center. NCDC rushed to cover for obviously corrupted surface temperature data by removing the instrument sites from the Internet to stem the flow of embarrassing photos of thermometers sited, for example, in asphalt parking lots.

Illustrative of the ties between the green establishment and rent-seeking industries with whom they jointly promote an agenda are Duke Energy and the Resources for the Future (RFF). Both promote the carbon cap-and-trade rationing scheme. RFF's president is former Congressman Phil Sharp (D-IN), who also sits on Duke's Board of Directors. Sharp was a director of Cinergy, a company acquired by Duke in 2006, headed by CEO and Chairman James E. Rogers. As discussed elsewhere in these pages, Rogers learned at the knee of Enron's Ken Lay how to cozy up to green pressure groups to advance a company's agenda.

Like T. Boone Pickens and a host of others who would benefit from taxpayers footing the bill for a regulatory and tax scheme premised in "global warming," Rogers puts his mouth where his money is. According to RFF's 2007 Annual Report, he is responsible for a contribution of an amount between $25,000 and $49,999. (Of course, while Carl Pope hitches rides in Pickens' jet, Hansen calls Rogers a potential killer for nonetheless wanting to build the odd coal-fired power plant which will cause global warming and, well, thereby kill people.[35] So, even saints aren't perfect and appeasement's unblemished record of failure continues.)

Similarly, consider the varied and sundry entanglements of the chairman of the board of Clipper Wind, which is working in Maryland to attain mandates and subsidies to plop down windmills on the mountaintops of scenic western Maryland. His bio on the company website reveals a case study in how the tentacles spread:

> Mr. Dehlsen served as an advisor to the Department of Energy's Wind Program, testified at the first U.S. Senate hearings on global warming, and served as a delegate to the Conference on Climate Change in Kyoto, Japan. After serving two terms on the Board of the American Wind Industry Association, he currently serves on the Board of the [pressure group] Worldwatch Institute in Washington, D.C. Mr. Dehlsen has a long-standing relationship with the University of California at Santa Barbara as a member of the Dean's Council of the Bren School of Environmental Science and Management and as a past member of the Chancellor's Council. With his wife, Deanna C. Dehlsen, he funded the Dehlsen Chair for Environmental Sciences at the University.[36]

Another coincidence is that Dehlsen, too, learned at the knee of Ken Lay.

The boards of directors of the various establishment pressure groups also reveal their wide-reaching relationships. For example Greenpeace USA is chaired by Donald Ross, who is also CEO of M&R strategic services, a lobbying firm. "In addition, Donald assists members of the Rockefeller family with personal philanthropy."[37] The Rockefeller family is increasingly known, in this context, for pouring millions into a campaign to insert a supposedly objective, independent consultant (Center for Climate Strategies) into state policymaking apparati. Greenpeace's board would be a disappointment, of course, without its own ties to left-wing academia, and Todd Gitlin fits the bill: former professor of sociology and director of the mass communications program at the University of California, Berkeley and a professor of culture, journalism, and sociology at New York University, and presently a professor of journalism at Columbia University. Natural Resources Defense Council's Board of Trustees is not simply populated by the earnest Hollywood types, but also James Gustave Speth (Dean of Yale's School of Forestry and Environmental Studies), George M. Woodwell (Founder and Senior Scientist with the Woods Hole Research Center—again, an advocacy group, not the research institution whose name it cribs), Columbia University professor Frederica Perera, and representatives of several *very* correct philanthropic foundations.[38] And so on.

The academic institutions have profited so handsomely from this game, in fact, that the dashing dollar figures found in global warming alarmism have led prestigious bodies of all sorts to get weak in the knees and rather goofy, even quite nasty as they fight to keep their beau.

All of this manifests the increasing tendency by environmental advocacy groups of infiltrating academic departments, institutions, professional societies, and even industry, a matter that has received little scrutiny thus far. If the shoe were on the other foot, things would be very different.

REALALARMISTS

Putting a bow on this package of interwoven relationships and back-scratching in pursuit of the elites' agenda (and largely at taxpayer expense) comes the leading alarmist weblog RealClimate.org. Seemingly established in 2004 to counter, of all things, Michael Crichton's novel, *State of Fear*, RealClimate serves as the popular science media's main touchstone for alarmist memes second only to Gore and his advisor Hansen—and we see here that this is really a distinction without a difference. This outlet is populated by none other than NASA's resident alarmist mouthpiece—and official spokesman for Hansen's GISS shop—Gavin Schmidt. Although RealClimate touts the unpaid nature of their writers' work, the time-stamps on Schmidt's often highly personal blog posts make quite clear that these actually come on the taxpayer dime, as well. Other RealClimate writers include "Hockey Stick" Mann and "Hockey Stick"-related Caspar Ammann.

It turns out that RealClimate.org is owned by an outfit that is in essence a non-profit public relations firm called Environmental Media Services (EMS), "dedicated to expanding media coverage of critical environmental and public health issues," whose Pittsburgh office houses the RealClimate server.[39] ActivistCash.com describes EMS as "the communications arm of leftist public relations firm Fenton Communications."[40]

EMA's listed registrant, Betsy Ensley, engages in the objective, non-partisan pursuit of "manag[ing] BushGreenwatch.org, a joint EMS-MoveOn.org public awareness website."[41] She also apparently ran WomenAgainstBush.org, and former Harvard string theorist (and still-hilarious climate blogger) Lubos Motl notes that when Ensley was campaigning against John Ashcroft her secretary was Kalee Kreider, now Al Gore's spokesperson.[42] MoveOn is of course in part a George Soros venture, and attentive climate realists recall the kerfuffle over Soros supporting Hansen's alarmism.[43]

Motl describes EMS as "primarily an organization to pay for junk science about food and beverages, often hired by food companies to damage their competitors."[44] This is known as "black marketing."[45]

This is not inconsistent with my own experience with Fenton, which I first encountered nearly two decades ago. Then, they were representing a "green" lawn care products company in a legislative effort to craft new federal laws creating a secure place in a market otherwise dominated by those whose products attain prominence through competition. This is a *modus operandi* that will sound very familiar by the time you finish this book. Fenton has also been associated with every questionable campaign, from chasing Alar off the shelves by leveraging weepy celebrities and fear tactics to promoting Mother Sheehan's tour.[46]

As critics note, the idea that RealClimate is just a bunch of unpaid "real scientists" is risible, given their methods of argumentation are often little more than smear, ridicule, cherry-picking science, and pronouncing themselves and their exclusive little climate clique as only the few "qualified" to have an opinion on man-made global warming. RealClimate's members, like Andrew Dessler of *Grist* and writers for the Soros-backed Climate Progress, perpetrate a unique form of "qualification thuggery" by which anyone skeptical of their agenda is unworthy to comment, typically because the skeptic does not affiliate with the UN IPCC. When the skeptic is an IPCC author or reviewer, well, he's still unqualified. And "mere physicists" such as Freeman Dyson, or chemists, or economists, are also unqualified, but only when they disagree. After all, Dessler is a chemist, and the IPCC's "chief scientist" is no such thing at all, as you'll see.

Absent agreement, this unholy alliance of activists, Big Science, and other vested interests responds so viciously to even the whiff of dissent that it is impossible not to wonder what it is they are afraid of.

LOCK 'EM UP

UN Environment Programme head Yvo de Boer apparently believes that it is "criminally irresponsible" even to encourage those who oppose the UN's agenda.[47] One is tempted to ponder where they are going with this mindset. He is not alone in indicating such thoughts, so we might ask, is this simple bombast and intimidation, or is it illustrative of the global warming industry's desires? Was it simple vigilante justice that, for example, the BBC reports police interrupted when stumbling upon "'a stash of knives and weapons' from [a] woodland near the Climate Camp" of activists?[48]

In September 2006, on CNBC's *Global Players* program, the CEO of a solar power company called for fellow guest, Competitive

Enterprise Institute (CEI, with which I am affiliated) President Fred
Smith to be locked up in jail for the crime of expressing doubt about
climate alarmism and schemes offered in its name. CEI writer Iain
Murray described that on the same panel, "James Hansen, head of
NASA's Goddard Institute for Space Studies, who has vociferously
complained in the media of being silenced by the Bush administration for his research on global warming, suggested—without a hint
of irony—that Mr. Smith should not even have been given such a
platform for his views."[49] The ultimate in establishment activists,
Canadian alarmist David Suzuki, also wants politicians who oppose
the global warming agenda to be thrown in jail.[50]

Left-wing author Alexander Cockburn's series on climate
change for *The Nation* magazine led to a "hysterical reaction"

THE MINISTRY OF TRUTH

"The global warming crowd does not take kindly to being contradicted,
either by critics or data. Of course, critics can be defamed and data can
be skewed. But unless the critics can be silenced, they can fight back
and expose phony data. When it begins to look like predictions of doom
are not turning out sufficiently catastrophic, a full Orwell is called for. The
media mobilize their templates to completely re-cast the information.

This process was fully in evidence yesterday when the global news
service Reuters spun a report in *Science* magazine (which has been quietly starting to warn its readership that maybe it would be prudent to
come in a bit from the end of the global warming limb) as if it confirmed
the seriousness of global warning, when in fact the report contained devastating information of flaws in the doomsters methodology and warned
that the disaster has been postponed."

James Lewis, American Thinker, *"Twisting Science to fit the global
warming template,"* September 2007

including "one individual, who was once on the board of the Sierra Club, [who] suggested I should be criminally prosecuted."[51] Even mainstream columnists in Australia wonder aloud about prosecuting climate change "denial" as "a crime against humanity."[52] It is analogized to Holocaust denial and even—somehow—abduction and torture of children (the latter alleged by a bishop in a letter to parishioners, no less).[53] A summit of Australia's "best and brightest," led by key policymakers and even attended by their Prime Minister, fielded a proposal to strip one's citizenship for the offense.[54] In one telling the idea is to start anew, relieving every Australian of his status and only re-issuing it to those who could prove they were "environment-climate friendly."[55] The slightly more measured Paul Krugman of the *New York Times* decreed skepticism to be "immoral."[56]

Condemnation, banishment, censorship, and imprisonment of dissenters are pretty heavy stuff. But "global warming" has become a billions-per-year business, accruing almost exclusively to the promotion of alarmism. The vested parties do not gently receive either dissent or challenges to this lucrative line of work—be the challenges real, merely potential, or simply imagined. It is not just the grant money and the otherwise non-existent "markets" that would be created under the proper regimes, either. Also tempting the beast is the authority the agenda promises, which remains so close to their grasp that the UN and its affiliated bodies and hangers on apparently can almost smell the accompanying corruption, and now join the nastiness.

As described later, calls for imprisonment or censorship also issue from high officials of government, not merely supra-governmental functionaries, journalists, and (other) activists. They are not only troubling, but often quite strange: some governments are teaming up to insist that climate change constitutes "human rights abuse,"[57] though the IPCC defines climate change to be, well, any change in the climate, "natural" or otherwise.[58] Imagine the consequences they hope to mete out in the event they successfully obtain some enforceable declaration that Man is responsible for the climate and an international regime is needed to sort things out.

"GETTING RID OF" HISTORY AND THE HISTORIANS

While such oppression may be surprising in the halls of government or the UN, college classrooms are another story. It is one of the world's worst-kept secrets that the tolerant, free-speech loving Left isn't too hot on academic freedoms if that means expressing climate skepticism. Consider the experience of Professor David Deming, a geoscientist at the University of Oklahoma who published an article, "Climatic warming in North America: analysis of borehole temperatures," reconstructing 150 years of North American temperatures from proxy (borehole) data.[59] He soon found himself with friends he never knew he had.

Deming reveals that "with the publication of the article in *Science*, I gained significant credibility in the community of scientists working on climate change. They thought I was one of them, someone who would pervert science in the service of social and political causes. One of them let his guard down. A major person working in the area of climate change and global warming sent me an astonishing email that said: 'We have to get rid of the Medieval Warm Period.'"[60]

This individual happens to be a UN IPCC lead author, and very soon that very same body did just that, with the now-exposed "Hockey Stick." This supposed awakening of knowledge to reverse 1,000 years of *accumulated knowledge from observations,* and even the UN's own prior assertion of climate history affirming it, came through a computer program interpreting more modern proxy data reconstructions. This was, of course, nonsense. Subsequent research has ratified the old, outdated thinking drawn from agricultural records, diaries, cultural artifacts, and the like that the

Medieval Warming was warmer than today and the Little Ice Age cooler, globally and not regionally.[61]

Deming came forward with his experience in the *Journal of Scientific Exploration*, withholding only the egregious correspondents' names. That he dared title this revelatory piece "Global warming, the politicization of science, and Michael Crichton's *State of Fear*" merely served to further enrage the alarmists, if not so much as to prompt the specific charlatans to fight back publicly.

Deming's revelation was not without cost, however, if only to him—though he to this day graciously will not flatly state that the subsequent alterations in his professional circumstances came about because of his outspokenness. He is willing to note how weather and climate are a big business on campus, with numerous research institutes relying heavily on government funding (and they recently requested $9 *billion* per year of your money, in addition). You decide whether retribution was behind his being "subjected to an involuntary transfer out of the OU geology dep[artment]. My office space was stripped from me, as well as one of my classes, and I was placed in a corner room in the basement."[62]

What is clear is that a comically threatening letter issued from attorneys for Oklahoma alumnus and wealthy donor Bob Stephenson, reminding the school of his financial and other efforts on its behalf. The barristers expressed Stephenson's displeasure that "Dr. David Deming is pursuing academic and personal interests outside of and not in support of the School's mission," vowing that "if his concerns are not addressed, please know that his efforts and donations on behalf of the School will not continue."[63]

For what it is worth, note that SEC filings state that one Robert L. Stephenson, as chance would have it, has significant interests in natural gas. Sort of like T. Boone Pickens, also the new Windmill King. The gas industry of course is one of the industries most aggressively pushing the U.S. to adopt carbon constraints in the name of "global warming"[64] (see Ken Lay's pioneering efforts in that vein in Rob Bradley's "Corporate Social Responsibility and Energy: Lessons from Enron"[65]).

Stephenson's lawyer closed by noting how it sure would be a shame if "a substantial number of other alumni" followed suit, as he sensed might occur if such outrages as Deming's continued. There is no indication that an offer of window insurance was also included. The lawyer did, however, give the impression that Mr. Stephenson was the patron of a colleague of Deming's, a "Dr. Slatt," whom Stephenson helped bring to the school as a program Director "with the professional expectation that faculty would follow the leadership of Dr. Slatt in support of the mission for [the School of] Geology and Geophysics."

One reasonable reading of this sequence is that an academic, upset with his colleague's public statements and advocacy including a revelation embarrassing to the global warming movement—though not to this individual personally—chose not to challenge the accuracy of the claim, but instead a wealthy donor leaned on the University. Deming had to go, and go he did.

But not all the way out, and not without a fight. The letter and other relevant documents released under an Oklahoma Open Records Act request are publicly available thanks to the Foundation for Individual Rights in Education (FIRE),[66] which assisted Deming in filing suit against the University of Oklahoma.[67] The professor tells me that, after settling out of court, he agreed to transfer to the College of Arts & Science, and that the University is now very supportive. A cynic might suggest that, after Deming found legal assistance, the school treats him almost as well as if he were spouting alarmism.

Deming's experience is by no means an isolated case. MIT's Richard Lindzen has cited the following litany of dissenters who have suffered for their outspoken questioning of alarmist orthodoxy: Henk Tennekes dismissed as director of the Royal Dutch Meteorological society, former World Meteorological Organization official Aksel Winn-Nielsen slandered as an industry tool by an IPCC official, and Italian researchers Alfonso Sutera and Antonio Speranza whose ability to raise research funds dried up after exhibiting a willingness to raise questions.[68] Storm-forecasting pioneer William Gray was suddenly told by Colorado State University, where he has long taught, that it declined to further handle media inquiries for their most sought-after expert.[69] The problem, it seems, is that every reporter now wants to ask about each storm *did the humans do it?*, and Gray is equally likely to give the wrong (from liberal academia's perspective) answer.

STATE CLIMATOLOGISTS LEANED ON, HUSHED, SACKED

Clearly, anti-warmist academics don't feel the heat solely within those hallowed halls, but wherever they are employed. Of particular concern to the alarmist establishment were state climatologists, who typically are university professors serving the function of providing data to the public. That position usually arises from a Memorandum of Agreement between the state, the scientist's university, and the National Climatic Data Center. Some state climatologist positions are statutorily created and some have budget line-items, as well, but generally it is this document that runs common to them. It states rather awkwardly that "the National Climatic Data Center of the [NOAA] officially recognizes the [State] Climate Office as the State Climate Office for the [State], with [name] as State Climatologist." This named individual "having been certified by the American Association of State Climatologists as an ARSCO, an official status as an AASC Recognized State Climate Office is hereby granted."

This makes it quite strange when a politician goes to lengths to insist that the state really does not have a state climatologist, as has increasingly occurred as part of a campaign to discredit and shut dissenting scientists up—or down—as needed.

In February 2007, Associate State Climatologist for Washington State Mark Albright found himself in hot water for expressing his scientific opinion on trends in snowpack melt without having first run his opinion past his boss. Check that: he got in trouble for rebutting in a *non-alarmist* email to colleagues, grounded in research, an alarmist claim by Seattle's mayor and global warming activist Greg Nickels in an op-ed. Nickels had made very specific and very deceptive claims that global warming is causing the Cascade Mountains to lose half of their snowpack—cleverly using a 1950s baseline—with the remainder expected to be cut in half again in thirty years.[70] Albright also referred to similar claims by the state climatologist as "the myth of the vanishing snowpack caused by global warming" in the Portland *Oregonian*.[71] Uh oh.

The state climatologist, Phil Mote, is a fairly typical, computer modeler-type global warming alarmist, which ensured that the assistant climatologist would not last in any formal capacity after offering his scientific opinion. A University of Washington atmospheric scientist—not a skeptic, for what that's worth—agreed to referee the competing claims. He sided with the more sober conclusion, affirming Albright's revelation that the alarmists were simply rigging the baseline to make their claim of melt, agreeing with Albright's assessment of a smaller loss, and even noting that if one chose a more modern baseline "there is a small *increase* in snow-water equivalent."[72] Subsequent research further validated this position, as well.[73]

Facts be damned, however, the idea that Albright continued to send data-based emails to colleagues about such things became too much for Mote, who tried to censor such communications. Albright objected, and, as reported in the *Chicago Tribune*, "was stripped of his state title, an unpaid post, [but] remains a research meteorologist at the University of Washington."[74] Albright's coworker, meteorologist Cliff Mass, said, "In all my years of doing science, I've never seen this sort of gag-order approach to doing science."[75] Stick around. In this field, you will.

We saw the same story unfold in Virginia, with State Climatologist Patrick Michaels, long the target of green ire. Michaels' sin is his fairly well-reasoned if still quite possibly overstated argument that, although slight warming over the past century has an appreciable human component and should continue, observations combined with computer models indicate any further warming would be mild.

His optimism about the future was also too much for the newly elected Democratic Governor of Virginia, Tim Kaine, who soon after taking office ratcheted up the effort to get Michaels removed from his statutory post.

Newsbusters noted how the media, which is highly attuned to political bullying and interference with substance and science, had no outrage to spare, and their sparse reportage on this buried the matters of political pressure and ignored the chilling effect of silencing critics.

George Taylor, head of the Oregon Climate Service at Oregon State University and as such that state's climatologist, faced the same reverse press-ganging, when Governor Ted Kulongoski remarkably stated that he wanted Taylor removed from his position because of his views. Taylor has published over two hundred research papers and two books, *The Climate of Oregon* and *The Oregon Weather Book*. Kulongoski does not boast of any, though he's surely just being modest.

As one paper kindly editorialized after the muck became hip-deep, "The governor and other Democrats wanted to sideline Taylor for not wholeheartedly going along with the prevailing theory of man-caused global warming, but evidently they didn't want to be seen doing so."[76] As a direct response to science not cooperating with politics, and being bound by their inability to simply bestow the title of state climatologist (that being up to the state university and NCDC), the politicians' solution was to create a *new* climate center tasked with the same functions as the statutorily created post that Taylor occupied.

Similarly, in the Blue Hen State, Chicken Little seems to be ruling the roost. University of Delaware's Dr. David Legates is that state's official climatologist according to the usual Memorandum of Agreement between him, the Governor Ruth Ann Minner, and the National Climatic Data Center. Legates, too, came under political pressure for daring to express his views on climate, again derived from research. Here, the elected politician proved to be the more responsible actor if only when compared to a media campaign to oust Legates, apparently orchestrated from within the state's bureaucracy.

Politicians with no expertise lean on scientists who derive their stances from actual research—sounds like a typical critique of the Bush administration, but it's more typical of Democratic governors facing realistic climatologists. These stories are far worse than a Bush administration official telling James Hansen to leave the policy statements to the policy people. Yet the latter made national news and was the subject of (utterly disingenuous) congressional inquiry as purported "muzzling!" and censorship; the former cases only made news to the extent that reporters were indignant about scientists daring to assert scientific positions that disagreed with politically obtained stances.

The lesson is that Hansen and other alarmists are free to say what they want about climate without any political thug telling them that *the scientific position is to be asserted by the politicians so put a sock in it.* He was merely told that the policy people speak to policy and, as much as he apparently would like to hold another job, he doesn't, and should stick to the one he has. There was no suggestion that maybe he should look for a new one.

These four scientists experienced the machinery of the state intervening to silence inconvenient climate speech. The cases neither are exclusive nor will they likely be the last state officials told by politicians that their science must conform to politics. The pols cannot tolerate that. There is much more at stake. As Michaels asked rhetorically at the close of the 1990 UK Channel 4 film "The Greenhouse Conspiracy," "Would you march down the road toward a policy which people have rightfully said requires an economic restructuring of the world knowing that the world was behaving opposite to what the basis for that policy said?"

ROCKET MAN

The green machine showed its fangs again in 2007 when NASA chief Michael Griffin dismissed the zealous global warmist presumption of amazing (and highly unlikely) anthropogenic powers. He also dared scoff at the implicit argument that we happen to live in a time with the ideal climate. It was to satirize precisely that fantasy as theorized by philosopher Gottfried Leibniz in his *Theodicy* that Voltaire created the character Pangloss.

Griffin dared wonder aloud in an interview on National Public Radio, of all places, "Whether [global warming] is a long term concern or not, I can't say. . . . To assume that it is a problem is to assume that the state of Earth's climate today is the optimal climate, the best climate that we could have or ever have had. . . . I think that's a rather arrogant position for people to take."[77] He had yet to meet arrogance, but soon would.

The *Washington Post*[78] and alarmist weblogs[79] were joined by Gore advisor and NASA scientist James Hansen[80] to leap in unison with frenzied outrage. The heat led Griffin to hurriedly affirm the observed warming trend the next day and to apologize, but at least he did so only for expressing his personal views and prompting a distracting controversy (Dr. Hansen, we're still waiting for yours).[81] He did not go so far as to scrape in shame over having *held* the views. In a vacuum this would not amount to much of a defense, but in this context Griffin's is in fact a relatively strong stand, what with the track record of so many who rush to proclaim, in appeasement, a full-throated cry of looming catastrophe after having angered the beast.

After the furor died down, Griffin admitted in an interview that he was surprised by the reaction to his having spoken what, in any open and honest debate, is a fairly basic statement that only the truly righteous could resent. Said Griffin, "I didn't realize it had approached the status where you can't express any sort of a contrary opinion or a comment without it being treated almost [sic] as a religious issue."[82] Now he knows. The point of the establishment's attack machine is to spread that knowledge so that fewer and fewer Michael Griffins of the world have any doubt that this will be the reaction. This approach toward achieving a dissent-free society has ritually failed in the long run, though there seems to always be one more faction with totalitarian instincts—recall the serial claims that dissent carries criminal overtones—to try their own hand at it.

EUROPE'S WITCH HUNTS, REVISITED

While the alarmists' totalitarian streak is, like the UK Royal Society affairs, appalling, these displays are less aberrant than one might presume. Consider how in 2007 a prominent French research scientist and academic was subjected to a formal if private trial by his academic peers, which proceedings were and remain hidden from public display for obvious reasons (they *do* have some shame). His crime was to have penned an op-ed in *Le Monde*, a major French daily, challenging alarmism.

Such attacks are less about the dissenters' science and more to do with singling out those who push back against the political consensus that the world is doomed unless certain institutions are empowered. Indeed, Bjørn Lomborg, who claims to believe that global warming is real, anthropogenic, and a problem—though not one

that ranks among the gravest global environmental worries—
attracts the "denier" label not because he questions the science
underpinning climate change, but because he doesn't conform to
the mainstream prescription.[83] Beginning in 2002, the Danish professor was treated to an inquisition clearly designed to cudgel him
into submission.[84]

As columnist and author James Glassman described Lomborg's
experience:

> They have gone berserk. Nasty, hysterical, paranoid—those are
> apt adjectives to describe the response to [Lomborg's first book,
> *The Skeptical Environmentalist*[85]]. *The Economist,* which,
> despite its own green leanings, lavishly praised Lomborg's book
> when it came out, last week reported that "Mr. Lomborg is
> being called a liar, a fraud and worse. People are refusing to
> share a platform with him. He turns up in Oxford to talk about
> this book, and the author (it is claimed) of a forthcoming study
> on climate change throws a pie in his face."
>
> The *World Resources Institute* has posted a special media
> alert on its website: "WRI is urging journalists to exercise cau-
> tion in reporting on or reviewing the new book, *The Skeptical
> Environmentalist.*" It's as though Lomborg were armed and
> dangerous. And, in a way, of course, he is: armed with facts and
> dangerous to a movement whose claims are rarely checked.
> *Grist* magazine, TomPaine.com, the so-called "Union of Con-
> cerned Scientists," and on and on—they're all trying to debunk
> Lomborg. There's even a site called www.anti-Lomborg.com.[86]

We urge caution in reviewing or reporting on a book. Cut down
trees to do so, sure; but the act of *analysis*? *Speech*? Impermissible
to environmentalists.

The green pressure groups World Wildlife Fund and the World
Resources Institute issued a Lomborg-bashing press release claiming

that his book was "riddled with misleading arguments and factual errors." These groups were seemingly unconcerned that their "industry" thrived by churning out endless pamphlets, popular media reports, and generally flimsy claptrap far less sourced than Lomborg's work. Still, they called it "pseudo-scholarship" because he relied in part on "articles that have not undergone scientific peer review."[87] Of course, turning this supposed standard of the alarmists on their own work would spell the end for their industry.

Consider one specific example of Lomborg's purported sloth and misleading arguments from incredible sources, his reliance upon an article from the *Bulletin of the American Meteorological Society*. This happens to be a peer reviewed journal, one which rarely allows rationalists to grace its pages. *Oh. Well*, the groups sniveled, *the piece had been rejected elsewhere*. That has certainly been the case with many published articles (the odds for which go up for "skeptical" pieces). It just happens to be untrue about this one. As we will see later, when pushed for facts the alarmists routinely make up claims on the spot.[88] So much for that concern with resorting only to confirmed facts.

Their claim that Lomborg is somehow factually deficient is particularly risible given the source. As Ron Bailey notes, the reviewers that *Scientific American* sicced on discrediting Lomborg phoned those whom he had cited to ask them if it was done accurately. For example, "Lomborg cites Paul Ehrlich and E. O. Wilson as supporting something called the Wildlands Project, which would reserve 50 percent of the North American continent as uninhabited wildlands. Pimm and Harvey asked Ehrlich if he supported such a plan. 'I know of no such plan,' replied Ehrlich. 'If there were one, I wouldn't support it.' Q.E.D."[89] Fortunately Bailey is able to help out, confirming an obviously distracted Ehrlich that in "The High Cost of Biodiversity" from the June 25, 1993, issue of *Science*, "The principles behind the Wildlands Project have garnered endorsements from such scientific luminaries as Edward

O. Wilson of Harvard [and] Paul Ehrlich of Stanford (who describes himself as an 'enthusiastic supporter')."[90]

Lomborg's detractors seem to be projecting their own deficiencies on him. Either that, or deep down they suspect that only a fool would rely on the elite peer-reviewed journals as authorities.

But worse was yet to come for Lomborg, who experienced behavior that the greens visit upon any who dare disagree. This does lead one to wonder if this isn't the ultimate sign that they lack confidence in their own racket. As Glassman also notes, "Back in the 1960s, campus radicals used to say that their demonstrations would provoke college administrators, the police, and government authorities into showing their 'true nature';" in the greens' case, this has been revealed as "a petulant, angry, selfish child that whines that it must have its own way."

Soon Lomborg found himself the subject of complaints before the Danish Committees on Scientific Dishonesty that he had, well, engaged in scientific dishonesty in his dissent from global warming alarmism in the best-selling tome. Among the complaining parties were writers—the ones whom *Nature* magazine had review Lomborg's book.[91] *Nature* then published a breathless piece announcing the charge titled "Ethics panel attacks environment book."[92] Ah, yes, *the ethics panel* did this. Further down the rabbit hole, the magazine claimed the committees "picked an appropriate target," but missed (that is, the truth prevailed, in a way).[93] Yes. The committees picked that target.

The pack was now set to howling, with *Nature* and other journals proceeding to style Lomborg as the moral equivalent of a Holocaust denier (and why not, the review had furiously if bizarrely claimed he "employs the strategy of those who, for example, argue that gay men aren't dying of AIDS, that Jews weren't singled out by the Nazis for extermination, and so on").[94] This is pretty rich from a publication that subsequently published work appearing to endorse extinction of the human race[95] (not to mention a piece on historical flooding concluding that the seemingly impending doom "might make Al Gore our Noah"[96]).

Scientific American, certainly as much as *Nature*, started the whole DCSD unpleasantness when Lomborg's inroads into the general media came to be of unbearable embarrassment to the vested establishment. That publication set in motion what was basically a character assassination by environmental doommongers (Stephen Schneider, John Holdren, John Bongaarts, and Thomas Lovejoy). Something simply had to be done. This should come as no surprise from a publication which hailed Al Gore's movie (which gets the cause-and-effect relationship between CO_2 and temperature—its very premise—*backward*) as "a paragon of clear science communication."[97]

In its January 2002 issue, *SciAm* published the (pretentiously titled) feature "Misleading Math about the Earth: Science defends itself against *The Skeptical Environmentalist*." In this eleven-page assault on Lomborg for daring to deconstruct the alarmist agenda, the four horsemen of climate alarmism purportedly representing "science" criticized him—oh, yes, and to some extent, his arguments, specifically as they pertained to global warming, energy, overpopulation, and biodiversity.[98]

> "Danish statistician Bjørn Lomborg, author of *The Skeptical Environmentalist: Measuring the Real State of the World*, sat down at a Borders bookstore in Oxford, England, to promote his controversial book. A pie was thrown in his direction. 'I wanted to put a Baked Alaska in his smug face,' said the perpetrator, 'in solidarity with the native Indian and Eskimo people in Alaska.' It was one of the more honest attacks on Lomborg and his book."
>
> Ron Bailey, Reason *Magazine*, May 2002

Reading like a slightly over-cast witches scene from *Macbeth*, the four strove to ensure that this Dane didn't get off Scot-free (so to speak) for sins both real (but small) and imagined, and would never become king of the environ-mental discussion they have so comfortably presided over. With per-ceptible insincerity *SciAm* sniffed in its pages that this ludicrously unfair mugging "should be a welcome audit. And yet it isn't."

This prompted a well-deserved firestorm of criticism largely centering on *SciAm's* obvious campaign to find activists to slam Lomborg with supposed critiques that largely skirted the substance of what he wrote. It then allowed Lomborg to respond[99] and its alarmists to rebut him as the final word. As Mark Steyn has dis-covered, this is precisely the standard called for by Islamic funda-mentalists trying to suppress speech that they don't like.[100]

So, four-against-none becomes eight-to-one. Reader reaction must have been severe. In a letter (that *SciAm* actually published, to their credit) Denis Dutton, cited as the Philosophy and Liter-ature Editor at New Zealand's University of Canterbury, assailed the enterprise's false construct and noted that the attack pre-sumed to define alarmism as science and skeptics as being out-side of science—even though science itself is inherently skeptical and indeed throws itself back to Medieval times upon abandon-ing skepticism.

> You have no intellectual warrant whatsoever to divide the world into two camps: "science," including the Lomborg critics you publish, plus their allies, Paul Ehrlich et al., and, apparently, "nonscience," including Lomborg, Matt Ridley, Lewis Wolpert and his many other allies. If you wanted to say "Environmental-ism (or The Green Movement) defends itself against *The Skepti-cal Environmentalist*," that would be acceptable. But there is no question that Lomborg and his allies are within science.[101]

Lomborg then detailed his detractors' own significant and embarassing inaccuracies in their rush to claim him guilty of pre-cisely that practice, exposing most of the claims as the visceral whines ritually spouted against every heretic, even if untrue in his case (*"denier" of the warming trend*, which he isn't; *rejects the UN process,* which regrettably he doesn't; *ignores specie loss*, which he actually instead overtly debunks).[102]

Lomborg closed by noting that his critics never addressed his concept of prioritization of risks, which is the underlying theme of his criticism of alarmist demands: the industrial processes so abhorred by his critics for purportedly warming the planet by a degree in a century-and-a-half have also brought unprecedented life-spans, reduced infant mortality, allowed sufficient wealth to be dedicated to environmental protection, and so on. But the well-being of people apparently has absolutely nothing to do with their calculus, but only occasionally their rhetoric.

The Committees ruled in January 2003, stating that "Objectively speaking, the publication of the work under consideration is deemed to fall within the concept of scientific dishonesty."[103] This opinion, such as it was, offered as evidence not analysis, but a *list of those who had criticized Lomborg*. One might call it a "litany" (and the ultimate low in the rhetorical sloppiness of appealing to authority).

As Charles Paul Freund wrote in *Reason* Magazine, "It's interesting to observe how impressively Denmark resolves issues of science that arise within its borders: by pronouncement. This saves a lot of time that is otherwise wasted on observation, experiment, analysis, and debate," noting sardonically how such "'pronouncement' business has a long and distinguished history."[104]

Schneider was apparently delighted that the ruling cited him—if not in any substantive way given its approach was to largely reiterate the *SciAm* gang-tackle. In this drama, Schneider was simply "a particularly respected researcher who has been discussing these problems for 30 years with thousands of fellow scientists and policy analysts in myriad articles and formal meetings." Schneider's delight was likely over the fact that they left his decades of "discussion" at that, with no mention of his contribution to the global cooling panic or subsequent dancing around of the same. Hmmm. That sounds like scientific dishonesty by the committees' standards.

Naturally, as reported by the BBC, "Although its ruling carried no penalty, Lomborg's opponents tried to use the judgement [sic] to get him removed from his post as director of Denmark's Environmental Assessment Institute."[105] The pattern does seem to be less one of substantive argument than of seeking to remove dissenters from positions of influence or authority. That is, it is personal. Period.

The headlines claiming Lomborg was convicted of dishonesty were halfway around the world, as Churchill said, before the truth got out of bed. "On close inspection, the Danish committee's statement makes no allegations of dishonesty by Lomborg. Instead, the analysis is based on an eleven-page article published last year in *Scientific American* magazine that found errors in the 2001 book."[106]

Despite their on-the-one-hand-it's-objectively-dishonest statement, the Committees' director stated, "The decision does not take a stance—nor is it supposed to take a stance—on whether Bjørn Lomborg's theories are right or wrong, no more so in fact than the decision elucidates whether his critics' theories are right or wrong."[107] So, the theories constitute dishonesty, but only in that the DCSD just went along in reiterating criticism of Lomborg; which somehow means, as the ruling states, "in view of the subjective requirements made in terms of intent or gross negligence, however, Bjørn Lomborg's publication cannot fall within the bounds of this characterization. Conversely, the publication is deemed clearly contrary to the standards of good scientific practice."

Got that? *We want to discredit him, but not so far as to actually go on record doing so, so we just repeat scurrilous invective and note with our official imprimatur that other people sure have said bad things about his work, which means it is "objectively dishonest." Except that he's cleared of said charge. Sort of.* One sees here not the courage that enabled the Vikings to depart Scandinavia to discover the world, but certainly a good example of why they might want to.

The champagne, like the greens' purported success in teaching Lomborg his lesson, wasn't to flow for long, and not simply because those bubbles represent a fearful release of the dreaded CO_2. Danes don't seem to care for the glare of international attention, or even genuine controversy for that matter. This episode certainly drew both, especially for the DCSD, which states in its annual report for 2002 of *l'affaire Lomborg* (written in 2003), "The decision gave rise to considerable debate."[108] Understated, those Danes. Except when coming after a heretic.

It seemed enough to admit, in the context of that invocation of Lomborg, that "the case prompted the Danish Minister of Science, Technology and Innovation to ask the Director of the Danish Research Agency to set up a working party, whose brief was to evaluate whether there is any need to adjust the regulatory basis for DCSD's future work." My wife who hails from Denmark assures me that the appropriate translation here is "look, someone [*deleted*] up, ok?"

The ultimate ruling on appeal to the Danish Ministry of Science, Technology and Innovation "reflected an overruling of DCSD's decision, was critical of DCSD in several respects," and remanded the matter back to the committee(s) which effectively ended the inquiry for reasons that sound an awful lot like an excuse trying to make things go away:[109] they concluded that "the DCSD has not documented where he has allegedly been biased in his choice of data and in his argumentation, and . . . the ruling is completely void of argumentation for why the DCSD find that the complainants are right in their criticisms of [his] working methods."[110] Put another way, the DCSD described this particular ruling as having "acquitted Lomborg *de facto* of scientific dishonesty."[111] That is to say that Lomborg was cleared of this spurious charge.[112] In response to this affair, Dutch scientist Arthur Rorsch and other academics wrote a damning assessment of the critiques of Lomborg.[113]

So, all ended well for the greater good, notwithstanding what Mr. Lomborg was put through but thanks to the uproar it caused, giving a black eye to such tactics and ultimately vindicating him, to boot.

PRIVATE JOURNALS

These same journals that helped lead the charge against the heretical Lomborg have a history of setting different standards for publication of inconvenient opinions, to the point of crafting transparent artifices to keep contrary views out of their pages. Pat Michaels regularly notes in his speeches how he exposed the journals' fetish for doom and exclusion of "skeptic" research papers. In his analysis of 115 relevant papers published over a particular year (mid-2005 and mid-2006) in the journals *Nature* and *Science*, Michaels found 83 of them claimed that global warming would be worse than previously suggested, 23 of them were neutral, and a mere 9, or under 8 percent, found that things were not as bad as previously thought. Meanwhile, hurricanes scarcely made landfall in the U.S. and by 2008 the cooling trend was so undeniable even the IPCC admitted it.

Despite observations supporting the skeptic or climate realist position, the alarmists tout this publication disparity as simply proving their point that the science is overwhelmingly on their side—for example, in *New Scientist*, which raised this point in an article titled so as to remove all doubt about Michaels' point, "Climate change special: State of denial."[114] Michaels notes instead that the laws of probability hold that this cannot be by mere chance, that new research would be close to evenly distributed in its conclusions.

The bias extends to how certain thought must be labeled, for example Scafetta and West's March 2008 article on solar variability being a main cause of climate warming was labeled as "Opinion" by *Physics Today*. When publishing the alarmist Gavin Schmidt's ode to climate models a year earlier, that tag was not applied but the piece was styled as an apparently objective review of the state of the deeply flawed beast.[115] Nor were readers informed that Schmidt is one of the producers of the alarmist RealClimate blog and a regularly high-pitched, and often nasty, activist.

Just as *Science* Magazine's publisher the American Association for the Advancement of Science is an activist group, the publisher of *Physics Today*, the American Institute of Physics, feverishly pushes the agenda. For example, it hosts a website on climate change by physicist Spencer Weart, who recommends readers to Schmidt's alarmist blog RealClimate, the Pew Center, and the IPCC for more information on global warming. He also lists some skeptical sites, finding his editorial voice to say, for example, "The industry-funded Cooler Heads Coalition offers arguments against the IPCC consensus; the Marshall Institute also gathers arguments motivated by conservative ideology."[116]

We have already covered how the American Meteorological Society has become actively alarmist, and detail elsewhere how this is not in fact representative of its despairing membership. Its *Bulletin of the AMS* (BAMS) is increasingly used in apparent synchronization with alarmist needs. For example, in early 2008 it joined the effort to proclaim the 1970s cooling scare as really just a "myth."[117] One of that article's three authors was Wikipedia's "gatekeeper" on global warming who has been demonstrated to continuously monitor the site and make changes scrubbing it for refutation of the alarmist thesis. AMS also moved helpful pieces through its *Journal of Climate*.[118]

All such bias is of course their right as private publications, but the role they play in this particular field of science does tweak the equation a bit. They go beyond their prerogative and stray into bias not merely in selection but when going so far as to, for example, avoid applying basic rigors of review to papers that fit the agenda.

IT'S JUST THEIR *NATURE*

The Lomborg affair is an extreme example of how the leading science journals have, in practice, increasingly altered their mission from providing unbiased research and reportage in favor of intimidating climate "skeptics" and advocacy for specific and drastic policies to curb CO_2 emissions.

This is further illustrated in the deeply troubling problems (noted elsewhere in these pages) John McLean and Douglas Keegan encountered while trying to obtain data. While more and more publications in other scholarly disciplines are requiring the archiving of data and methodologies and making it accessible through the Internet as a condition of publication, most climate science publications do not yet require even minimal transparency.

In the face of increasing questions about the integrity of surface temperature data, the UK's Hadley Centre repeatedly "refuse[s] to release lists of the [temperature] stations used in compiling their global data sets or in their papers claiming the data shows no urban adjustment is needed."[119] Certain fast-tracked AMS pieces, and one in *Nature,* seemed part of an effort to cover for this glaring problem in maintaining the alarmists' claims of a Man-made, twentieth century trend of increasing surface temperatures.[120]

When U.S. congressmen sought to reconcile challenges to the 2001 UN claims to having a "smoking gun," the IPCC's head knew enough to run for the protective pleats of *Nature*'s skirt. They provided his response, such as it was, in a piece titled "Climate change: is the US Congress bullying experts?: Climate chief Rajendra Pachauri responds to US demands for information."[121] Apparently *Nature* believes that it's mean when the people who paid for something that turns out to be bogus ask the parties involved to explain how this happened.

Despite everything revealed in these pages about the reality of the scientific debate, of which leading alarmists are obviously aware, *Nature* penned an editorial claiming that by using "specious scientific findings" skeptics "worked to establish a bogus scientific debate," and use "unscrupulous determination to deny the facts" countering "the consensus view of climate researchers."[122] The actual consensus that does exist is that temperatures have risen a degree in 150 years since the end of the Little Ice Age and, all other things being equal, more CO_2 and Man's contribution of GHGs should play some role. That's it, and we spend billions trying to narrow it down further, but skeptics don't deny it.

Further, according to *Nature* the skeptics "deliberately set out to take maximum advantage of media gullibility." At this point one is tempted to remind the alarmists that they don't believe in media bias. Just its ignorance, apparently. *Nature's* punch line then denounces this campaign to "confuse and delude the U.S. public on global warming."

Still, the figures noted above leave it more apparent that journals such as *Nature* are the ones actively engaged in an effort to create the phony paradigm, going to great lengths to provide a skewed representation of the state of the science. For example, a 2003 submission to *Nature* explained how populations actually fare better with hot weather events, with mortality not increasing but rather dropping with the frequency of the events, for the simple reasons that individuals and society as a whole learn to respond.

Examples include Chicago and France. Heat waves in 1995 and 2003, respectively, had killed many people; when similar heat waves occurred in both places a few short years later, the results were very different. In fact, urban mortality has dropped as cities got warmer. People figure things out. To oversimplify the larger picture, obese people discern that high noon is not the time to go jogging or mow the lawn.

Nature, with a history of publishing alarmist papers, particularly those addressing the likelihood of massive casualties resulting from a warmer world, passed on the piece which was so unworthy that it went on to win the Association of American Geographers' 2004 "Paper of the Year" award (Climate Specialty Group).[123]

Consider a November 2004 paper published by *Nature* claiming to have developed a method of using grape harvest dates for estimating any individual year's summer temperature in Burgundy, France, back to 1370.[124] It asserted that 2003 saw by far the warmest summer there in more than seven centuries (a period mostly, though not completely, fulfilled by the Little Ice Age). This is a very desirable outcome for the alarmist agenda. It is also apparently unsupportable, but *Nature*'s peer-review process didn't even go so far as to check basic facts.

Mathematician and independent researcher John McLean was sent the paper by someone seeking comment from a mathematical perspective, and discovered among other problems that "the authors' estimate for the summer temperature of 2003 was higher than the actual temperature by 2.4°C (about 4.3°F). This is the primary reason that 2003 seemed, according to the authors, to be so tremendously warm."[125] Yeah, that would do it. In short, "the authors had developed a method that gave a falsely-high estimate of temperature in 2003 and falsely-low estimates of temperatures in other very warm years. They then used those false estimates to proclaim that 2003 was much hotter than other years."

Given the similar practice employed by James Hansen in going back into the record and emerging with prior years now being cooler and more recent years warmer, thereby enhancing a warming trend, this might be unremarkable but for one thing. When McLean asked paper author Isabelle Chuine what data was sent to *Nature* when submitting the paper, "Dr. Chuine replied, 'We never sent data to *Nature*.'" McLean stresses that the truth or falsehood of the paper's claim is not as important as the systemic flaws it revealed. He states that outside of the medical sciences it turns out to be common both for researchers to submit papers without including the supporting data and for peer reviewers to lack the requisite mathematical or statistical skills needed to check the work. The vaunted "peer review" doesn't wear scrutiny well.

So here we see the world's most prestigious science journal illustrating how desired yet unsupportable outcomes can get published. And *Nature* has proven that outcomes such as this are most definitely the sort they are more comfortable with.

Further revealing their service to the alarmist community, when famed debunker Stephen McIntyre let it be known that he had been invited to make a single post on *Nature's* blog in reply to a discussion about the Hockey Stick that had, amazingly, failed to mention Stick debunkers McIntyre and McKitrick's work, alarmist feathers were ruffled and the next day *Nature* rescinded the invite.[126] Can't have "other" views represented, even of those who know more about a particular subject that *Nature* otherwise finds worthy of coverage.

Benny Peiser, who has gained great notoriety among the alarmist industry for chronicling their foibles, argues that the advocacy and editorial bias compounds itself through confirmation bias. That is, they not only spout their own dogma as fact but seek to affirm it through the work of others, while also keeping inconvenient thought from the light of day.

Peiser claims that a careful examination of the leading journals' publishing record reveals how science editors, like others, tend to favor the publication of papers confirming, rather than questioning, their publicly stated beliefs. He also notes that this phenomenon is fairly well-established among climate scientists, as shown for example by the regularity with which they are now accused of running statistical models and framing their data so as to predictably confirm their hypothesis. It extends to peer review, the reviewers being selected by the very same editors, and being "more likely to accept evidence that supports their own prior belief while rejecting arguments and data that may challenge these convictions (Kaptchuk, 2003)."[127]

Peiser says this is to be expected. "After all, research into confirmation and other biases has shown that the scientific method incorporates an inherent tension between hard data and their interpretation by scientists with deeply held convictions." The logical conclusion affirmed by anecdotal information is that this dissuades submissions, as well.

As the editors, alarmists, and their apologists note, the evidence affirming this practice is largely circumstantial—no editor has yet to pen a note explaining that, due to the enormous stakes both financial and reputational, they must pass on a "skeptic's" submission. But we didn't say they were stupid. Only biased.

POPULAR SCIENCE CULTURE

This cynical advocacy cloaked in science extends beyond peer-reviewed journals, of course, into the popular science media which also bared its fangs in *l'Affaire Lomborg*. John Rennie, editor of *Scientific American*, publicly airs his preferred level of intellectual vigor, deriding dissenters as "denialists" and offered a brow-furrowing caution that to "give them even one paragraph in a 10-paragraph article would be to exaggerate their importance."[128]

The editors of *New Scientist* try to square the indispensable principle of falsification with their belief that its application to the man-made warming thesis would simply undermine political attempts at mitigating climate disaster. Their haughtily stated position, in an editorial titled "Nowhere to turn for climate change deniers," is that "some scientists are challenging our ideas on climate change, which is vital if we are to progress. But to overturn present thinking will need very strong evidence because, as the IPCC states, confidence in the idea that anthropogenic warming is changing our world has never been higher."[129]

That is, others must be allowed to speak, but not so much that they are effective. What is important is the mission, and catastrophism is the pony to ride. Yet even this silly effort to appear in favor of debate is only half-hearted given that the latter element— a zealous defense of the apocalyptic climate consensus—ensures that the former cannot be satisfied at any meaningful level. Instead, a staunch resistance must continue against allowing those critical researchers a forum for rebuttal or attempts at falsification.

The point of turning the reality of uncertainty on its head, of citing it as a reason *not* to look before one leaps but to row faster in the direction of the agenda and its energy and lifestyle policies, is the breathtakingly primitive, "It's a fair bet that much of what we do not yet know for sure will turn out to be scarier than most of us like to imagine."[130] Yet these people like to imagine *apocalypse*, making this even more difficult to swallow.

For these reasons, "environmentalists...are horrified" when, for example, large deposits of clean-burning fuel are discovered because, although "a cleaner-burning fossil fuel than coal or oil," huge quantities of combustible natural gas "represent 'captured' greenhouse gasses that some believe should remain locked under the sea."[131] Finders keepers, return to sender, ashes to ashes, and all that.

Writers Stuart Blackman and Ben Pile documented the balance *New Scientist* shows. In 2007, "to expound his theory that the world will witness sea level rises of five metres this century (the IPCC estimates between 18 and 59cm), NASA's James Hansen [was given] a 3,000-word feature in *New Scientist*. In contrast, when the same magazine, in the same month, reported on Harvard scientist Willie Soon's paper in the journal *Ecological Complexity*, which challenged received wisdom that climate change is imperilling [sic] polar bears, the scientific argument was ignored in favour of speculation about Soon's alleged links to the oil industry, and that the research was part of an orchestrated campaign to undermine the environmental movement's use of the polar bear as an icon."[132]

Even more disturbing, and illustrative of how the hierarchy of these journals will seize any opportunity to advance a cause, the respected peer-reviewed journal *Climate Research* published a paper supporting the longstanding and broadly held view that the past millennium's climate was rather variable, including the Medieval Warm Period and Little Ice Age.[133] This paper—which worked its way through four reviewers, all of whose comments resulted in changes acceptable to them, and the editor—received the opprobrium of the global warming industry.

Ultimately, alarmist editors resigned from the publication on the specious grounds that the journal, having seen one of its papers criticized, needed to publish an editorial on the matter. Actually, the demand was for a piece in time for a Senate hearing called to review the scientific controversy. Apparently, one side of the aisle felt they'd be really helped out if a peer-review journal teamed up with them, to publicly flog itself for having allowed a paper to be published, through the peer review process, which the publisher had reviewed and found appropriate, but which was attacked by alarmists upon publication if hardly on its substance. It doesn't get much more brazen than this.

The rush call for a hair-shirt editorial was circulated on Friday evening (U.S. Eastern time). A draft was circulated *condemning the practice of publishing papers that are subsequently criticized*, for Monday publication. It was prompted by an email from the Democratic staff director of the U.S. Senate Environment Committee seeking assistance for the upcoming hearing on Tuesday.

Additionally, the alarmists called for appointment of an editor in chief with the power to override the peer-review process and publish or refuse to publish pieces on his own determination, contrary (by definition) to scholarly journal practice. The complaints, distilled, were best encapsulated by the buffoonish pomposity of Michael "Hockey Stick" Mann at that Senate hearing that the editorial was supposed to support. Granted the "last word" by Senator James Jeffords, embracing him as "my witness," Mann seethed that "my understanding is that Chris de Freitas, the individual in question, frequently publishes op/ed pieces in newspapers in New Zealand attacking IPCC and attacking Kyoto and attacking the work of mainstream climatologists in this area. So this is a fairly unusual editor we are talking about."[134] *He publishes op-eds against Kyoto, and he's free to walk the streets?*

AUTHOR! AUTHOR!

Climate rationalists regularly claim that researchers who produce dissenting work find a more difficult path to publication in the journals' pages. "The difficulties of getting published are compounded when one is working in a contentious area with policy implications—climate change, for example. An author can face endless hassles with referees, and with editors who often openly display their prejudices in editorials."[135] Although *Science* ran Oreskes' claims—in "essay" form for the apparent reason, in hindsight, that it could not pass even the degraded standards for peer review—it also rejected German Professor Dennis Bray's survey revealing tepid support among scientists for the claim that Man drives climate, while another rejected Klaus-Martin Schulte's review of the 500+ papers published after Oreskes' search, only 7 percent of which agreed with her "consensus."

Science also rejected a paper by William Livingston and Matt Penn, solar scientists with the Tucson-based National Solar Observatory. The pair predicted a dud of an upcoming sunspot cycle that would reveal the beginning of another extended down period in solar activity. "[T]he punch line: That last long-term down period, 1645-1715, coincided with the Little Ice Age, a period of bitter cold winters."[136] *Oh, no you don't. Science* dismissed the piece as a mere "statistical argument." Meaning it shared an awful lot in common with pretty much all else that they publish. Of course, Livingston and Penn also have been proven quite correct so far on sunspots, with that fiery ball in the sky which we are to ignore for climate purposes remaining oddly quiet. Coincidentally, it's cooling, too.

Hey. We all make mistakes; it just seems that the elite journals make them with somewhat greater regularity in their insistence on a particular industry-building agenda.

Pat Michaels noted, as far back as 1990 in the Channel 4 (UK) film *The Greenhouse Conspiracy*, his experience with getting work of his published that ran contrary to accepted argument:

> MICHAELS: People who have a point of view which may not be the politically acceptable point of view are going to have problems. That's not surprising. I have had experience with editors where I have asked questions as to why something [a paper submitted for publication] was rejected and this has occurred with more than one journal and have been told that your papers are held to a higher standard of review than others. I've literally been told that.
>
> INTERVIEWER: On what grounds?
>
> MICHAELS: Because of what they say.[137]

But the alarmists deny this bias exists, because nobody can produce a rejection letter saying, "We cannot run your piece because it casts doubt upon our viewpoint."

Yet it remains undeniable that claims of selective impediments to publishing critical work are not uncommon. Scientists with whom I have spoken typically report, for example, having papers continuously "delayed for publication because of petty issues related to it, [as opposed to having them] rejected."

As the narrator of *Conspiracy* concluded:

> It may not quite add up to a conspiracy. But certainly a coalition of interests has promoted the greenhouse [warming] theory. Scientists have needed funds; the media, a story; and governments, a worthy cause.
>
> And beyond that, is it the millennium that encourages notions of an apocalypse? Or simply that in a world without belief, we need a catastrophe to give us something to believe in.[138]

In response, the fabulously alarmist and well-funded James Hansen dismissed the notion, oddly citing himself as one of those who has suffered for "sticking [his] neck out." His evidence, without hint of irony and apparently in all seriousness, was that when he first pushed the panic button of man-made warming in 1981—the gravy train being one of "cooling" at the time, though as Hansen surely knew the atmosphere's temperatures had already by then reversed—his claim ran against the grain and, he implies, cost him his funding (from which he seems to have amply recovered).

The bias is so damning that BBC environment correspondent Richard Black set out to marginalize the charge. Black, like his employer, is aggressively skeptical of the skeptics and understandably invokes their inability to produce such written proof. His is a worthwhile tale, for it represents one of the few casting calls for examples of bias in the scientific institutions, including the journals. It is also instructive for the depths to which the alarmists and their defenders must go to deny the obvious.

Black boldly, or not so, "invited sceptics to put their cards on the table, and send me documentation or other firm evidence of bias."[139] Nearly a year later he followed this up with a piece announcing that no evidence of bias to his satisfaction had been provided. Rather, he specifically found "one first-hand claim of bias in scientific journals, not backed up by documentary evidence; and three second-hand claims, two well-known and one that the scientist in question does not consider evidence of anti-sceptic feeling. . . . If there is an anti-sceptic bias running through the institutions of science, it is evidently keeping itself well hidden."[140]

The truth is that Black doesn't seem to have looked beyond his inbox, which is somewhat revealing about the sincerity of his quest.

Tim Worstall, a popular (also UK-based) blogger on Black's beat—specifically the intersection of economics and environmental issues—noted after Black's initial call in December 2006[141] the fairly glaring experience of James Annan,[142] which on its face represents precisely what Black purported to be auditioning.

Annan submitted a paper to the *Journal of Geophysical Research Letters*, which is actually known to be far more accommodating to the work of skeptics than *Science* or *Nature*. The paper analyzed the central issue of climate sensitivity, "essentially, how much should average temperature change if atmospheric CO_2 doubles from pre-industrial levels. There has been any number of attempts to work this out for it is an extremely important number. Much of the work of the IPCC depends upon it, of course, as do things like the Stern Review and so on."[143]

Annan employed a new method, revising earlier estimates of sensitivity, which dramatically reduced the likely range and, it should be said, is far more consistent with observations than the IPCC's assumptions.[144] As noted in the discussion of Stephen Schwartz later in these pages, this is a very big deal. Though Annan's piece was peer reviewed, with two of the three reviewers recommending publication, the editor would not accept it for publication (a year later, as observations continued to confound the notion of a highly sensitive climate, *GRL* did publish Schwartz's work revealing a climate sensitivity of a fraction of the IPCC's claim). As critical as this and other failures to find placement may be for possible bias, they are also important because only upon publication can they even possibly be considered by, for example, the IPCC (though as covered, *inter alia*, in the discussion about IPCC conflicts, the best way to have one's work considered is to author the IPCC chapter).

Black, like others, circled the wagons to defend the alarmist franchise and only accept as contradictory evidence that with which no one could disagree. Unlike most alarmists, however, Black elected not to stoop to going *ad hominem, ad nauseum*, on Annan, but instead ignored the example altogether. He elected to limit his evidence to several examples e-mailed to him, each of which quite clearly failed to rise to the level of material bias (in his estimation), all instead having alternate explanations. He also explained away well-known examples related to him second-hand. These included refusals by *Nature* and *Science* to publish the McIntyre/McKitrick and Peiser critiques, respectively, of the Hockey Stick and the Oreskes "consensus" essay. That those critiques were well-known was marked down as a substantive demerit, which tactic is on a par with the rhetorical device of appealing to authority. They, too, were also explained away as not rising to anti-skeptic bias, or at least were understandable to Black, in hindsight.

Dismissing critics on the grounds that the alarmists have already heard of them, and those they haven't heard of on the grounds they haven't—a clever two-step of *Oh, that guy* and *Who are you, again?*—is another trick of the alarmist trade.[145] Black offered some potentially valid points (if applied to all comers, which he does not do) and, with rather greater frequency, some clever and not so clever stabs at "la[ying] to rest" what he admitted was "the most damaging accusation raised by the skeptical community."[146]

Individual scientists and the scientific establishment have created tremendous risk for themselves. They used claims of increasing certitude over catastrophism to make "climate" a multi-billion dollar enterprise wholly dependent upon policymakers not being made fools of. Yet that outcome would befall every party involved if the "consensus" claims wavered after more than a decade of claiming "proof" which only pathological nut jobs would insist on disputing.

Such varied anecdotes and exhibits are proof of nothing except a pattern of impediments to gaining publication of dissent, be it in the form of research papers or corrections to unsupportable alarmist claims. If a similar pattern exists among alarmists I have yet to hear of it, but await it with a mind as open as Richard Black's.

CHAPTER 4

Stifling Everyone's Speech

Even Their Own

AL GORE, THE MOST OUTSPOKEN PROPHET of climate doom, fears scrutiny of the details of his alarmism. He cancels interviews when his handlers cannot control the questioning in advance and bars the media from his talks, [1] preferring instead to bombard the public through imagery and repetition. He is by no means alone.

In July 2008, after I and a lead author for the United Nations' Intergovernmental Panel on Climate Change both traveled across the Atlantic for the express purpose of debating "global warming" policy, we sat down for a pre-debate joint interview with a Madrid journalist. Though an academic, the IPCC functionary poured forth with unsupportable statements, tortured her own stance with illogic, and was quickly embarrassed by our back and forth, which nonetheless remained cordial. Yet by the time I walked back into my hotel room, the phone was ringing, with news that she no longer was willing to debate me. Unless certain conditions were met, that is.

She would only speak *after* me. I was not permitted a rebuttal. She also insisted in advance that she would not respond to me, on the grounds that I do not hold a PhD. She would only respond to the audience which, I presume, all held PhDs. I reminded our hosts that they could tell her to pound sand and that I was happy to debate an empty chair, but would not adopt equal petulance and left it to them. During my presentation she pointedly crumpled lozenge wrappers, repeatedly dropped a metal coaster on the dais, sighed, engaged in conversations with a colleague in the audience, ran a pen across her notebook's spiral binder, and otherwise sought to distract the audience from my arguments in any way other than by addressing their substance.

It was not a good showing by their team, but several years of these people led me to conclude it was nonetheless a fairly typical one. One former advisor to Prime Minister Margaret Thatcher, Lord Viscount Monckton, has a wealth of similar experiences, adding how the head of Greenpeace for Europe adamantly insisted on speaking second during a debate at the Cambridge Union, and the deputy leader of the UK Liberal Democrat party simply opted to not appear at all at a major scheduled event.

Best, Monckton relates how a Greenpeace representative whom he debated on Al Jazeera television "begged the presenter not to talk about the science because, he said, I'd be able to cite learned papers going back to 1963. He didn't know I was listening in on the line."

Monckton describes these collective experiences as "a heartening admission that they know the game is up, scientifically speaking." But the alarmist industry goes much further, engaging in outright efforts to censor those who dare disagree with its tenets or agenda. This includes the impediments placed in the path of climate realists to speak, participate, and even to publish, and the implicit—and sometimes explicit—threat of retaliation experienced by academics and government employees, discussed elsewhere.

These efforts also rise to simple thuggery and occur in even the best of families. For example, 2006 saw possibly the lowest moment for the scientific establishment since their pursuit of Bruno, Copernicus, and Galileo. The august UK Royal Society—which is in fact Britain's oldest taxpayer-funded lobby group—demanded that dissent cease over their party line of catastrophic Man-made global warming, and for dissenting think tanks to be financially isolated by their supporters. While they were at it, they also sought funding details for various groups. The Royals also demanded that what constitutes "science" be redefined at least when the term applies to "catastrophic Man-made global warming."

Specifically, the Society sent a letter to ExxonMobil making certain demands regarding the company's actions in relation to the Society's official, if undemocratic and scientifically curious, position.[2] The BBC's former online science editor, Dr. David Whitehouse, wrote that the Society "demands EssoUK stop giving money to groups and organisations who do not believe that human activities are totally responsible for global warming. It also asks EssoUK to provide details of all the groups it funds so that the Royal Society can track them down and vet them, 'so that I can work out which of these have been similarly providing inaccurate and misleading information to the public.'"[3] He reminded us of Einstein's caution that "Unthinking respect for authority is the greatest enemy of truth."

Indeed. The Society also put out a "guide to facts and fictions about climate change." This lecture directed at the media slavishly bows in fealty to the United Nations' pronouncements of near-certitude about lurid future scenarios—which are risible, as described elsewhere in these pages—and disparages calls by thousands of scientists for sobriety as "extreme" and unworthy of consideration.[4] Oddly, the alarmists, shrieking that the UN's IPCC is insufficiently catastrophic, are spared the Society's opprobrium as extremists. Such tough talk is reserved for others who dare urge caution against those in positions of responsibility rushing panicked toward a severe agenda on such flimsy evidence.

These attempts to bully away debate reflected their view that dissent must be squashed—abandoning nearly four hundred fifty years of translating the Society's motto, *Nullius in Verba*," as "on the word of nobody." The Society actually, if quietly, dropped such old fashioned beliefs, choosing to "distanc[e] science from the scholasticism of the ancient universities, and stress[] that scientific knowledge is based on appeals to experimental evidence rather than to the word of authority figures."[5]

In lieu of such outmoded thinking, former Society president Robert (Lord) May, also an ex-chief scientific advisor to the UK government, announced that "the motto is now best translated as 'respect the facts'"—*their* "facts"—such that, "Like any political body, the Royal Society would prefer that policymakers and the public take the word of nobody but itself."[6]

As Stuart Blackman and Ben Pile of the UK group Climate Resistance put it:

> The custodians of the facts will jump on anyone they deem guilty of not respecting those facts. The Royal Society and its most prominent members have recently been taking it upon themselves to make statements—via open letters, the media, and public debate—about the moral character of those who dare to challenge the climate orthodoxy. And in doing so they often display a flagrant disregard for the facts themselves. . . . Other so-called 'deniers' are, the Royal Society tells us, the work of the Devil, or at least his modern, secular equivalent, ExxonMobil (Ward 4.9.2006; Royal Society 2005).

At the time of the effort to intimidate ExxonMobil and anyone else paying attention, the Royal Society's then-Senior Manager of Policy Communications Bob Ward avowed how, "It is now more crucial than ever that we have a debate [sic] which is properly informed by the science. For people to be still producing information that misleads people about climate change is unhelpful. The next IPCC report should give people the final push that they need to take action and we can't have people trying to undermine it."[7]

No, we can't have science being subject to skepticism or challenge; that would be too much in keeping with science's tradition.

The Society's president, Lord Rees, nonetheless had the temerity to baldly assert obeisance to the principle that "in science the time for debate is never over."[8] This only begins to reveal the tennis match that is his logic. While Rees emphasized that politics and science must remain distinct, he argued that policy must be based on the political concept of "scientific consensus," then further made plain that this consensus is provisional. That is a reasonable proposition in theory, though one, in this context, that has proved an embarrassing and discrediting spectacle in practice.

This is to say that, while claiming to draw a distinction between politics and science, Lord Rees called for them to be used in each other's service; *our position today on A is B, and as such please do C; subject to change tomorrow* ("royal" society, indeed). Rees did not say whether political expedience drives changes in science or science's desires drive the politics; he also failed to decree if there is to be a general rule or if this should be tackled *ad hoc*. This raises the hoary spectacle of past disasters from which the continent seems to have learned few lessons.

As *Financial Times* columnist John Kay put it, in one of his series of pleas for reason among a movement that seems to have supplanted Judeo-Christian beliefs as the dominant theology in Europe:

Consensus is a political concept, not a scientific one.... The processes of proper science could hardly be more different. The accomplished politician is a negotiator, a conciliator, finding agreement where none seemed to exist. The accomplished scientist is an original, an extremist, disrupting established patterns of thought. Good science involves perpetual, open debate, in which every objection is aired and dissents are sharpened and clarified, not smoothed over.... It is easy to see why the president of the Royal Society might want to elide that distinction, but in doing so he turns the organisation from a learned society into a trade union. Peer review is a valuable part of the apparatus of scholarship, but carries a danger of establishing self-referential clubs that promote each other's work.[9]

Lord May also publicly censured newspapers such as the *Daily Telegraph* and the *Daily Mail* for publishing the occasional skeptical article or commentary and, as reported by publisher of the CCNet update Dr. Benny Peiser, resorted to personal intimidation against respected writers such as the naturalist David Bellamy, columnist Melanie Phillips, and science writer Michael Hanlon.

That same year the Royal Society's then-vice president, Sir David Wallace, warned the British media not to publish anything that distorted the official view of climate science: "We are appealing to all parts of the UK media to be vigilant against attempts to present a distorted view of the scientific evidence about climate change and its potential effects on people and their environments around the world. I hope that we can count on your support."[10] Or else the *Royal We* would not be amused.

MORE ROYAL PAINS AND HIGH SOCIETIES

The Royal Society's efforts at censoring and bullying dissent were merely an escalation of its running campaign to intimidate scientists from speaking out over "warming." In 2005 the group drafted a statement intended to influence political events, specifically a G-8 meeting where the UK was insisting that "climate change" be a top priority for a gathering of the world's largest nations.[11]

This was a politicized tract insisting on policy actions, the prescription of which is of course slightly outside the realm of science.[12] This exercise lacked any assessment of relative risks, but instead proclaimed that agreement on global warming's reality is at hand, which therefore "demands prompt action." Naturally, this means an even more prominent role for the Society's membership.

The effort was so bad that the Russian Academy of Sciences publicly applied the smack-down, beginning with the group's membership chastising its president for participating in the misrepresentative stunt and flatly stating that he should not have signed on. Even the then-president of the U.S. National Academy of Sciences, Bruce Alberts, privately wrote the head of the Royal Society to condemn the use to which the joint effort was put, calling the their presentation of the statement "quite misleading."[13]

> "America's National Academies of Science, the UK's Royal Society and the acronymed jumble of United Nations agencies have increasingly abandoned traditional roles as science 'advisers' in favour of actively lobbying for their quantitative models and scenario extrapolations to be public policy planning tools. In effect, scientific institutions have evolved into 'special pleaders,' as vested in the rightness of their recommendations as any influence-seeking industrial trade group or bar association."
>
> *MIT researcher Michael Schrage in the* Financial Times

This is by no means the lone organization promoting an alarmist statement clearly implying agreement by and in the name of their memberships but upon which those members never were granted a vote. Science is not a democracy, but the intent of this practice to deceive is transparent.

The American Association of State Climatologists stands out among relevant professional associations for its sobriety and lack of apparent desire to exploit the global warming hysteria for professional or personal gain.[14] This might be why you don't hear its position touted. What makes the media's ignoring of this group most odd is that alarmists insist that only "climate scientists" or, often, "climatologists" may comment on the matter as opposed to, say, meteorologists. Yet they turn around and invoke as evidence of scientific consensus the aggressive lobbying and public affairs campaign of none other than the American Meteorological Society (AMS).

THE WEATHERMEN

The story of AMS deserves telling as an example of how "consensus" occurs in professional organizations. AMS describes itself as "a professional and scientific society that promotes the development and dissemination of information and education on the atmospheric and related oceanic and hydrologic sciences and the advancement of their professional applications."[15] It also has escalated its advocacy campaign, however, spurring open rebellion by its membership. More sober members who don't want their name attached to AMS's alarm have despaired to me that they have nowhere else to go, because AMS certification is considered *de facto* a requirement for on-air meteorological jobs.

In 2006 the AMS decided it was time to craft a scary global warming announcement. Its council quietly appointed an *ad hoc* drafting committee of ten authors with five alternates. Their names were not published, though AMS said in a response to a complaining AMS Fellow, "We do not consider the writing team a 'secret' per se; we are happy to provide the names of the folks working on this if someone asks as you have, but we view the resulting statement as a community effort."[16] Enjoy that one for a moment.

The (appointed) committee chair had final say on the product, under consultation with the AMS council, to which this drafting committee provided a position statement for review. They then posted that version[17] for comment on the AMS home web page they use for such postings[18] for thirty days.

The AMS simply posted its draft statement on the website, with no specific notice sent to the very membership whose names and reputations are implicitly associated with the statement. One council member tells me that though he was told, at a meeting, of a "record number" of comments received about this position, "most of them negative" and many of them strongly negative, he was not given access to them.

There is no publicly available AMS record of these deliberations, consistent with their website's general paucity of information on the organization outside of an organization chart and member contact information. Despite the volume of comments and what is described by an involved party as "an exhaustive internal effort to catalogue then respond to the comments, in the end little substantive change was made to the statement." The comments generally were rejected on the basis of oral assertions that "most papers disagree with this." AMS members, including those on the council, with whom I spoke were also unaware of any record of these workings.

There was in fact plenty to dispute about this supposed consensus statement. Roger Pielke Sr., the climate scientist and AMS fellow who is by no definition a "skeptic" (though he does reject alarmism), did his best to spread word of the effort.[19] He took to his Climate Science blog, popular among the community, to note AMS's request for comment within thirty days and publicly offered his displeasure. Backing up his charges with details, Pielke called their draft "scientifically incomplete and misleading," and particularly disputed three key statements having to do with attribution of climate change to humans and to carbon dioxide, generally.

On the latter he took AMS to task for apparently being behind on recent science. He also assailed the statement for apparently misunderstanding climate models, and noted that the sources the AMS claims to rely on actually differ in key respects. He objected at length to the AMS statement relating to the impact of land use, urbanization, and other localized factors. He called for more work to be put into it, decrying how a small group of like-minded people were behind this, leaving too short a period of time for people to argue points on something that was simply sprung on them. He insisted that more review was in order before the council put the AMS brand to such claims—that would of course be used politically and for policy purposes as representing more than it actually did.

Pielke said, "On professional statements by scientific societies, if they insist on this, they should be voted on by all of the members. I would vote to reject the current AMS Statement since it is seriously biased in its presentation."[20] AMS had no more interest in subjecting its stance to a vote of the people for whom it was presuming to speak than they did in reaching out to specifically notify them that they would be so speaking. Pielke Sr.'s well-respected voice was not alone, but it was in vain.

When the alarmist outcome became a *fait accompli*, Pielke wrote:

> The Report which was approved by the AMS Council represents the views of a few tens of the members of the Society...
>
> 1. This Statement does not represent the spectrum of views on climate change of the members of the American Meteorological Society.
> 2. There are members on the Committee who have a clear conflict of interest in preparing an objective Statement (see, e.g., *http://www.azstarnet.com/metro/158175*).
> 3. The Statement was not voted on by the members of the American Meteorological Society. Thus, as with all such statements, it will be embraced by those who agree with it and used for political advocacy, but dismissed as deficient by those whose views were excluded.[21]

The bottom line was that the AMS ultimately asserted a position drafted by "a few tens" of its members, which was objected to by its general membership vocally and in great numbers but loved by the global warming industry. This rises to the level of knowingly misrepresenting the views of much its membership for whom such statements implicitly speak, essentially on the grounds that these few know best.

The AMS even urges a form of "Climate Re-Education" to straighten out the thinking of misguided climate realists. The gang at Climate Skeptic noted a piece in the Bulletin of the American Meteorological Society titled "Climate Change Education and the Ecological Footprint." "The authors express concern that non-science students don't sufficiently understand global warming and its causes, and want to initiate a re-education program in schools to get people thinking the 'right' way." Instead of seeking to better educate kids on the details of the carbon cycle, distinguishing human impacts from natural variability, or improving climate modeling, the advocated curriculum "has very little to do with meteorology or climate science. What they are advocating is a social engineering course structured around the concept of 'ecological footprint.'"[22]

Part of this re-education might include disavowal of the 1970s "consensus" on global cooling, which BAMS also weighed in to rewrite as a "myth."[23]

AMS's new president is Tom Karl, the man who stood by Al Gore's side as the then-vice president held a regular series of public events declaring a climate emergency. Karl has no MD or PhD to his credit but has in recent years and without apparent protest from his colleagues begun styling himself as "Dr.," apparently coincident with being awarded an honorary Doctorate of Humane Letters from North Carolina State University (in 2002), though as early as 1997 has posted a *curriculum vitae* claiming to have earned an academic PhD—which the "Dr." typically connotes—from N.C. State in 1978.[24] N.C. State officials wrote me saying that "Thomas Richard Karl took some post-baccalaureate courses here at NC State. He was not in a degree program." I suspect that a

> "The National Academy of Sciences, the American Meteorological Society, the American Geophysical Union and the American Association for the Advancement of Science all agree that humans are forcing global temperatures upward."
>
> Willamette Week, *in a hit piece on Oregon State Climatologist George Taylor*

> "I am a member of the American Meteorological Society and a Certified Consulting Meteorologist. No one asked my opinion before crafting the Society's statement. I understand the same is true of the others. And again, the human influence is acknowledged by scientists everywhere; it's the DEGREE of influence that is being debated."
>
> *Taylor, in response*

climate realist would not find such tolerance among his peers for this claim to the Dr. credential.

Former Gore Senate staffer Anthony Socci leads the way for AMS on the climate policy issue, among other things, by chairing a series of one-sided congressional briefings or seminars. Recent briefings ran the spectrum—of alarmism, that is, not of opinion—ranging from *Arctic Sea Ice Melt and Shrinking Polar Ice Sheets: Are Observed Changes Exceeding Expectations?* (guess); *Hurricanes and Climate Change: What's Resolved and What Remains To Be Resolved?* (the open question being how horrifically are we enhancing the storms); and *Effective Communication: Persuasion and the Science of Social Influence to Multiple Lines of Evidence: The Scientific Case for Global Warming and its Causation.*[25] In short, AMS is as much as anything else an advocacy organization pushing the alarmist case for global warming.

When I visited its website in late October 2007 the upcoming event, *Impact of Global Warming on Precipitation Trends, and the Human Signature of Those Trends*, was teased with a Photoshopped image of London so inundated by flooding that only the tops of famous landmarks such as Parliament with Big Ben's tower were exposed. *See, if you keep refusing to take the bus and insist on those holidays, why, it'll rain so much that the Thames swallows London!*

As one AMS member told me, "I have never seen the society so aggressively pushing advocacy efforts. It will be their downfall."

A SILENCING ALARM

We will see how the alarmist industry fights to stifle dissent, subjecting critics to their nastiness and even "investigations," making the path to publication in the journals, for example, more difficult on top of the heavy pressure to go along so all can continue getting along on the gravy train. "Skeptic" websites such as ClimateAudit are subjects of regular "denial of service" attacks designed to silence their opinions and information. CO2Science.org received such attacks after they released notice of a movie questioning the climate "crisis."

In March 2008, as the Heartland Institute gained notoriety for its New York conference for climate realists, someone forged Heartland's e-mail domain name to send millions of SPAM messages to servers worldwide. This of course results in the target's server being hit with millions of rejections at once, overtaking its ability to function. In short, they silenced Heartland at the moment when the group was drawing attention to the "skeptics'" cause. Later, Heartland was hit with an "SQL injection attack," under which a hacker entered and modified the titles of documents—which, left unmolested, might be found by people seeking to learn the other side of this issue—such that Heartland lost about a month's worth of work. Before that, anyone seeking to browse Heartland's site or several key documents was redirected to a vile home page that, shall we say, addressed a different lurid fetish than climate alarmism.

Now we see Gore advisor James Hansen—who perpetrates the remarkable feat of being both a media darling for his outlying tales of catastrophe, while also claiming to have been "muzzled"—seek a promise from politicians that the deeply vested "big science" bureaucracy be removed from democratic accountability, freeing them to unleash even greater alarm than Hansen has already wrought.[26] He has proven an ability to say whatever alarmist thing he wishes so long as he sticks to his discipline, unlike fellow employees of the federal government holding different views.

For example, one scientist at the Department of Energy signed a letter addressed to the UN, along with 100 others, advising the "adaptation" approach to climate change. This letter was posted on a "skeptic" group's website. Within minutes a colleague had complained to management, and the scientist received a phone call insisting that he have his DoE affiliation removed. His superior frantically inquired, "Are you aware—people have been FIRED for things like that????"

Then there was the time Hansen tried to get climate realist Dr. John Christy booted from a Senate panel, conditioning his own appearance on Christy's removal?[27] Were there consequences then, when he refused a call to assist congressional oversight on the grounds that he claimed a doctor's appointment which, he noted, he would move if Christy were bumped?

There are no repercussions for such irresponsible behavior because Hansen proves his worth as a public servant with his alarmism and name-calling (though Charles I and Bertholt Brecht certainly would both appreciate a government employee with a set policy agenda, who finds that agenda thwarted by the popular assembly, setting out to get rid of the problem).

There's also Hungarian physicist Ferenc Miskolci, who resigned his affiliation with NASA claiming that the agency refused to allow him to publish his work countering the alarmist position.[28] He had been a researcher with NASA's Ames Research Center and, after resigning, published his research supporting Brookhaven National Labs scientist Stephen Schwartz's assessment of a far-less sensitive climate, in a peer-reviewed journal in his homeland.[29]

So they want to stifle the speech of those who disagree and have special rules applicable only to themselves. Not surprisingly, we see they also have a history of suppressing their own words.

THE USE OF A PHONY, CRONY "CONSENSUS"

This claim of "consensus" as a tool to stifle debate is unique to the issue of global warming, of course, and its use is quickly moving from deceptive to hysterical. Author Peter Foster put it well: "Invoking the authority of science and the democratic value of 'consensus' are again both designed to cut off rational analysis. This leads to the strange phenomenon of the discussion of policy alternatives becoming delinked from likely results."[30]

Indeed the very notion of peddling the issue as *concluded* due to science-wide agreement is a bit odd, argues climate expert Richard Lindzen, because "global warming consists in so many aspects, that widespread agreement on all of them would be suspect, *ab initio*."[31]

Regardless, this battle cry of *consensus* leaves us facing Gore's proposed "solutions" which would cost the world on the order of $34 trillion to bring a projected cost of climate change—something that Yale's William Nordhaus estimates in a "do nothing" scenario might cost $22 trillion—down to $12 trillion. In short, at a cost of $46 trillion Gore would leave us twice as bad off as the nightmare scenario the alarmists say awaits us. But on the bright side, they would finally get their lifestyle and Statism agenda in place.

We are told that the supposed consensus of today is real, contrary to those embarrassing stories from the 1970s popular press and even a cover story in *Science Digest* all assuring us how "the world's scientists are now agreed" on a catastrophic Man-made cooling which represented a phony, media-created consensus,[32] despite there being far broader and more vehement dissent among scientists today than there ever was about the cooling panic.

Far from being an indication of strength, this insistence on claiming "consensus" is a glaring admission of weakness, an effort to "move on" from scientific inquiry. *Financial Times* columnist John Kay explained the oddity of "consensus" in science: "We do not say that there is a consensus over the second law of thermodynamics, a consensus that Paris is south of London or that two and two are four. We say that these are the way things are."[33] Professor Robert Carter makes the same point: "We do not usually say that there is a 'consensus that the sun will rise tomorrow.' Instead, the confident statement that 'the sun will rise tomorrow' rests upon repeated empirical testing and the understanding conferred by Copernican and Newtonian theory."[34]

This rallying cry to shout down discussion arises from a phony analysis in an "essay" titled "Beyond the Ivory Tower: The Scientific Consensus on Climate Change," by history professor Naomi Oreskes published in *Science* Magazine.[35] Yet the tenacious insistence on "consensus" not only will not go away, or even find its way to be correctly stated, but continues to grow in its mythology with help from leading alarmists who seem to see it simply as a platform from which to spring spectacular fibs about a calamitous future. In fact, although the claim simply denotes a general agreement,[36] alarmists even interchange it with *unanimity*.

Hyper-alarmist Robert F. Kennedy Jr. is so desperate that discourse cease that he has manufactured a spectacular "consensus" lie. On ABC's *Good Morning America* he stated:

The National Academy of Sciences did a study an inventory, three years ago, of all of the scientific documents that had—the peer-reviewed, refereed scientific documents that had been published in the previous decade, over 10,000 documents, 10,000 scientific studies. All of them agreed on the basics: that global warming exists; that human beings are causing it; that it's upon us now; and that its impacts are going to be catastrophic. In the scientific community, there was literally zero dissent.[37]

This is untrue from top-to-bottom, as Kennedy is either remarkably confused or intentionally conflates and inflates. With this statement he apparently equates activist Naomi Oreskes' disproved and retracted claim with the National Academies of Science. Then he wildly inflates the number of papers that Oreskes claimed to have reviewed (about 900). In short, he just made this up in service of shouting down dissent that might draw attention.

By the way, note how "the basics" include that global warming, *caused* by Man, *will* be *catastrophic*. Precisely what would the deluxe package include?

Professor Dennis Bray of Germany and Hans von Storch polled climate scientists to rate the statement, "To what extent do you agree or disagree that climate change is mostly the result of anthropogenic causes?" on a scale of one to seven, seven indicating strong disagreement. They received responses from 530 climate scientists in 27 countries, of whom 44 percent were either neutral or disagreed with the statement (29 percent said that warming is *not* mostly the result of anthropogenic causes). "These results, i.e. the mean of 3.62, seem to suggest that consensus is not all that strong and only 9.4% of the respondents strongly agree that climate change is mostly the result of anthropogenic causes." (*Science* Magazine helpfully refused to publish the findings, by the way).[38] Other surveys reach similar conclusions.[39]

Further, it is worth noting—since the media found it completely unhelpful for their purposes to publicize it—that an October 2007 survey of the U.S. scientists listed as IPCC contributing authors and reviewers affirmed that "the notion of a meaningful scientific consensus on global warming is ludicrous."[40] According to JunkScience's Steven Milloy, who headed the group doing the research, "The survey results indicate that when asked routine questions about the climatic role of manmade CO_2, the IPCC scientists responded for the most part with the Pavlovian manmade-CO_2-is-bad view seemingly demanded of them by the IPCC. But when you ask questions that are off the IPCC script, the supposed consensus seems to readily fall apart."[41]

It seems that when pushed off of the talking-point script, IPCC-affiliated scientists reveal that those areas that we are led to believe are matters of scientific agreement have little support—for example that we are experiencing unprecedented warmth (44 percent disagree), that a cooler climate than today would be better (14 percent agree, while over 60 percent acknowledge there's no such thing as an ideal climate), that Man is the principal driver of climate change (only 20 percent accept that quasi-religious assertion).

IF SILENCE IS CONSENT, THEN SILENCE THE DISSENTERS

The alarmists even go so far as to insert themselves in the process when researchers seek to publish data that would reflect poorly on the alarmism but otherwise has nothing to do with them. Their fight over the claim of consensus seems as if they are protecting the queen bee, fully aware that once it falls their entire colony goes with it. So when Dr. Klaus-Martin Schulte, a surgeon and researcher at King's College Hospital in London affirmed as absurd the notion of scientific agreement on global warming, its causes, and impacts, the alarmists had to make sure he couldn't get published.

Schulte assessed what the *current* literature was saying on the matter by reviewing 528 papers *addressing* climate change (not just obscurely referencing the phrase, as with Oreskes) published from 2004 to February 2007. This covered the period since May 2005 when the IPCC closed the Fourth Assessment Report's window for research eligible for complete and open consideration by authors and reviewers alike.[42]

Schulte found that "a mere 38, or 7%, explicitly support the consensus. *Daily Tech*, an online magazine, says the ratio goes to 45% 'if one considers "implicit" endorsement (accepting the consensus without explicit statement).' While only 32, or 6%, of the papers reject the consensus outright, *Daily Tech* blogger Michael Asher reports that the 'largest category (48%) are neutral papers, refusing to either accept or reject the hypothesis.'"[43] Hardly *consensus*.

Asher wrote that "the figures are even more shocking when one remembers the watered-down definition of consensus here. Not only does it not require supporting that man is the 'primary' cause of warming, but it doesn't require any belief or support for 'catastrophic' global warming. In fact, of all papers published in this period (2004 to February 2007), *only a single one makes any reference to climate change leading to catastrophic results*"[44] (emphasis in original).

No such results can be allowed to stand without assault from the alarmists and their apologists. They therefore came after Schulte's findings, but not on the substance, which for them would be asking far too great a change of habit. Besides, his findings are fairly straightforward: *what articles say what and how many*? Instead, they argued *against it being published*, and received word from the editor of the journal to which it had been submitted, *Energy and Environment*, that it was "nothing new" and "not of interest" to her.[45]

Note what this represents: research is offered for publication affirming that Oreskes's "consensus" claim was wrong. Alarmists get wind of this and insert themselves into the publication process to argue against it, not on its substance but rather on the grounds that it is too similar to an earlier exposé of Oreskes, (which had errors of its own which were subsequently acknowledged).

That remarkable pretzel of illogic notwithstanding, the piece was not published, on those grounds that it was nothing new. Which is on its face true. That Oreskes' claim was false is well established—after all, she had to correct it in the same pages in which it was published. Schulte's analysis was actually only "new" in that it confirmed that Oreskes's argument *remained* wrong over time, what with her survey purporting to cover from 1993 to 2003, and Schulte's from 2004 to early 2007.

A similar episode occurred in mid-2008 when the American Physical Society newsletter *Physics and Society* dared post a paper by former Thatcher advisor Monckton, calling the alarmist hypothesis into question by examining the key calculation underlying climate models: climate sensitivity.[46] As its editor Jeffrey Marques wrote in explanation, "There is a considerable presence within the scientific community of people who do not agree with the IPCC conclusion that anthropogenic CO_2 emissions are very probably likely to be primarily responsible for the global warming that has occurred since the Industrial Revolution. Since the correctness or fallacy of that conclusion has immense implications for public policy and for the future of the biosphere, we thought it appropriate to present a debate within the pages of P&S concerning that conclusion."

That sort of productive scientific discourse could not be tolerated. According to *The Register* (UK), "within a few days, Monckton's piece carried a health warning: in bright red ink: 'The following article has not undergone any scientific peer review. Its conclusions are in disagreement with the overwhelming opinion of the world scientific community. The Council of the American Physical Society disagrees with this article's conclusions.'"

APS's claims that Monckton's paper was not peer reviewed and that its own disclaimer followed a peer review of Monckton appear to be false.[47] In fact, it seems that APS posted its disclaimer as a result of just one day of pressure from an email campaign.[48] All of which provided a fascinating science experiment on its own.

The spoken word is also intolerable if those words aren't of the proper kind. In the spring of 2006, when it was announced that I would be speaking at "Spain's Harvard," Universidad Carlos III de Madrid, the Marxist student association protested my appearance and, to try and minimize attendance, worked with the administration to organize a counter-event. Those who attended were actually rather civil, if apparently hoping to intimidate me with their presence and glaring.

Should censorship fail, at least speakers can be shouted down. A typical example of how actual efforts to speak are treated was on display in Hartford, Connecticut, when meteorologist Art Horn was scheduled to speak at the city's public library. The word went out for an organized protest, apparently to demonstrate against his ability to speak.[49] He describes the protesters' response as quite predictable, *where do you get your money, you can't possibly be sufficiently credentialed* (the same question obviously also demanded of Drs. Gore, DiCaprio, and Morrissette), and a lot of interrupting from the floor while he was speaking. "There was considerable tension and outright anger in the back of the room. It was as if I was attacking their religion." He was.

Noted physicist Freeman Dyson has felt the fury of the global warming alarmist industry for failing to throw his considerable academic weight behind it. He asserts that environmentalism has replaced socialism as the leading secular religion. "Unfortunately, some members of the environmental movement have also adopted as an article of faith the belief that global warming is the greatest threat to the ecology of our planet. That is one reason why the arguments about global warming have become bitter and passionate. Much of the public has [therefore] come to believe that anyone who is skeptical about the dangers of global warming is an enemy of the environment."[50]

DON'T QUOTE ME

When two experts published a list of over 450 scientists who had "documented doubts of Man-made global warming scares" through peer-reviewed papers that run counter to the alarmist mantra, the response was typical. The list, put out in 2007 by the co-authors of *Unstoppable Global Warming: Every 1,500 Years*—the physicist Dr. Fred Singer and Dennis Avery, PhD, an agricultural economist—included the hundreds of qualified researchers, their home institutions, and the peer-reviewed studies they had published in professional journals providing historic or physical proxy evidence that:

1) Most of the 20th century warming was caused by a long, moderate, natural cycle rather than by the burning of fossil fuels;

2) The sun's varying radiance impacts the earth's climate as more or fewer cosmic rays create more of fewer of the low, wet clouds that act as the earth's thermostats, deflecting more or less solar heat out into space.

3) Sea levels are not rising rapidly nor are they likely to;

4) Wild species are not being driven to extinction but rather are increasing wildland biodiversity;

5) Fewer rather than more humans death are likely in a warmer world, since cold is far more dangerous and the earth is always warming or cooling;

6) Food production is likely to thrive as well, rather than collapsing due to climate overheating; and/or

7) Storms are likely to be fewer and milder as the declining temperature differential between the equator and the poles reduces their power. [51]

Most alarming of all to the warming industry was that some of the work cited was by their very own noted alarmists, including lead bloggers on "RealClimate." One of them on the list demanded that the Hudson Institute remove the compendium from its web site, threatening litigation and chanting his belief that global warming is Man-made and a disaster. That's all well and good, but Hudson merely posted his name and paper with a brief statement of its con-clusions. In Avery's news release announcing the list he specifically says that not everyone on the list is a "skeptic," but that their writ-ing in peer-reviewed journals supports an alternative view of cli-mate change to Man-made catastrophe.

The alarmist's challenge wasn't to that description or replication of the piece's abstract. It was to being *associated with the implica-tions* of the writings, that the catastrophist case is not in fact some-thing uniformly supported among the literature (it isn't even remotely supported by any balance of the peer-reviewed work, of course). Remember why this is important. With the agenda's price tag, no element of doubt is permissible. So, it appears, even alarmist scientists either talk a different talk when subject to peer review or they had recently changed their minds.

A similar example came in August 2007 when spokesman Marc Morano of the Senate Committee on Environment and Pub-lic Works staff (Minority) released a 4,000-word paper titled "New Peer-Reviewed Scientific Studies Chill Global Warming Fears."[52] FOX News Channel picked up on the document, prompting the alarmists to take out after it with the assistance of the left-wing activist group "Media Matters."[53] Apparently, cer-tain authors cited in the report were upset about being associated with the heading, "Sampling of very recent inconvenient scientific developments for proponents of catastrophic man-made global warming."

Their article in question was a new peer-reviewed study on surface warming and the solar cycle in the *Journal of Geophysi-cal Research Letters*, and was accompanied by a write-up of the study taken from *New Scientist* online, written by a fairly alarmist writer for that publication. This reviewer had recently penned, for example, the global-warming inspired "Is the U.S. headed for an environmental 9/11?"[54] He summarized the GRL work:

The study found that times of high solar activity are on average 0.2 degrees C warmer than times of low solar activity, and that there is a polar amplification of the warming. This result is the first to document a statistically significant globally coherent temperature response to the solar cycle, the authors note. Authors: Charles D. Camp and Ka Kit Tung: Department of Applied Mathematics, University of Washington, Seattle, Washington, U.S.A. Source: Geophysical Research Letters (GRL) paper 10.1029/2007GL030207, 2007.[55]

There we have it, in an alarmist's own words: temperature responds to the sun. Naturally one of the authors responded to the attention by claiming that the study actually proves *Man-made warming*. This possibly manifests what I will call the Wunsch effect, whereby scientists quoted accurately or whose work is cited accurately feel the heat from the alarmism industry and claim they were misunderstood (more on Wunsch below). While no one but Dr. Wunsch can be certain that this accurately describes his own experience after appearing in *The Great Global Warming Swindle*—and it is not likely that he or anyone else subjected to that process would acknowledge it if so—it does seem to be a fair assessment of what happened, there as here.

I say here, too, because the paper at issue is in fact a key tool for debunking climate alarmism. Its analysis specifically illustrates how low levels of solar activity tend to yield a lower global temperature than does high solar activity over the eleven-year solar cycle, and that these effects hold for fifty years or so of the full record available. In fact, as Morano's report accurately reflected, the paper also said that with the solar activity, one can also expect polar amplification—warming or cooling will be greater at the poles than in the middle. This means that the observed polar amplification of the slight warming can by no means be simply chalked up to greenhouse gases as the alarmists would have us believe. The authors could not stand the conclusions being cited, even if simply on their face and accurately, by "skeptics."

It happened yet again when a Competitive Enterprise Institute advertisement accurately cited research affirming the truism of ice mass buildup in Greenland, in addition to ice loss on the coast (with recent data confirming the ice is at the same level as in the 1920s to the 1940s). Their point was simply that there is more to the "climate" story than the public generally hears, which is exactly what the very title of the paper claimed.[56] As is typical, the author disingenuously labored to claim that the group was being disingenuous by citing his research.

Yet again, none of the voices expressing outrage about work being accurately cited were heard assailing Al Gore for distorting scientific research to claim it stood for the precise opposite of what it showed.

DON'T QUOTE ME, II

The phenomenon extends beyond citing published works. For example, MIT's Dr. Carl Wunsch agreed to be interviewed for a movie by filmmaker Martin Durkin, which ultimately was titled *The Great Global Warming Swindle*.[57]

The film emphasized research that largely fingers the sun as the principal driver of historical changes in the Earth's temperature (a very dangerous proposition to the global warming industry). Like Gore's movie, the film is convincing and compelling but it makes (far fewer, far less damning) mistakes; also like *An Inconvenient Truth* (*AIT*) a few of its moments are open to valid criticism in addition to quibbles about what can be argued with such confidence or, in some instances, even credibly. Without placing too much weight on the project—again, in contrast to *AIT*'s cheerleaders who cite that polemic by a politician as deliverance of climate truths—it is worth noting that, in this specific context, it is hardly dirty pool that Durkin made mistakes or even put things in the light most favorable to one's thesis. *AIT* established the tone and standard for what's acceptable when arguing these issues publicly. Viewed this way *TGGWS* safely clears the (fairly low) bar set by Gore.

Credible argument is no longer the relevant standard, at least in the climate debate. Instead, there is "consensus" that must be obeyed—unless of course you have a more dire prediction, which then becomes the storyline; witness *AIT's* claims to sea-level rise, hurricanes, you name it. What is uniformly lost in most attacks, however, is that one ought to prefer mistakes over outright fabrications such as Gore's, to the defense of which the usual alarmist cheerleaders ran.

For example, *Swindle* overstepped what one might be able to state with assurance in a courtroom about, say, what ice cores reveal about temperature reconstructions. This was one of Durkin's attackers' principal complaints.[58]

Durkin was subjected to withering attacks because his overall message was the wrong one. The former president of the UK Royal Society falsely told the crowd at an environmental festival that Durkin had been behind films denying that HIV is linked to AIDS.[59] Durkin and his film were also subjected to a spate of 265 complaints about the film to the UK Office of Communications (OfCom), which regulates the airwaves. This is not unusual in Euroland, where the greens and their speech code are several years ahead of their partners in the U.S.

The *Swindle* complaints mostly alleged misrepresentations or a failure of due impartiality (seriously). OfCom tossed all of the misrepresentation claims, that is, it concluded that Durkin did not materially mislead viewers as alleged and widely reported (the BBC became particularly exorcised). Further, none of the complaints alleging partiality was upheld. OfCom said instead that Durkin should have provided those whom he interviewed a few more days to respond to a draft of the film.[60] (Certainly Al Gore extended that courtesy to Phil Cooney, whom he slandered in *AIT*?) In sum, "bruised egos, but no offence."[61]

Affirming the alarmists' desire to simply stifle dissent, *Guardian* columnist George Monbiot responded to the ruling in outrage, as well as apparent ignorance of OfCom's assessment. "By broadcasting programmes that appear to manipulate and even fabricate evidence, Channel 4 has impeded efforts to forestall the 21st century's greatest threat. For how much longer will this be allowed to continue?"[62]

One of the complainants was Dr. Wunsch, upset about his portrayal. In *Swindle*, Wunsch is filmed in his office explaining, *inter alia*, how the oceans are connected to temperature changes and atmospheric gas concentrations. His explanation is a very inconvenient one, that when oceans warm up, they release CO_2 and when they cool they absorb it. This goes a long way toward the devastating reality (for Gore) that, historically, temperature increases precede atmospheric CO_2 buildup, not the other way around as is required for their Man-as-agent-of-doom thesis.

Wunsch's useful insight included, "The models are so complicated you can often adjust them in such a way that they do something very exciting" and:

Even within the scientific community you see it's a problem. If I run a complicated model and I do something to it, like melt a lot of ice into the ocean and nothing happens, it's not likely to get printed. But if I run the same model, and I adjust it in such a way that something dramatic happens to the ocean circulation like the heat transport turns off, it will be published, people will say this is very exciting, it will even get picked up by the media. So there is a bias, there's a very powerful bias within the media and within the science community itself toward results which are dramatizable....

The earth freezes over. That's a much more interesting story than saying well you know it fluctuates around, sometimes the mass flux goes up by 10 percent sometimes it down by 20 percent but eventually it comes back. Well, you know, which would you do a story on? I mean, that's what it's about.

Wunsch's admission of the bias and explanation of how modelers, among others, are incentivized to "tweak" their parameters to produce headlines (and, implicitly, funding) were damning and, upon reflection, he apparently regretted them.

When the movie became somewhat of a sensation upon its release—and by this time bearing a title causing the alarmist industry and other elites no small amount of discomfort—Wunsch first rushed out a "Partial Response to the London Channel 4 Film *The Great Global Warming Swindle*."[63] The *Guardian* reported his arguments that "his comments in the film were taken out of context and that he would not have agreed to take part if he had known it would argue that man-made global warming was not a serious threat. 'I thought they were trying to educate the public about the complexities of climate change,' he said."[64] The film clearly did this, but in polemic style.

Climate scientist Fred Singer noted that Wunsch's beefs were "without cause: What he said on the program was scientifically correct. His statements were not altered or edited in any way. And they agreed with the skeptical views he has always expressed. So what was his complaint about? He didn't like the general tenor of the program—which was politically incorrect—certainly in Cambridge, Mass. I am disappointed in Carl. He is much too good a scientist to be concerned about public opinion at MIT."[65]

Wunsch had actually not been taken out of context at all. He does however seem to present a model of scientists possessed of an almost-understandable fear of being associated with the hated skeptics.

In what might have been the most revealing aspect of the *Swindle* kerfuffle, the *Independent* (UK) conducted an "investigation" into Durkin's use of the many graphs in his movie, shrieking that "[a] Channel 4 documentary that claimed global warming is a swindle was itself flawed with major errors which seriously undermine the programme's credibility, according to an investigation by the *Independent*. *The Great Global Warming Swindle* was based on graphs that were distorted, mislabelled [sic] or just plain wrong."[66] There is more than a touch of hyperbole in this

> ### TROLLING FOR GRANTS
>
> "If you want to be an eminent scientist, you have to have a lot of grad students and a lot of grants. You can't get grants unless you say, 'Oh, global warming, yes, yes, carbon dioxide.'"
>
> *Reid Bryson, the "father of scientific climatology"*

account by the activist *Independent*. But, okay, that's a reasonable standard: the media must expose mislabeled, distorted, or just-plain-wrong graphs. *Sometimes.*

Oddly, no such journalistic ventures tracked Al Gore's movie, which notoriously ran two graphs across the stage/screen, which combination of data are indispensable to his thesis that CO_2 and, now, Man drives climate. One graph represents temperature for the past 650,000 years recreated from proxy data, and the other shows atmospheric carbon dioxide concentrations, also recreated from proxy (ice core) data, which he wisely elects to not superimpose on the first; instead, he cheekily runs one physically above the other on the stage-wide screen before which he struts.

In the film, Gore smirks, "Now one thing that kinda jumps out at you is, do you they ever fit together? Most ridiculous thing I've ever heard." Then he flatly states, "The relationship is actually very complicated. But there is one relationship that is far more powerful than all the others. And it is this. When there is more carbon dioxide, the temperature gets warmer."[67]

Though the obvious implication is false, the statement itself might be generously read in one way so as to be considered literally true, just as with the claim that "the more people put on bathing suits and go to the beach, the temperature gets warmer." There is a correlation, to be sure. As regards Gore's stretcher, it is fair to say that compared to cooler periods, warmer periods often (but not always[68]) had higher atmospheric CO_2 levels. But if you, unlike Gore's audience, have independent sources of information, this claim is transparently misleading: according to that data *it warms first* and the increased concentrations of CO_2, released from the oceans as they warm, comes second.

Temperature cools first, too, then CO_2 levels drop, reabsorbed by the cooler oceans. The cause and effect that Al Gore works so hard to imply is actually the precise opposite of what the very data he cites suggests, as plainly noted when it was published in *Science* magazine. Finally, Gore's own advisor, to whom he attributes another chart in the movie, admits—when pushed—that this actually isn't his work at all.[69]

So, in a movie that makes news, draws audiences, wins awards, leads to a Nobel Peace Prize, and is made *mandatory viewing* in all secondary schools in England, Al Gore knowingly (it is reasonable to presume from these factors) misleads students on the key premise of his theory, which error was well known by the time the government determined that all pupils must see it. No newspaper finds that worth even reporting, let alone pursuing an "investigation" as done against a one-off documentary aired on television. Apparently, trying to scare kids into supporting government policies deserved no scrutiny; it is another matter entirely when someone else is exposing the fodder as unsupportable. Further, despite the efforts to make every school kid see Gore's film, Member of the European Parliament from Sweden Anders Wijkman sought to bar *Swindle* from being shown as *not the kind of speech that ought to be tolerated in that building.*

Durkin, by the way, withheld release of the DVD of his film until an error was corrected; Gore never altered his glaring non-truths.

With the scientific establishment baselessly harrumphing that Gore pretty much got things right even though detailed deconstructions of Gore's whoppers exist, including by Gore supporters no less,[70] it is quite clear that science is willing to pimp itself out for the cause.

MORE SAUSAGE-MAKING

We've seen several examples of alarmist revision of the historical record. The most obscene examples come with those whom the alarmists had failed keep to quiet but, having died, can no longer fight back. High-profile examples of alarmists revising a deceased's views or attributing a deathbed conversion to alarmism include Gore's Harvard professor Roger Revelle[71] and, more recently, pioneering scientist and founder of NASA's Goddard Institute for Space Studies (now headed by Gore-pal Hansen) Robert Jastrow,[72] and "father of climatology" Reid Bryson,[73] all of whose positions were perverted by alarmists once they could no longer object, frequently before the body was even cold.

MIT's Lindzen also notes the even more obscene example of prominent skeptic William Nierenberg, a past director of the Scripps Oceanographic Institute, in whose honor the Nierenberg Prize was created. Now annually awarded to an environmental activist, "[t]he most recent recipient was James Hansen who Nierenberg detested."[74]

We have also seen how alarmist scientists fancy themselves policymakers, which must explain how they mimic the lawmaker's practice of reaching back into the record of events to "revise and extend" their remarks. As that window into the sausage factory, C-SPAN, describes the practice, "Asking to Revise and Extend allows a member to add to or edit his/her floor remarks in the *Congressional Record* . . . [the practice means] Making changes to the words actually spoken on the floor."[75] It was only a matter of time before the alarmists appropriated this tactic for themselves.

Then–global cooling, now–global warming alarmist Stephen Schneider provided the following gem in an interview with *Discover* magazine: "We have to offer up scary scenarios, make simplified, dramatic statements, and make little mention of any doubts we might have.... Each of us has to decide what the right balance is between being effective and being honest."

Although Schneider claims to be perfectly happy to have others quote him on his past utterances, we will see that his actions reveal a belief that the record must instead be expunged.

For background, as noted Australian "climate skeptic" John Daly wrote, "During the Ice Age Scare of the 1970s, Schneider was one of its foremost advocates," having published among other things a book titled *The Genesis Strategy* warning of the coming glaciation, a phenomenon he posited in articles as deriving from the burning of fossil fuels.[76] He offered encomium on the cover of Lowell Ponte's *The Cooling*, a book claiming that the 1940s–1970s cooling telegraphed the coming Ice Age.[77]

He wrote a 1971 paper titled "Atmospheric Carbon Dioxide and Aerosols—Effects of Large Increases on Global Climate," attributing cooling to aerosol discharge.[78]

In short, Schneider has a long association with the previous cooling panic.

Remember that.

Schneider objects when people invoke his balance-honesty-with-effectiveness quote, claiming he is being taken out of context. So, here is the context:

> On the one hand, as scientists we are ethically bound to the scientific method, in effect promising to tell the truth, the whole truth, and nothing but—which means that we must include all the doubts, the caveats, the ifs, ands, and buts. On the other hand, we are not just scientists but human beings as well. And

like most people we'd like to see the world a better place, which
in this context translates into our working to reduce the risk of
potentially disastrous climatic change. To do that we need to get
some broadbased support, to capture the public's imagination.
That, of course, entails getting loads of media coverage. So we
have to offer up scary scenarios, make simplified, dramatic
statements, and make little mention of any doubts we might
have. This 'double ethical bind' we frequently find ourselves in
cannot be solved by any formula. Each of us has to decide what
the right balance is between being effective and being honest. I
hope that means being both.[79]

In context, Schneider's meaning remains seemingly clear and
unchanged—there is an ethical downside to expressing doubts,
about catastrophic Man-made warming or, phrased alternately,
there is an ethical imperative to make simplified dramatic statements and tell scary stories even if one doesn't fully believe them.
This ethos is apparently affirmed by the great lengths to which he
now goes to ensure that his most troublesome past statements are
not invoked, even with the context provided.

It's a common theme: an alarmist is reminded of a past statement, and so he claims that rascally skeptics are taking alarmists
out of context. For example, when asked about having likened
Bjørn Lomborg to Hitler, IPCC head Rajendra Pachauri said, "I
was misquoted. That was taken out of context."[80] Not to quibble
but, which is it? And, if the latter, in what context is that not still
hysterical, buffoonish, and inflammatory? Never mind, move on,
no need to mention it again, etc.

Yet it is also not uncommon for the alarmist industry to advocate a rather liberal use of language. As we see elsewhere, the
BBC's Roger Harrabin circulated an internal memo offering ways
to distort the UK High Court having thoroughly debunked all of
the money claims in Gore's movie *An Inconvenient Truth*, a ruling
also discussed elsewhere in these pages. Consider the UK's Institute

for Public Policy Research's relatively candid 2006 report, "Warm Words: How are we telling the story of climate change and can we tell it better?" In this Orwellian appeal we learn that "the task of climate change agencies is not to persuade by rational argument but in effect to develop and nurture a new 'common sense'... to work in a more shrewd and contemporary way, using subtle techniques of engagement.... The 'facts' need to be treated as being so taken-for-granted that they need not be spoken."[81] "Facts" in quotation marks is a good tip-off about such people.

For example, *EOS*, the official journal of the American Geophysical Union, in 2008 published a piece by someone from a group called "Climate Communication." Her counsel included a Schneider-like plea to scale back a bit on the caveats, and that bothering with uncertainties amounts to no more than offering "weasel words." For example, "Saying human activity 'contributes' to global warming makes it sound like human activity might be only a minor contributor. It would be more accurate to say 'most of the warming...."[82] Further, "Avoid using the word 'debate' in connection with climate change. It reinforces the mistaken notion that there is a debate about basic issues that are settled science. When referring to the whole issue, try something like 'the urgent challenge of human-induced climate disruption' rather than 'climate debate.'"[83] It was only fitting that this piece ran above another article focusing on what this is really all about: ever widening the spigot of taxpayer dollars. (Even more appropriate is that the U.S. Climate Change Science Project brought this woman—who previously wrote Laurie David's alarmist HBO special "Too Hot Not to Handle"—on board as "senior editor and team coordinator" to help sell an election-year climate change screed.[84])

Schneider not only remains true to the alarmists' penchant for stifling troublesome speech and rewriting the past, but now insists even that all discussion of his now-infamous admission about honesty-vs.-effectiveness be suppressed. Specifically, Schneider sought removal of reference to his claim from a chapter for *From Climate to Chromosomes* submitted by Delaware State Climatologist Dr. David Legates, a book in which Schneider also had a chapter.[85] This episode offers a very troubling example of how alarmists will demand and bully their way even to censor *their own* words.

Schneider approached the book's editor, asking to review the submission of other authors contributing to the work, apparently to see if any dared mention him. Legates had in fact offered the famous quote, for the proposition that Schneider believes that the climate issue puts scientists in a double ethical bind, in that extreme or exaggerated claims or scenarios are superior tools to gain the attention of and action by policymakers and the media. Legates then noted that Schneider historically protests use of this comment as being taken out of context, as it is often used without including his "hope that means being both." So Legates included the comment in its context.

The editor admitted to having "mixed feelings about passing along chapters at this late stage, since our book is about controversies and dialog, [but] we sent the chapters to Schneider." Schneider claimed that by using his own words, even in context, Legates misrepresented him. He insisted that the passage be struck or he be permitted a rebuttal in the book, in addition to his own contribution. As you might suspect, this is unusual.

The editor suggested that Legates just go along with the first option of not mentioning Schneider's past claims, assuring him it wouldn't alter his argument at all. Balking, Legates offered to withdraw the quotation if Schneider no longer believed it. He also asked how it is possible to misrepresent someone by quoting him in full context, noting, "But I am not willing to remove something just because he objects."

Apparently Schneider had not actually changed his position, and the editor countered Legates by implying that inclusion of

Schneider's own quote, of which he clearly is embarrassed but in full context, violates the advice against including "inflammatory language focused on individual scholars." He did not explain how this was so. Further, he oddly stated that context was *not* sufficient—though that had long been Schneider's complaint—but instead that to use Schneider's own words, in context, still required "relevant elaboration and clarification" (implicitly, as acceptable to Schneider, who insisted in e-mails to the publisher that "[t]he quote does not 'speak for itself' as [Legates] asserts," again contrary to previous demands that indicated a belief otherwise so long as the statement is read in-context). In sum, "things will move more quickly and more smoothly if we just remove a small piece of your text." Because an alarmist doesn't want it in there. Being an alarmist apparently means never having to say you're sorry, because you can just pretend things never happened.

The editor then went on to also strangely argue that Legates should acquiesce because none of the chapters "makes any attack on you," and again advising against "personal attacks," implying that quoting Schneider when he doesn't want his still-held beliefs to be aired anymore is to *attack* him. In closing, the editor flatly stated that "I want you to simply drop the text." Legates held firm and, in a surprise happy ending, the book came out with Schneider's quote intact.

This is not the first time that Dr. Schneider has uncomfortably dealt with his own past alarmism which, when recorded for posterity, isn't all that helpful to his present cause. Back in 1990 when being interviewed for the film *The Greenhouse Conspiracy* he expressed some apparently conflicting emotions when confronted with his past writings over what he has said and is now willing to say.

NARRATOR: You do accept that, sort of 10–15 years ago, people were talking about a global cooling not a global warming.

SCHNEIDER: Yeah. People were talking about global cooling 15 years ago, but not everybody. *I* was one who was not sure. (emphasis Schneider's)

NARRATOR: You say you didn't believe in global cooling but in your first book you said, "I've cited many examples of recent climatic variability and repeated the warnings of several well-known climatologists that a cooling trend has set in—perhaps one akin to the Little Ice Age." Well that was just 14 years ago.

Schneider appears on camera to be less than comfortable, but then quickly changes his tune to *of course I was one who was sure.*

SCHNEIDER: Yeah. I said that because at the time it was true. But you gotta be honest. You gotta tell things the way they are. I don't mind people quoting what I had to say in the '70s.

NARRATOR: But doesn't all of that add up to saying that you're asking governments to spend billions of dollars on a view which is different from one you had a decade ago.

SCHNEIDER: I don't see any problem in saying that people learn. I'm not embarrassed about the view I had a decade ago.

This is reminiscent of *Newsweek's* claim, that their contribution to the 1970s cooling panic, while wrong, wasn't *journalistically inaccurate.* Admittedly, there was a little bit of journalistic "gotcha" going on there, if with someone who has made himself vulnerable to such gambits. But, first he says he wasn't one of those folks who bought into that global cooling thing, until confronted with the fact that he actually did repeat precisely those warnings, but he is not at all embarrassed about having that quoted at him—which is somehow probably why he first said he hadn't bought into it. Until confronted with his past views. At which point—when on camera—he says he doesn't mind being quoted from before. And when off camera and confronted with an even more infamous assertion, he has a very different opinion, to the point of leaning on publishers (and as we see, filmmakers) to pretend it never happened.

Some habits die hard, and in 2008 Schneider was still seeking to censor his own words, this time after having given an apparently embarrassing interview to filmmakers makers Phelim McAleer and Ann McElhinney. Thinking better of the exchange, he had Stanford (where he gave the interview and otherwise allowed himself to be filmed) deny permission to use the footage. (The duo had previously faced environmentalist censorship when green groups pressured outlets to not screen their work, so Schneider's reaction was not a complete surprise.)[86]

Similar episodes include one particular peach from Gore adviser Hansen, who seemingly explained that it's now safe to move from his own "scary story" period on to the "I wanna do policy!" phase with the public's and policymakers' attention (and budgets?) having been secured. To wit, "Emphasis on extreme scenarios may have been appropriate at one time, when the public and decision-makers were relatively unaware of the global warming issue. . . . Now, however, the need is for demonstrably objective climate forcing scenarios consistent with what is realistic under current conditions."[87]

Not only did he later fall off the wagon and resume promiscuous use of catastrophist scenarios but, as one state climatologist opined to me, "Hansen is woefully mistaken to argue that extreme or blatantly false scenarios ever are or were appropriate to garner the attention of the public—indeed, such stances smack of 'the ends justifying the means' and are anathema to the scientific process." Humorously, according to Legates, Schneider suggested to the *From Climate to Chromosomes* editor that Hansen also be permitted to object to inclusion of his own uncomfortable admission in the book, which had come back to bother him, too.

Hansen's view expressed above is quite similar to that of his pupil, Gore, stating, "Nobody is interested in solutions if they don't think there's a problem. Given that starting point, I believe it is appropriate to have an over-representation of factual presentations on how dangerous it is, as a predicate for opening up the audience to listen to what the solutions are, and how hopeful it is that we are going to solve this crisis."[88] Most of that which Gore demands be disproportionately aired falls under the heading of a prediction or projection, generally from a computer model which, for whatever reasons, the alarmists cannot separate from "fact."

Unlike Schneider, Gore hasn't sought to reinterpret his words. But then again, Gore refuses to subject himself to situations where he might be asked to, even canceling interviews with those whom he had originally, it seems, presumed to be "friendly." Hansen, meanwhile, is a media darling, but apparently doesn't get asked such questions. Someone, no doubt, is yet again muzzling him.

CHAPTER 5

Poisoning the Little Ones

Propagandizing Your Children

"We need to get kids young. That's where it started with me. I can remember watching documentaries in which I learned about mass extinctions of species in rain forests. That emotionally engaged me as a young kid, and I said to myself, 'When I grow up, I'd love to make a difference in this field.'"

Leonardo DiCaprio

THE CHILDREN ARE VERY IMPORTANT to the environmentalist industry, for their use as emotional props—*why, you don't want to* kill children, *do you?*—and to mobilize what's called Pester Power—turn the kids into mini alarmist-pesterers, and suddenly, you're reaching every home, from the inside.

Mobilizing pester power entails an intensive assault through the classroom though the alarmists aim even their advertisements at children,[1] as do their rent-seeking Big Business partners. Gang Green know full well the rationale under which children are largely exempted from societal norms, such as bearing legal consequences for their actions: they do not possess judgment.

This "education" is not solely aimed at creating future believers, but also at employing present-day cute lobbyists for pet

181

causes, who will assail their parents' lifestyles, and their parents themselves. This pester-power approach is increasingly bearing sour fruit in the U.S. and abroad.[2] As *Spiked* Magazine wrote:

> [P]recisely because they are children, they are more receptive to these messages and less able to think critically about them.... It's difficult to see this as anything other than an attempt to turn children into eco-warriors who will judge their parents' behaviour and lecture them to do better, rather like the spies in Orwell's *Nineteen Eighty-Four*—or a green version of China's Red Guards, perhaps. In one online discussion of the problem, Lisa from Perth in Scotland reports that her kids are so worried about climate change that they have even asked her if she still wants to be cremated.[3]

Adopting a unique approach to the intimacy of parenting, Al Gore's co-producer Laurie David wrote an open letter to her own children stating: "We want you to grow up to be activists."[4] *Open letter reminding you to pick up your room to follow.*

Similarly, the Somerset (UK) County Council sent local primary schools an indoctrination team to scare the dickens out of children—sorry, "to raise awareness of the urgency of climate change"—ranging in age from seven to ten.[5] The Council's Climate Change Education Officer (seriously) spilled the beans by admitting the goal is to "inspire children to take this message home to their families, friends and communities." There's nothing like starting kids off early on lifetimes of being friendless nags who are insufferable at family gatherings.

Rent-seeking industries are equally shameless in their effort to create a league of wealth-fearing snitches. For example, European energy company *npower* launched a campaign "to enlist as 'climate cops,' to root out 'climate crimes,' and thus 'save the planet.'"[6] This included color ads in the Sunday paper sections and "[i]n a luridly-designed website, mimicking the style of 'yoof' cartoons, it offers a bundle of downloads, including a pack of 'climate crime cards', urging its recruits to spy on families, friends and relatives, inviting each of them to build up a 'climate crime case file' in order to help them ensure their putative criminals do not 'commit those crimes again (or else)!'"

Thankfully, or possibly just wisely, the "or else!" is left unspecified but the "climate cops" are encouraged to keep detailed written records for a "Climate Cops HQ"—aw, that's so cute—so the crimes would presumably be revealed at your hearing. "And for those 'climate cops' that successfully perform the 'missions' set (or turn in their own parents), there is the reward of 'training' in the 'Climate Cop Academy.'"

Those in industry not on board are of course also targets. NASA's self-appointed climate change education officer, Gore-advisor James Hansen, expresses his "hope that [industry] will hear more from the young generation, and [looks] forward to our policy makers appreciating and acting upon the concerns of young people."[7] Toward that end he offers the sober message, "If we cannot stop the building of more coal-fired power plants, those coal trains will be death trains—no less gruesome than if they were boxcars headed to crematoria, loaded with uncountable irreplaceable species."[8] *Now, sleep well.*

The players complement each others' efforts, as shown by Hansen joining with a green pressure group to challenge school text books daring to mention existing doubts over causation, or the one that mentioned "greater warmth will make it easier and cheaper to grow crops and avoid high heating bills."[9] One can't risk the possibility that our kids aren't bombarded with enough of the Gore message.

We also see how "Nonprofit organizations like the National Wildlife Federation have compiled information booklets and lesson plans for teaching climate change to kids at all grade levels."[10] Gosh, norms certainly do change with the fashions. Recall the Left-wing outrage over bringing Channel One news tailored for children into classrooms because it was possible to trace corporate sponsorship to the operation? Why, those corporations might be peddling beliefs...like, say, the National Wildlife Federation and FoE. Presumably it is also appropriate, and acceptable to NWF et al., that the National Rifle Association do the same? (we know the answer: no. Not even an Eddie the Eagle mascot teaching gun safety, because that could lead to hunting).

While these groups, the UN,[11] and European Union[12] have long published books designed to frighten children into becoming little Gore-bots hectoring for the alarmist agenda, the same pap is now becoming the stuff of U.S. textbooks and even mandated in school curricula. Leading children's publisher Scholastic Books has a contest for teachers to out-alarm each other—and their young charges—with the most convincingly hysterical among them taking home cash prizes.[13]

When a concerned parent contacted Scholastic for the names of scientists they consult with, after six months of foot-dragging the publisher cited Dr. Dan Lashof from the pressure group Natural Resources Defense Council, Dr. Susan Joy Hassol who wrote Laurie David's alarmist "Too Hot not to Handle" HBO Special, Dr. Mark Spencer, and pressure group Environmental Defense's Dr. Michael Oppenheimer. All of them, in fact, appear to be activists who generally make the Gore-style "lawyer's brief" case of one-sided and exaggerated alarmism, refusing to deviate from Man-made warming orthodoxy. That's such strong "science" it was thrown out of court as unsupportable, so you can see why a less mature audience is far preferable.

Scholastic refused to provide the parent with names of the relevant editorial committee. You can draw your own conclusions about how balanced that must be.

Third graders in the U.S. have been subjected to indoctrination straight out of an earlier time—on a different continent—with songs glorifying the movement and its tenets, repeating back chants such as "We must preserve this exquisite wonder for many years to come. Global warming is a serious issue. We must all try to stop it. Remember, every small change will make our Earth a better place."[14] The Heartland Institute, a free-market think-tank in Chicago, got to see the fruits of this first-hand, when, as part of a class project, sixth graders were led to write letters denouncing Heartland as "you horrible people."[15]

So kids can't say a pledge of allegiance to the United States in school, but they are engaged as Young Pioneers in a political movement and compelled to pray fealty to the state of modern environmentalism.[16] Gaia is more relevant in our schools than God. Governments mandate that schoolchildren view *An Inconvenient Truth*, which is apparently an interdisciplinary tool: one Canadian student was subjected to *AIT* in four separate courses (possibly even science class, of all places).[17] At least the UK courts intervened to demand that, if such poison is served, it be accompanied by an antidote.[18] Not to miss out, however, librarians are now putting the hard sell on the tots to check out the book, DVD, and earthy rap sessions about our stolen future.[19]

We shouldn't be surprised by any of this. It would be unrealistic to have expected that this opportunity for spoon-feeding the end-of-days Mother Lode to the most vulnerable—and useful—audience would escape the environmental industry's longstanding campaign to turn children into hectoring chatterboxes. The repetitive "are we there yet?" is to mean, *have you arrived at the politically correct lifestyle?*

But it does seem a bit much that the American Academy of Pediatrics joined the fun, warning of the disproportionate impact of global warming on kids, urging pediatricians to educate lawmakers on this inegalitarian calamity.

Not for the purpose of frightening the kids, of course, but because "'Anticipated direct health consequences of climate change include injury and death from extreme weather events and natural disaster; increases in climate-sensitive infectious diseases; increases in air pollution-related illness; and more heat-related, potentially fatal, illness,' the [AAP] report said. 'Within all these categories, children have increased vulnerability compared with other groups.'"[20]

A *USA Today* article reported, "'We already have change, and certain bad things are going to happen no matter what we do,' said lead report author Katherine Shea, a pediatrician and adjunct public health professor at the University of North Carolina-Chapel Hill. 'But we can prevent things from getting even worse. We don't have the luxury of waiting."[21] *Of course we don't, dear.* Try that line out for yourself next time they leave your kids in the waiting room with back issues of *Highlights* for an hour just to get an MMR shot.

Of course, for every alarmist hoping kids can be part of the hysteria, there's one arguing kids are part of the problem. The Medical Journal of Australia published an article calling for massive "baby tax" to account for all the CO_2 those critters will emit in their lifetime.[22]

TV REALLY DOES MAKE KIDS DUMBER

The media, as mentioned earlier, also operate with our most vulnerable in mind. CNN's "Planet in Peril," the heavily-promoted special discussed in Chapter 3, was a fairly typical four hours of alarmism packaged with the ritual, beautiful imagery to distract the mildly curious from searching out actual data or otherwise pressure-testing the claims. But pouring this bilge into the classroom was an express purpose of the network, which separately produced and promoted free "Peril" materials via CNN Student News.[23]

The children's cable television channel Nickelodeon has joined the fashionable business of frightening children about the alarmist case for global warming.[24] Longtime newshound Linda Ellerbee took her show on the road for Nick to produce a special program dedicated to scaring them into badgering their folks about global warming, by presenting needy cases as purported results of "climate change."[25] This takes it a step further, pinning poor peoples' plights on parents. Yes, the weather, or climate (not "climate change"), has always been among the greatest threats to the world's poor, though historically the best societal response has been wealth creation and technological advances making all parties more adaptive to always unpredictable, often severe weather—which is something that we do know we will continue facing in the future.

Making energy more scarce has a less-stellar track record. Unfortunately, if the alarmists have their way, the past responses of name-calling and witch-burning to explain crop failures will look like the good old days compared to the desired response of leaving the world a poorer, less-resilient place which must deal with it.

But, heck, it might get ratings.

Reaching out beyond the classroom, the Australian Broadcast Corporation created a children-specific site, inviting them to calculate "how big a greenhouse hog are you?" As described by writer Ben O'Neill, the fun continued when they mouse-clicked the skull and crossbones "to find out what age you should die at so you don't use more than your fair share of the earth's resources." The website also discusses "cultural imperialism" and "how much your lifestyle sucks." An outraged if attentive reader of meteorologist Anthony Watts's website noted, "What is most disgusting about this is that ABC ignores their own published Code of Practice, [specifically] 'In providing enjoyable and enriching content for children, the ABC does not wish to conceal the real world from them. It can be important for the media, especially television, to help children understand and deal with situations which may include violence and danger. Special care should be taken to ensure that content which children are likely to watch or access unsupervised should not be harmful or disturbing to them.'"[26] So much for standards.

He also notes that the ABC site, purporting to target children approximately nine years of age, provides the footprint of the "sustainable greenhouse pig" against which the children should measure their own wretchedness. That footprint happens to be the emission total achieved by the average Aussie child at nine and one-third years of age. "In short, the site tells kids that they should die at age 9.3 years." Stay classy, ABC.

Hollywood, naturally, has long aimed at the shamuses in short pants, with absurdities ranging from the aptly named *AI: Artificial Intelligence* to the recent *Happy Feet*, *Arctic Tale* and of course Leonardo DiCaprio's dreary flop *The 11th Hour*, apparently his contribution to assist the greens' "need to get kids young."[27] "I want the public to be very scared by what they see. I want them to see a very bleak future."[28] Decried by one lawmaker as "a 'scarefest' aimed at kids,"[29] fortunately *11th* Hour's box office take was such that DiCaprio's investors were the most alarmed of all.

Disney's teen siren Miley Cyrus "wants America to wake up and deal with global warming...though she's not quite sure what that means. At least, that's what she admits in a song—dubbed an 'eco-anthem' by some" on her 2008 musical CD "Breakout."[30] Meanwhile, Internet videos claim that the North Pole is melting leaving Santa and his elves to drown,[31] and Greenpeace has their "angry kid" TV spot clearly designed to sic the tots on their folks in fury. That the angry kid also appears to be the go-cart driving "tween" in the hilarious "Warren Wallace/Mike Wallace" GEICO ads does slightly confuse matters, what with the luxury of Busch League car racing not making Greenpeace's list of acceptable practices.

HOLIDAYS IN HELL

They say if you can terrorize just one child with death-camp analogies, or indoctrinate them to view people who dispute your scary stories as denying the Holocaust, you've succeeded. Or maybe it just seems like some environmentalist must have said that. Consider how the holidays reliably bring out the worst the alarmist industry have to offer. From their Halloween-based guilt trips— "The most frightening part of Halloween is what it is doing to our planet"[32]—to their assault on non-sustainable Thanksgiving,[33] Autumn is just their warm-up for the Big Kahuna of Christmas as an excuse for scare campaigns and indoctrination.

Just in time for Noël a purportedly educational tome titled *When Santa Turned Green* rolled out. "It's November up in the North Pole and everything's going along smoothly at Santa's workshop until he discovers a leak in his roof. Santa soon learns that this little leak is connected to a far bigger problem: The North Pole is melting because of global warming! Faced with the reality of what this could mean for Christmas—not to mention the planet and the future—Santa is determined to turn things around."

> **BA-HUMBUG**
>
> "Let's not beat around the bush: Christmas is a carbon catastrophe and the reason is our ludicrous culture of present giving."
>
> *BBC writer Justin Rowlatt, in "The ethics of Christmas presents," December 21, 2007*

As if society was in short supply of encouragements to resent the parents without telling your kids that the minivan that gets them to soccer practice safe and comfortably is really trashing the elves' workshop.

School children in Wales were banned from exchanging Christmas cards, "in the name of saving the planet and its 'wretched' Africans."[34] With this move, environmentalism officially overwhelmed the holidays with political correctness gone mad. We see here at the Evan James Primary School that environmentalism managed to supplant the rest of the PC twaddle as a meta-excuse.

"The reasons for not having cards are endless," head teacher Nicholas Daniels claims. Although one could speculate that a big motivating factor was to remove the crushing burden of handing out the cards from teachers ("We are a big school. We have 68 pupils in two classes in year six. The magnitude of cards is horrendous"), Daniels' argument was explicitly moral. "We did take a strong moral ground on the matter. . . . We knew we would face opposition but we decided to do this on moral and environmental grounds. Cards in school cause litter problems and can become a popularity contest about who gets the most."[35]

What with burghs ranging from the picturesque Berkshires resort town of Great Barrington to Brooklyn pulling the plug on public holiday lighting, it should go without saying that the greens also implored others to light one less menorah candle during Hanukkah in the name of salvation of a different sort. "The campaign calls for Jews around the world to save the last candle and save the planet, so we won't need another miracle."[36] No mention was made of the fact that Al Gore's Nobel flight to Oslo—and Mercedes limo whisking away just his luggage—occurred during the festival of light. It does seem that these folks are going to need that miracle, though a good start would be engaging in just one less annoying campaign to step all over the joy of others.

SCHOOLS OF CROCK

Perversely, it just seems natural that fully half of the children in the land of mandatory viewing of Al Gore's *An Inconvenient Truth* report sleep loss due to fear over "global warming,"[37] a malady also reported among U.S. schoolchildren.[38] Apparently one in seven UK schoolchildren also already blame their parents for "global warming," thanks to the fact that the schools have adopted Gore's tone and message in all corners of their curriculum.[39]

In what is certainly a coincidence we also see that "Britons may be banned from drinking 'traditional milk' in favour of the long-life variety in order to save the environment, according to a gov-

ernment strategy...to reduce the amount of carbon emissions....
'The milk chain should enhance the development, marketing and
placement of UHT [NB: that is ultra-pasteurized, boxed] milk
products. The move could see less refrigeration by outlets, but consumers will still have to cool the milk in fridges once the carton has
been opened.'"[40] Refrigerators? *Murderer*!

The Commonwealth remains spiritually unified, with New
Zealand having no fewer than ten separate government agencies[41]
frightening its schoolchildren with sophisticated offerings of
alarmism[42] so comprehensive as to also provide a questionnaire for
Nanny State to check which schools and pupils are doing their
duty.[43] Not surprisingly, the U.S. EPA also has followed suit, with
its own climate-change-for-kids materials available at EPA.gov.[44]

TEACHING THEM TO TALK REAL GOOD

Google the lovely phrase "spew CO_2," which is the new activist
and media favorite to describe the act of emitting carbon dioxide—without massive quantities of which there would be no life on
Earth (and to which Man contributes only at the margins). This
search will yield more than 50,000 returns; "spew carbon dioxide" provides tens of thousands more including, right up top, the
delicately titled "Teachers' Guide: How much do you spew?"[45]
This tract is produced by the University Corporation for Atmospheric Research (UCAR), "a nonprofit consortium of research universities on behalf of the National Science Foundation and the
university community."[46] This means it is a taxpayer-dependent
outfit sucking your dollars and spewing alarmism.

Alternately you might join over three million others and view
the hysterical YouTube video posted by a high school teacher
styled "Most terrifying video you'll ever see" that, it admits up
front, makes Al Gore and his fever dream look like that of a sis-
sified Pollyanna.[47] I had hoped that was some strange code for

"dishonest," but instead it seems that someone who has custody of children for several hours every day finds Al Gore too calm and rational. The National Education Association seems inclined to agree.[48] It occurs to me that a safer option to subjecting my kids to professional educators is home schooling. And by that I mean sealing them in a drum with Alec Baldwin and a furious badger. Much safer.

The alarmist hits just keep on coming, for example from the North American Association for Environmental Education (NAAEE), revealing that no environmental education is complete without instilling in children "possible consequences" and "*global responsibility*" (emphasis in original)—the former term a red flag for alarmist scenarios, the latter which we will see is a synonym for the loopiest enviro-dogma in print or spoken word. Also on tap are the "hidden environmental costs of driving" and, most important, ensuring that the kids become activists.[49]

The NAAEE article about how to teach "climate change" reveals their stab at balance succumbing instead to more subjective standards. These include that, in the acceptable curriculum, "Scientifically and socially credible positions and explanations are covered thoroughly, while other positions are also mentioned. (Balanced presentation does not mean giving equal time and space to every opinion or perspective, but treating major positions fairly)." Educators are to seek out "materials [that] communicate areas of consensus among scientists or other experts."[50] Gee, whatever socially acceptable claims of consensus could they be alluding to?

This educators' group demonstrated "balance" by turning to "a management consultant whose practice focuses on climate-change issues and corporate social responsibility,"[51] which is to say, someone who possesses a particular point of view and whose livelihood depends upon the extant alarmism. This one's particular point of view is that although we're killing the planet we can tell kids this in a way that doesn't scare them. Instead, he counsels, kids can negotiate splitting any year-over-year reductions in the energy bill with their parents, and get mom to dry the clothes on a line. He's not much on facts, but he's got chutzpah.

This dedication to balance was also illustrated in the NAAEE decision to link to a compendium of alarmist resources as their selected reading for teachers.[52]

The group boasted a graduate of one of Al Gore's training sessions to present the *An Inconvenient Truth* slideshow, "including updated data" at their 2007 Annual Meeting.[53] I have debated one of the graduates of Gore's Climate Camp graduates, the training at which includes rehearsing a provided script and instruction on how to evade and if necessary discredit questioners who challenge alarmism. So I'm willing to bet that, although this presentation occurred more than a month after the UK High Court bounced the substance of *AIT* as propagandistic, not educational material, these updates didn't include redacting the portions of the movie laughed out of Court. The other NAAEE highlights were: "Teaching the Greatest Challenge to Sustainability: Climate Change" (the presenter was listed as "Tim Grant [Green Teacher]"); and "Global Warming, Blogs, Web Design, and Teaching."

The program teased the 2008 convention in Wichita—tempting, but, not quite Bali...these guys would never cut it up in the big leagues of the IPCC—as offering instruction in how to teach the children about "Environmental Justice, Environmental Health, and Climate Change: The EE Challenge of our Lifetime."

Another group calling itself the National Environmental Education Foundation merely offers more of the same,[54] but they'll soon be able to do so in a noisier fashion as it appears that The Weather Channel (naturally) tossed them $2.5 million to improve climate awareness, *a la* TWC of course.[55] Presumably this means breathlessly "on the 'eights'" and with lots of shots of severe weather *coming to your school soon*!

Taking these lessons to heart, California's legislature decided to mandate the instruction of global warming in its public schools. I am confident that this does not mean exploration of how it has been much warmer many times before in Man's history, how the current warming peaked in 1998, or that the mandate was passed in the fourth straight year of cooling. Talk about "we must act now!" This was so heavy-handed, even über-green poseur Governor Arnold Schwarzenegger vetoed it.

Is it working? One ten year-old lectured a local newspaper reporter during her school's science fair that "carbon dioxide gas, overflowing landfills and people who don't conserve and recycle are ruining our planet through global warming."[56] Others scribble, as part of their educational requirements, notes to politicians detailing the desperate efforts of the (vastly expanding) polar bear population "to cope with arctic changes brought on by global warming caused by human-produced carbon dioxide emissions."[57] This assignment should be no surprise from their teacher, molder of young minds, who articulated her own insights about this suggestion, brought to her by a child after being "taught climate change lessons." "When he first said it, I was like, 'Wow.'" Did I mention that was the teacher?

Wow, indeed. The glowing stories abound in local papers of children writing either terrified odes to stave off the destruction they are promised will be nigh, or simply being forced to regurgitate alarmist pabulum and adopt alarmist advocacy to pass their classes.[58] Ten-year-old Hunter Sahaprio-Throckmorton was awarded the title of "The Most Philosophical Fourth Grader in America" after penning an *AIT*-inspired poem written from the perspective of the planet, proclaiming its own death and warning of dead bodies soon to be seen floating in the seas courtesy of global warming.[59] Kids can be so cute. How can you resist twisting their adorable little minds to advance an agenda?

One high school biology teacher wrote to a well-known skeptical meteorologist, despairing over the resistance he meets from brainwashed lads and lasses when explaining how there might be a reason that the climate changes other than CO_2. Oh, and he mentions that "It is difficult to speak out since I am not yet tenured at this school and the majority of my co-workers, including those who would decide my future employment, consider Al Gore to be a hero and those who disagree with him as heretics." But experience shows that this gentleman's insistence on anonymity only proves to our alarmist superiors that he doesn't exist. And if he publicly spoke out it would only prove him unfit for the job. Such a comfy world, theirs.

It gets worse, as Congress is now considering a measure to cure "nature deficit disorder" with "environmental literacy" training as a graduation requirement.[60] Once again, it appears that literacy means acquiescence to or at minimum parroting of a particular agenda and worldview. So it is clear that the greens are winning the battle to impose their ideology in the schools (as well as in films and on the menu), all the way up to instilling fear and loathing of parents and prosperity.

And market-based messages or the notion that increased wealth creation and indeed consumption improve living conditions—even among those peoples being used as poster children to scare the little ones sleepless? We just don't hear those.

As Professor Allen Quist put it: "It seems, that in the run-up to the festive season, children will just continue to learn all the wrong 'facts of life': that consumption is bad, that the 'poor little black babies' in Africa need you to sacrifice your Christmas cards so they can have a goat, that the environment poses absolute limits to human development, and that normal human interactions pose a threat to our basic sense of well-being."[61]

PICK ON SOMEONE YOUR OWN SIZE

The alarmists are more open now about their agenda to churn out half-pint climate nags than they ever have been before. John Stossel discovered the extent of this abuse when taping his October 2007 *20/20* segment on Al Gore's alarmism.

STOSSEL: Children are frightened.

FRIGHTENED CHILD: I worry. My mom worries.

CHILD: The water might rise and and [sic] it might flood the whole town.

CHILD: We won't be able to survive for long...

GORE: Sea level worldwide would go up 20 feet.

CHILD: Yeah. Maybe even like the height of this building.

CHILD: We'll probably just, like, drown and, we'll die.[62]

Apparently, it's not only, like, scary, but certain to occur, and kids have learned not to let any dark forces sprinkle the pixie dust of skepticism or critical thought on them in the rare chance that they are able to obtain a moment of sleep amid the trauma.

AD: Some say irreversible consequences are 30 years away.

STOSSEL: This Ad Council PSA says ignoring the coming crisis is like putting our kids in front of a train.

AD: That won't affect me (terrifying cacophony, indicating you are being hit by a train)...

STOSSEL: What are you most worried will happen?

CHILD: We'll all die.

STOSSEL: Are there some people who say this isn't true?

CHILDREN: Yes.

STOSSEL: Might they be right?

CHILDREN: No!!! (in unison)

STOSSEL: How do you know they're not right?

CHILD: Well, 'cause, the Earth is getting hotter.

STOSSEL: Where do you learn this?

CHILD: I saw the Al Gore, um, video.

California saw this indoctrination and raised it with some activism even before Sacramento chose to ride the popular wave with a mandate. Local media in Marin County (of course) reported in November 2007, "Elementary school students join fight against global warming." It seems that, in order to fiddle with the globe's thermostat, "Teachers, parents and volunteers helped organize the assemblies and participated in the skits to help raise awareness about global warming and what people can do about it."[63] This was repeated in often hysterical form and in public schools nation-wide during the Left's January 2008 "Focus the Nation" effort, funded by usual suspect ideological activist organizations.[64]

So, just like Gore's extensive travel on private jets if rather *unlike* Thanksgiving skits, these are environmentally okay. Somehow. Clearly, schools no longer teach (possess?) logic, only dialectics.[65]

In all likelihood this theater included little in the way of aware-ness-raising about what people can do to change the earth's tem-perature, given that no one claims that any restriction or set of mandates ever proposed would have that effect. It seems that the school instead preached the usual lifestyle-policing. One major practice the teachers recommended is to nag their parents and, bet-ter yet, inform on them. "Rancho [Elementary School] students will be given bilingual 'Cancel-a-Car' coupon books filled with ways they can fight global warming. Once the coupons are returned to school, teachers will track what conservation efforts are made and the date. Teachers will help monitor the progress."[66]

Hmmm. Now, Marin County isn't all that far from the home of one Michael Newdow, who taught us that including "under God" in the Pledge of Allegiance heaped unbearable pressure on children to conform and constituted the heavy-hand of the state impermissibly trying to mold little theists through the teachers, whose presence—to borrow a phrase—"will help monitor the progress." Yet, "Three nonprofits...are implementing the program and hope to introduce it to 25 Marin schools by the end of the year." Certainly if Mr. Newdow gets wind that these "non-profits" are affiliated with any church, he'll be on them like Al Gore on a private jet. *Right*?

I'm kidding, of course, because we all know that eco-fundamentalism is a blessed faith, while the Nativity (and too many menorah candles) must be chased from the public square. After all, the world *was* much warmer back when Christ walked the Earth, during the "Roman Warming" and, let's face it, that simply cannot be coincidence.

READING IS FUNDAMENTAL-IST

Lynn Cherry of the Center for Children's Environmental Literature e-mailed a revealing announcement of a dinner/discussion in Palo Alto, California. The gabfest was facilitated, naturally, in cooperation with the Society of Environmental Journalists:

> A children's book can often have more impact on society than an ephemeral newspaper or magazine article; children's book classics can stay in print for half a century or more and reach thousands or even millions of children, shaping values and culture. A League of Conservation Voters study found that adults got most of their environmental information from materials

their children brought home from school. Hence, children's books can educate parents as well as their target audience. Information in children's books written on a third grade reading level is understandable to most adults and can play an important role in the general public's science literacy.

These books targeting children, and thereby in fact openly targeting adults, have dropped most pretense of subtlety and typically employ fear as their principal medium of communication. But the alarmists go beyond corrupting the kids' stories and peddling their staple of mantras and gooey drivel, and actually fudge the facts and misrepresent the science in order to frighten and mobilize children who do not possess the adult's intellectual or even physical abilities to second-source or fact-check.

Consider the example of Gore's co-producer Laurie David, who followed the utterly disingenuous and on occasion dishonest film with a book aimed at the little ones. Finding scientific distortions even more brazen than those in the movie, the Science and Public Policy Institute revealed how "in order to contrive a visual representation for their false central claim that CO_2 controls temperature change, David and co-author Cambria Gordon present unsuspecting children with an altered temperature and CO_2 graph that falsely reverses the relationship found in the scientific literature."[67]

Specifically, one ought to have suspected that Al Gore was up to something when he ran two lines across the screen behind him in his film, claimed a cause-and-effect relationship, and then forgot to superimpose them. Instead he kept them a safe distance apart. Gore was correct to insist there was a relationship between the temperature line and the CO_2 concentration line, as measured over the past 650,000 years according to ice core data. The relationship, however, was the *precise opposite* of what he suggested: historically, *it warms first*, and then CO_2 concentrations go up. This could be because when the air gets warmer, then seas get warmer, and the water releases its dissolved CO_2; when it cools, the seas cool, absorbing CO_2. It isn't even close: the lag between temperature and CO_2 is centuries-long.[68]

Gore's wording and visuals were cleverly deceptive—he implied, without stating (because it would be false to say so) that CO_2 increases are followed by temperature increases. The reason he didn't source his claim is that the literature doesn't support it. Somehow believing only the young would bother to open their effort targeting children, David and Gordon weren't so clever. Their book included the two lines, but dared superimpose them, and even stated the phony relationship more outlandishly than Gore did in his film. The reason that temperature appeared to follow CO_2 proved to be because *they reversed the labels in the legend*. The very paper they invoke makes quite clear that it stands for the opposite of that for which purpose David and Gordon cite it.[69] Whoops.

They pitched their book claiming that it contains "urgent information" for kids on global warming. Apparently this "urgency" fallback they have for everything is so great as to even preclude proof-reading. Or else they were lying.

David was nonplussed that anyone would dare question her claims, even such a whopper as reversing the cause-and-effect, which had already telegraphed itself for a year in the risibly phony movie. Of course, she had during that period been encouraged by supportive scientists falling over themselves to insist that it "got all the major points right." Ah, but welcome to the rough-and-tumble, full-contact world of children's publishing, where fact-checking is so alien to those who push alarmist twaddle that David hailed it as a sign of desperation. "Apparently the climate change 'skeptics' have grown so desperate in their attempts to hide the truth from the American people that they've taken to spending hours scrutinizing a children's book, trying to marginalize the urgent information it contains about global warming."[70]

She is not amused that one would dare look into claims—aimed at children, no less—of the world coming to an end, posing the question, then, *what* is *worthy of inquiry*? Further, using the "reasonable man" standard, which act is more one of desperation: fact-checking claims in a book targeting children that are facially erroneous (to adults who know what they're talking about) by a woman recently having been exposed as having participated in aggressively misrepresenting the science in a related piece of work—or the underlying act of making such claims, itself?

That you likely arrived at a different answer than Ms. David reveals a principal distinction between the global warming activist and the rest of the world. Her publisher Scholastic privately admitted the "accidental" error to a colleague of mine, promising to correct the chart in the next edition. Given that the bogus chart represents the entire premise of the book—CO_2 drives temperature—this should prove an interesting challenge. Regardless, all of this simply guaranteed an invitation to her and her co-writer/accomplice to pollute the "Green California Schools Summit."[71] What is it about that place?

As if the allergic reaction to accuracy weren't sufficiently illustrative of motivation and character, the blogger at ConservativePublisher.com brought the public's attention to a "jaw dropping" interview with Ms. David in *Publisher's Weekly*, "mak[ing] it clear that her Sept. book is meant to indoctrinate children."[72] David admitted to a sympathetic *PW*[73] how "kids also are the number one influence on their parents, so if you want to reach the parents, go to the kids."[74] Elsewhere, David revealed "I know how powerful my kids are. When they want something, forget it—all the resistance in the world isn't going to help you."[75]

President and chairman of World Ahead Media Eric Jackson responded to David's admission, "As opposed to marketing a book to parents and saying this is an informative resource to teach children about an issue, they are going directly to kids to indoctrinate them with a political agenda.... The book is clearly political.... It is a political issues book that is being presented directly to children under the guise of science. This is an inappropriate way to approach curious and impressionable children."[76]

In September 2007 the *Los Angeles Times* provided a round-up of some green books produced for kids, predictably titled "For Earth's sake" and noting that the ages-11-and-up version of *AIT* had just been released, fawning that "Gore's tone is dignified and elegant."[77] Sort of like that guy who broadcast the Hindenburg explosion.

Such a paean in the face of all available evidence (and judicial decree very soon thereafter) is not surprising since the *Times* also described the book as "aim[ing] to educate kids about rising temperatures, how human activity is affecting the Earth's climate and humanity's responsibility to reduce greenhouse gases in the atmosphere." The *Times* suddenly discovered the art of understatement, as well, vowing, "The aim of these books is to prevent children from feeling like powerless victims of environmental degradation and to turn them into active citizens."

The piece, written by Sonja Bolle, "a freelance book editor and children's book reviewer," continued with its blinkered view of Gore's already-debunked alarmism being imposed upon children. It gushed, "The illustrations are beautiful, even when they're documenting grim realities; the attention to visuals shows the book's origins as a slide presentation. Gore's memory of his mother reading her children Rachel Carson's classic, *Silent Spring*, which argued, in Gore's words, that mankind 'now had the power to seriously harm the environment,' gives a sense of history to the environmental movement."

Here we go again. Oddly, a piece written by someone dedicated to childhood literacy doesn't flinch at Gore's claim that his mother read him a children's book that came out in 1962, when Gore was fourteen (alternately raising the question of how a child still being read to in his teens soon makes the leap to Harvard). This practice presaged those memorable times he has reminisced about when she rocked him to sleep with the "look for that union label" jingle, written when he was twenty-seven.

In a nod to balance clearly written with teeth clenched, the *Times* then revealed that an alternative viewpoint exists. "Presenting itself as an antidote to the alarmist views of environmentalists is *The Sky's Not Falling!: Why It's OK to Chill About Global Warming* by Holly Fretwell, a natural resources policy expert and self-described optimist." The *Times* apparently was unable to discern from her book whether Fretwell *really is* an optimist or just calls herself one (she could be lying, you know; women who write global warming children's books have been found to do such things). The review continued with a touching dismissal of Fretwell's concern really being for businesses, not science or the precious Earth. Subsequent paragraphs wax on in a *Times* ode to California's environmental regulators. All that is missing are the sneer-quotes around "antidote" and "optimist." *Nothing to see here, parents, move along.*

THE COLD-HEARTED NORTH

In October 2007 *Energy and Environment News* reported how "Schoolteachers across Alaska are being fed exaggerated and false global warming alarmist materials to distribute to their students, thanks to the taxpayer-funded University of Alaska-Fairbanks."[78] The materials include hoary predictions of doom made all the worse because the exaggerated scenarios come from the UN's IPCC, a group subject to broad criticism even "by its own participating scientists, for exaggerating its forecasts of future warming. Even so, IPCC models predict nowhere near the warming Alaska teachers are told will occur even in the 'best case' scenario."[79]

Of course, in the process of forging little advocates out of school-age charges, the materials "also direct teachers to 'Ask students to

> **NOT TEXTBOOK MATERIAL**
>
> The Arctic in the 1930s was as warm as or warmer than it was in the late twentieth century.
>
> *Source: Polyakov et al. (2003)*

discuss what happens when temperatures rise.' The answer key lists numerous negative predicted consequences, but fails to mention any of the real-world benefits experienced in the past 100 years, such as increasing crop yields, forest expansion, and desert shrinkage."[80]

So as to not be out of step with the IPCC in other areas—if remaining woefully uninformed of numerous exposés of past IPCC mistakes or misdeeds—"teachers are given temperature graphs for the past 1,000 years in which the Medieval Warming Period has been erased from the record," while it also joins the campaign to get rid of the equally unhelpful Little Ice Age, claiming that period got a mere 0.2°C cooler than when we know Viking settlements successfully farmed Greenland hundreds of years prior.

Despite the alarmists' dismissal of those who challenge their prophesying if the "skeptic" is not a practicing scientist (but then again, even when they are), "In a lesson plan titled 'Alaska's Changing Climate,' teachers are directed to alarmist news articles written by non-scientists claiming polar bears are being stressed and threatened by polar ice. Real-world evidence shows polar bear numbers are increasing rapidly throughout the Arctic."[81]

No global warming alarmism is complete without wrenching tales of frozen things melting, and in a "Student Worksheet: Greenland Melting," the materials misleadingly claim that "Greenland's ice sheet has begun to melt again....In 2001, Greenland's ice sheet was losing about 50 cubic km of ice per year. By 2005 the melting had increased to 220 cubic km per year." This is at best a truncated and selective presentation of the relevant data given that temperatures in the northern nether regions in the past have been as high as 6°C warmer than today, Greenland warmed more and faster in the early twentieth century,[82] its glaciers have largely been receding for a century,[83] and the purported acceleration in regional melt in 2005 was a short-lived anomaly that is no more.[84]

TALK ABOUT NIGHTMARES

After having trotted out indoctrinated children as props at all manner of gatherings for more than a decade the UN had the temerity to announce its dog-and-pony show for the 2007 "Kyoto" talks with the claim, "For the first time—let's hear what the world's youth and children have to say about climate change and the impact it will have on their future."[85] First time, eh? So, in addition to all of its other problems, the UN's short-term memory is shot. Or else they take us all to be as trusting as the children they manipulate, at least until those children wake up as adults to discover how they've been used by the population and lifestyle axe-grinders.

As we have seen the alarmists acknowledge, all of these efforts are the bottom-up leg of Big Green's campaign to impose its agenda, by creating what the *Wall Street Journal* has called "Inconvenient Youths: Eco-warrior kids [who] go after parents for 'environmental offenses.'"[86] And its impacts are serious, all right, if not necessarily all of the sort intended by the puppeteers, or else they are merely those that they decided constitutes acceptable losses and a cost of doing (harm against) business.

The alarmists' practice of reflexively seeking to strike fear in kids' hearts in order to push their ideological agenda—such as when the Soros-funded Center for American Progress blamed a tornado ripping through a Boy Scout camp on global warming, despite zero authority or reason to support such a claim[87]—how can they pretend to be surprised, let alone distressed, at the outcomes?

We see impressionable youths suffer public breakdowns when "testifying" before cynical congressional panels about the horrors they are sure await them,[88] and become so maddened by it all as to literally become clinical head cases. Australian columnist Andrew Bolt reported that 2008 saw the first diagnosed case of "climate change delusion." "Writing in the *Australian and New Zealand Journal of Psychiatry*, Joshua Wolf and Robert Salo of our Royal Children's Hospital say this delusion was a 'previously unreported phenomenon'....'A 17-year-old man was referred to the inpatient psychiatric unit at Royal Children's Hospital Melbourne with an eight-month history of depressed mood... [and] visions of apocalyptic events.' 'The patient had also developed the belief that, due to climate change, his own water consumption could lead within days to the deaths of millions of people through exhaustion of water supplies.'"[89] Certainly, in hindsight, all of these consequences to children are entirely predictable.

Yet the *Journal* brings our attention to the travails of a seven-year-old confronting dueling fears of the dark and global warming, manifesting themselves in a ritual, moral struggle over a tiny night-light. "His father describes the indoctrination as border[ing] on the obsessive: 'He sees the cutting down of a tree as a sacrilegious and awful event.'"

Denver first-grade student Fiona Henderson apparently found religion at church after a minister pushed kids toward EPA's global warming website "where kids can click on a drawing of an Earth with a bandage on it to learn about greenhouse gases. Fiona, 6, started pestering her parents, John and Margit, to use the lights less often. She walked around shutting off lights, told her father not to drive to work and now gives 25 cents from her $1.50 weekly allowance to various environmental causes. 'She's not so much upset as strident—"Turn off that light! Turn off that light!" says Mr. Henderson. 'We ended up having conversations with her that it's OK to use energy.'"

Wait until the teacher hears about that.

Investor's Business Daily was only partly right when describing the cynical imposition of this parade of horribles upon children as child abuse.[90] Previously, that was prohibited, not mandated, by the state, which ought to leave children free to dream about clowns and puppies and other joys of youth.

CHAPTER 6

Big Government

How Government, Politicians, and Alarmists Abuse Power in the Pursuit of Power

"The 'climate change' hysteria has proved a godsend for prod-noses and punishment freaks. I doubt there is a single country on earth where the entire political class has so completely taken leave of its senses over alleged global warming. Here in Britain, it has been seized upon as an exciting new weapon with which to inflict more taxes, fines and regulations on us."

Columnist Richard Littlejohn in the *Daily Mail* (London)

THE GLOBAL WARMING INDUSTRY is made up of lifestyle nags and nanny-statists seeking further interventions against the intolerable exercise of individual liberties, joined by rent-seeking industries petitioning the state to create markets and mandates and enhance subsidies. Their common objective is expansion of government power.

Government is not only their *end*, it is their *means*. Bureaucrats and elected officials offer some of the most odious examples of alarmist bullying and scheming. Further, local, state, and national governments, joined by supranational bodies, adopt the absurd as official policy in order to advance their agenda while also quietly funding private parties to ratify their claims and their cause.

SCARING YOU OUT OF YOUR LIBERTIES, 101

How did we come to this point of shrieking to the heavens about the need to urgently impose a dramatic overhaul of society?

In short, the environment is the latest alleged victim of capitalism to whose defense the Statists rush to offer salvation. Add to this the substantial drop in the 1990s of the decade-long spike in the price of carbon-based fuels—and, therefore, a substantial drop in the justification for billions in subsidies and mandates for the "alternative" energy industry; within five years there was an organized "global warming" movement out of Washington seeking to re-increase the price of carbon-based energy.

Peter Foster of Canada's *Financial Post* explains how this began with a series of environmental agreements and initiatives all based on the notion that the world was running out of various resources or, similarly, was on a fast track to permanently despoiling them. The response was "state control over capitalist enterprise on the basis that it is both morally suspect and practically unstable."[1] "Global cooling," followed by "warming," then later "climate change" and now—thanks to Al Gore and his advertising campaign—the "climate crisis," were simply the ideal vehicles.

Why would governments leap on board? A simple combination of the environmentalists' noise machine threatening their peace, and the delights that this agenda promised for bureaucrats and policy-makers "to stay relevant, busy, and in power.... The policy process became self-feeding."[2]

Some scientists, seeing the monster that has been unleashed, note for example that "the present alarm on climate change is an instrument of social control, a pretext for major businesses and political battle. It became an ideology, which is concerning."[3]

Lord Anthony Giddens was an advisor to the Kyotophilic administration of Tony Blair, whose government was quite possibly the most alarmist that global warming has yet seen. Giddens described the preferred approach to impose the desired policies in terms of "the phenomenology of risk, which applies not only to risks of global terrorism but to other risks. In order to manage risk, you must scare people...even if that risk is what one might call a low probability but high consequence risk."[4]

It is thus not surprising that the UK was first to advance the notion of individual carbon ration coupons during this, the war against climate change.[5] One UK scientist wrote to me in response, deriding "the introduction of a second currency with everyone having the same allowance—wealth redistribution by having to buy carbon credits from someone less well off." Prime Minister Gordon Brown even threatened retailers that he would force them to cut down on climate-changing plastic bag use if they did not voluntarily do so with sufficient ardor.[6] And you thought that the world's incredibly shrinking politics had hit bottom with "school uniforms" and feeling your pain.

It is little wonder, then, that UK citizens appear to be the first who believe in large numbers that carbon police lie in their future. They are no doubt comforted by the head of that massive nanny state's Energy Savings Trust (seriously), who says that such heavy-handedness "need not be the case." If people get with the program on their own, that is.[7]

In this context, such deprivations of freedom are just fine even for the pan-leftist movement apoplectic about any encroachment upon civil liberties sold in the name of fighting global terrorism. In fact, the global warming agenda poses a far greater threat to individual liberties than those measures.[8] As columnist Mark Steyn notes, "It's fascinating to observe how almost any old totalitarian racket becomes respectable once it's cloaked in enviro-hooey. For example, restrictions on freedom of movement were previously the mark of the Soviet Union et al. But in Britain, they're proposing limits on your right to take airline flights to other countries—and, as it's in the name of environmental responsibility, everyone thinks it's a grand idea. [The zero-population growth crowd's] views are the logical *reductio*."[9]

The idea is of course to go slightly further than pushing you off the airplane. Carbon Sense Coalition in Australia offered the following compilation of extant proposals to use that country's laws to modify behavior in the name of global warming:

- Ban open fires and pot bellied stoves
- Ban incandescent light bulbs (what about those candles on birthday cakes?)
- Ban bottled water
- Ban private cars from some areas
- Ban plasma TV's
- Ban new airports
- Ban extensions to existing airports
- Ban "standby mode" on appliances
- Ban coal fired power generation
- Ban electric hot water systems
- Ban vacationing by car
- Ban three day weekends
- Tax babies
- Tax big cars (are big people next?)
- Tax supermarket parking areas
- Tax rubbish
- Tax second homes
- Tax second cars
- Tax holiday plane flights
- Tax electricity to subsidise solar [power]
- Tax showrooms for big cars
- Eco-tax for cars entering cities
- Require permits to drive your car beyond your city limits

- Limit choice in appliances
- Issue carbon credits to every person
- Dictate fuel efficiency standards
- Investigate how to reduce production of methane by Norway's Moose (what about those belching whales?)
- Remove white lines on roads to make motorists drive more carefully (no kidding!)[10]

Barack Obama's policy advisor Jason Grumet therefore rather understated things in admitting, "This is going to require a kind of social commitment the likes of which we haven't seen in this country since World War II."[11] But of course, these restrictions in practice seem to be upon the masses, not the Apparat, the bossiest of whom who continue commuting daily in private cars and even private jets,[12] generally refuse to disclose emissions by the institutions of government, and claim phony reductions when it suits them to nag others.[13]

The red flags are many and signal that we should listen when the economist Vaclav Klaus, president of the Czech Republic, says that global warming "has become a new religion or new ideology and in that sense I think it's justified to compare it with other ideologies."[14] By this he means the communism that his country suffered under for decades—because of how the warmists' agenda "threatens to undermine freedom and the world's economic and social order." The same holds true for Vladimir Putin's former economic advisor Andrei Illarionov, when he flatly compares Kyoto and other CO_2 rationing schemes to one of history's most notorious catastrophes, the Soviet five-year central planning scheme called "Gosplan."[15]

It is precisely for such a philosophy that aspiring Green Party politicians say things like:

I think the key thing I want to say is this: that the population issue HAS to be faced, because we have reached the limits to growth. If one is serious about ecology and about localisation, one has to be serious about restraining population. It is not proven that this can be done entirely by voluntary means. We may have to think, e.g., about limits to family size.... As I have argued in several posts during the last week, there is no voluntary-based way of reducing fossil fuel use.... That is going to require political action on an unprecedented global scale—it will make Seattle [the barbarous rioting in opposition to liberalized trade] look like a walk in the park.[16]

During the negotiations over a successor to the Kyoto Protocol, Friends of the Earth sent forth their messenger to remind us that "a climate change response must have at its heart a redistribution of wealth and resources."[17] After all, *that* is the point—not impacting the climate, as any analysis of the Kyoto's climactic effect reveals.

This threat of stealth socialism and the doomsday cultishness of warming alarmism were so spectacularly displayed in a Kyoto Protocol negotiation—during which UN Secretary General Ban Ki-moon threatened that the world risks oblivion if it refuses to bow to the Kyoto agenda,[18] that someone at the Vatican leaked the content of Pope Benedict XVI's January 1 address three weeks early. His remarks "launched a surprise attack on climate change prophets of doom, warning them that any solutions to global warming must be based on firm evidence and not on dubious ideology."[19] Goodness, does this mean the alarmists will call the Pope a heretic?

The final straw for the Pontiff may have been the contemporaneous remarks by one particular island nation's leader, demanding that other countries bestow upon his government many millions in the name of rising sea levels caused by global warming (while also building beachfront hotel resorts), and threatening that unless the wealthy acceded to these demands "the entire world will face sufferings that will far exceed the nightmare of the Tsunami."[20]

At this point we recall economics professor Bruce Yandle's description of the melding of otherwise incompatible interests in pursuit of governmental policies which both favor, as "Baptists and Bootlegger" coalitions, which in this case means the tag-team by the Enrons of the world with green pressure groups.

Who profits from alarmism? Many folks, but we can thank South Carolina senator and enthusiast of global warming alarmism Lindsey Graham for succinctly if accidentally reminding us how it is possible to do the right thing for the wrong reason. In a March 2008 speech to the Nuclear Energy Institute he observed, "The one way to gather support for nuclear energy is to embrace climate change because there's no way anyone can deny nuclear's place at the table as it provides a source of energy that doesn't pollute the planet." Yes, Senator, they figured that out some time ago.

About the same time it also was helpful to read that "leading green thinker Mayer Hillman [says] that rationing is the only way to prevent runaway climate change" because, "When the chips are down I think democracy is a less important goal than is the protection of the planet from the death of life, the end of life on it. [Carbon rationing] has got to be imposed on people whether they like it or not."[21] What with this being a global agenda, there are still some upsides. For example, "'The Chinese live in a totalitarian state,' [Hillman] points out. 'You don't

"Gore's off-planet fantasies about being some kind of new Timelord who speaks for the human species expose the anti-democratic strain in the politics of environmentalism. Many green-leaning leaders and spokesmen claim that the threat facing the planet is so dire that normal democratic debate and processes must be suspended in order to deal with it. Dictators of old used to impose states of emergency in order to freeze democracy; today's eco-megalomaniacs use the more PC phrase 'planetary emergency' in an attempt to justify allowing small groups of people to override the 'obstacle' of individual nations' democratic processes."

Brendan O'Neill in Spiked Online

have to persuade the Chinese, you've got to persuade the Chinese Government.'" How true. But could you at least try not to *smile* when you say that?

Hillman is by no means the sole alarmist noting the glories of communist China as a model for their green utopia. The authors of the 2007 book *The Climate Change Challenge and the Failure of Democracy*, admiringly vow that global warming can be effectively dealt with only by "an authoritarian form of government."[22] In the United States, the Left's lawyers have already crafted a blueprint to bypass our system's checks and balances such as the constitutional requirement that the Kyoto treaty be ratified before it is implemented, and even to get around the need for ratification entirely.[23] It is proving simply too problematic that the elected representatives refuse to do to the taxpayer what no free society would do to itself absent a threat of doomsday.[24]

It is perhaps for reasons of such reality that, we are told, we must go from "suffering" economic slowdown and "enjoying" economic growth to suffering the growth and enjoying the slowdown.[25] Toeing the popular "too important for democracy" line, green mouthpieces increasingly lament how, given current political freedoms, the necessary revolution might not be feasible. This is probably true, given our reluctance to even broadly accept their baby-step proposals of wearing rayon clothes, preferably hand-me-downs or consignment store purchases, to fight global warming.[26] Further, given how environmentalists regularly reject any proposed response that doesn't require significant changes in lifestyle and/or population (carbon capture and storage, CO_2 "scrubbers," nuclear power), their desired society will likely not come about voluntarily.

Vaclav Klaus's research led him to note the modern environmentalist practice of evoking a sense of peril "of undreamed-of magnitude" creating the obligation "to act quickly (possibly right now), without paying attention to details or costs of the newly employed measures."[27] Stop and ponder all of the environmentalist threats you have heard that carried the breathless insistence that "we must act now!" The answer is *all of them*. Global warming is merely the latest, best excuse for energy controls and economic interventions. And not just for energy. When confronted with overwhelming evidence that the economic costs of pretending to control the weather make the "mitigation" agenda politically unrealistic, alarmists respond by turning the alternate, certainly more rational approach of "adaptation" into an excuse for socialized medicine.[28]

To paraphrase a PhD economist with whom I work, in the global warming agenda we are dealing with a premise that, once adopted, leads to no other conclusion than to accept government control of nearly every aspect of our lives. This is nearly as much a reason that libertarians and conservatives are immediately suspicious of the agenda as for the Left's feverish embrace of it. Recall how throughout Europe the fallen communists found refuge in the "Green" parties. Doing its part if also ignoring history, the *New York Times* intones how we should fear the fall of communism in Cuba because it will mean such bad things for the environment[29] (poverty, despite all outward appearances, is apparently "green"; disregard what we found behind The Wall when it came down).

Does that sound extreme? Well, note how global warming is the political Left's Holy Grail. Global warming makes "market failure" completely ubiquitous if through the artifice of government fiat, raising it from a special case to a reason to regulate or tax every aspect of life. The claim is that everything we do emits CO_2, but we don't bear the costs of our emissions—global warming. The free market and the price system aren't working, then, so we need government intervention. This is why the alarmist industry gravely threatens our liberty. Just as its advocates regularly admit, if often in unguarded moments.

Making this eco-fundamentalism more dangerous is its particular appeal which allows it to advance in ways that pure, announced socialism fails. In this form, the proposition is no longer that industrial civilization is a pox upon the poor, but instead that its very instruments will bring ruin to the rich whose behavior destroys the earth. This appeal to self-interest resonates with people who otherwise reject the assault on capitalism as an evil exploiter of the weak.

In fact, as chairman of the George Mason University Economics Department Donald J. Boudreaux notes, "Al Gore, Robert Kennedy, Jr., and too many others...write and speak as if the material prosperity that capitalism brings is either not threatened by increased government power, or is of only small importance when compared to the threat of global warming."[30] The practical experiences of Klaus, Illarionov, and millions of others, however, speak to the contrary.

THE KYOTOPHILES' "LEVEL PLAYING FIELD" OF "GLOBAL GOVERNANCE"

The lowest-hanging fruit in this discussion has long been the November 2000 assertion by France's then-President Jacques Chirac that the Kyoto Protocol was "the first component of an authentic global governance." I was in the room in The Hague that day when he so praised Kyoto, only to thereby bury its chances for a while in the U.S. Before Chirac, the then-EU Environment Minister Margot Wallstrom had said, "Kyoto is about [the] economy, about leveling the playing field for big businesses worldwide." When confronted with these giddy admissions alarmists roll their eyes at what we are to dismiss as mere hortatory cheerleading by Europols.

Except, Kyoto is a Europe-driven endeavor. Further, Europe's experience puts meat on the bones of this rhetoric. So, consider further claims from other EU quarters. UK Prime Minister Gordon Brown came to the U.S. in April 2008 to hawk a post-Kyoto treaty that "must include an international carbon market as the surest and most efficient way to achieve our aims—eventually generating up to $100 billion dollars a year to fund 'green' development."[31] The meaning of that call for an international fund to put us all on a diet of preferred energy sources is clear. Brown's colleague, German Chancellor Angela Merkel, is a native of Communist East Germany, who learned the realities of socialism the hard way. She is considered a mild conservative in the very relative scheme of European politics, if still a proponent of the statist agenda. But she let the cat out of the bag when addressing the matter of international climate regimes during a speech in Kyoto. "The question is…what kind of measure do we use to create a just world?"[32]

So that's what this is about, moving things around a bit to create a "just world." Given who will be doing the judging, the answer to her question is *the imaginary kind*. President Klaus took the rare step of assailing how Frau Merkel enables alarmism, saying that although she is merely one among many "politicians, journalists and scientists [who] are exploiting an unproven issue for their own advantage…. 'She [also had] lived in a socialist society and she knows the dangers of ideologies that are aimed against freedom…. Utopia is an excellent escape for politicians because they can busy themselves with far-away goals and don't have to worry about immediate problems,' added Klaus. 'Climate change is an excellent issue for that escape.'"[33]

This is rough stuff in the clubby diplomatic world, and clearly he pulls no punches. Noting how environmentalism has become the vehicle for those who abhor individual liberties, Klaus quotes Marek Loužek of the Czech Centre for Economics and Politics, in the English version of his own book *Blue Planet in Green Shackles*, as saying that environmentalism "strives for the reform of the social order and for the removal of social and environmental injustices created by the operation of free markets."[34] Klaus also notes how numerous researchers have chronicled the striking similarities binding Fascist and Green Party ideologies and even slogans.

Writer Janet Biehl summarized well the Euro-statist mindset: "The ecological crisis is resolvable only through totalitarian

> "The most dangerous man to any government is the man who is able to think things out for himself, without regard to the prevailing superstitions and taboos."
>
> *H.L. Mencken*

means" and "an ecodictatorship' is needed,"[35] the obvious reason being that no free society would do to itself what the green agenda requires. As green guru Paul Ehrlich noted with a colleague, among the U.S. Constitution's deficiencies are the lack of the principles of mandatory population reduction in rich countries and poor alike; that "the overdeveloped countries must be de-developed" and "the underdeveloped countries must be semi-developed"; and most ominous that "[p]rocedures must be established to monitor and regulate the world system in a continuous effort to maintain an optimum balance between the population, resources and the environment."[36]

Leading environmentalist voices such as *The Guardian's* George Monbiot echoes the "too important for democracy" line, and the hysterics are increasingly open in supporting the idea that "global warming" policies are the perfect excuse for circumventing democratic institutions, imposing the agenda through unaccountable supranational bodies.[37] The notion is that we just can't trust democratic institutions and need a supranational, unaccountable institution, even if administered through central banks of the various nations so loathed by the anti-globalist environmental movement.

The notion that climate change is a suitable vehicle for pursuing other means such as Chirac's dream of "global governance" or "a just world" found another adherent in Christine Stewart, Canada's environment minister at the time of Kyoto's agreement. She swooned to the *Calgary Herald* in 1998 that "no matter if the science is all phony, there are still collateral environmental benefits" to global warming policies.[38] Actually, she has no idea what she is talking about, as carbon scarcity schemes are widely recognized as the least efficient (most expensive) means to achieve reductions in actual pollutants such as sulfur and mercury. What Ms. Stewart and others toeing this line presumably mean is that there are *ideological* benefits to imposing the agenda even if the science is phony.

This may help explain why governments fund groups to lobby for the global warming agenda, including even more such taxes and "trading" (rationing) schemes. For example:

> The European Commission is giving millions of pounds of taxpayers' money to environmental campaigners to run lobbying operations in Brussels, the BBC has learned. Among the organisations to benefit is Friends of the Earth Europe (FoE), which received almost half of its funding from the EU in 2007.... In 2006 the EU gave more than 7.7m euros (£5.5m; $11.2m) to at least 40 environmental organisations to help them lobby in Brussels. They included big campaign groups such as WWF (World Wide Fund for Nature) and FoE Europe. They are both in the Green 10, a powerful environmental lobbying network which works closely with the European Commission, the European Parliament and the Council of Ministers.[39]

Or, as leading Danish newspaper *Berlingske Tidende* revealed, one might do what the previous (Social Democrat) regime did, and have a governmental department pay outside "researchers" and academics to agitate about how climate change requiring massive state intervention is *too* Man-made.[40] Such nefarious work, this, of paying researchers to advocate a particular position while pretending to be independent—someone ought to check and see if that is something about which the alarmist industry has ever expressed an opinion? I kid, of course, as this is the first thing said about anyone who dares challenge alarmist dogma with data.

You really can't blame the particular agency involved, Denmark's energy department, which you have to understand oversees a *quarter of a billion dollars per year* in subsidies just for windmills alone—small country, huge amount—and the larger social agenda hinges in great part on this gambit succeeding. *Sorry, just can't risk having the fiefdom brought down with facts.* Denmark's Environment Minister under the succeeding coalition government of (classical) liberals and conservatives also even "openly admitted that the greenhouse gas levy was a source of income for the state and no longer an environmental measure."[41]

Fallen alarmist Dr. David Evans of Australia was an early climate modeler for the state, only to ultimately walk away from the task after realizing that the data simply didn't support the faith, the industry it had created, or certainly the agenda. He writes:

> ... the idea that carbon emissions were causing global warming passed from the scientific community into the political realm, and actions started to happen. Research increased, bureaucracies were formed, international committees met, and eventually the Kyoto protocol was signed in 1997—with the aim of curbing carbon emissions.
>
> And the political realm, in turn, fed money back into the scientific community. By the late 1990s, lots of jobs depended on the idea that carbon emissions caused global warming. Many of them were bureaucratic, but there were a lot of science jobs created too. I was on that gravy train, making a high wage in a science job that would not have existed if we didn't believe carbon emissions caused global warming. And so were lots of people around me; and there were international conferences full of such people. And we had political support, the ear of government, big budgets, and we felt fairly important and useful (well, I did anyway). It was great.[42]

Yet the true nature of the agenda became inescapable, and to his credit he walked.

What a terrific racket. Establish an agenda that demands giving people like you greater budgets, and even control over economic and individual liberties. Then you fund bureaucracies and outside groups who have created a financial stake in the agenda (fundraising, consultancies, emission verification, etc.), and turn to them for "objective advice" that what you are doing is necessary and must be enhanced.

This is big money, and a staple of modern university budgets. No wonder "The University of California system, for example, is preparing to spend $500 million [in taxpayer dollars] to create a think tank to analyze global warming and the Public Utilities Commission has adopted a decision which will spend $600 million more for a separate think tank to study the issue. That's $1.1 billion being spent to just 'think' about the problem at the same time the State of California is moving forward with regulations that may or may not work but will cost businesses and consumers billions of dollars to implement."[43] So taxpayer dollars are being lavished on a university project to declare a pressing need for even more taxpayer dollars, spending on universities, and regulations. Shame.

THINK GLOBALLY, TAX GLOBALLY

A full decade after Chirac's "global governance" remarks, the transfer and indeed redistribution of wealth remain the driving rhetorical and programmatic force behind negotiations for a "global warming" treaty. At the December 2007 Kyoto talks in Bali the idea was pushed yet again. This time it was formally presented by the Swiss, if touted, as always, by green pressure groups (who no doubt would find themselves recipients of certain portions of the tens of billions of dollars the tax sought to redistribute, as they've designed consultancies for themselves under Kyoto).[44]

As an alternative, economist Ross McKitrick proposes that policymakers consider a tax (at the country level) directly tied to temperatures: no warming, no tax; big warming, big tax.[45] Given there has been no warming in a decade and how, upon scrutiny of their behavior, it is difficult to believe that most of the global warming industry actually believe their doomsaying, this will certainly go nowhere.

Reason magazine's Ron Bailey scoured the Bali discussions, listening to the proposals. He reported another iteration, an idea floated by a UN-accredited climate counselor called Greenhouse Development Rights Framework (GDR). Their plan involves a climate "consumption luxury tax" to be levied on every person on the planet earning beyond a "development threshold" of $9,000 per year.[46]

This has long been a consistent theme, manifest at all of the Kyoto talks that I have attended over the years. It is grounded in the notion that wealthy countries are that way in large part because they went through stages of industrialization that involved putting, or rather returning, large amounts of the trace gas CO_2 into the system. As Bailey notes, this means that—under the anthropogenic warming theory—that leaves less space for poor people to emit as they develop.

"In one scenario, Americans would pay the equivalent of a $780 per person luxury tax annually, which amounts to sending $212 billion per year in climate reparations to poor countries to aid their development and help them adapt to climate change."[47] Most global warming activists would blink, not at the amount of the price tag but that these folks bothered to attach one at all.

Of course, nowhere do the demanded reparations scenarios recognize that the rich world's consumption is and will remain the principal source for poor countries' own development, such as it is. But-for our carbon footprint, most of these countries would simply be corrupt kleptocracies *without* export markets.

Bailey ran the numbers and came to a total annual "climate reparation" from rich to poor countries of over $600 billion. "This contrasts with a new report commissioned by the U.N.

Development Program that only demands $86 billion per year to avoid 'adaptation apartheid.'"

Why, foreign aid has worked out so splendidly, why *not* massively increase it? It is no more absurd than increasing the school system's budget in the District of Columbia, where we see a similar relationship between money spent and despair.

Adding such new huge sums to the wretched waste that already exists in this transfer of wealth from the poor in rich countries to the rich in poor countries asks us to continue ignoring that poor countries are poor in great part because of their regimes' refusal or inability to provide a transparent judiciary and respect for property rights, and so investors see the risk as outweighing the reward. These are the parties who will receive and, ahem, administer the new booty of "climate aid" or reparations.

"The [GDR report's] authors do not go into any specifics about what kinds of institutions—private, public, or partnerships— would annually transfer $212 billion to poor countries from the U.S. Considering that the $2.3 trillion spent on foreign aid in the past 50 years has largely failed to generate economic growth or permanent improvements in living standards for most people living in poor countries, the institutional question is not trivial. By some estimates lifting trade barriers could produce benefits of $600 billion annually, reducing the number of people living on $2 per day by 144 million."[48]

Bailey notes that one woman in the audience warned that such climate aid would simply vanish into the kleptocrats' pockets, not lift poor people out of poverty. "But the touching faith of climate campaigners in the efficacy of international and national bureaucracies is immune to such realities," Bailey concluded.

Of course, "tax" is not a word that greatly assists their cause so the greens strive to craft softer, more appealing approaches such as "an atmospheric trust to slow global warming." Alternately called a "sky trust" by the global governance set, this entails establishing a supranational body to manage a global rationing or cap-and-trade scheme. We actually have one of those, called the UN, but it has a sufficiently shady history as to not warrant trust of the target of this scheme, the U.S. public.

Regardless, after this unnamed body auctions off the ration coupons its "trustees distribute some fraction of this sum back to the world on a per-capita basis. This would give political cover to countries like India and China, while simultaneously giving them incentive to use the most climate-friendly energy sources possible." This, too, is called redistribution of wealth, from successful states to unsuccessful ones.[49]

Naturally, the Third World joins those playing off of the slavery reparations argument to wrench more direct wealth transfers from the West in the name of global warming, on top of the more indirect argument for transfers via Kyoto's existing mechanisms. "Rich countries must give poor nations more aid to help them overcome the impact of global warming, international experts have told an EU conference.... 'There is here a phenomenon of an extreme injustice,' [UN Development Programme chief Kemal] Davis said. 'There is an issue of historical responsibility which we cannot escape.'"[50]

Indeed, one Chinese diplomat makes expressly clear that "negotiations on a new treaty to fight global warming will fail if rich nations are not treated as 'culprits' and developing countries as 'victims.'"[51] Brazil's President Luiz Inacio Lula da Silva also weighed in, calling the Third World "victims of deforestation"—which, obviously, is a *developing*-country practice, not something rich countries do—and "victims of the global warming." "Although Lula admitted the importance of preserving the environment, he said it was necessary to take into consideration the social and economic needs of local populations,"[52] complaining that "rich countries consume 80 percent of the natural resources of the planet. They have to pay a trade-off to poor countries for them to conserve the environment."[53]

Bolivia's president was even less circumspect, arguing that in the name of saving the planet, well, "we have a duty to put an end to the capitalist system."[54]

Drill down into any given story, negotiation or discussion, and you will see that all of this is directed at the U.S. After all, by merely outperforming Europe when it comes to actual emissions performance and climate research, the "climate criminal" U.S. is engaged in "climate racism," "climate terrorism," and "climate genocide."[55]

ABUSING THE INSTITUTIONS OF GOVERNMENT IN ORDER TO EXPAND THEM

Anecdotes abound of big government advocates using the global warming issue as another excuse to get more of what they want: more and bigger government. Senate Majority Leader Harry Reid of Nevada touts massive federal ownership of a state's land as a virtue for enabling massive deployment of windmills in the name of global warming, which is to say, ritually devaluing the land as few private landowners would;[56] it's a good thing for the birds that those things don't turn very often. San Francisco appointed a "city climate chief" at a $160,000 salary, on top of the at least two dozen other city employees already purportedly working on climate change issues.[57] The Taxpayers Alliance in the UK has found that, e.g., the London Borough of Tower Hamlets—the poorest borough in London—has fifty-eight such bureaucrats on its payroll.

Clearly, just as you've got to spend money to make money, the big-government crowd needs to flex some to gain more. I at first found it humorous when, in a federal court in California, the state's attorney general Bill Lockyer sought all e-mail communication between auto companies and a list of eighteen climate skeptics, including me. The basis for the request was that I and "a few other high-profile greenhouse skeptics have proven extraordinarily adept at draining the issue of all sense of crisis."[58] I would blush but, if the circus we are witnessing around us is one drained of the crisis atmosphere, I would hate to see the results of us skeptics being only moderately adept. Knowing as I do that, at least in my case, there were no communications, this was pure fishing and an effort at intimidation.

Lockyer's trial lawyer pals have big plans for "global warming" by the way. Australian "human rights lawyer Julian Burnside says wasting electricity could become a criminal offence in the foresee-able future.... 'If we come to general agreement that part of the problem is that people are using too much electricity, then you have to create a regime that encourages people to use less electric-ity, you might make it an offence to waste electricity,' Mr. Burnside told ABC Radio."[59] Lawyers teaming up with the state—here, state AGs—to, as Burnside put it, "target large companies" is a lucrative and growing field, chasing jobs away from those on the lower rungs of our economic ladder to those in dirtier, often highly corrupt countries. Presumably this benefits human rights.

In the U.S., "Research by [law firm] Arnold & Porter shows that about 100 climate change-related lawsuits have been filed in the United States so far. And an activist at an ABA conference designed to prime the industry for its next boondoggle, crowed that "global warming litigation is the next asbestos and tobacco for lawyers in America."[60] Just what our economy needed.

NON-DISCRIMINATING HATRED

While more than willing to trot out anti-skeptic chestnuts, the global warming industry actually just hates *people*, period. Espe-cially the kind that are born. Remember, while normal people see a human being and see a soul and a mind and a set of hands, global warming activists and environmentalists generally just see a stom-ach, one that is going to cause their precious Gaia heartburn. As such, they want government to get to work making you pay dearly for your sins.

Mark Steyn somehow isolates the humorous angle in even the most heartbreaking tragedy—and, when the greens are involved, you're guaranteed both. He wielded his rapier to bring our attention to "something new that took hold in the year 2007: a radical anti-humanism, long present just below the surface, [which] bobbed up and became explicit and respectable."[61] Steyn cites examples including the UK's Optimum Population Trust storming that "the biggest cause of climate change is climate changers—in other words, human beings"—*other* human beings, they mean, what with warming alarmists Ted Turner, Al Gore, and the like typically procreating in numbers recklessly disregarding Gaia—and academics calling for "voluntary child-reduction."

This fear and loathing of the diaper set, Steyn expounds, is rooted in the philosophy that "'every person who is born . . . produces more rubbish, more pollution, more greenhouse gases, and adds to the problem of overpopulation.' We are the pollution; sterilization is the solution. The best way to bequeath a more sustainable environment to our children is not have any. What's the 'pro-choice' line? 'Every child should be wanted'? Not anymore. The progressive position has subtly evolved: Every child should be unwanted."[62]

As my colleague Iain Murray points out in his book, *The Really Inconvenient Truths: Seven Environmental Disasters Liberals Won't Tell You About (Because They Helped Cause Them)*, it is not an accident that the head of the Sierra Club was once political director of Zero Population Growth. It is, after all, the global warming movement whom we have to thank for renewed calls to tax babies. The most recent version Down Under wants to ding you breeders a $5,000 per-child birth tax, plus $800 in annual carbon tax for each child born after your second.[63] Elected climate crusaders in the U.S. also reveal their moral compulsion to modestly propose and even extend this insanity, so why stop there? In addition to those levies, they ought to call for elimination of the dependent child tax credit for all children, elimination of federal income, health, education, and nutrition entitlement benefits for children after the first two, and a new $1,000 car tax on each that seats more than four.

One professor saw the Aussies' proposed carbon tax and raised the pot with "carbon credits" for those who get sterilized.[64] As Steyn noted, "That would be great news for female eco-activists boasting in London's Daily Mail how they had their tubes tied and babies aborted to save the planet."[65] Other revealing advocacy includes "Melbourne University population guru Prof. Short [saying] 'We need to develop a one-child family policy because we are the global warmers...[and]...Climate Care is offering to offset emissions from jet travel by hiring poor Indians to use manual treadle pumps—once used in British prisons—rather than diesel pumps to pump irrigation water: 'Sometimes the best source of renewable energy is the human body itself.'"[66]

Of course, this also requires elimination of the home mortgage interest deduction for houses larger than 3,000 square feet, a version of which has the endorsement of the Democratic chairman of the U.S. House of Representatives' Energy Committee. By offering a government-sponsored per *family* living space quota—not even *per capita*—the movement and its political patrons reveal their anti-people philosophy.

In truth, anyone who crunches the numbers must admit that is impossible to meet the 70 percent emission-reduction targets in the leading U.S. Senate global warming bills without population controls.[67] As economist Ross McKitrick details in a (at publication, still draft) paper for the Competitive Enterprise Institute, barring some miracle technology making zero-emitting energy as affordable as fossil fuels, reducing U.S. emissions by the demanded quantities while maintaining today's standard of living provided by fossil fuels means cutting our population by more than half of what it is projected to be, down from today's 300 million to about 170 million.

To put this in perspective, note that only Haiti and Somalia currently produce emissions at a level even remotely consistent with what's required for an 80 percent reduction in the world's emissions. "If everyone in the world lived as they do in these two countries, we'd have the emissions challenge licked."[68]

No U.S. politician has dared utter the specifics of the agenda carried out to these obvious next-steps, but its adherents across the pond aren't so bashful, given the repellent infection of their body politic with the enviro-bug. London's *Mirror* reported:

> People should stop having babies to combat global warming, a top Liberal Democrat said yesterday.Chris Davies reckons population control would be far more efficient than trying to cut pollution.And the North West MEP wants his plan to be considered by the EU. He said all governments should look at measures to discourage people having large families.[69]

Davies had written in a local paper, "What's the single most effective thing couples can do to play a part in combating global warming? It is to have no more than one child."[70]

Again with the China-idolizing. Indeed, leaders from Europe and the UN recently lauded China's demand that it be given credit due to its emission "reductions" (sic), though they clearly mean "avoidance," achieved due to its coercive one-child policy. Reuters reported:

> Efforts undertaken by developing countries (i.e. Brazil, China, India and Mexico) for reasons other than climate change have reduced [sic] their emissions growth over the past 3 decades by approximately 500 million tonnes of carbon dioxide a year," according to a technical (UN) summary seen by Reuters.
>
> ...China's one-child per couple policy introduced in the early 1980s, for instance, had a side-effect of braking global warming by limiting the population to 1.3 billion against a projected 1.6 billion without the policy. "This has reduced

greenhouse gas emissions," [China's EPA chief] told a conference in Oslo last month.[71]

Elsewhere, "China says its one-child policy has helped the fight
against global warming by avoiding 300 million births, the equivalent of the population of the United States.... China, which
rejects criticism that it is doing too little to confront climate
change, says that its population is now 1.3 billion against 1.6 billion if it had not imposed tough birth control measures in the late
1970s."[72] However, "Beijing says that fewer people means less
demand for energy and lower emissions of heat-trapping gases
from burning fossil fuels."[73]

Ever bashful of boasting, China made clear that "this is only an
illustration of the actions we have taken." Of course. But, please
spare us the details of the rest of your program.

Now, should we accept this horror then the U.S. is entitled to a
large claim of emissions avoided, too, given Al Gore's assertion in
Earth in the Balance that "any child born into the hugely con-
sumptionist way of life so common in the industrial world will
have an impact that is, on average, many times more destructive
than that of a child born in the developing world."[74] As my colleague Myron Ebell commented, "The Chinese are correct that
they have done more than anyone to [avoid] emissions through
their reprehensible population control policies. We could make the
same claim about our unlimited abortion policies."[75]

Still, allow me to suggest that the suburban, "soft" environmentalists among you, nodding in acceptance at politicians who push
the global warming hype as sounding like they care and maybe
deserve your support: Ask yourself, is this a game we should be
playing?

Apparently, *yes*, at least according to the greens. "We must end
world population growth, then reduce population size. That
means lowering population numbers in industrialised as well as

developing nations."[76] Given that women and other minorities are both, well, majorities of the population, surely this would disproportionately harm them? Possibly the UN could investigate itself for promoting such policies. There must be some kickbacks they can arrange as part of the process.

This agenda of the global warming activist is often phrased far less delicately; the above offering is courtesy of an advocate who was granted prominent placement for his views by the ultimate in establishment media, the quasi-governmental BBC.

As you see, the global warming movement is about a lot of things, and these things often change depending upon to whom you are speaking. The General Electric executive might not be so keen on openly pushing Chinese coercive family-planning policies, just as some environmentalists may not be so hot on the massive subsidies and mandates that GE seeks for their products *to save the planet*. But it demonstrably is *not* about the climate.

> "Global warming is quickly becoming the one-stop shop for almost every variety of social engineer and closet authoritarian who hankers to boss the rest of us around. Those who want to dictate where Americans live, including the size of their houses and lots, what they drive or whether they drive, and even what they eat, need only link their goal to the campaign against global warming to infuse it with moral force. You don't have to be a global warming skeptic (I'm certainly not) to be disturbed by this trend."
>
> *Vincent Carroll*, Rocky Mountain News, *October 16, 2007*

AMERICAN ROYALTY

Presumably because they are rarely exposed to the Euro-candor discussed above, many American elites fawn over the prospect of molding this nation along the lines of our intellectual, moral, and environmental superiors, the Europeans. It was in apery of this crowd that an official press release on United States Senate letter-head blared, "Rockefeller and Snowe Demand That Exxon Mobil End Funding of Campaign That Denies Global Climate Change."[77] Speech that contradicts or simply disagrees with politicians pushing the global warming agenda is apparently a very dangerous thing. How else to explain the use of taxpayer-funded resources to "Demand that the World's Largest Oil Maker Make Public Its History of Funding Climate Change 'Skeptics'"?

In 2006, these two senators, Republican Olympia Snowe of Maine and Democrat Jay Rockefeller of West Virginia, teamed up to threaten the CEO of ExxonMobil, a company that the green industry had identified as public enemy No. 1 for its failure to completely buckle to their wishes. Both senators sit on the powerful Senate Finance Committee, which writes tax legislation, and unleashed this letter and media campaign at the same time that anti-energy forces and their allies were openly discussing efforts to specifically target energy producers for major tax hikes. The point was clearly made.

Using language like "demand" and "'come clean' about its past denial activities," these two deep-thinkers, who it is fair to presume have never read a peer-reviewed climate-related research paper in their lives, also demanded in code that ExxonMobil join the legions of rent-seeking and appeasing industry who support the alarmist agenda (demanding that "the corporation take positive steps by a date certain toward a new and more responsible corporate citizenship").

Among ExxonMobil's "denial" activities was to give financial support not exclusively to "environmentalist" groups (as we euphemize the anti-energy, anti-growth, anti-people industry) but to also have supported others including the Competitive Enterprise Institute whose insistence on an open debate about climate science and policy constitutes "climate change denial" (actually, neither

Big Government235

CEI nor I receive, or at the time received, support from ExxonMobil, yet oddly I and CEI are still around, which surely causes great confusion at meetings in the fever swamp).

First, these senators had obviously not exactly steeped themselves in ExxonMobil's stance on climate change any more than they had kept current on the company's assertions of what groups it supported. So here we see some of the CIA's noisiest critics making that Agency's search for WMDs appear thorough and accurate by comparison. Our Potomac Sages apparently relied for their wisdom on press releases from green groups and the UK's Royal Society, as their boogeyman corporation also did not deny that climate changes and is changing, nor did it deny that Man likely has some role.

In fact, ExxonMobil's "denial" had sunk to the vicious levels of, well, pledging only $100 million to Stanford University "to[ward] researching new options for commercially viable, technological systems for energy supply and use which have the capability to substantially reduce greenhouse emissions,"[78] and more still to green pet projects. The company's crime was to *support speech* of others who honestly state that neither the science nor the wisdom of policy responses are settled ("climate change denial front groups").

That had to be attacked, and at your expense. The reason was simple: although the previously Exxon-supported CEI (as were many others including green pressure groups) hardly "denied" climate change the senators complained that it had "made it increasingly difficult for the United States to demonstrate the moral clarity it needs across all facets of its diplomacy." That is, thanks to other voices being heard, the public was sufficiently informed so as to make it risky for such scolds to burden the family budget with the Kyoto agenda to satisfy the vanity of political elites. The important point here wasn't accuracy, of course, but intimidation, and ensuring that people who insist on facts be knocked out of the debate.

As my CEI colleague Marlo Lewis wrote, the Snowe-Rockefeller missive was "a follow-up to a letter sent to ExxonMobil's British subsidiary by the Royal Society of London urging the company to stop funding organizations that 'misinform the public' about climate change. Since the Royal Society gets most of its funding from the British Government, Snowe and Rockefeller should at least have wondered what *raison d'etat* the Royal Society might be serving."[79]

Lewis suggested that possibly "Snowe and Rockefeller should have written a letter to the Royal Society reminding that body that (a) the U.S.A. is no longer a British colony, and (b) the U.S. Senate does not appreciate foreign meddling in our internal affairs."

The *Wall Street Journal* smelled the rat and weighed in, saying, "Washington has no shortage of bullies, but even we can't quite believe an October 27 letter that Senators Jay Rockefeller and Olympia Snowe sent to ExxonMobil CEO Rex Tillerson. Its message: Start toeing the Senators' line on climate change, or else.... This is amazing stuff. On the one hand, the Senators say that everyone agrees on the facts and consequences of climate change. But at the same time they are so afraid of debate that they want Exxon to stop financing a doughty band of dissenters who can barely get their name in the paper.... The Senators' letter is far more serious because they have enormous power to punish Exxon if it doesn't kowtow to them. A windfall profits tax is in the air, and we've seen what happens to other companies that dare to resist Congressional intimidation."[80]

The *Journal* also noted one of the alarmists' many double standards, without which their movement would be a mere, embarrassing footnote in history: "Imagine if this letter had been sent by someone in the Bush Administration trying to enforce the opposite conclusion? The left would be howling about 'censorship.' That's exactly what did happen earlier this year after James Hansen, the NASA scientist and global warming evangelist, complained that a lowly twenty-four-year-old press aide had tried to limit his media access. The entire episode was preposterous because Mr. Hansen is one of the most publicized scientists in the world, but the press aide was nonetheless sacked."

"DO SOMETHING ABOUT THESE PEOPLE"

While the Rockefeller-Snowe comedy act was extreme, it was not isolated. The leader of another of the UK's major political parties encouraged the government to "do something about" skeptics, suggesting the government boycott industry that dares to support such speech:

> I ask the Secretary of State to consider what to do about the remaining climate change deniers, who include multinational corporations. . . . I ask the House: should we be buying fuel from people such as ExxonMobil? I do not want even indirectly to be helping to fund bodies such as the International Policy Network and the Competitive Enterprise Institute. I do not think that the Government should do so either.[81]

On the heels of a spectacularly unsuccessful private sector boycott of ExxonMobil's UK subsidiary by others holding the same extreme view that companies need to fall in line with whatever is fashionable, this gentleman sought to use government (which is to say taxpayer expenditures) as a way to teach a rough lesson about speech. This dwarfs petty efforts by Team Gore to date such as leaning on Nashville authorities to deny his critics their right to speak against his agenda in ways highlighting his shameless hypocrisy.[82]

Australian politician Kelvin Thomson leaned on individual companies, expressing his sincere hope that they know better than to support dissent. Doing his best Brando-as-Corleone, he wrote that global warming is bad for us and seemingly indicated that supporting people who oppose him might be even less healthy:

> [G]lobal warming is happening, it is man-made, and it is not good for us....I am writing to ask whether your company has donated any money to the Institute for Public Affairs, the International Policy Network, the American Enterprise Institute, the Competitive Enterprise Institute, the European Science and Environment Forums or any other body which spreads misinformation or undermines the scientific consensus concerning global warming. If your company has donated such money in the past, is it continuing to do so? If so, I request that your company cease such financial support.[83]

Using the bully pulpit of elected office in a slightly different fashion, recall how back in the States it was liberal Republican congressman (now retired) Sherwood Boehlert who embarrassed himself and ultimately set the entire alarmist movement back by years when he enlisted the National Academies of Science in his service to weigh in on the controversy surrounding the IPCC's "smoking gun," the "Hockey Stick" from its 2001 Third Assessment Report.

Boehlert requested the NAS involve itself, not to examine the taxpayer-funded claim which had come under such withering and obviously discrediting criticism, but to take out after those questioning it! The result of this effort to intimidate the individuals exposing the fraud was to completely defrock the "Hockey Stick," which supposed "smoking gun" was without ceremony dropped from the next IPCC Report.[84] This was typically clumsy of such bullying if more satisfyingly counterproductive.

In the Spring of 2007 I was slated to speak on a panel in the European Parliament in Brussels, which debate and discussion would be followed by a screening of the film *The Great Global Warming Swindle*. Reflecting the free-speech tolerance of alarmists, generally, Swedish MEP Anders Wijkman sought to block the screening. He failed, thanks to the dogged persistence of one of the biggest thorns in the Eurocrats' sides, Roger Helmer, MEP from the UK.

Al Gore, of course, has a long history of using the powers of governmental office to bully critics of his alarmist views, whom he also has a continuing record of smearing.[85] His legacy lives on in the myriad "investigative" activities undertaken by Congressman Henry Waxman. In early 2007 Waxman held a hearing on "Political Interference with Science: Global Warming." The principal objective seemed to be to smear former White House aide Phil Cooney for doing his job as Chief of Staff at the Council on Environmental Quality. Cooney was demonized for reviewing and editing the office's policy work product on climate change— specifically, the latest edition of *Our Changing Planet*, which plainly stated in its subtitle, "A Supplement to the President's Fiscal Year 2004 and 2005 Budgets"—as a non-scientist, just as were his two predecessors under the Clinton-Gore administration, even if he did so with more extensive formal educational credentials.

The politics of the issue, however, are what matter. The climate reports under Clinton-Gore were so useless as policy tools, and also in violation of their statutory authority, that they led to litigation (by yours truly) which resulted in agreement by the government to attach a disclaimer to them. Humorously, to this day the alarmists alternately dismiss and hyperventilate over that achievement.

Yet no media frenzy or political outrage ensued over those documents' obvious politicization, outside of three lawmakers who joined CEI as plaintiffs. No hearings, no congressional attorneys demanding depositions.

Are such intimidation tactics worth it? As one talk show host skeptically asked while I was promoting *The Politically Incorrect Guide™ to Global Warming*, "Isn't this a lot of trouble to go to just to stop progress?" You might think so, yes. But stopping progress, depending on how one views progress, isn't necessarily the goal. The goal is instead the same thing driving politicization of any issue, particularly by the "progressive" Left: control and imposition of one's ideology.

The transparency of the goal will surely prove this movement's downfall. Remember how even in the UK, where the broadest polling on the matter seems to have occurred, most of the public admit to having been scared by global warming alarmism yet also see the agenda as simply an excuse to impose revenue-raisers on the public, cloaked in green guilt.[86] In the U.S., despite the hundreds of millions spent to frighten the public into accepting the agenda, Gallup found that global warming ranks ninth among twelve environmental concerns—with concern having fallen in 2008 compared to 2007.[87] Those who live by the hype also die by it: safe drinking water, the lack of which has not been an actual threat in the U.S. for decades, comes in first. So, 48 percent of Americans claim they are unwilling to spend even a single penny more in gasoline taxes to reduce greenhouse gas emissions, and 76 percent aren't willing to spend as much as 50 cents. The latter is an actual proposal, if the most radical to date, which nonetheless wouldn't according to anyone do a thing about the climate.[88]

The U.S. and UK experiences do not appear to be aberrant, with the Canadian government also having spent $26 million in 2004 on a campaign to convince the public to change their behavior in the name of global warming, only to see it completely flop.[89] All of which is to say that the public gets it. As other research (that for some reason shocked the alarmists) reveals, the more people learn about "global warming" the less alarmed they are about it.[90]

A CASE STUDY IN ABUSING GOVERNMENT
TO GROW GOVERNMENT: "STAGECRAFT"

As Rockefeller, Snowe, Waxman, Boehlert, and others make plain, the United States Congress is particularly fevered (and bipartisan) in its effort to capitalize on the global warming panic that it does so much to foster, and whose membership seeks to so greatly benefit from. For decades, members of Congress have used their platform to try and frighten the public into accepting legislative salvation in the form of wealth confiscation and redistribution, and otherwise push pet programs and pay off constituencies.

The PBS series *Frontline* aired a special in April 2007 which, as noted elsewhere in these pages, revealed how brazen the agenda-driven media can be to construct the necessary artifices for their story. It also lifted the curtain on the sort of illusions that politicians and their abettors originally employed to kick off the campaign.

Frontline interviewed key players in the June 1988 Senate hearing at which then-Senator Al Gore rolled out the official conversion from panic over "global cooling" to global warming alarmism. *Frontline* interviewed Gore's colleague, then-Senator Tim Wirth (now running Ted Turner's UN Foundation). Apparently comforted by the friendly nature of the PBS program, Wirth freely admitted the clever scheming that went into getting the dramatic shot of scientist James Hansen mopping his brow amid a sweaty press corps. An admiring *Frontline* termed this "Stagecraft."[91]

SEN. TIMOTHY WIRTH (D-CO), 1987–1993: We knew there was this scientist at NASA, you know, who had really identified the human impact before anybody else had done so and was very certain about it. So we called him up and asked him if he would testify.

DEBORAH AMOS: On Capitol Hill, Sen. Timothy Wirth was one of the few politicians already concerned about global warming, and he was not above using a little stagecraft for Hansen's testimony.

TIMOTHY WIRTH: We called the Weather Bureau and found out what historically was the hottest day of the summer. Well, it was June 6th or June 9th or whatever it was. So we scheduled the hearing that day, and bingo, it was the hottest day on record in Washington, or close to it.

DEBORAH AMOS: *[on camera]* Did you also alter the temperature in the hearing room that day?

TIMOTHY WIRTH: What we did is that we went in the night before and opened all the windows, I will admit, right, so that the air conditioning wasn't working inside the room. And so when the—when the hearing occurred, there was not only bliss, which is television cameras and double figures, but it was really hot.

[Shot of witnesses at hearing] WIRTH: Dr. Hansen, if you'd start us off, we'd appreciate it.

The wonderful Jim Hansen was wiping his brow at the table at the hearing, at the witness table, and giving this remarkable testimony.

[nice shot of a sweaty Hansen]

JAMES HANSEN: *[June 1988 Senate hearing]* Number one, the earth is warmer in 1988 than at any time in the history of instrumental measurements. Number two, the global warming is now large enough that we can ascribe, with a high degree of confidence, a cause-and-effect relationship to the greenhouse effect.[92]

This dialogue speaks for itself, though it is worth noting Wirth's excitement about having heard of some scientist *who had identified this before anyone*, "this" being a new excuse for imposing a long-held agenda. At least when climate rationalists find holes in the alarmist thesis, *identifying something before anyone else*—for example, a cooling trend, a relationship between the sun and temperatures, corrupted siting of surface temperature measuring instruments, etc.—is characterized as fringe; given that it runs against the pols' agenda, this also means it is ignored. Hansen therefore had to be the focus of some media-enabled showmanship.

PHILIP SHABECOFF, *NEW YORK TIMES*, 1959–1991: If he hadn't said what he had said, it would not have become the major issue and scientists would not have taken it up the way they did after that. It was a major breakthrough. Certainly, it was a major political breakthrough.

JAMES HANSEN: I said that I was 99 percent confident that the world really was getting warmer and that there was a high degree of probability that it was due to human-made greenhouse gases. And I think it was the 99 percent probability statement which got a lot of attention.

TIMOTHY WIRTH: I mean, this was a very, very brave statement. I mean, he was on the edge of the science. He's working for the federal government, and certainly, this was not cleared, you know, far up the line, what he had to say. So the summary of what Jim Hansen had to say that year, plus the fact that it had gotten so much attention—but I thought we were going to move a lot more rapidly than we did.

DEBORAH AMOS: *[voice-over]* As it turned out, the country had more immediate concerns. In 1991, the first President Bush launched the first Gulf war. Then global warming seemed to stop—briefly.

So, best of all, from the perspective of people like the typical *Frontline* viewer, the Wirth/Gore/Hansen show worked. Or, would have, according to *Frontline*, had that clever George H. W. Bush not started a war three years later to distract us all from Congress's zeal and brilliance.

THE BUREAUCRACY BLOB

Not every step on Big Green's path to Big(ger) Government is quite so facially extreme as jailing or censoring us skeptics, as we shall see many actually call for. But the specter of using the power of the state as the means to reach the end of evermore of the same is rapidly increasing. Behold Tom Boggus, "associate director for resource development with the Texas Forest Service, [who] told attendees it was pointless to debate whether pollution is linked to climate change. 'Global climate change is a fact because the policymakers say it is, regardless of what you may think.'"[93]

As a practical matter, Boggus is correct. And it is not merely the elected policymakers who are reaching for the brass ring of global warming governance. In early 2008 internal battles took place within the U.S. Environmental Protection Agency, whose career employees were positively giddy with excitement over the opportunity dangled before them by the Supreme Court to regulate carbon dioxide emissions. CO_2 would surely be the most ubiquitous emission they could ever hope to have authority over, and the Court ruled that they either exercise it, or explain why not. It was the timidity by EPA's political types over explaining why this was neither wise nor warranted which got them before the Court in the first place, so this was a rather ominous choice.

It was also an obvious one, at least to the career employees at EPA: *regulate, and fast!* Lost in the discussion was that EPA was neither ordered to do so nor was it given a timetable to respond to this choice.

This mess springs from the Supreme Court's reckless 5–4 decision in April 2007 in *Massachusetts v. EPA*, decreeing that CO_2 is an "air pollutant" under the Clean Air Act (CAA) on the grounds that although the Act lists what it considers pollutants, it also defines the terms "air pollutant" and "air pollution," and in so doing used wording that the Court deemed broad enough that Congress probably really intended CO_2 as well, if without saying so.[94] Dissenting, Justice Scalia noted that this opinion means that EPA also should consider regulating everything "from Frisbees to flatulence" as pollutants.

Please Justice Scalia, don't give these people any suggestions.

As 2008 continued, there was an obvious urgency among the global warming industry, including politicians who sought the agenda but not so badly as to actually vote for the thing, to ensure that this regulatory behemoth like so many before it came under a Republican administration. One reason explored further below is that imposition of even one strand of the alarmist braid of "warming" demands will yield exorbitant costs, for no detectable environmental benefit, climatic or otherwise. It would be a coup to extract that as a Bush legacy, details of the mess which they could take credit for cleaning up later. (That there would also be massive environmental detriment is worth mentioning, given for example how plowing of fallow land, increased fertilizer use, food price inflation [and riots], and energy poverty all follow when food crops become fuel crops by government fiat.)

As Holman Jenkins of the *Wall Street Journal* noted in the context of related legislation, responsibility for the perils of this agenda are well understood by its champions. "Don't doubt that this is precisely the chasm that keeps Mr. Gore from running for president. He could neither win the office nor govern on the basis of imposing the kinds of costs supposedly necessary to deal with an impending 'climate crisis.' Yet his credibility would become laughable if he failed to insist on such costs. How much more practical, then, to cash in on the crowd-pleasing role of angry prophet, without having to take responsibility for policies that the public will eventually discover to be fraudulent."[95]

These considerations were clearly on the mind of EPA bureaucrats as they promptly lurched into action after the ruling and with apparent certainty about two things. First was that regulating CO_2, with or without tacking on a Frisbee fee or a fart tax, portends future political disaster with its logical conclusion of essentially mandating de-carbonization of the U.S. economy. Being impossible, under foreseeable technologies, without devastating economic dislocation and human suffering (which also always brings environmental degradation), the second certainty was that they had to set the rulemaking ball in motion under the Bush presidency. Allowing things to proceed deliberately would mean that the next administration, one that the D.C. bureaucrats were convinced at the time would be a Democratic one, would be saddled with proposing such rules.

Therefore when the Bush administration proposed to put the matter out for public discussion in a rulemaking, the howls about dangerous dallying echoed across the Potomac. Oddly, these were particularly shrill from lawmakers who for some reason couldn't bring themselves to simply enact clear requirements in lieu of tortured readings of a law never meant for such a use. Once again, a politician they dismissed as an idiot had beaten them at their own game. Unfortunately, that didn't really end the matter but only shifted the onus.

Things are a little more difficult on the Hill with the Democrats' eldest member, Energy and Commerce Committee chairman John Dingell of Michigan, wondering aloud at a hearing "that if climate change is really the transcendent challenge his party says it is, then Congress should bother to pass legislation, not outsource policy to the Environmental Protection Agency," as the *Journal* put it.[96] The simple truth is that enacting this scheme risks discrediting the Democratic Party on economic matters for decades, and so they opt to shriek like Banshees about a supposed crisis, if one that they do not wish to confront. This is the same calculus achieved when they assessed the impacts of the scheme's forerunner, the plan to socialize medicine (the resemblance shared by charts of the respective bureaucracies is uncanny). The longstanding charge against them, as being dangerously under the sway of the Moonbat elements of their political base, would stick. The *Journal* labeled this their "crocodile outrage."

As of this writing it is only fair to acknowledge that the EPA could have shown an even greater abandonment of measure, but some adults obviously waded into the process. Yet it appears quite possible that by the time you read this the EPA, under one president or another (neither Senator Obama nor Senator McCain appear interested in stopping this train), will be formally in the process of pointing at the statute and saying that *these consequences were Congress's doing.* And therefore, *since we must,* the EPA will regulate CO_2 which will also, as a matter of the Clean Air Act's construction, necessitate regulating nearly every facet of American life from automobiles to obtaining construction permits.

The Heritage Foundation summed things up as, "In effect, an endangerment finding for carbon dioxide under section 202 of the Clean Air Act would lead to a regulatory scheme far more extensive than those Congress has wisely rejected. The economic impacts and public anger could be unprecedented and would leave a highly unfortunate legacy for this Administration."[97]

You haven't heard the punch line yet. Iain Murray pointed out, "There's slightly more to this than meets the eye," that if a 2007 study attributing increased CO_2 emissions to divorce holds up, "and it has to (I've been arguing for years that enviros need to consider the emissions effects of divorce if they want to be consistent), then the EPA actually will have an interest in your divorce, as you increase emissions by going ahead. Who knows, the day may come when you have to file papers with the EPA as well as the Court."[98]

It must be of immeasurable fury to the environmentalists to find themselves backing into a pro-family position.

SURELY CONGRESS WILL SAVE US?

Clearly, despite the noisy show being once again produced on Capitol Hill, Congress continues to be daunted by the politics of taking direct responsibility and specifically imposing this "wrenching transformation of society." And well they should be. But this only leaves it to unelected judges and bureaucrats to work their mischief, which is where we stand as of this writing. As such, whether Congress would ever impose such a yoke on individual Americans and the economy is no longer the issue of gravest importance. The courts have stepped in at the behest of politically activist state attorneys general, offering the EPA yet another promotion from sleepy backwater agency created by Executive Order (thanks *again*, Nixon) to arbiter of all that is and might be.

That doesn't mean that the congressional posturing does not include a few legislative gestures about which tubs are thumped. 2008 saw the third failed effort to pass a Senate bill along these lines because, as admitted by one of its chief proponents, Senator Joseph Lieberman: "It's hard to imagine that [his bill] will not cost—over time—these (electric power and industrial) sectors, hundreds of billions of dollars to comply with the demands of this bill."[99] Only the most hard-bitten interventionist can convince themselves that this doesn't mean the average ratepayer and consumer foots the bill when all is said and done.[100] The Congressional Budget Office agreed, noting the $1.2 trillion tax hike that the bill's restrictions represent over just ten years.[101]

Ever helpful when it comes to expanding its own authority, the EPA weighed in to dismiss the economic impacts of this scheme (*why, no, it wouldn't hurt* our *budget at all!*).[102] Consider those periods since 1980 when the gross domestic product (GDP) in the wealth-creating, or productive, sector of the economy contracted for two or more consecutive quarters—a recession—as well as several periods when we experienced non-consecutive quarters of negative growth. That turmoil saw GDP shrink in a range from about 1 percent to about 3 percent. Yet these were also quite short. With energy-rationing schemes such as Kyoto and the failed 2008 Lieberman-Warner Senate bill the express objective is to go much further. These proposals call for this to continue, in perpetuity, reducing GDP *several percent per year* and reducing household disposable income by thousands of dollars, on average, periodically deepening the hit with a required level of GHG emissions commensurate with our economy in about 1910 (an 80 percent cut, or approximately one billion metric tons).[103]

This is quite obviously not a trajectory that is politically sustainable. The actual goal of today's politicians, however, is to facilitate a claim they "did something" which really means "doing nothing" to affect the climate. It's posturing. And I'm not receptive to the *OK, but it's a first, necessary step* argument from people who viscerally reject offshore and Alaska drilling on the grounds that, well, that alone wouldn't solve the problem.

As Pat Michaels' World Climate Report blog summed it up: "[I]f the entire world (including the United States) fully met their emissions reduction obligations laid out in the Kyoto Protocol (which, by the looks of things, few if any countries will actually achieve) that the amount of future global warming that would be 'saved' would amount to about 0.07°C by the year 2050 and 0.15°C by 2100."[104] That amount of warming delayed for a few years at such tremendous cost is actually too small for scientists to distinguish from the "noise" of inter-annual temperature variability.

It should go without saying then that legislation pushed by Lieberman and others, daring to stumble just one big step down the Kyoto staircase on the (relatively speaking) cheap, would be even less climatically meaningful. So, all such approaches are all pain, no gain. According to Michaels, "Recall that EPA calculates that the climate bills will reduce future atmospheric CO_2 concentrations by 23 to 25 [parts per million]...the climate bills 'save' about 60% of 0.15°C or just less than one tenth, that's 0.1, degrees Celsius. One tenth of one degree Celsius for an enormous economic hit."[105]

Lieberman's colleague, chairman of the Senate Energy Committee Jeff Bingaman, has also put forth proposals in the name of pretending we can put a thermostat on the wall of the world. On the heels of Lieberman's admission of trillions of dollars in regulatory taxes, Bingaman offered his own, including that "cap and trade" schemes will "increase...the price of energy across the board," that "a substantial cost will ultimately be passed on to consumers," and that the less inefficient, if also more transparent, carbon taxes are politically unworkable.

So they know that the politically riskier tax would hurt you less, but heaven forbid they be the ones who end up paying for their actions.

This was placed on plain view for anyone who cared by one well-versed industry player, as if industry spending such enormous sums to lobby for this were not testimony enough. Consider how the CEO of German utility Vattenfall, "Lars G. Josefsson, who is also an adviser to German Chancellor Angela Merkel, said higher electricity prices are 'the intent of the whole exercise....If there were no effects, why should you have a cap-and-trade system?' But consumers ask why four big utilities that dominate the German market got to keep the money."[106] Yes, they would do that, wouldn't they?

Senator Bingaman's comments were less to remove doubt about such things than they were directed in part at halting an alternative version of the scheme that at least tells the government to *sell* the emission quotas, rather than simply giving the ration coupons to well-heeled interests (namely, big utilities that have made billions in windfall profits on the back of ratepayers under Europe's scheme).

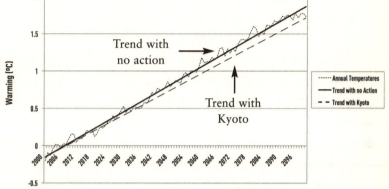

Attaining the targets of the Kyoto Protocol would barely slow warming, according to the models alarmists use.

Bear in mind that rent-seeking companies, which particularly in this context are utilities, are generally on the wrong side of every environmental issue including at the state level. An example is Duke Energy, which has very comfortable relationships with the green pressure groups whose agenda for the next few decades they in great part share, the state environmental regulators where they operate and the utilities commissions. Duke's CEO James Rogers was after all a senior Enron official back in the days when Enron was acquiring companies that would only make real money in a world burdened with "global warming" regulations—windmills, solar panels, emission credit trading operations—in anticipation of aggressively lobbying for precisely that. The infamous internal Enron memo describing the 1997 negotiations in Kyoto included the following: "Enron now has excellent credentials with many 'green' interests including Greenpeace, [World Wildlife Fund], [Natural Resources Defense Council], German Watch, the U.S. Climate Action Network, the

European Climate Action Network, Ozone Action, WRI, and Worldwatch. This position should be increasingly cultivated and capitalized on (monitized)[sic]."

Ken Lay's global warming staffer John Palmissano noted that, "if implemented, this agreement will do more to promote Enron's business than will almost any other regulatory initiative outside of restructuring of the energy and natural gas industries in Europe and the United States." Therefore, Kyoto "is exactly what I have been lobbying for," and "This agreement will be good for Enron stock!!"

When Rogers left for Duke, he took Lay's political business model with him, which can be gently described as getting out in front of issues and shaping them. This is why one former colleague of both Lay's and Rogers' tells me that "'Enron Lives,' when it comes to climate alarmism," in the high offices of Duke Energy.

So, these companies get on board with the spate of new regulations they help mold, building in the ability to pass costs along to rate payers without having to go through a rate hearing. When plans emerge to make them buy their goodies, well, suddenly *this matter requires further deliberation, let's not be hasty*. Then they engage in expensive public relations campaigns bragging about how green and responsible they are and how they were in favor of legislation that imposed the regulations on themselves, meaning imposed costs on the customers.

Therefore it should be no surprise to see Duke donating to activist organizations even at a few million dollars a pop. For example they recently gave $2.5 million to the highly politicized Duke University Nicholas School of the Environment to "develop policies to address the problems of global climate change." In practice, this means provide ammo and engage activists to bang the alarm bell for policies that Duke not only benefits from under today's "green" branding craze but directly, in terms of the carbon and other regulatory schemes that the School and its activists help advance.

Given such realities it is not a revelation that politicians are willing to heap a more expensive, more inefficient way of doing something stupid (under any approach) in order to reduce their own political exposure while pushing an agenda. It is just something that policymakers and savvy green pressure groups generally go to great lengths to mask as opposed to admit.

Again, given the impossibility of any climatic impact all of this can only be designed to burnish political credentials, pay off constituencies and extend fiefdoms.

The good news is we will at least give the career bureaucrats at EPA the power they've always sought.

CONCLUSION

There is no shortage of government officials, both real and aspiring, willing to claim that we can become richer by rationing emissions—which for as far as we can project, even according to adherents of Man-made warming theory, unavoidably means rationing energy use.[107] For example, presidential aspirant and Senator Hillary Clinton conducted a listening tour of the landscape of rent-seeking industry looking to cash in on this sort of government intervention in the energy and manufacturing sectors of the economy, with a system of quotas and vouchers with which she is quite familiar. She concluded, "I believe America is ready to take action, ready to break the bonds of the old energy economy and ready to prove that the climate crisis is also one of the greatest economic opportunities in the history of our country.... It will be a new beginning for the twenty-first century."[108]

Not to be left looking sober and rational, Senator Barack Obama proposed a program styled upon the Depression-era Works Progress Administration under which the state will "take some of the money that's generated from fining polluters, and we are going to spend billions of dollars on solar, wind and biodiesel"—yes, it's criminal we have yet to do that, plus—"We will hire young people who don't have a trade and give them a trade" of certain chores including...*wait for it*..."changing light bulbs."[109] How many bureaucrats does it take to change a light bulb? Just wait until they're slacker, unionized federal bureaucrats.

These rackets will certainly offer a "new beginning" for some. Enron had planned on it until the unpleasantness. Now the companies that picked at the carcass, like GE and BP, push the scheme, with great help from friends in government. ABC reporter John Stossel fairly summed up this agenda for his *20/20* expose' on Al Gore's brand of global warming alarmism:

> I suspect that next year's government boondoggle will be massive spending on carbon-reducing technology.It reminds me of George Mason University Economics Department Chairman Don Boudreax's suggestion that such schemes really mean "government seizing enormous amounts of additional power in order to embark upon schemes of social engineering—schemes whose pursuit gratifies the abstract fantasies of the theory class and, simultaneously, lines the very real pockets of politically powerful corporations, organizations, and 'experts.'"
>
> He is so right. The abstract fantasies of the theory class will soon send huge chunks of your money to politicians, friends, activist scientists, and politically savvy corporations.[110]

Along the way, however, certain other interest groups will attain the co-benefit of imposition on the masses of long-held policies, and state-assisted suicide of speech, seeing as how all of these abstract fantasies apparently justify the repellent efforts by government to use government to stifle debate and marginalize potential opposition to their continuing encroachment upon our economic liberties.

Spiked's Brendan O'Neill summarizes the efforts aptly. "As in all attempts at censorship, from Torquemeda to [British] New

Labour's religious hatred legislation, this is about controlling how people think and what people say. And it is an attempt to win the argument without having to have the argument; to win it with the blunt instruments of demonisation rather through than free and open discussion."[111]

Let's conclude the discussion of government as the ends and the means of the global warming industry with the counsel of Czech President Vaclav Klaus. Specifically, recall his remarks at the Ambrosetti Forum, Villa d'Este, Itálie in September 2007, titled, "Global Warming Hysteria or Freedom and Prosperity?"

The threat I have in mind is the irrationality with which the world has accepted the climate change (or global warming) as a real danger to the future of mankind and the irrationality of suggested and partly already implemented measures because they will fatally endanger our freedom and prosperity, the two goals we consider—I do believe—our priorities.

We have to face many prejudices and misunderstandings in this respect. The climate change debate is basically not about science; it is about ideology. It is not about global temperature; it is about the concept of human society. It is not about nature or scientific ecology; it is about environmentalism, about one—recently born—dirigistic and collectivistic ideology, which goes against freedom and free markets. I spent most of my life in a communist society which makes me particularly sensitive to the dangers, traps and pitfalls connected with it.[112]

CHAPTER 7

Stupid Science Tricks[1]

Keeping that Gravy Train Chugging

"Climate scientists need there to be a problem in order to get funding."

Climate scientist Dr. Roy Spencer, NASA's Space Flight Center, *The Great American Swindle*

"We [climate-related scientists] have a vested interest in creating panic because then money will flow to climate science."

Dr. John Christy, *Swindle*

"There's one thing you shouldn't say, and that is, 'this might not be a problem.'"

Dr. Richard Lindzen, *Swindle*

RARELY, IF EVER, has the scientific establishment seen a gravy train the likes of global warming. The money flowing into studying the issue is jaw-dropping: federal taxpayer expenditures on climate-related research for the entire panoply of related inquiry is now pushing up against $6 billion per year, more than taxpayers send to the National Cancer Institute and even more than our government spends on AIDS. Add private research dollars, and you put to shame those fever swamps surrounding paranoid flicks like *The Constant Gardener*.

Now ask yourself this: would this money keep flowing from governments and international institutions if scientists concluded tomorrow that Man's influence on climate is likely within natural variability or "background noise"? Or that anthropogenic effects on climate change are real but not catastrophic or substantially different than we have faced and will always continue to face?

Do you think scientists—or at least those most disposed to mug for the camera and canoodle with green pressure groups and reporters—don't ask themselves this question? Is it likely they pause before answering it? As long as Man-made greenhouse gases *really matter*, the people who study greenhouse gases and technologies that would benefit from the government action will be flooded with taxpayer money. Understanding this dynamic is key to understanding why science has been corrupted. And it *has* been corrupted by the global warming scare.

Indeed, many scientists have come forth to blow the whistle on their fellow practitioners and on their profession. Increasingly, scientists are willing to detail how a colleague putting forth an alarmist result cannot explain the result, has deliberately put an alarmist spin on it, or even has fudged it altogether.

Considering these funding streams created over the years which require that there be a global warming problem, we should not be surprised. We actually *did* see this coming thanks to the frankness of media-favorite Dr. Robert Corell (famous for citing a snowmobile falling through the ice as proof that the Inuits' thousand-year way of life was being stolen from them). According to one participant in the room at a 1990 conference at the University of Oklahoma (back before the global warming industry had fully glimpsed just how gilded their lily would become), Corell stressed how they must not miss this golden goose, as their field had never before seen funding like that which was going to be involved here.

Well, the word clearly got out, as you will read. Massive increases in federal funding sought to keep pace with the hysteria, which it in turn was of course only feeding. A positive feedback loop, you could call it.

Imagine the damage to the institution of science and to individual careers should the doomsaying be proven as faulty as "skeptics" now allege. This fear is certainly behind the increasingly erratic behavior of the alarmist industry as it scurries to protect its franchise. No claim is beyond them to make, and no trick too outrageous to try.

In this context we now hear that the weather—whatever it ends up being—is exactly what they predicted, or at least what we should expect in the overheated world of which they have warned us. Scientists line up to encourage media hype about global warming causing hot weather and cold weather, rain and drought, fire and flood, and of course every severe weather event—because we know these never happened previously.

It is a rather sad *Rainman* routine: absolutely, positively everything is *definitely, definitely global warming. Definitely.* Typically

---

"Prior to Bush the elder, I think the level of funding for climate and climate-related sciences was somewhere around the order of $170 million a year, which is reasonable for the size of the field. It jumped to $2 billion a year, more than a factor of ten, and yeah, that changed a lot . . . a lot of jobs, it brought a lot of new people into it who otherwise were not interested. So you developed whole cadres of people whose only interest in the field was that there was global warming.

"We're all competing for funds and if your field is the focus of concern, you have that much less work rationalizing why your field should be funded."

Dr. Richard Lindzen, quoted in The Great Global Warming Swindle we get the caveat that *of course no single event can be attributed to "global warming,"* followed by the ritual pause and "but," as in *but this is precisely what we would expect.* To call that intellectually dishonest would be unfair to intellectual dishonesty.

Another approach for scientists is to say things like, "The [Antarctic] Peninsula is the fastest warming place in Antarctica."[2] That's true because, well, the peninsula is home to the 2 percent of the continent which *isn't* cooling. Clever. When observations trend along the same lines as climate model projections, then these observations *confirm* the models—or, more humbly, they "are consistent with" the models.

Climate scientist Roger Pielke Jr. translates this claim: "an observation, with its corresponding uncertainty range, overlaps with the spread of the entire ensemble of model realizations," which is meaningless because "the greater the uncertainty in modeling—that is, the greater the spread in outcomes across model realizations—the more likely that observations will be 'consistent with' the models. More models, more outcomes, greater consistency—but less certainty. It is in this way that pretty much any observation becomes 'consistent with' the models.'"[3] The result is that no observation is ever *inconsistent* with computer model predictions.

So the "consistent with" claim itself is not only meaningless, Pielke points out, but it also reveals how "from a practical standpoint climate models are of no practical use beyond providing some intellectual authority in the promotional battle over global climate policy."[4]

Models claim for example that both poles should be warming first and most; this is the "polar amplification" shown by all general circulation climate models (which are discussed in detail elsewhere). Unfortunately for them, Antarctica is *cooling.*[5] Similarly rainfall[6] and GHG concentrations behave[7] inconsistently with the models. These models also predict erosion in Bangladesh when in fact land mass has built up,[8] they predict warmer ocean temperatures which have cooled,[9] and incorrectly judged the Northwest

Passage.[10] In short, cheerleaders for models cherry-pick those items on which the blind pig finds the acorn, hailing them as *affirming* the models and greenhouse warming theory. They, at best, ignore those areas where models are—by their logic—affirmed as being wrong in their assumptions, feedbacks and operations.

When observations indicate either slower change, no change, or a change in the opposite direction than models project, then we're told the comparison is untimely or unfair. When we notice increased Andean snowpack, why that's just cherry-picking.[11] Indeed, major checklist items are dismissed as insignificant when the change is in the wrong direction, for example when the ocean's warming trend had *stopped*, and even cooled slightly.[12] What was heralded as a harbinger of things to come, well, no longer is really all that important.

When it comes to climate, a comparison between observed data and model projections is legitimate only when the observations support the forecasts. Directly and indirectly the alarmists insist that there simply must be something wrong with the *observations*, given they don't conform to modelers' expectations, which is probably the best example of our geek class taking the "second life" and avatar nonsense a tad too far.

These scientific contortions and excuses, plus data "correction" and "gap-filling" among other torture of the numbers and rationalizations may be best understood by first considering the bigger picture.

HOW LOW DO THEY GO?
A SNAPSHOT OF THE ALARMIST BASICS

In this whole business, there is a hypothesis to be tested: Manmade (anthropogenic) carbon dioxide emissions are causing dangerous global warming. Where is the control experiment with results that show the relation between CO_2 and ambient temperature? That's a pretty obvious question, yet no one has ever claimed to establish it outside of PlayStation computer models, as even famed botanist-*cum*-ostracized skeptic, David Bellamy has noted.

The global warming industry has been built up on the assumption that some level of greenhouse gases would be devastating—but those charged with telling us what that level would be refuse to do so. The original global warming treaty of 1992 was built upon avoiding dangerous warming by keeping atmospheric greenhouse gas concentrations below some unstated level.[13] The Kyoto Protocol incorporated this premise by reference. *What is the maximum allowable GHG concentration?* was the original question posed to the Intergovernmental Panel on Climate Change (IPCC). Answering that question inherently requires affirmation of the hypothesis. No answers were forthcoming.

The IPCC, which is styled as a scientific body and makes scientific proclamations (but admits it performs no scientific research) actually twice refused to answer the question. The closest it comes is to offer desired *policy* prescriptions which might avoid this level of GHG concentrations—while never telling us what the dangerous level would be. Here we see the first signs that, like certain bossy climate scientists, the IPCC saw its true mandate as something different from its simple job description.

Perhaps the IPCC can't answer the question because, as even Al Gore's movie affirmed, GHG concentrations go up and down regardless of Man's will or actions—and therefore are out of our control. The fact that they continue to go up this decade while temperatures are now going down—reminiscent of the 1940s through 1970s—is confounding, but somehow still "consistent with" climate models that earlier supposedly proved we would get *warming* with increased CO2.

The greenhouse warming hypothesis is of course testable, and you would think that climate scientists would, well, test it—that being "the scientific method" and all. This has proven too great a hurdle, however, for the very well-funded alarmist industry.

The first question: is it warming? Well, yes and no. In fact, "both": you just tell me your agenda, and I'll provide you that agenda's most suitable baseline year.

The early, Kyoto-era alarmists shrieked to the heavens that the planet had warmed (1 degree Fahrenheit) "since 1860!" In this case, it wasn't that the American Civil War had much to do with the temperature but that this is approximately when the Little Ice Age is agreed to have begun its exit from the world stage. Therefore it is a politically useful if largely meaningless baseline. Similarly, the 2004 Arctic Climate Impact Assessment selected the baseline year of 1966 for its own deeply alarmist and far too clever claims of catastrophe.[14] This seemingly arbitrary figure was quite plainly chosen on the basis of being the coldest Arctic year on record, thereby inherently presenting a warming trend just like "since 1860!"[15]

It is warming since the end of the last ice age (10,000 years ago), cooling since the Roman Warming (2,000 years ago), also cooling since the Medieval Climate Optimum (1,000 years ago), warming since the Little Ice Age ended, cooling since the mid-1930s, and warming since the 1970s (it is warming since the sun came up this morning—maybe even thirty degrees, and somehow without massive specie loss). But the last decade—during which, thanks largely to Man, atmospheric CO_2 concentrations have increased by fifteen parts per million (4 percent)—has seen no warming.[16] Now, alarmists will be the first to tell you *ten years is too short to declare a trend*. They are right about that, but that was also true when the short periods showed *warming*—but back then, it was *a clear sign*. All of this earns the theory an F.

After the claim of a warming trend, the second step is presenting the parade of horribles to result from warming (angrier and more frequent storms, frozen things melting, etc.). As the UK High Court found regarding key Al Gore anecdotes, these claims are either unsupportable or fall within natural variability. Frozen things do melt, and some are melting; they are also growing, often very nearby their retreating brethren. It seems that Gore and crew stretch the truth because the truth isn't scary (which has led to alarmists pleading for a "major climate event,"[17] a phony concept to begin with given that climate deals with long-term trends, not weather events). Failed again.

Attempting to move beyond the anecdotal or circumstantial, the alarmists then say they've got computer model projections. These models are not evidence, as they can produce whatever outcome the modeler chooses—and they happen to choose warming—but have proven incapable of credibly hind-casting past climate, without designing the program to fit known outcomes. Basically, the models are rigged. They are very expensive guesses about the future, but most certainly not *evidence*.

The ugly truth is that even ignoring recent cooling, and regardless of how they monkey with the baseline, temperatures have consistently failed to rise as fast as the IPCC predicts—with 95 percent certainty—they should be rising. This presents a problem more obvious to the layman and policymakers: models tell us of continued warming while the world experiences cooling at the same time the sun goes remarkably quiet and continues (as of this writing) to put off its long-awaited next cycle. In short, the models either do not understand the climate, or despite admitted, weak understanding of the key variables and mechanisms, they do understand it to some credible extent, but have the climate's sensitivity to carbon dioxide wrong.

The specifics of the failure and even fraud of the climate models, detailed below, reveal that these programs which provide the premise of the warming agenda are tools whose output is not subject to verification, and whose utility is mostly in their political application.[18] Strike three.

And of course at the day-to-day level, we see the institutions of science gaily spouting—since at least 1992—both the mantra that "the science is settled" and claims of monumentally important breakthroughs, sometimes as silly as "Global warming could plunge North America and Western Europe into a deep freeze, possibly within only a few decades."[19] Nowhere do they even bother attempting to reconcile the talking point of "settled science" with (real claims such as) "that's the paradoxical scenario gaining credibility among many climate scientists," or the regular contradiction and replacement of fashionable scares.

Why do the errors—ranging from the basic statistical variety all the way to borderline fraud—nearly all come down in support of the theory that Man is causing dangerous warming? Why would highly intelligent, highly educated individuals stoop as low as revealed in these pages?

Many factors are at play, beginning with the formidable professional and other financial interests they have in pushing alarmism. But the *Wall Street Journal's* Holman Jenkins asks, "What if everyone believes in global warmism only because everyone believes in global warmism?"[20] Or, as Tolstoy noted in his own time, "I know that most men, including those at ease with problems of the greatest complexity, can seldom accept even the simplest and most obvious truth if it be such as would oblige them to admit the falsity of conclusions which they delighted in explaining to colleagues, which they have proudly taught to others, and which they have woven, thread by thread, into the fabric of their lives."

Imagine if Tolstoy had met an IPCC Lead Author.

LEAVING NO STONE UNTURNED

The ploys that alarmists use to convince the public of *certainty* and *crisis* range from the very simple to the elaborate. Vast resources and venom are employed to create the pretense of professional agreement, marginalizing the substantial disagreement as daft or venal. Oddly, even by scientists, the substance of challenge is largely ignored, though tremendous resources are employed to attack and discredit the challengers.

At its more sophomoric, for example, scientists artificially mold the discussion in the lowbrow online crossroads of popular information, Wikipedia.[21] Although this open-source, basic resource is not a scientific reference by any measure, it is the sort of gateway to the issue where the alarmists prey on the masses.[22]

Skeptical scientists and writers have seen their (undisputed) factual corrections reversed and suggestions that the science is not "settled" deleted, at times by "official" Wikipedia editors. Personal attacks on climate realists are also common practice in this Internet "resource," including through biographical pages for prominent "skeptics." Wiki's rules against these practices are apparently mere suggestions when it comes to climate.

OTHER TRICKS OF THE TRADE

Tactics more sophisticated than the clever baseline selection are also routine. Past temperature observations are adjusted, re-adjusted, and adjusted again for good measure. The reason given: accounting for changes in the time of observations, missing data, type of instrumentation, changes in station siting, and urban warming.

Outside parties have identified mistakes both inadvertent and—as with Al Gore's debunked claims—apparently intentional. Often the errors are excused as no big deal. Even when the claims are corrected, this comes only after evasive maneuvers by the alarmists. The jockeying rarely stops, however, and even these corrections, though acknowledged, turn out later to have been quietly reversed to their pre-corrected state. In short, scientists treat the data like they do claims on Wikipedia.

In the course of just one year, intrepid "skeptics" and even not-so-skeptical researchers uncovered an embarrassing series of errors and inaccuracies, adding to a growing list of claims which have required substantial corrections to the record.

It is not surprising that the alarmists' mistakes, biases, or revisions of historical data tend to be of the sort that create or enhance the appearance of a Man-made warming trend. The only downward revisions the scientific establishment seems capable of are the corrections imposed on them when they are caught.

Somehow this kind of chicanery yielded a 100 percent increase in taxpayer funding for climate-related research under George W. Bush, seemingly in the vain hope that appeasing the beast would soothe its hunger for catastrophist alarmism. As should be expected, the opposite proved true.

RIDICULOUS, ON THE SURFACE

We saw an embarrassing example of the simplistic depths to which the scientific establishment will sink to advance global warming alarmism in the wet and cool summer of 2007. The embarrassing tinkering was revealed by the creative new website SurfaceStations.org, set up by meteorologist Anthony Watts, providing unwelcome scrutiny of the reliability of our temperature measurements.

You see, there's no such thing as "global temperature" or even "U.S. temperature." There are, instead, weighted averages from adjusted readings from many different measuring stations. Now, clearly it matters how and how often instruments are maintained, and of course where they are sited. Place your measuring equipment in the wrong places and you could, well, help start a global warming panic.

Evidence began percolating that the U.S. network's reliability was not all that it was cracked up to be, with a bias derived from misplacement. Soon, a full-blown scandal erupted—such as is possible when the revelation betrays the alarmist cause—exposing the expensive U.S. surface measurements as quite possibly not much more than one more tool in the global warmers' kit to frighten the taxpayer into at long last accepting a radical lifestyle agenda.

Watts had issued a call for individuals to photograph each of America's 1,221 official surface stations. As the first snaps came in, he noticed a preponderance of ridiculously sited instruments. This yielded, among other shots, a priceless photo of a measuring station in Tahoe City, California, near the heat islands of a tennis court and parking lot. Oh, and it was five feet from a metal trash burn barrel. The blogosphere has also shown us the great station in Hopkinsville, Kentucky (facing page): next to shrubbery contrary to standards, which is child's play compared to the fact that it abuts not just a brick building, but the chimney. The station overhangs not only a black asphalt pad but an air conditioning fan blowing hot air. The Weber barbeque grill right below, however, is the ultimate touch.[23]

Another icon is the Arizona measuring station smack in the middle of an asphalt parking lot. (And as you consider the warming trend, note that this one wasn't always in the middle of a parking lot.) Common sense warns this would produce a warming bias among the U.S. network (which, remember, is the world's least unreliable). See the site yourself.

Officials at the National Climatic Data Center did, and were not amused, reacting to these developments as would any guilty-minded organization: by suddenly pulling the location addresses from publicly available resources.

Watts took them to task.[24] Soon enough, realizing that the cover-up almost always compounds the crime, NCDC again made the locations publicly available.[25] They continued, however, refusing to post photographs of Historical Climate Network sites that it acknowledged that it had in its possession, despite calls from reputable climate scientists to do so in the name of transparency and in the face of such questions.[26]

The white canister is a measuring station in Hopkinsville, Ky. Yes, that's a Weber grill below it. (Courtesy of Anthony Watts)

TUSCON, ARIZ.—Moving a temperature measuring station to an asphalt parking lot is a fine way to prove global warming. (Courtesy of Anthony Watkins.)

The brazenness of the act nonetheless prompted me to file a request under the Freedom of Information Act seeking the internal deliberations behind such apparent trickery. Although this facially only implicated a very small potential group of staff whose e-mail record would be searched, and going back only about a month,

NCDC circled the wagons and sought nearly $5,000.00 in search fees in a clear effort to impede the scandal from growing.

Remember this when you hear the climate science establishment carping about how science will suffer if they aren't freed from the shackles of oversight of how they spend your billions.

Rubbing it in on NCDC, Watts' inquiry arose out of his tests to see if there is an impact from the semi-gloss latex paint instead of whitewash for the white slat-vented boxes (called "Stevenson Screens") that house the thermometers in the U.S. network. It does make a difference, it turns out, accounting for as much as half of the surface warming detected since the late-'70s "cooling" panic.[27] When did this switch occur? 1979.

As we will see, there is no shortage of corrupting factors. This merely affirms the enormous grain of salt with which you must take the claims of precise measurements of mean surface temperatures, and "record" years by a few hundredths of a degree. As of this writing, NCDC has capitulated to reality and asked Watts to assist them in cleaning house. Surely this is more than an effort to co-opt a very principled, effective watchdog.

DISCONTINUITY

While absurd station placements give us plainly corrupted readings, the bigger problem when you're talking about trends is uniformity and continuity of the network of measuring stations. It turns out we don't get great scores on that, either, and it's no secret.

The problem of continuity has been known for years, at least since Ross McKitrick charted a dramatic, worldwide closure of more than one-half of the planet's surface stations during 1989–91, as illustrated, below.

Those station closures coincided with a dramatic apparent jump in global surface temperatures in the 1990s—the "hottest decade ever!" according to agenda-driven alarmists. Not a warming trend,

MEASURING STATIONS CLOSE, MEASURED TEMPERATURES RISE

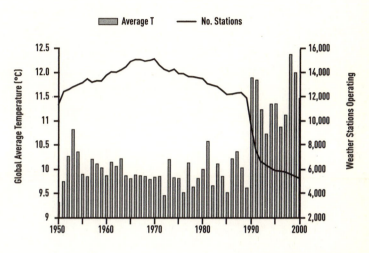

(Source: Ross McKitrick)

mind you, but an abrupt shift upward. While other closures were implicated, it seems this temperature shift can be partly attributed to having closed thousands of cold-weather latitude stations in Canada and Siberia when, for example, the Soviets/Russians found themselves with bigger concerns than maintaining thermometers in Novaya Zemlya.

To further understand this phenomenon, note the aggregate number of months with data missing from the 110 Russian stations that remained open, represented in the following chart from McKitrick and Michaels (2007)(see following page).

REVISIONISTAS

In this most recent election season, you may have seen shirts or stickers with Barack Obama's mug and logo, blaring "CHANGE HISTORY." It's an odd exhortation, when you think about it—except in climate science, where we learn the past is often subject

MISSING OBSERVATIONS IN RUSSIA

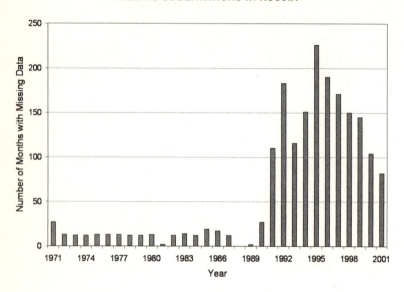

Total number of missing monthly observations each year for the 110 Russian weather stations reporting weather data continuously from 1971–2001 (McKitrick and Michaels).[28]

to revision, either for political purposes or because of the inexactness of measuring "global" temperatures over time.

Without announcement, in August 2007, a government agency rewrote the past. Only this time it wasn't to enhance a warming trend, but the opposite—thus, no press releases.

Here's the story: NASA reports temperatures and trends through its Goddard Institute for Space Studies (GISS). GISS is run by Gore-advising, John Kerry-endorsing Dr. James Hansen, the "father of global warming" for his 1988 testimony also discussed elsewhere in these pages. (As an example of how GISS spends your tax dollars, its top three "News and Features" during a visit to their homepage while researching for this book were "Global Warming and Violent Weather," "Climate Approaches Dangerous 'Tipping' Point," and

"Climate Change and Summer Heat Waves."[29] *Be very worried. Oh, and we probably need more money.*)

Hansen's dexterity with history is well established. In 2000 he declared that "we can predict with reasonable confidence that the record annual and decadal temperatures for the contiguous 48 U.S., set in the 1930s, will soon be broken."[30] Lo and behold, this visionary published a paper the next year, in which he revealed a major adjustment to U.S. surface temperature records, as a result of which 1998 was moved up in the hierarchy of "hottest years on record" right up front in a statistical tie with 1934. As the twenty-first century and Hansen's work both marched onward in their inexorable drive to history, in the words of Stephen McIntyre, "1998 continued to make small gains and the 1934 record was finally broken [in] 2005—by a rejuvenated 1998."[31] This says it all.

Of course Hansen is not alone in this pattern of behavior, as former Virginia State Climatologist Pat Michaels has noted. Temperature "records have been revised a number of times, and I examined the two major revisions of these three records. They are the surface record from the United Nations' Intergovernmental Panel on Climate Change (IPCC), the satellite-sensed temperatures originally published by University of Alabama's John Christy, and the weather-balloon records originally published by James Angell of the U.S. Commerce Department. The two revisions of the IPCC surface record each successively lowered temperatures in the 1950s and the 1960s. The result? Obviously more warming—from largely the same data."[32]

After noting similar treatment for balloon and satellite data, Michaels concluded "There have been six major revisions in the warming figures in recent years, all in the same direction. So it's like flipping a coin six times and getting tails each time. The chance of that occurring is 0.016, or less than one in 50. That doesn't mean that these revisions are all hooey, but the probability that they would all go in one direction on the merits is pretty darned small."[33]

This did, however, make the odds pretty good that more revisions would follow.

Hansen's Y2K problem

While the rest of the world escaped any Y2K problem corrupting their computers or bank account, Hansen seems to have had his own unique data problem at the turn of the millennium involving that similar unfounded panic, catastrophic Man-made global warming—a problem that, *Surprise!*, allowed him to claim more warming than was justified.

The story begins with some more measuring-station problems, but it is far broader that that. In July 2007 some curious "skeptics" spotted an apparent anomaly in surface temperature measurements at certain stations beginning in 2000. The first site to catch their eyes was Detroit Lakes, Minnesota, which showed a bizarre jump following a data gap.[34] Investigation revealed that this correlated with the physical environment surrounding the measuring apparatus having been altered, specifically by moving some heat pump/air conditioning units from a rooftop to directly next to it. This occurred on May 5, 1999. The readings for the next month came in as the second-hottest June on record, followed by the hottest July in seventy years.

Coincidence, to be sure. Further, it turns out that the equipment had first been relocated to a warmer place, even without HVAC venting corrupting the readings. For one thing, it's next to a swamp, warming the nighttime ambient air temperatures.

It turns out that those conditions weren't the only thing pushing up the reported temperatures from Detroit Lakes—James Hansen was pushing them up, too. In 2007, Hansen's revisions moved the station's temperatures upward 0.8°C. This wasn't the only station whose readings were being adjusted, either.

Hansen wasn't fudging data—he was fixing a mistake he had made. A pretty big mistake. It turns out that, beginning in January

2000, inapposite data sets had been spliced together when the U.S. government changed the way it recorded temperatures.

In short, Hansen was sticking together two incongruous sets of temperature data: a pre-2000 set that had been adjusted for various factors, and a post-2000 set without any adjustments—raw data. The necessary adjustments to correct the shift in systems used was not performed, however, and this on average created an artificial warming. The way Hansen laid them out, it looked like a post-millennium/post-Bush inauguration rise in temperature. In truth, Hansen had failed to conduct a basic statistical adjustment required to meld A on B, such that the spike was more like a milder version of switching from Celsius to Fahrenheit. Hansen was forced to correct his post-2000 data, with some stations going up, but the net adjustment of the national average being downward—an adjustment that oddly found no interest among a media obsessed with the tales of post-2000 warming which, now, were without support.

Media ignorance notwithstanding, it was a very big deal[35] and the attention from skeptics proved quite uncomfortable for Dr. Hansen, who has never been shy about a media spotlight.

Some measuring stations saw discrepancies 1°C or higher,[36] with the largest step occurring for the Douglas, Arizona, station into which Hansen was forced to bring the reported average temperature down 1.75°C (2.8°F) over six years[37]—remarkable considering the basis for the present global warming hysteria is over an increase totaling about 0.6°C (1°F) over 150 years.

Again, the distribution throughout the measuring stations was not uniform but bimodal, meaning that some of the errors actually made a few stations cooler.[38] But it is also crucial to note that GISS's (Hansen's) adjustments quite clearly do not achieve the ostensible purpose of an adjustment—removing the bias from U.S. measurements—but instead seem to enhance the appearance of a warming trend.

Columnist Mark Steyn, among others mocked the episode, which involved Canadian Stephen McIntyre, describing the situation as "just another immigrant doing the jobs Americans won't do, even when they're federal public servants with unlimited budgets."[39]

You could tell how big a deal this revelation actually was by how hard and fast the usual suspects rushed to dismiss it. Also instructive was the way their media enablers, after a respectful period of mourning in silence, then found sufficient interest in the matter to provide space for the alarmists to dismiss it.

This was very dangerous stuff. After all, one of the alarmist movements' money quotes was Al Gore's claim that nine of the ten "hottest" years on record occurred in the past decade. At least as far as the continental United States was concerned, NASA no longer considered 1998 the hottest year, as they had trumpeted. Suddenly, past breathless press releases about individual, recent years were overtaken by an admission that, after fixing the mistake, the warmest year was 1934 (the years are only "hottest" when they're recent, and merely "warmest" when they're long ago) followed by 1998 and then 1921 third. *O, mighty warming trend!* In the final analysis, the 1930s had four of the ten warmest years, leaving the 1920s, 1950s, and the current decade each as home to one of the top ten years, with the remaining three in the 1990s.[40]

As meteorologist Joe D'Aleo put it:

The adjustment made was primarily to the temperatures in the years post-2000 for which the average year declined by 0.15C. NASA GISS's Gavin Schmidt and James Hansen have responded to the media that the adjusted downward correction of 0.15 deg C was not significant.

If one accepts that as true and examines the new US temperature curve since 1930, one finds a trend of only 0.12C (0.22F) for the 77 years of measurement. Thus, according to the recent judgment of Schmidt and Hansen's, the warming in the United States over the past 77 years has also been "insignificant."[41]

D'Aleo notes that after McIntyre caught Hansen's error and GISS adjusted temperatures down, the National Climatic Data Center then adjusted them back up.

The alarmists show remarkable flexibility here in other ways, as well. Now 0.15°C was insignificant, though a decade prior to this incident they were ecstatic when they found an error far smaller—but in the opposite direction—in the temperature data collected by weather satellites.

It seems that, similar to Hansen's simple statistical adjustment that was forgotten, the scientists maintaining the orbiting thermometers had failed to account for orbital decay, or the yearly minute downward drift.[42] When the effects of drift were added into the observations, the inconvenient cooling that the satellites had detected dropped from 0.04°C per decade to 0.01. This upward correction of *three-hundredths of a degree* but still showing no warming, somehow led the alarmists to declare vindication and that the disagreement between the atmospheric temperature measurements (which are the data which matter) and surface temperature measurements (which, as explained in these pages, really don't) had for all intents and purposes been erased. No, it hadn't. The disagreement was *narrowed*; the important point the alarmists sought to diminish is that it still exists.[43]

In 2007, the significantly larger 0.15°C was now so miniscule according to Team Hansen as to warrant no discussion, and certainly no press releases. It therefore seems that whether an adjustment to temperature records is newsworthy is dictated simply by which direction it works. Welcome to the world of convenient alarmist logic, rationalization, and double standards.

Nothing lasts forever

Hansen took this debunking by McIntyre about as well as you could expect: he lashed out at critics in a blog post to which he linked from NASA's website (since taken down), thus revealing yet one more fine line he straddles as a zealous agenda-activist on the public payroll.

In his response, Hansen derided the correction as insignificant and likened global warming skeptics to "court jesters," whose claims were unworthy of his bother. Yet, following this remark, the skeptics on his trail noticed a series of revisions on Hansen's government web-based datasets of past claims of temperature observations, all unannounced of course. This prompted McIntyre to quip it is no wonder Hansen can't joust with jesters, when he's so busy adjusting his adjustments.

Playing whack-a-mole

Hansen wasn't going to let some data correction poke a hole in what he *knew* was true.

An alert participant in the campaign to photograph the USHCN stations noticed that one particular site he was reviewing, "pristine by climate monitoring standards" in part because it had not been physically moved in ninety years or otherwise modified, was inexplicably and suddenly adjusted by GISS at what proved to be a curious moment. He found that both the raw data and the adjusted numbers had just been revised, and then again.

This seemed straight out of a Hollywood movie—though the roles would certainly be reversed in any movie about "global warming," in which a "well-funded denial machine" *a la News-week's* fever dream would be the one manipulating data from the past and even the present. "We had a citizen trying to figure out why a climate site with good data was 'adjusted', and then the data changed right in the middle of him looking at it."[44]

Soon, the growing truth-squad was on the case, catching data as it was being changed across many surface temperature measuring sites. As McIntyre noted on September 13, "Since August 1, 2007, NASA has had 3 substantially different online versions of their 1221 USHCN stations.... The third and most recent version was slipped in without any announcement or notice in the last few days—subsequent to their code being placed online on Sept 7,

2007."[45] (McIntyre's reference to "their code being placed online" was to NASA's response to his demands for transparency in its adjustments.)

Ominously, as a result of this continuing evolution of data for *past temperature observations*, "Hansen has clawed back most of the [temperature] gains of the 1930s relative to recent years—perhaps leading eventually to a re-discovery of 1998 as the warmest U.S. year of the 20th century."

Within days, this prediction was proven prescient, with the NASA U.S. temperature history—that is, the past—*again* changing so as to move 1998 back up and into a tie with 1934 for the warmest year on record in the U.S.[46] It's a tenacious year, that 1998.

Individual (year) liberties

While Hansen and his allies covered this embarrassing revelation by diminishing the importance of mere hundredths of a degree (while such magnitudes, when useful to sounding the alarm, are trumpeted as significant), they also worked to diminish the use of what had been their metric of choice all along. That is that Hansen, dismissing this correction that was for all practical purposes imposed upon him, sneered at the impropriety of focusing on single years although as already noted *it is precisely this focus on single years that kept Hansen in the spotlight*. Sure enough, Hansen soon forgot this pivot[47] in his rush to bang on about the importance of 2007 temperatures.[48]

While the *New York Times* never covered NASA's correction, they managed to then cover Hansen's response to the ensuing mockery. In the story about what a non-story this really is, Team Hansen was permitted to note without challenge that they rarely, if ever, discuss individual years, particularly mere regional findings like those for the United States (the lower forty-eight are only 2 percent of the planet's surface, after all). "In general I think that we want to avoid going into more and more detail about ranking of individual years.... As far as I remember, we have always discouraged that as being somewhat nonsensical."[49]

They say the mind is the second thing to go, so here's a quick review for Hansen and company conducted by my colleague Iain Murray—such a search apparently not occurring to the *Times*'s reporter—revealing the following selections from the NASA web site:[50]

- "2005 Warmest Year in a Century,"[51] which actually even employed a table of individual years, which Hansen we now know "always discourage[s]." NASA dismissing that was just one more way of muzzling the poor guy.
- "The highest global surface temperature in more than a century of instrumental data was recorded in the 2005 calendar year in the GISS annual analysis." Global surface temperature trends—2005 Summation[52]
- "2006 was Earth's Fifth Warmest Year,"[53] employing such a table yet again.
- "Earth Gets a Warm Feeling All Over,"[54] focusing on the individual year 2004, with one of those always-discouraged tables focusing on, well, individual years.
- "Global Temperature Trends 2003,"[55] beginning with the always-discouraged focus of "The year 2003 is the third warmest year in the period of accurate instrumental data"; and prominently mentioning the two warmer years.
- "Global Temperature Trends 2002,"[56] beginning with the always-discouraged focus of "The 2002 meteorological year is the second warmest year in the period of accurate instrumental data."

Racing Hansen to the bottom, his cheerleaders over at RealClimate soon found it convenient to also disparage (other) people as "misguided" for bothering to try and find meaning in *eight* years of temperature.[57] Once again, what's important was neither consistency nor accuracy but that you accepted their stance and contortions.

In truth, far from "in general" or "always" discouraging the practice, it seems that James Hansen fairly revels in focusing on individual years;[58] he and his ilk just don't appreciate it when others do the same if it is to point out problems with the alarmists' claims. Then, the practice falls out of favor.

Further rushing to Hansen's defense, the *Times* reporter claimed in an on-line discussion that "those releases you cite from NASA all (pretty sure) highlight *global* temperature record, not United States regional trend (which was the focus of McIntyre and the focus of my story)." True, but a *non sequitur*, given that Hansen never said that it was inappropriate to focus on individual years *from the U.S.*, but condemned the practice, period. Murray exposed this, leading the *Times'* reporter to change the subject.

We are the world... or, aren't we?

So, what about that "it's only the U.S.!" fallback argument to minimize the import of the correction forced on Hansen and NASA? Is it, as it seems, merely a transparent affirmation that a fact's relevance is determined by whether it supports or refutes the alarmist thesis?

Back in 2001, Hansen made a correction of the average U.S. temperature and wrote about it:

> Although the contiguous U.S. represents only about 2% of the world area, it is important that the analyzed temperature change there be quantitatively accurate for several reasons. Analyses of climate change with global climate models are beginning to try to simulate the patterns of climate change, including the cooling in the southeastern U.S. [Hansen et al., 2000]. Also, perceptions of the reality and significance of greenhouse warming by the

public and public officials are influenced by reports of climate change within the United States.[59]

So we see that Hansen certainly knows the importance of data (and reporting) of climate change within the U.S., even if he diminishes it when it works against him. Note also the subtle implication upon *global* temperature claims of such errors in the world's least-unreliable record. McIntyre noted in conclusion about Hansen's zig-zagging on the importance of corrections to U.S. data, that, just "a few years ago, Hansen et al thought that a restatement of U.S. results, amounting only to an upward re-statement of about 0.32°C per *century* was worth publishing. However, it seems that an error amounting to a downward step [involving a few years] of 0.15°C is immaterial."[60]

All that changed between the two scenarios, of course, was the implication for Team Hansen's thesis (and their industry).

ADJUST THIS

Writer John Goetz reported a particularly concerning aspect of Hansen's adjustment: "Replication is a base tenet of science. So far NOBODY has been able to fully replicate what Hansen does with his adjustments....This code would not pass muster in many organizations, because if it was used for mission critical operations, people would die. Yet it is used to formulate climate policy."[61]

One party involved in the issue, a statistician, emphasized to me Hansen's inherent conflict in being both the official predictor of U.S. temperatures and the adjuster—not to mention his heavily, privately underwritten advocacy of huge reductions in CO2 emissions. As Dr. Fred Singer has also noted, "Hansen's data manipulation brings home an essential truth about modern politics: he who controls the statistics controls the high ground. It does not matter what the reality is—what matters is how that 'reality' is portrayed."[62]

Hansen has already acknowledged the importance of how the U.S. press covers his issue, and has proven very adept at influencing it, if apparently assisted by the likes of George Soros and his affiliated pressure groups.[63] All of this comes further into focus when one realizes how Hansen's output has disagreed with that of the other outlets.[64]

While the media present "global temperature" or "sea temperature" figures as precise measurements, it's clear that this is foolhardy. There are obvious problems, gaps, and duplication within all of the data sets, the rationale behind none of which are apparent.[65] They are routinely the product of "adjustment," as discussed, which we know is dictated by the party doing the adjusting. As such, any claims arising from that source ought to carry error bars and notify readers that the derived figures are approximations.[66]

Instead, these precise-sounding claims are treated as gospel by the media and alarmists. Rather, they are so treated when they show warming either at first or, as is increasingly common, upon receiving gentle ministrations. Also, of course we know the data are revisited and mysteriously changed when they are less cooperative.

The UN IPCC cites as "proof" of human CO_2-caused warming the claimed increase in global temperatures of about one degree Fahrenheit over approximately 130 years—supposedly lying outside natural variability. That is, while natural cycles do occur, nature doesn't typically change *like that*, and so it must be unnatural, meaning *of human influence*. Hansen says the IPCC is far too conservative.

Unfortunately for the IPCC and particularly Hansen, the measurements are burdened by an agreed uncertainty of more than 0.3°F. This means that possible observed values could vary by as much as 66 percent of the total change—they are after all subject to "corrections" and "adjustments" in the form of orchestration by custodians such as Dr. James Hansen. In other words, it is equally likely that the recent warming since the end of the Little Ice Age may not be outside of natural variability, but instead may fall nicely inside the "expected" band (and much research cited in these pages supports this latter assessment). All of which only heightens the silliness of this entire conversation about whether the warming is big or small revolving around a few hundredths of a degree.

All of this tells us that, unseemly appearances notwithstanding, it is clear that even per the UN's standards the present climate could still be *entirely* without any human influence; this seems unlikely considering that at least through the urban heating effect humans impact global temperatures at some level. What does seem increasingly likely, however, is that the influence is very small and indeed just a fraction of that of solar influence[67] (despite "a rich tradition of near 20 years of IPCC inspired attempts to trivialize the solar/climate link"[68]). The solar influence and its interaction with cosmic rays[69] are together increasingly prominent climate drivers, just as CO_2's influence is battered by emissions and temperatures having of late gone their separate ways.

The point, however, is that even the UN's own sources indicate it should not have made the conclusive, "money" claim that climate change has conclusively been outside of natural variability.

MAKING THE CITIES DISAPPEAR

Just as alarmist scientists and their politician cohorts need to diminish the importance of the Sun in heating the planet, they need to minimize the effect that, say, covering an area with asphalt has on the temperature right where they've placed (or moved) the measuring instruments. That is, they need to downplay the role "urban heat island" (UHI) effect plays in driving up average temperature readings.

The alarmists' dismissal of urban warming is disingenuous and often heavy-handed. It's not paving they want to regulate nearly so much as it is energy. Besides, taking care of the latter solves their problems with the former.

In brief, the UHI, is as follows:[70]

In cities, steel and concrete walls absorb the sun's heat. Over night, these walls and paved surfaces radiate this heat back into the air, thus offsetting the nighttime cooling that would occur. This can cause cities to have nighttime temperatures as much as ten degrees warmer than rural areas. The same is true of nearby water, but states such as Michigan have chosen to site a host of instruments next to sewage treatment plants. The result is higher ambient night-time temperatures at the site, which account for half or even more of a station's recordings. That's a phony warming signal.

Obviously, more and more of the world is being urbanized: paved, built up, and covered in concrete. So the instruments placed near people have to be adjusted—here we go with that again—and there is evidence that those adjustments are insufficient. Also, the UHI effect appears not only larger, but also broader than the adjusters have taken into account, however lucky they are with their adjustment program (the record for which is miserable). Physicist T. R. Oke (1973)[71] and climatologist Douglas Hoyt (2002)[72] have shown that even towns with much smaller populations can experience urban warming, especially in winter (towns of 1,000 can see warming of up to 2°C). Geologist Kenneth Hinkel (2003) showed how even the village of Barrow, Alaska, with a population of 4,600, has seen a winter warming of 2.2°C compared to the surrounding rural areas.[73]

IPCC author Dr. John Christy testified about this before Congress: "Many studies have shown that the nighttime low has warmed more rapidly than the daytime high in most regions. The cause of this nighttime warming, however, is more consistent with the effects of human development of the surface and consequent influence on the near surface air (e.g. urbanization, farming, aerosol pollution) rather than greenhouse warming."[74]

Jim Goodridge, who was California State Climatologist, found an increase of more than 4°F since 1910 in California counties of more than 1 million residents. Counties with populations between

100,000 and one million experienced a mild warming of 1°F since 1910. Counties with populations below 100,000 witnessed a warming over the same period of time of 0 degrees. Consistent with other research, Goodridge concluded that "long-term temperature trends are clearly a function of urban population density. There are few temperature-measuring stations located in places with no heated buildings, pavement, or night lights in their view shed."

This is important because the relevant authorities use a deeply flawed system plotting grid boxes on a map to determine an average temperature. But we don't uniformly measure the planet and those places we do measure are rather perversely chosen. IPCC expert reviewer Dr. Madhav Khandekar writes in an e-mail that even the influential paper by Phil Jones in the *Journal of Climate* (January 2003) showed "significant warming trends are present in only 10–20% of the available grid boxes." Says Khandekar, "a close look at these boxes reveal that for land-areas, most of these

CO2 RISING. TEMPERATURE NOT.

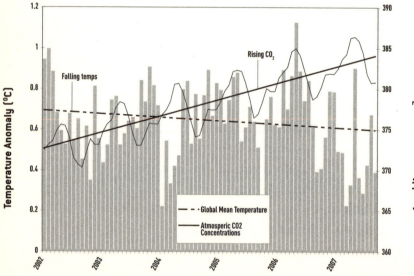

Sources: Carbon Dioxide Information Analysis Center, NASA GISS

boxes are in the vicinity of large cities and urban centres of the world.... So in essence the statistically significant warming is primarily due to urbanization and land-use change and NOT due to increased greenhouse gases."

This phenomenon was affirmed by research published in late 2007 revealing that while California may have warmed at a rate of 0.13°C per decade over the past half century, heavily urbanized stations showed warming at a significant rate with many rural locations barely warming, not warming, or even cooling. "Some of the largest temperature increases occur in the vicinity of urban centers, particularly for minimum temperatures. Few rural stations show significant increases in minimum or maximum temperatures."[75]

If you were looking for a cause of warming here, it wouldn't be greenhouse gases, which have a tendency to scatter around the world rather than sit above the cars, stadiums, and other sources that emit them. This data becomes very problematic for those who would pin the planet's future on our CO_2 emissions. Thus, the alarmists had to reply.

The IPCC, in order to diminish the urban heat island effect, turned to professor Wei-Chyung Wang of the State University of New York at Albany, and his collaborator Phil Jones. As described by a critical researcher, "The paper of Jones et al. is one of the main works cited by the IPCC to support its contention that measurement errors arising from urbanization are tiny, and therefore are not a serious problem."

But there are problems with the road the IPCC took to get there.

In August 2007 that independent researcher, Douglas J. Keenan, publicly accused Wang of fraud for his work on Chinese temperature measuring stations—work that included the same Jones paper the IPCC relied on.[76]

Wang was the lead author of one of the impugned papers, and a contributor to Jones' influential paper (Jones, by the way, is infamous for his refusal to allow others access to necessary background data to check on his work, until forced to by statute). Keenan later published his analysis of the misfeasance and its implications in a peer-reviewed journal, *Energy and Environment*.[77]

Keenan states, "There is conclusive evidence that some important claims that Wang has made in some of his published work on global warming were fabrications.... The term 'fabrication' is formally defined by the U.S. government to mean *making up data or results and recording or reporting them*. Fabrication is one of the three officially-defined types of scientific misconduct (the other two being plagiarism and falsification)."[78]

In short, Wang claimed that the measuring stations he relied on were not moved, and did not experience changes in instruments or observation times during the relevant period; or, if a few experienced such changes, it was rare. But Keenan detailed questions about the reliability and even possible *non-existence* of particular surface temperature data that the papers claimed in support of an appreciable warming trend.

Wang and Jones claim they used data from eighty-four stations, but the very authority they cited claims that station histories for forty-nine of the eighty-four stations (or *nearly 60 percent*) are not available. One cannot claim that the stations were never relocated—or anything else about them—when one knows nothing about their history.

Keenan also asserts that the records indicate at least half of the thirty-five stations for which historical data does exist had been moved, sometimes frequently. At least one of them moved five times over thirty years. A station whose history includes relocations cannot provide historical data. Combined, these two claims, if true, completely undercut the utility of data relied upon by the IPCC and others for their alarmist case.

Keenan cites a statement from the U.S. Department of Energy and the Chinese Academy of Sciences that "few station records included in the [Chinese] data sets can be considered truly homogeneous [i.e. have no significant changes in location, instrumentation, etc.]. Even the best stations were subject to minor relocations or changes in observing times, and many have undoubtedly experienced large increases in urbanization."

Keenan offers details partially absolving the otherwise maligned Jones of complicity, at least at first. When the papers were published in 1990, "it appears very likely that Jones knew nothing at the time." But then Jones co-authored a study in 2001, using two meteorological stations in China (at Beijing and at Shanghai). That study noted station relocation, and that this substantially affected the measured temperatures.

> Thus, by 2001, Jones must have known that the claims of Wang were not wholly true. On 19 June 2007, I e-mailed Jones about this, saying "this proves that you knew there were serious problems with Wang's claims back in 2001; yet some of your work since then has continued to rely on those claims, most notably in the latest report from the IPCC." I politely requested an explanation. I have not received a reply.[79]

The original sin appears to be Wang's. From the moment of his publication onward, it does seem in hindsight that the data just appeared too good to be true, which is catnip to alarmist bodies such as the IPCC.[80]

Time and again in the global warming context, something that is too good to be true is also too good to turn away from, and the failure to scrutinize such a juicy claim ultimately backfires[81] when the truth ultimately comes out despite efforts to block it.

IT'S NOT THE HEAT; IT'S THE STUPIDITY

IPCC claims of increases in the global mean surface temperature, heavily influenced by the Jones paper[82] that Wang co-authored, presume that overall urbanization effects are insignificant. Even invalidating Jones would not in itself invalidate the IPCC's presumption of minimal UHI influence.

For example, IPCC defenders note their reliance on Tom Peterson's 2003 work concluding that "no statistically significant impact of urbanization could be found in annual temperatures,"[83] but that finding isn't even supportable from his own data as supplied to Steven McIntyre. Unfortunately for Peterson, the ever vigilant McIntyre found that the raw temperature measurement from Peterson's data set actually did reveal a very large urbanization effect of about 0.7°C over the last century. The study's author avoided showing these raw numbers in his study, in favor of adjusted results that suffer under scrutiny.[84]

In fact, McIntyre's review concludes that all twentieth century warming might be attributable to UHI.[85]

Unfortunately, the IPCC's 2007 report dismissed the findings of McIntyre's old colleague Ross McKitrick, published along with Michaels, also showing twentieth century warming is accounted for by warming from urban areas. The IPCC said this relationship was coincidental, and that the Arctic Oscillation accounts for warming being largely centered in urban areas. As McKitrick wryly notes, the IPCC doesn't even try to blame the Arctic Oscillation for what's going on *in the Arctic*; but to explain why cities are warmer, well, that's their answer.

McIntyre and Roger Pielke Sr. have written dozens of times about this in recent years given that Peterson's paper is at least partially responsible for the warm bias in the global and now U.S. climate data bases. The IPCC and the data centers instead continue to accept Peterson and reject the many peer reviewed papers and other work by Pielke, McKitrick, and Michaels, Anthony Watts and others exposing the data as contaminated by urban and local land use factors and poor siting.

Keenan notes yet another study relied upon by the IPCC, by David E. Parker at the UK's Hadley Centre,[86] has also since been strongly criticized including in the peer-reviewed literature. Keenan notes:

> Since the publication of Jones et al. (1990), there have been several studies on the effects of urbanization on temperature measurements in China. The most recent study, in 2007, is by Guo Yu Ren and colleagues at the Laboratory for Climate Studies in China.[87] This study concludes that a large part of the warming that has been measured in China is due to the effects of urbanization on measurement. (The study is also supported by the analysis of He et al. (2007) for the years 1991–2000.)[88]

It isn't that the alarmists ignore urban warming, but disingenuously pretend that it is less important than it really is. In fact, "Because GISS was able to accumulate a 0.5 degree Celsius error (in the difference between 1998 and 2007 temperatures) during one decade and because the older measurements of temperature resembled those of GISS, it is conceivable that the whole 20th century warming by 0.6 degrees Celsius is due to similar errors."[89] Urban warming is not just real and almost certainly much greater than the alarmists are willing to entertain, but any "adjustments" made to account for it remain just that, adjustments, subject to human error, bias, and simple design flaw.

Keenan fairly concludes that "none of this means that the conclusion of the IPCC is incorrect. It does suggest, though, that a re-evaluation of the evidence would be appropriate."[90] Of course the IPCC has, like the rest of the warming industry, aggressively worked to ensure that no such review of the evidence be part of their operation. The IPCC refuses to accept more recent, more reliable data, apparently because such data doesn't support their position that the urban effect is minimal.

This further reveals the *modus operandi* of what is touted as the gold standard and latest in scientific thinking on climate change.

In the end, however, we see the familiar, self-serving refusal by the IPCC and friends to acknowledge that the warming from urbanization—completely distinct from "greenhouse" or what's commonly known as "global" warming—might be significantly enhancing (or constitute the entirety of) the surface warming since the 1950s.

In short, the IPCC goes to great lengths to dismiss the obvious, distorting influence of urban heating upon the surface temperature record for the apparent reason that to admit its real influence undermines the enterprise and even threatens the panel's very existence. Such defense of the indefensible, however, seems more likely to be the global warming industry's downfall than its salvation.

CHAPTER 8

The Intergovernmental Panel on Climate Change

The UN's Four-Alarm Liar

"We have to get rid of the Medieval Warm Period."

University of Arizona professor and IPCC lead author Jonathan Overpeck in an e-mail to a colleague he assumed was on board.

WE CAN THANK THE FRENCH for many things: great whines, John Kerry, and of course their former president Jacques Chirac outing the Kyoto Protocol with praise of it as "the first component of an authentic global governance."

That may not sound like such great shakes to you but, having been in the room in The Hague where he gave his ode to Kyoto in November 2000, I can tell you that this vision is shared by many global warming alarmists. This occurred at a meeting hosted by our supposed future global governors—the United Nations—and there wasn't a dry non-American eye in the house. To little surprise, that same gang has also been the source of some of the worst alarmist deceptions.

Whenever our media or our politicians—agitating for an international or mere federal scheme to constrain energy and freedom in the name of saving the planet—need an unimpeachable, disinterested, expert source claiming that climate catastrophe is upon us, the ultimate resource is the United Nations body called the Intergovernmental Panel on Climate Change, or IPCC. Though touted as a "scientific body" it is indeed an inter*governmental* panel, one which openly if infrequently admits it conducts no research.[1] Instead of research, it performs advocacy, specifically in favor of a global warming treaty, which is precisely what it was expressly chartered to support.

The specific shortcomings and misanthropy of the IPCC are legion. They rank among the most brazen, not just in climate science but in all of science. The IPCC's misdeeds are among the most craven in the UN's pantheon of wretchedness. Begin with the words of Sir John Houghton, who oversaw each of its first three much-touted reports, "Unless we announce disasters no one will listen."

The unsupportable advocacy from these supposed sages of science begins with their threshold dishonesty of putting forth a lurid and alarming "summary," drafted by a few dozen people who often are activists—and encouraging claims that these conclusions represent the consensus of thousands of "the world's leading scientists" from the world over.

The IPCC in its summaries bends the facts—by exaggeration, omission, and oversimplification of nuanced issues. When their authors lay out a range of future scenarios, limited to those fitting their narrative of course, the organization works with the media to hype the least probable but most powerful scenarios precisely because of the stark picture they paint. For example, the IPCC regularly fosters alarm over the notion of a drought-stricken future, regardless of certain inconsistencies between that and the mechanics of a warmer world with more evaporation and increased atmospheric moisture. Droughts dominate any list of the worst climate-related disasters of the twentieth century, and the prospect of drought is the best way to get attention. Alarming scenarios sell, and the IPCC has proven expertise in at least identifying scenarios they know worry the public. This is little different than Al Gore claiming a likely, massive sea level rise because of its impact on individuals' psyches and despite his claim being so utterly improbable and unsupported that it is a complete misrepresentation of the data.

While the IPCC purports to represent the objective, peer-reviewed consensus of the latest in climate science, not one IPCC document, conclusion, or assertion can claim more than about one hundred authors. The "summary" document on impacts, regularly cited by the media as agreed to or written by "thousands" of scientists, actually has fifty-one authors.

On the rare instance where the IPCC admits fallibility, it soon finds a way to reverse the admission. For example, the deeply flawed computer models infect the IPCC's entire product and have to be covered for. Models provide the basis for the science, or Working Group I Assessment Reports (the product of which are in turn used as the basis for the Working Group II and II Assessment Reports). The 2001 Third Assessment Report clearly acknowledged the reality that, "In climate research and modeling, we should recognize that we are dealing with a coupled non-linear chaotic system, and therefore that the long-term prediction of future climate states is not possible."

This was pretty damning given the importance of models to the IPCC and entire global warming industry. As a result, they had to be watered down in the next report, the Fourth Assessment Report. There, the language was as follows: "More generally, the set of available models may share fundamental inadequacies, the effects of which cannot be quantified."[2] That is, while the IPCC cannot quantify the models' weaknesses it will nonetheless claim certainty about their output. Yet even this diluted acknowledgement that models (still) do not have predictive or forecasting ability belies the loudly trumpeted claims of growing confidence in the models. As discussed below, it is increasingly inescapable that the models on which the IPCC bases its alarm are useless for the task to which they are put, and the IPCC knows it.

As *Investor's Business Daily* admitted in an editorial, "We have a grudging admiration for the IPCC and the rest of the alarmists who have successfully turned global warming into the bogeyman of the 21st century. Their drumbeat of disaster has put them into a position from where they can shut out and shout down the opposition and not be challenged for it. It won't last forever, though. At some point, the public will realize the sky is not on fire and begin to shrug at the believers' antics. But the everyday man is never safe. Zealots, as they always do, will find another threat to hype, and they will swear that it will be worse than any of the faux cataclysms that came before."[3]

A LONG HISTORY OF REWRITING HISTORY

For the moment, let us consider the origin and nature of the IPCC beast as opposed to its specific failings. Philip Stott, emeritus professor of biogeography at the University of London, offers a tidy summary of the endeavor from its origins to the most recent flailing. He notes that it sprung from the "post-modern period of climate change angst" which itself derives, like so many wonderful movements and -isms, from the late-1960s.

Stott regales how the "global cooling" scare was in full swing by about 1973,[4] among other fashionable and increasingly hysterical claims, all of which would prove unfounded. By the year 2000 the U.S. population would be down to only 22 million, compared to the 302,824,000 estimated to be hanging around in 2007. No Michael Moores were to be in evidence, either, as the average American's caloric intake would be a mere 2,400 per day. Since then alarmist fashions changed only a matter of degree, so to speak, and with the weather.

In 1987, the scare abruptly changed to 'global warming,' and the IPCC was established (1988), issuing its first assessment report in 1990, which served as the basis of the United Nations Framework Convention on Climate Change (UNFCC). The second assessment report was then issued in 1995, the third in 2001, and, of course, the draft fourth assessment report on Saturday. In essence, the Earth has been given a 10-year survival warning regularly for the last fifty or so years. We have been serially doomed. So it comes as no surprise to note that the latest IPCC Draft Report's panel yet again declares that action must be taken within a decade or so if we are to save the world from 'global warming.'[5]

In part because the IPCC so slavishly promotes a particular agenda, its critics call it corrupt. To be sure, there are parallels to other UN offices which have abused their mandate and the public trust.

Consider how the IPCC increasingly seeks to stifle dissent, both among its own participating scientists (detailed below) and the media. In late 2007 the IPCC dragooned authors to the Mediterranean city of Valencia, Spain, presumably to motivate the drafters by depositing them amid the horrors of a warmer climate. The lavish November confab was intended to produce ammunition for the December meeting of the IPCC's partner group, at which the world would keen over the call to action (in, of all other inhospitable places, the tropical resort of Bali). Clearly, our climate warriors are willing to brave any conditions, and along the way spew untold tons of carbon dioxide, in the name of hectoring (other) nations to legislate away the freedom of millions of people to occasionally vacation almost as if they were an IPCC grandee.

It was at this event that UN Secretary General Ban Ki-moon audaciously proclaimed looming disaster—derived from a summary of three different summaries already trumpeted over the course of the year, all of which were written by a handful of bureaucrats and pressure group lobbyists. His claim that "today, the world's scientists have spoken, clearly and with one voice"[6] was soon exposed, though not for lack of the UN trying to keep such criticism quiet.

You see, in Bali the two things that they were not willing to brave were non-fawning scientists or skeptical press. The organizers denied media credentials to *Environment & Climate News*, which "has been in continual publication for 10 years; is sent to more than 75,000 elected officials, opinion leaders, and environmental professionals in the United States; and is one of five newspapers published the by 23-year-old Heartland Institute."[7] *E&C News* was kicked out.

By coincidence, the publication happens to be openly skeptical of alarmism and the IPCC. Representatives from a sound science coalition were also bounced. Later, their promised media event was abruptly barred from taking place.[8]

This is one way to create "consensus." That same day, looking around and seeing none in disagreement—as those types were kept outside—the head of the UN Environment Programme Yvo de Boer crowed that "the heyday of the climate skeptic has been put to rest once and for all, and political momentum and global public awareness for climate change have never been higher."[9] None of the censorship, by the way, was covered by the West's establishment press. "Skeptic" press had of course already been neutralized.

The same week that Ban Ki-moon declared the UN's indispensability in saving the world from a growing climate crisis—upon which one of its offices depends—in a completely unrelated development the UN office that obtains increased money and authority depending on the extent of the AIDS epidemic was forced to admit it had long grossly overestimated the global infection rate by more than 40 percent. This latter pattern of exaggeration appeared to date back as far as UNAIDS' founding in 1995. Yet, just as with the UN's climate arm constantly claiming things are much worse than before (even when the underlying work actually tones down prior projections), the UN only the year before had reported infections rising faster than "even our worst estimates," and warned of the "dangers of inaction."[10] "'There was a tendency toward alarmism, and that fit perhaps a certain fundraising agenda,' said Helen Epstein, author of 'The Invisible Cure: Africa, the West, and the Fight Against AIDS.'"[11] This should sound rather familiar. In fact, it is increasingly apparent that this same *modus operandi* is employed by the UN IPCC and its parent the UNFCCC.

The IPCC's many substantive flaws are also predictable results of a biased process. The Summary of the IPCC's inaugural Assessment Report (1990) dismissed the satellite data, which showed no abnormal warming. The next IPCC report (1995) was exposed as having had significant alterations made to the text after being approved by the scientists, in order to convey the impression of a human "finger print" in global warming. Next, the 2001 IPCC report hyped the now-discredited "Hockey Stick" graph as a "smoking gun" proving highly unusual twentieth century warming, apparently due to Man. The 2007 IPCC report minimized the growing scientific evidence that warming and cooling cycles over the eons tends to correlate with solar activity and changes in the Earth's orbit. In short, it seems that the IPCC is monomaniacal to conclude that Man is hurtling the planet to a fiery end, regardless of the totality of the evidence.

As to the original sin, an analysis released by Dr. Fred Singer's Science and Environmental Policy Project (SEPP) revealed that the IPCC was distributing claims in a Summary for Policymakers that were not supported in either the underlying report allegedly being summarized or a later supplement.[12] This allegation revealed not just how the Summary is used to distort the work done by the hundreds and even thousands whose agreement the IPCC claims, but the enterprise's general credibility and specifically its misuse of "peer review" as the term and practice are commonly understood.

Dr. Frederick Seitz, a longtime figure in America's scientific establishment, wrote an op-ed in the *Wall Street Journal*, titled "A Major Deception on Global Warming," detailing these changes made to the IPCC's Second Assessment Report (1995) *after* it had been approved.[13] Seitz revealed that, although the IPCC report carries heft due to having been the topic of review and discussion by many scientists, "this report is not what it appears to be—it is not the version that was approved by the contributing scientists listed on the title page. In my more than 60 years as a member of the American scientific community, including service as president of both the National Academy of Sciences and the American Physical Society, I have never witnessed a more disturbing corruption of the peer-review process than the events that led to this IPCC report."

What transpired was that "more than 15 sections in Chapter 8 of the report—the key chapter setting out the scientific evidence for and against a human influence over climate—were changed or deleted after the scientists charged with examining this question had accepted the supposedly final text," even though nowhere of course do IPCC rules provide for such tricks. In Seitz's assessment, "nearly all [of the changes] worked to remove hints of the skepticism with which many scientists regard claims that human activities are having a major impact on climate in general and on global warming in particular." These included deleting the following qualifications or expressions of uncertainty, which Seitz described as included at the request of participating scientists to keep the IPCC honest:

- "None of the studies cited above has shown clear evidence that we can attribute the observed [climate] changes to the specific cause of increases in greenhouse gases."

- "No study to date has positively attributed all or part [of the climate change observed to date] to anthropogenic [man-made] causes."
- "Any claims of positive detection of significant climate change are likely to remain controversial until uncertainties in the total natural variability of the climate system are reduced."

In response, the relevant lead author Dr. Benjamin Santer, whom Seitz says made the changes, wrote a letter in the *Journal* that did not deny that the changes were made as alleged.[14] Instead, he offered numerous assertions, none of which rebutted Seitz's specific claim but instead dismissed Seitz as not having participated in the drafting and dismissed his qualifications. Santer defended the IPCC's work, not from the specific allegations but generally as balanced, comprehensive, and objective.[15] He said that even though the deletions were made after authors had agreed on the language their *content* remained, such that the final reviewed and approved version and the altered, published version were "equally cautious."

It turned out that the stealth editors had in fact been prevailed upon to make these supposedly meaningless changes. This left the ultimate question still outstanding, which was how Seitz's revelations could be immaterial given that the IPCC goes through the painstaking pretense of obtaining line-by-line agreement?

The rush to discredit Seitz's recitation of what transpired was typical. Stephen Schneider also wrote to the *Journal* in complaint—which only seems fitting given his infamy over the alarmist's imperative of touting "scary scenarios," making "little mention of any doubts," and deciding the appropriate balance "between being effective and being honest." His letter recited what Seitz exposed, followed by the somewhat juvenile retort, "Similar claims of procedural improprieties have been made by the Global Climate Coalition, a consortium of industry interests."[16] The substantive nature of this rebuttal was typical of alarmists, apparently to spare the masses from wading through actual details. The facts remain what they are, however, and the principals' explanation (and Schneider's amusing attempt at diversion) did not change what Dr. Seitz revealed about the IPCC enterprise,[17] and portended what was still to come from the IPCC bag of tricks.

BACKWARDS IS AS BACKWARDS DOES

In 2007, the myth of the IPCC was exposed. It began with the IPCC issuing the first of many dribs and drabs of its "Fourth Assessment Report," the Summary for Policymakers of its Working Group I on "The physical science basis of climate change."[18] It attained all of the lurid coverage that it was designed to generate. The actual underlying work purportedly being summarized was not in fact yet completed, but was released months later and then again also in stages for maximum hype. This is how the IPCC works: summarize first, then produce; if the scientists producing the underlying Assessments aren't on the same page, seek changes to "harmonize" the underlying work with the pre-written summary.

By the end of the year, the summaries were summarized *once again*, this time somehow yielding the most apocalyptic coverage and diplomatic clucking yet. This product was the Synthesis Report (SR) accompanied by its own pithy, hysterical Summary for Policymakers (SPM) "based on a draft prepared by" forty scientists, who we will presume agreed to the Summary though they did not write it.[19]

Writing "summaries" before completing the text being summarized enables the IPCC hierarchy to hype unsupportable claims, such as the conclusion that CO2 drives warming. Professor Delgado Domingos, for instance, points out that a recent IPCC scientific report states "that in Antarctica the temperature rise preceded the rise in carbon dioxide emissions, but that is omitted in the report for policy makers."[20]

The tone of the summaries combined with the IPCC's claim to 95 percent certainty that Man was driving climate change prompted independent researcher John McLean to review the IPCC process, starting with a very basic inquiry:

> But did anybody actually read the report in detail and check the evidence on which the claim was made? At the time this would have been extremely difficult because the Summary for Policy Makers was released well in advance of the detailed document on which it was based, but prudence would have dictated waiting for that evidence before accepting that pivotal claim.
>
> When the Working Group I report was finally released in May 2007 anyone who reviewed the principal finding, that mankind was responsible for the increase in temperature, should have been appalled by the absence of concrete evidence.[21]

We don't actually know how to assess the rather brazen "money claim" that greenhouse gasses have very likely caused most of the warming over the past fifty years. This is because, as McLean found when reviewing the crucial Chapter 9 of the WG I ("science"), at most *five* independent scientist reviewers agreed with the claim. Four of them turned up in his review of reviewers with vested interests in the outcome and the other made a single comment for the entire 11-chapter report.[22]

Here we find a hint as to why the IPCC trumpets its "summaries" of reports before the reports are produced. That way, when the alarming summary comes out there is no way to check the lurid claims for months, until the actual underlying work by the scientists is produced and released, to far less notice. By that time, the summary's claims are firmly embedded in the media's and politicians' minds. You can't unring the bell, even if one day environmental journalists do something completely out of character and dig beyond press releases and summaries and into the substance of a matter.

Columnist and climate skeptic Melanie Phillips picked up on this practice, noting: "But here's the really wicked thing. It appears that the IPCC intends to make the scientists falsify the science." She quotes an appendix on IPCC procedures:

> The content of the authored chapters is the responsibility of the Lead Authors, subject to Working Group or Panel acceptance. *Changes (other than grammatical or minor editorial changes) made after acceptance by the Working Group or the Panel shall be those necessary to ensure consistency with the Summary for Policymakers or the Overview Chapter* [my emphasis]. These changes shall be identified by the Lead Authors in writing and made available to the Panel at the time it is asked to accept the Summary for Policymakers, in case of reports prepared by the Task Force on National Greenhouse Gas Inventories by the end of the session of the Panel which adopts/accepts the report.
>
> Let's pause for a second. The IPCC has said that the authors of the scientific papers will have to change their findings if they depart from the summary in order to bring them into line with it. In other words, research which apparently shows that the panic over man-made global warming is exaggerated, misleading, and wrong is to be altered to support the summary's view that man-made global warming is even worse than previously thought.[23]

Concludes Phillips, "We are repeatedly told that there is simply no evidence to counter the man-made global warming theory and that the argument is over. This, it would seem, is how they are ensuring that it *is* over—by proposing to doctor the evidence. If they believe the evidence really is conclusive, just what are they so worried about?" That is a good question, and one that the alarmists are most reluctant to answer.

NOT VERY DIPLOMATIC

In 2002 the recently installed IPCC chairman Rajendra Pachauri revealed the character of this outfit by now known for fudging content, and which would soon be caught exaggerating qualifications. He was confronted with what should have simply been a challenge for the scientists, but which the IPCC viewed instead as an embarrassing problem to be attacked. Two experts of impeccable pedigree had offered a well-reasoned critique explaining their view that the IPCC report had serially and substantially overestimated reasonable projections of human CO_2 emissions. That was important because the emissions scenarios were one factor in producing the IPCC's lurid "story lines" used to create fanfare.

Pachauri may have been new but he also knew how the game was played at the UN. This after all is a body that goes so far as to claim that global warming is causing an increase in rich older men taking younger brides, elopement, high school dropouts, and sexually transmitted disease.[24] Pachauri's response to the allegations was not to investigate but, after apparently being dissatisfied with the efficacy of ignoring them, to use the offices of the IPCC to start a smear campaign against those who dared bring the facts to his attention. Thus the world was introduced to a man who would also argue that there are only "about half a dozen" skeptical scientists left in the world.[25] Possibly it was to help enlighten Pachauri on what participating scientists really believe that the official IPCC reviewer comments were finally made public in 2007.

The gents who were interested in checking the math underlying "the greatest threat facing Mankind" were former head of the Australian Bureau of Statistics Ian Castles, and the former head of the Economics and Statistics Branch of the Organization for Economic Cooperation and Development (OECD) David Henderson. They went through formal channels, sending respectful letters[26] (knowing Henderson personally, I can attest to his unflinchingly genteel nature).

Pachauri—certainly a gentleman in his own right as revealed by his subsequent comparison of Bjørn Lomborg with Adolf Hitler (of course)[27]—lashed out during the "COP-9" Kyoto negotiation in Milan, Italy with a press release to the nearly 200 media outlets attending the confab. It claimed that "disinformation" was being spread by "so-called 'two independent commentators'" (Pachauri does not reveal whom he is quoting).[28] Reflecting the IPCC's ire over the audacity of someone questioning it, this was *one of only two press releases the IPCC would publish that entire year.*[29]

Pachauri's argument was intemperate, in which he vowed that it is "factually incorrect" to claim that the IPCC's *projections of the future* are unrealistically high, because they were "carefully chosen." Of course, projections about the future are not "factual" in any sense no matter how carefully their basis is chosen. Regardless, the greens praised his reflexive downpour upon those who dare criticize alarmism.

Pachauri closed his press release with the remarkable claim that "there is absolutely no reason to believe that, in the longer term, lower economic development would, all other things being equal, result in lower emissions." That's not only facially absurd, but is directly disputed by Alan Greenspan among many others (including industry being cudgeled with emission reduction mandates in Europe). In fact, retarding economic development is the *only* demonstrated way to reduce emissions over any period of time given available and foreseeable technologies (the models being the collapse of the Eastern bloc economies with the fall of the Soviet Union and shuttering East Germany industrial capacity after reunification).[30] Pachauri seemed to also be inartfully defending against the professional consensus, and practical experience, that cutting emissions of heat-trapping greenhouse gases under a cap-and-trade scheme risks economic harm, and that CO2 emission reductions "can only occur with much lower levels of economic activity."[31]

Since this episode Pachauri has subsequently gone on to claim, again in the face of no warming over the past decade—which mere months later he would admit—that "what is particularly worrying [about 'global warming'] is that it is accelerating."[32] And ignorance is strength, Winston.

It is tempting to sympathize with the frustration that our friends at the UN must feel over the issue which had held so much promise for their fiefdom. Not only has the past decade seen the atmosphere's temperature turn uncooperative, but also no one new is agreeing to join the handful of countries caught up in the Kyoto Protocol fiasco attempting to "level the playing field for big businesses worldwide."[33]

With his choler and his instincts Pachauri certainly ought to feel right at home in the UN bureaucracy. After all, Libya was awarded a two-year term on the Security Council in October 2007 instead of the Czech Republic, which it seems was rejected due to its President Vaclav Klaus, just before the decision, quite publicly questioning awarding the Nobel Peace Prize to Al Gore and the IPCC.[34] Klaus had of late also been outspoken against global warming alarmism, specifically noting that it is a vehicle for the kind of statism that the eastern half of Europe was still crawling out from under.

The departed UN Secretary General Kofi Annan had been well-known for seizing on the global warming issue for political gain, pandering to anti-Americanism.[35] The head of the United Nations Environment Programme and longtime UN bureaucrat, Yvo de Boer, warns that "ignoring warming"—defined as not accepting the UN's demanded response, which happens to benefit the UN though it's less clear if the environment or anyone else would be better off—would be "criminally irresponsible."[36] UN special climate envoy Dr. Gro Harlem Brundtland declared it "completely immoral, even, to question" the UN's claims to scientific "consensus."[37]

What with the UN IPCC being just another vehicle to advance the agenda, Annan's successor, Ban Ki-moon, took things several steps further.

BAN MOON, RISIBLE

Though Pachauri's incivility came in a defensive crouch, when it comes to going on offense no claim has been too grotesque for the UN to make, from capitalizing on natural disasters of every variety to Mr. Ban blaming Man-made global warming for ethnic cleansing in Darfur[38] because of increased desertification caused by rich countries. (This is only more reckless given that deserts actually should retreat in a warmer world, like the cooperative Sahara seems to have done during the recent, slight warming trend.[39])

For the IPCC's smash-bang hoopla in Valencia over the November 2007 summary of its "Synthesis Report," Mr. Ban affirmed not only that he does not understand the underlying facts and arguments, but that he seemingly does not care and is instead in thrall to the idea of Kyoto's collectivization.

Ban used his pulpit as Secretary General to gather the media and frantically declare that this process that conducts no actual research and a document revealing nothing not already long in print instead offered proof that "we are on the verge of a catastrophe" and "we are nearing a tipping point."[40] He also declared that "one path leads to a comprehensive climate change agreement, the other to oblivion. The choice is clear." *Surely you accept my policy demands that happen to call for a vastly expanded role for our little outfit; you wouldn't want to be one of those people in favor of oblivion, now, would you?*

For Ban's promotion of this summary-of-the-summaries the IPCC issued a "scientific 'instant guide' for policy makers, stating more forcefully than ever that climate change has begun and threatens to irreversibly alter the planet."[41] That is, *with no new work supporting it* the IPCC found a way to more forcefully than ever state the very same things that had already been released over several events in the previous ten months, all of which purported to summarize work published anywhere from two to six years before. But at least they haven't resorted to alarmism or desperation tactics.

"Welcoming the report, [Ban] said climate change imperils 'the most precious treasures of our planet.' The potential impact of global warming is 'so severe and so sweeping that only urgent, global action will do,' Ban told the IPCC after it issued the report."[42]

So, Ban is not a big fan of sovereignty-hugging super powers refusing to toss the keys to him and his bunch at the UN. But he was too busy making cracks like the one about computer model scenarios being "as frightening as a science-fiction movie. But they are even more terrifying, because they are real,"[43] to notice that the report he trumpeted in fact "noticeably reined in its predictions of future doom and gloom (less sea-level rise, lower temperature rise, admissions of serious problems in its climate models, and so forth)."[44]

> "Yes, we have to face it. The whole [IPCC] process is a swindle. The IPCC from the beginning was given the licence to use whatever methods would be necessary to provide 'evidence' that carbon dioxide increases are harming the climate, even if this involves manipulation of dubious data and using peoples' opinions instead of science to 'prove' their case. The disappearance of the IPCC in disgrace is not only desirable but inevitable.... Sooner or later all of us will come to realise that this organisation, and the thinking behind it, is phony. Unfortunately severe economic damage is likely to be done by its influence before that happens."
>
> *IPCC Expert Reviewer*
> *Dr. Vincent Gray*

Mr. Ban invoked Antarctica as his case study, having just gone there and having been told that he was witnessing ice melt that was so rapid that "sea levels could rise by six metres...almost overnight in geological terms" (meaning "millennia," per the text). Or, they could not. Mr. Ban was apparently never informed that the Antarctic ice has reached a record mass for modern measurement which, regardless of how long or short such a period is, is another way of saying it isn't melting.

"In short: It's the truth battle of the Nobel Prize winners! Who has the least inaccurate but terrifyingly real science-fiction movie story to tell? Is it Al Gore's *An Inconvenient Truth*? Or will it be Ban Ki-moon's An Unreadable Synthesis?"[45]

Bryan Leyland, chair of the economics panel of the New Zealand Climate Science Coalition, summed it up with his call for Ban "to recognise facts from his own life experience":

The worst case scenario described by the IPCC is that the world will warm by a maximum of 4°C in the next 100 years. That is an exaggeration, but let's accept it for a moment. According to the World Meteorological Organization, the city of Seoul, where Dr Ban Ki Moon comes from, on the hottest day of its mean temperatures, has a maximum of 29.5°C and a minimum of 22.1°C. The Finland city of Helsinki, the home of Nokia, on its coldest day, has a maximum of -2.9°C and a minimum of -9.3°C. That's a spread of, at maximum of 32.4°C, and at minimum, 31.4°C. Yet people live happily and productively in both cities, and would scoff at any suggestion that they could not handle a difference of 4°C, up or down, spread over the next 100 years.[46]

It is true that some places on Earth including Tokyo, Sao Paulo, Minneapolis and Rio de Janeiro have seen annual mean temperatures rise by 2 to 4°C since 1880 and, other than that bridge in Minnesota the alarmists told us collapsed because of global warming, it seems to have been a calamity-free trend. Meanwhile, "in the Southeastern United States, more than 90 percent of recording stations in Georgia, Alabama and Texas show a marked cooling trend of several degrees since the 1880s."[47] More embarrassing, the planet has cooled slightly since Kyoto was agreed[48] (talk about climate sensitivity, the pact hadn't even gone into effect yet and had already bullied temps into submission!).

Regardless, asking the UN chief to inform his judgment with his own life experience is of course unrealistic. His personal experiences aren't harrowing and don't come from computer models and as such have no place in this discussion.

THE TRUTH ISN'T SCARY

A collection of scientists seeking to temper escalating UN rhetoric on the issue then reminded the Secretary General that the most lurid IPCC claims are found in the only IPCC product that most anyone will ever read, the summaries, prepared by a relatively small core writing team which is a small fraction of the full roster of contributors and reviewers the IPCC would have the public believe made the claims contained therein.[49]

Exposing how material this point is, consider the following statement, which is arguably the most important of the whole UN climate process and certainly one of the media's most aggressively embraced: "Most of the observed increase in global average temperatures since the mid-20th century is *very likely* due to the observed increase in anthropogenic greenhouse gas concentrations."[50] (emphasis in original) As with everything else in the UN process, at most several dozen authors produced the statement (in this case, fifty-one: thirty-three drafting authors and eighteen contributing authors).

Of course thousands did *not* sign off on this, but only sixty-two scientists reviewed the chapter in which this statement appears, of whom fifty-five had serious vested interests, leaving only seven expert reviewers who appear impartial. In addition, almost 60 percent of all the comments from official IPCC reviewers concerning this crucial chapter were rejected by IPCC editors. This does not rise to the level of "peer review," and the claim that 2,500 independent scientist reviewers agreed with this statement, or any other statement in the UN climate reports, is patently false.[51]

Implicit in IPCC lore is that it must poll the tens of thousands of scientists and social scientists around the world qualified to assess the validity of the Summaries, risible on its face. Therefore the IPCC is simply not in a position to claim "consensus" on or majority support among the world's experts for any of their claims that Man is driving global warming or their projections of costly effects.

This can be easily established. Claims to the contrary, however, cannot. Fortunately for the IPCC, they are never challenged on this and in fact they have been left comfortable to merely imply the authorship of "thousands," which is then mythologized by their helpful media, politician, pressure group, and rent-seeking industry partners.

AND YOU ARE...?

It is of course difficult to get a handle on what the universe of relevant scientists believe, given that one of the alarmists' many double standards is to tout absolutely anyone who agrees with them as a "world's leading scientist" for these purposes while dismissing even the most learned parties as unfit to comment on the matter. Supposedly, somewhere over two thousand such creatures form the IPCC chorus of agreement about future doom.

In addition to only a few dozen scientists writing the IPCC assertions attributed to the authorship of many, the stature of this "over two thousand" was rocked by the revelation that most of them, the Expert Reviewers, for the most part did not bother participating in any tangible way beyond allowing their name to be glorified (for example, by commenting).

For example, McLean found that of the fifty-four non-governmental representatives reviewing the critical chapter that attributed recent warming to human activity, nearly one-third of them made just one comment, thirty-one of whom had a vested interest in the report as editors or having papers cited therein. Twenty-six of these reviewers authored or co-authored papers cited in the final draft of the IPCC report, ten of them even explicitly mentioned (that is at minimum relied upon with a complete lack of objectivity, and at worst simply promoted) their own papers in their review.[52]

This recalls the old line of "waiter, the food was horrible, and the portions too small!" Only a handful of reviewers actually offer substantive comment, and among those most are conflicted out or, rather, would be in any transparent or credible process.

Further, those who did comment were as a general proposition simply dismissed when their edits criticized the preordained conclusions, as detailed below. And of course a far greater number of relevant scientists than fifty-one have written to the UN specifically in protest of such claims to scientific agreement.[53]

The IPCC also exposes the folly of the alarmists' qualification thuggery. Despite how its participants are hailed, their biographies reveal they hardly are dominated by the hard sciences—let alone "climatology"—as you are also led to believe. Reconciling the rhetoric with the actual composition of the IPCC begs troubling questions. Such as, *why would an economist (or anthropology TA) sign off on a physicist's work?* The answer is he wouldn't and he never has. A general rule is that the more vocally someone supports the IPCC enterprise the less they typically know about it. Mistakes come easy to people too busy waiving a document, yelling "consensus!" to actually read the thing.

The fact of the matter is that the "climate" field covers many and varied areas, making numerous disciplines relevant to its work and in many instances the most appropriate practitioner is a stat-istician—dealing, as this does, with mathematics, data reconstruc-tion and projections. This explains why at least three-fourths of the IPCC's participants come from fields which, when practiced by climate rationalists, leave them disqualified as unfit to comment. It doesn't explain, however, why their peers who do play the IPCC game *are* qualified, as world's leading experts no less. Also, those IPCC authors and reviewers who do come from the hard, physical sciences include people who have, e.g., advocated "get[ting] rid of" the more inconvenient aspects of the historical climate record.

"Consensus" cheerleaders specifically dismiss the opinion of theoretical physicists, such as world-renowned Freeman Dyson. Leading alarmist organ *Grist* magazine keened, "Expertise mat-ters. Not everyone's opinion is equally valid.... [Dyson] simply does not have the relevant specialist knowledge. That also applies [sic] the large number of social scientists, computer programmers, engineers, etc., without any specialist knowledge on this prob-lem."[54] This author of this, Andrew Dessler—a chemist, by the way—specifically dismissed Dyson also because he had posited the concept of powering space vehicles through a series of nuclear explosions. How absurd. Lock the kook up. Next thing you know he'll probably say that this is what drives submarines.

Here's where it gets uncomfortable. Who dares break it to the IPCC's shrillest champions that their scripture is authored by indi-viduals of Dyson's background (if not quite his prominence)? For example, consider authors such as theoretical physicist Sivan Kartha,[55] left-wing economist Tariq Banuri,[56] as well as futurists and social advocates *cum* Gore advisors?[57] Could it be that even the loudest proclaimers of "consensus" now see the supposed rel-evant universe of experts as unqualified for the job?

All of this was on embarrassing and high-pitched display when Senator James Inhofe and others released a list of what grew to 500 peer-reviewed scientists whose recent work challenged the supposed consensus of catastrophism. The warmists howled that this document was facially discredited by including individuals who, it turns out, merely held the very same professional training as the IPCC authors. That is to say that, yet again, the warmists beg the question of which time they're lying. Engineers, chemists, economists, statisticians, physicists, computer modelers, and so on either are relevant, or they are not. Nowhere else, outside of an elementary school playground, is relevance determined by whether someone agrees with you.

The alarmist oracle "Climate Progress" whined the loudest (this is a band of left-wing activists in a project of George Soros's Center for American Progress, helpfully affirming global warming's role in the "progressive" agenda[58]). "'Padded' would be an extremely generous description of this list of 'prominent scientists.' Some would use the word 'laughable.'...For instance, since when have economists, who are pervasive on this list, become scientists, and why should we care what they think about climate science?"[59]

Hmmm. Good question, posed by someone whose bio boasts that his own expertise of the panel is *having been interviewed about the IPCC*, if apparently never having checked who it consists of. The warmist peanut gallery swarmed to complain about inclusion of non-"climatologists" like economists, and also engineers, and meteorologists. This represents staggering ignorance of the subject matter given that climatology is a very and artificially narrow field (with about eighty PhDs in the U.S., let's say a few hundred worldwide—which falls somewhere short of 2,500). So, strike atmospheric scientists, climate modelers and frankly most of the world's "climate scientists" from the ranks of the qualified.[60]

It is unclear what this means for high-profile alarmist heroes, like IPCC Coordinating Lead Author Kevin Trenberth, a mathematics graduate who then pursued the very same field of meteorology that alarmists now insist is utterly irrelevant for someone hoping to play climate scientist.[61] Similarly, chemical engineer

Thomas Ring was among those whom the alarmists specifically dismissed; he has authored several scientific papers for *Oil and Gas Journal* and is a member of both the American Institute of Chemical Engineers and Tau Beta Pi (the national honors society for engineers). Yet he was assailed as *just a chemist*—you know, like Dessler—with the alarmists mocking his discipline as irrelevant.[62] Irrelevant if the chemist challenges alarmism, that is, because mere chemists round out the very ranks of IPCC Lead Authors[63] and, as we have already seen, are among the noisiest spouters of alarmist dogma.[64]

Also, when the alarmists failed to find any peer-reviewed articles on climate change bearing Ring's name, this absence was cited as proof that he is unqualified to comment on the topic. More on that complaint, momentarily.

Recall how the alarmists find the notion of economists opining on climate laughable? It only gets funnier. The IPCC's head Rajendra Pachauri—often falsely described as a "climatologist" by the *New York Times* and[65] *USA Today*,[66] canonized as "the scientist leading research into the issue,"[67] and elsewhere called the UN's "chief climate scientist"[68]—has no peer-reviewed climate science articles to his credit for the very simple reason that he is not a climate scientist or anything close to it.[69] He is, in fact, an *economist and industrial engineer*. For an interventionist perspective on energy or economics, he's your guy. Climate science, well, not so much. He has, however, sat on a lot of boards, taught business school, and worked for the UN an awfully long time. He might even have stayed at a Holiday Inn Express last night.

We already know what they think about engineers but the alarmists, apparently unaware of their leader's background, mewled that *economists are the least-qualified of all to pronounce on climate issues*.[70]

Hard to believe, but the more you look, the better yet it gets. The gang over at the UK's Climate Resistance saw how the alarmists were getting their knickers in such a knot over having their illusion of IPCC climate expertise and consensus deconstructed and stooping to new depths of hypocrisy in their usual insistence about who is and who is not a climate scientist. The CR team reviewed the backgrounds of their countrymen listed as contributing to the IPCC. First looking at the most recent Assessment's "Working Group II"—"Impacts, adaptation and vulnerability"—they found that, using the alarmists' standards, it seems you'd be lucky to find many scientists in this crowd at all.

Of the UK's fifty-one contributors to AR4 WG II, five were economists, three epidemiologists, five work in civil engineering or risk management/insurance, and five are zoologists, entomologists or biologists; seven had specialties in geography, and just ten have specialties in geophysics, hydrology, climate science or even modeling. "But there were 15 who could only be described as social scientists. If we take the view that economics is a social science, that makes 20 social scientists" out of fifty-one total.[71]

Further scrutiny revealed that these "world's leading experts"— in fields like anthropology and transport management to whom we defer for decisions regarding our sovereignty and energy policy on the basis of their thoughts on climate change—were quite often "research associates at best" (teaching assistants) with little to no publication credits to support their supposed world leadership. Now, what about that requirement of peer-reviewed articles on climate science as a precondition to comment as an expert?

At this point the alarmist cries out at the unfairness of criticizing the relevance and scientific credentials of the 1900 participants in Working Groups II and III, which by definition are not about the science of climate change at all (that's WG I's turf, though its team is heavily laden with computer modelers, also diminishing that crowd's claim to climatology fame). WGs II and III merely run with WG I's conclusions. But this proves too much about the claim of *two thousand of the world's leading climate scientists*—the vast

majority of them having nothing to do with climate science what-
soever. This is only the beginning of why the global warming industry relies so heavily on name-calling and shouting down opposition;
they aren't very good with facts. They might bear in mind the old
counsel against lying due to the difficulty of keeping one's story
straight later.

Within weeks of this revelation the *New York Times* subtly
shifted to writing about the *400-member IPCC*, with no mention
of where the other 2,100 went.[72] Someone might ask.

The above also struck a nerve with one alarmist activist who the
UN trots out to shout the consensus to the heavens, and to his
credit he publicly offered a couple of amazing yet, at the same
time, not overly surprising admissions:

> It got me thinking: I'm an environmental scientist, but I've never
> had time to review the "evidence" for the anthropic causes of
> global warming. I operate on the principle that global warming
> is a reality and that it is human-made, because a lot of reliable
> sources told me that, and because I read it in learned journals.
> When I said, in my opening speech for the launch of UNEP's
> Global Environment Outlook-4 in Beirut: "There is now irrevo-
> cable evidence that climate change is taking place..." I was
> reading from a statement prepared by UNEP. Faith-based sci-
> ence it may be, but who has time to review all the evidence? I'll
> continue to act on the basis of anthropic climate change, but I
> really need to put some more time into this.[73]

Yes, please do. And tell your neighbors. If you're going to give
speeches as an authority on the "greatest threat to Mankind," etc.,
you might want to check the claim out first.

Manifesting how absurd this support-by-association game
extends, consider Pasteur Institute Professor Paul Reiter, a leading
expert on malaria who had to threaten legal action against the

IPCC to have his name removed from the list of "2,000 of the world's leading scientists" who supposedly backed its summary. His reason was simple: he doesn't support the claims at all, but "instead argu[ed] that it was a 'sham.' The IPCC 'make it seem that all the top scientists are agreed, but it's not true', he said."[74]

Given these truths and others described below, all of which are available for anyone who cares to look, it is implausible to assert with a straight face that authorship by a few dozen scientists and some government representatives, working in coordination with a handful of pressure group lobbyists, represents an "overwhelming consensus." As one might expect, a group that lies so flagrantly about the basics is probably telling real whoppers about the big stuff.

IPCC SCIENCE, FICTION

Two prominent IPCC claims in the latest round of hype beg for scrutiny. The first was the bold step of the IPCC now claiming a 90 percent to 95 percent probability that human emissions of carbon dioxide are having a significant effect on climate—although our emissions are about 2 percent to 3 percent of the total CO_2 produced each year and, when combined with all other anthropogenic GHG emissions, still is only responsible for about a *quarter of one percent* of the greenhouse effect. (Oddly, the IPCC now plans a Fifth Assessment Report with even *better* results, for 2014;[75] this is doubly odd given their claim of certainty).

This particular claim and its grave implications received great media attention. Recall that an October 2007 survey of U.S. scientists listed as contributing authors and reviewers of the IPCC's "Working Group I," "Climate Change 2007: The Physical Basis" found that only whopping 20 percent of respondents claim to believe that human activity is the principal driver of climate change.[76] This did not attract the media's attention.

Is such a claim of more than 90 percent confidence supportable, two decades after James Hansen's claim during the "stagecraft" appearance at a Senate hearing of 95 percent certainty that *Man-made* global warming was underway? In short, no.

First, Hansen's claim at that time remains true today, that "The forcings that drive long-term climate change are not known with an accuracy sufficient to define future climate change."[77] These forcings are the basis for computer models, which in turn are the basis of the IPCC's claims. As IPCC author John Christy described this claim, "We are not told here that this assertion is based on computer model output, not direct observation. The simple fact is we don't have thermometers marked with 'this much is human-caused' and 'this much is natural.' So, I would have written this conclusion as 'Our climate models are incapable of reproducing the last 50 years of surface temperatures without a push from how we think greenhouse gases influence the climate. Other processes may also account for much of this change.'"[78]

Statistician William M. Briggs writes the IPCC's confidence is "*conditional* on the model that [is] chosen being *true*. Since it is rarely certain that the model used *was* true, the eventual results are stated with a certainty that is too strong. As an example, suppose your statistical model allowed you to say that a certain proposition was true 'at the 90% level.' But if you are only, say, 50% sure that the model you used is the correct one, then your proposition is only true 'at the 45% level' *not* at the 90% level, which is, of course, an entirely different conclusion. *And if you have no idea how certain your model is, then it follows that you have no idea how certain your proposition is.* To emphasize: the uncertainty in choosing the model is almost never taken into consideration."[79]

In fact, the IPCC admits (on pages unread by journalists) that when it comes to the nine mechanisms that can force climate change (called "forcings") the body possesses a low to medium "level of scientific understanding" (LOSU) for seven, and a high

LOSU for only two. Then it somehow excludes *water vapor alto-gether* from its list of greenhouse gases,[80] given that water vapor is responsible for somewhere above 95 percent of the greenhouse effect and is closely related to clouds—another key forcing the IPCC does not understand.

The IPCC need not bother with such trifles because it admits that the impact of water vapor on climate change "is not well understood."[81] Middlebury College professor Jim Peden states that this is similar to concluding that the human race is all male, after eliminating females from consideration in gender demographics because "they are not well understood." This also indicates the IPCC believes that without Man the planet might just be well below freezing at the moment. Surely it was before we came along?

To make matters worse, as climate scientist Dr. Roy Spencer asks, rhetorically, "Why are ALL of the 20+ IPCC climate models more sensitive in their total cloud feedback than published estimates of cloud feedbacks in the real climate system (Forster and Gregory, *Journal of Climate*, 2006)? If the answer is that 'there are huge error bars on our observational estimates of feedback,' then doesn't that mean that it is just as likely that the real climate system is very insensitive (making manmade global warming a non-problem) as it is to be as sensitive as the IPCC models claim it is?"[82] All of which is to say, in sum, that the IPCC still isn't even sure what the major drivers of climate are, or at least have just changed their collective mind about

---

MODEL OF CORRUPTION

"For years I have called these computer models scientific money-laundering. They take unproven assumptions, plug them into something they call a model, and then get results they claim to be proven…
The models are built on the assumption that anthropogenic effects drive the climate, and so they therefore spit out the results that… anthropogenic effects drive the climate."

www.Climate-Skeptic.com

it while also demonstrably misplaying those which they include, but they've always "known" enough to demand that you bow down before the agenda the group was expressly chartered to support.

Worse, after the IPCC Valencia show was over and the Bali circus of Kyoto talks was just beginning, an important paper from a respected climate scientist (Kiehl 2007) seemed to admit that *the anthropogenic forcings in the twentieth century used to drive the IPCC simulations were chosen to fit the observed temperature trend.*[83]

CAN'T HANDLE THE TRUTH

Beyond the IPCC's game-rigging and hypocrisy are its ethics. It happens that not only are the IPCC products not written or even substantively reviewed by thousands of leading experts, but its expertise is questionable as are the conflicts with which it is riddled and that contribute to apparent corruption of the process and its product.

Consider the level of expertise typically shown by IPCC reports. Professor Scott Armstrong is a leading expert on forecasting at the University of Pennsylvania who, along with Professor Kesten Green of Monash University's Business and Economic Forecasting Unit in New Zealand, conducted an audit of the section relevant to their expertise, Chapter 8 of the IPCC's Working Group I ("science") report, "Climate Models and their Evaluation." They found no evidence that the IPCC authors were aware of the primary sources of information on forecasting. They also found that there was only enough information within the IPCC report to make a judgment on 89 of the total 140 forecasting principles as described in Professor Armstrong's book, *Principles of Forecasting*. Of the 89, the IPCC violated 72.[84]

As a result of what he found, Armstrong didn't merely criticize the claims and their claimants. He put his money where his mouth is by challenging the IPCC's co-Nobelist Al Gore to a $10,000 bet, based on climate predictions. After Gore initially dismissed the challenge by saying that he was too busy, Armstrong suggested that Gore could simply review a list and "provide a checkmark beside a leading climate model" he claims supports the alarmist case. Months later, upon prompting, Gore's mouthpiece replied that "Mr. Gore simply does not wish to participate in a financial wager" (though he has in fact placed a heavy financial bet already on his scare campaign). "Armstrong responded that it was fine by him and that we could 'merely do it for its scientific value.' The spokesperson said that she would ask Mr. Gore . . . . Professor Armstrong [still] awaits Mr. Gore's response to the revised challenge."[85]

Renowned sea-level expert Nils Axel-Mörner reviewed the list of experts performing the IPCC's section on sea-level rise, and was amazed to discover that he had never heard of these so-called "world's leading experts."

What Mörner uncovered supports Dick Lindzen's experience that some actual leading experts are too disgusted with the IPCC anymore to bother, and then some. "[T]he IPCC might have doctored data to show a sea-level rise from 1992 to 2002. 'Suddenly it changed,' Mörner said of the IPCC's 2003 sea-level chart, which is intended to convince the public that warming due to man's activities is melting ice that will cause the oceans to rise to dangerous levels. The change 'showed a very strong line of uplift, 2.3 millimeters per year,' which just happens to be the same increase measured by one of six Hong Kong tide gauges. Mörner said that particular tide gauge is 'the only record which you shouldn't use' because 'every geologist knows that that is a subsiding area. It's the compaction of sediment. . . . Not even ignorance could be responsible for a thing like that,' he said. 'It is a falsification of the data set.'"[86]

So, to make its case the IPCC managed to use the one data set that was obviously corrupted. Clever. And also, as Mörner has long noted, by no means restricted to that Hong Kong set.

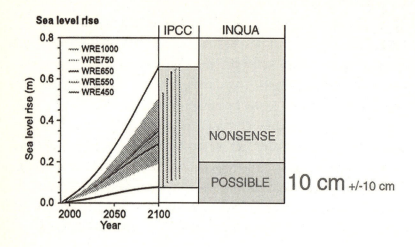

Chart courtesy of sea-level expert Nils Axel-Mörner

All of these red flags have led to scattered inquiry into what might well be described as a scam, or at minimum deceptive advertising. For example, consider the aforementioned Reiter, who heads the Insects and Infectious Disease Unit at the Pasteur Institute and before that the entomology section at the Dengue Branch of the Centers for Disease Control. In short, he is a real "world's leading scientist" in his field, having worked as an officer of the Harvard School of Public Health, served on the World Health Organization's Expert Advisory Committee on Vector Biology and Control, and was lead author of the Health Section of the U.S. National Assessment of the Potential Consequences of Climate Variability and Change. But he had had enough of the IPCC's politicization and amateurish tricks.

Reiter found himself nominated by the U.S. State Department as a Lead Author for the relevant health chapter, only to see two scientists with no specialty in vector-borne diseases selected instead despite (because of?) the increasing IPCC emphasis on global warming supposedly leading to a dramatic rise in, say, malaria and Dengue fever.

Like Mörner, Reiter wanted to know how individuals of whom he largely had never heard found find themselves counted as world-leading experts. As reported in the *National Post*, Reiter "wrote the IPCC with a series of detailed questions about its decision-making process. It replied: 'The brief answer to your question below is "governments." It is the governments of the world who make up the IPCC, define its remit and direction. The way in which this is done is defined in the IPCC Principles and Procedures, which have been agreed by governments.' When Prof. Reiter checked out the 'principles and procedures,' he found 'no mention of research experience, bibliography, citation statistics or any other criteria that would define the quality of "the world's top scientists."'"[87]

The IPCC also presents glaring conflicts of interest. Climate scientist Roger Pielke Sr. poses a thought experiment, putting into stark relief the scandal that consumes the IPCC and indeed "climate science."

If instead of evaluating research in climate, suppose a group of scientists introduced a new cancer drug that they claimed could save many lives. There were side effects, of course, but they claimed that the benefit far out weighed these risks. The government than asked these scientists to form an assessment Committee to evaluate this claim. Colleagues of the group of scientists who introduced the drug are then asked to serve on this Committee, along with the developers.

If this occurred, of course, there would be an uproar of protest! This is a clear conflict of interest.

Yet this is what has happened with the IPCC process! The same individuals who are doing primary research in the role of humans on the climate system are then permitted to lead the assessment! There should be an outcry on this obvious conflict of interest, but to date either few recognize this conflict, or see that since the recommendations of the IPCC fit their policy and political agenda, they chose to ignore this conflict. In either case, scientific rigor has been sacrificed and poor policy and political decisions will inevitably follow.[88]

Here's another thought experiment, this time involving our judicial system which strives for fairness, including in the jury selection process. Imagine the (justifiable) outcry should even one of these reviewers cited as having conflicts be permitted to judge claims litigated against the IPCC's merits, due to their obvious personal stake. But it is precisely such a stake that the IPCC seems to find most appealing in its reviewers.

History proves that these conflicts are real and greatly diminish the quality of the IPCC as a useful tool for anything other than propagandizing, as was illustrated most vividly in the Hockey Stick affair arising from production of the Third Assessment Report (TAR). Then, chapter author Michael Mann inserted his work, which clearly did not withstand scrutiny when it finally was received, after the fact. It made its way into the Technical Summary and was given prominent placement on the second page of the Summary for Policymakers. It was the "smoking gun," only to wither under the slightest test.[89] In fact, some congressmen simply asking for substantive backup was enough to get the "smoking gun" demoted to one exhibit in a flurry of obfuscation about the prior assurance of aberrant twentieth century warming and regional Medieval warming.[90]

The TAR also supported a paper that labored at the unconvincing argument that pre-1940 warming—inconvenient to the alarmist cause—was of human origin. This work, too, contained fundamental errors in its statistical analysis and, like the Hockey Stick, quietly disappeared from the next IPCC report.

When the IPCC's Hockey Stick finally received detailed scrutiny, experts empanelled by the Chairmen of the U.S. House Committee on Energy and Commerce and the Subcommittee on Oversight and Investigations and the National Academies of Science thoroughly discredited it.[91] Both heard that Mann's "decentred methodology is simply incorrect mathematics,"[92] and that "Mann's assessments that the decade of the 1990s was the hottest decade of the millennium and that 1998 was the hottest year of the millennium cannot be supported by his analysis."[93] The IPCC hadn't bothered to look.

Representatives of both Wegman's committee and the NAS panel concurred on the "spurious trend in the proxy-based reconstruction" the IPCC previously hyped.[94] Wegman et al were particularly blunt. "Overall, our committee believes that Mann's assessments that the decade of the 1990s was the hottest decade of the millennium and that 1998 was the hottest year of the millennium cannot be supported by his analysis."[95] Their analysis noted that the claims by the "Hockey Stick's" critics can be replicated, but that Mann's cannot:

We have been to Michael Mann's University of Virginia website and downloaded the materials there. Unfortunately, we did not find adequate material to reproduce the MBH98 materials. We have been able to reproduce the results of McIntyre and McKitrick.[96]

The panel took specific aim at the scientific establishment that promoted and then circled the wagons around the "Hockey Stick," for apparent ideological—and decidedly not for scientific—reasons:

[The] fact that their paper fit some policy agendas has greatly enhanced their paper's visibility. . . . The 'hockey stick' reconstruction of temperature graphic dramatically illustrated the global warming issue and was adopted by the IPCC and many governments as the poster graphic. The graphics' prominence together with the fact that it is based on incorrect use of [principal components analysis] puts Dr. Mann and his co-authors in a difficult face-saving position.[97]

In conclusion, Wegman et al. offered suggestions to avoid such scandalous abuses in the future, which the IPCC process quite clearly rejects. These include more intense scrutiny and review as opposed to visceral fawning derived from a desirably doomsaying conclusion. "It is especially the case that authors of policy-related documents like the IPCC report, *Climate Change 2001: The Scientific Basis*, should not be the same people as those that constructed the academic papers."[98] Good luck with that.

The second recommendation for "a more comprehensive and concise policy on disclosure" derived from the rampant conflicts and incestuous nature of the IPCC and climate science, generally. Wegman et al. also rejected the practice of climate alarmists to refuse access to their codes and data.[99] Finally, they recommended that climate scientists stop keeping statisticians at bay when it is precisely that expertise needed to confirm (or expose) their claims, which are at their essence statistical in nature, as is the case with drug trials.[100] In short, they found the IPCC to be the poster child for conflicts of interest.

Some establishment press did actually pay attention when former IPCC Lead Author and NOAA hurricane expert Christopher Landsea resigned his participation, writing to the IPCC in an open letter addressed to all colleagues, "I am withdrawing because I have come to view the part of the IPCC to which my expertise is relevant as having become politicized. In addition, when I have raised my concerns to the IPCC leadership, their response was simply to dismiss my concerns."[101]

Specifically, Landsea was asked by a particular Lead Author, the aforementioned Kevin Trenberth, to provide the write-up for Atlantic hurricanes. He did this, only to then see news reports of Trenberth—who was in possession of the relevant work, and had performed no original research of his own—publicly offering contradictory, unsupportable, alarmist conclusions about global warming impacting hurricanes. When Landsea got wind of this he objected, and one of the scientists scheduled to participate dropped out of the event for reasons unspoken. Then, after first reviewing transcripts to ensure that what he read Trenberth as saying was not mere media hype, Landsea wrote, "I personally cannot in good faith continue to contribute to a process that I view as both being motivated by pre-conceived agendas and being scientifically unsound." He pleaded with the IPCC to affirm that the report would adhere to the science and not such sensationalism. They declined to offer any such reassurance, and he resigned with rather pointed language at this corruption of science.[102]

Landsea made clear, however, that "my concerns go beyond the actions of Dr. Trenberth and his colleagues to how he and other IPCC officials responded to my concerns. I did caution Dr. Trenberth before the media event and provided him a summary of the current understanding within the hurricane research community. I was disappointed when the IPCC leadership dismissed my concerns when I brought up the misrepresentation of climate science while invoking the authority of the IPCC."

Other prominent scientists who have distanced themselves from the IPCC include Wil Alexander, John Christy, Vincent Gray, Zbigniew Jaworowski, Marcel Leroux, Richard Lindzen, Nils-Axel Mörner, Hans Oerlemans, Paul Reiter, and Roy Spencer, while many more have criticized its process. Former Netherlands Foreign Ministry official and IPCC expert reviewer Hans Labohm published a more extensive list (in German, so the names clearly translate if not their specific critiques).[103]

PEERLESS PEER REVIEW

The IPCC boasts that "the reports by the three Working Groups provide a comprehensive and up-to-date assessment of the current state of knowledge on climate change."[104] Yet, the IPCC actually excludes research produced later than two years prior to its own publication,[105] except to include alarmist material. The two years preceding its 2007 AR4 were notable for the non-alarmist science emerging, and therefore very good to ignore. Had the IPCC been more objective it could have also informed the public of significant if inconvenient new findings casting further doubt on its hypothesis of dangerous human-caused global warming, including Schwartz's empirical confirmation of climate sensitivity to a doubling of CO_2 at no more than about one degree Celsius of warming, and the discovery of important errors in NASA's U.S. surface temperature records which, when corrected, show the 1930s to be the hottest period in the last century.

Were the IPCC interested, it also could have considered recent research providing an updated and enhanced understanding of how tropical weather and clouds act as planetary cooling thermostats (Spencer et al, supporting Lindzen's "Iris effect"[106]); the effect on climate of natural oscillations over decades;[107] mechanisms whereby solar wind and magnetic effects may significantly influence climate;[108] and how the impact of incoming energy from the Sun is amplified near Earth's surface.[109] So it may be a lot of things, but scientific research as the media portray it, and "up to date" as it calls itself, it is not.

Expert reviewer Khandekar details how, as an invited reviewer for the IPCC 2007 documents he pointed out several recent peer-reviewed studies which were completely ignored by the IPCC authors. To his dismay, they ignored all of his comments and suggestions for major changes in the first order draft (FOD), and sent along a Second Order Draft with essentially the same text as the FOD. He concludes:

> This is not an acceptable scientific review process. I have been an editorial board member for two international journals (*Climate Research*-Germany and *Natural Hazards*-Netherlands) and have reviewed more than 100 manuscripts submitted to

these journals in the last 10 years. In no case was the manuscript accepted without full exchange of communication with the authors through the editorial offices in Germany and Netherlands, respectively. This is the essence of peer-reviewed process and is the standard procedure for any scientific journal. Unfortunately IPCC bypasses this process by claiming United Nations immunity. This is unacceptable.

... The IPCC and its authors have closed their minds and eyes to this evolving science which points to solar variability as the prime driver of earth's climate and not the human-added greenhouse gases. [110]

All of the preceding in turn raises the question: is the IPCC subject to the vaunted "peer review" it claims? In short, the answer is *no*, beginning with the very basics. Reiter explains how the IPCC turns peer review "on its head." "In professional science, the names of peer reviewers are kept confidential to encourage independent criticism, free of recrimination, while the deliberations of the authors being critiqued are made public.... [But in the IPCC process] 'The peer reviewers have to give their names to the authors, but the deliberations of the authors are strictly confidential.' In effect, the science is spun, disagreements purged, and results predetermined."[111]

As his numbers cited earlier affirm, John McLean's analysis of the 2007 AR4 WGI ["The Physical Science Basis"] found that "The IPCC's editors could—and often did—reject the peer-reviewers' comments, a reversal of the normal practice in scientific peer-review. Analysis of the extent of the editors' refusal to accept criticism is difficult because the expressions of rejection come in many forms, some were partial and others were rendered otiose by the rewriting, restructuring or deletion of sections of text."[112]

He states that even if one merely considers comments that were greeted with "rejected," "reject," and "disagree," an analysis of the comments still "reveals that the number of peer-reviewers' comments that were rejected by the IPCC climate-templars aver-aged 25% (min. 9.5%, max 58.1%) of all comments on the Second Revision."[113]

McLean describes most rejections as being of "dubious nature," which is to say unsubstantiated. Some were simply absurd. "In several instances, reviewers invited the IPCC to express its conclusions with less certainty, and provided evidence in support of more caution given the uncertainties inherent in climate science. In almost every such instance, the IPCC's reviewers flatly rejected the reviewers' suggested moderations of its conclusions. *Some comments were rejected on the ground that there was not enough space.* Given the unconstrained length and supposed importance of the IPCC's assessment report, this ground of rejection is not compelling."[114]

It appears that the IPCC are also keeping their reasons for rejecting many dissenting reviewer comments secret, or else they simply lack justification.

> Reviewers would cite references in the learned journals challenging the IPCC's conclusions, but in almost every instance they were told that a greater number of references supported an alternative argument. The correct approach, at the very least, would have been to insert in the assessment report a mention of the references that challenged the IPCC's conclusion.
>
> Reviewers who made brief proposed amendments would often be brushed off by being told of just one paper that contradicted the suggested amendment. In at least one response *the IPCC's editors made reference to a document that had not been subjected to peer review at all.*[115] [emphases in original]

The IPCC's summary rejection of so many expert reviewers' comments flaunts the response contemplated by "peer review," which is to make the necessary change to the document or substantively explain why the comment is wrong and the change inappropriate.

While reviewers had to justify the textual amendments which they were putting forward, the responding editors were under no corresponding obligation to justify their rejections of the reviewers' proposals.[116]

The IPCC summarily dismissed comments drawing attention to natural climate forces (e.g. El Niño influences, or the natural 'blocking high' that triggered the 2003 European heat wave).[117] Highlighting its self-dealing, conflicted, and arrogant approach, the IPCC even cited its own inadequately reviewed reports—that is, they underwent nothing such as is required for actual publication in a peer-reviewed journal—as the authority supporting its dismissal of comments.[118]

Simply performing McLean's analysis required piercing a veil of secrecy, the need for which is amply explained by what McLean found. Events indicate that it really was a Freedom of Information request by "Hockey Stick" co-debunker Steve McIntyre that prompted the IPCC to, for the first time, make publicly available the reviewers' comments and editors' responses for the WG I report. This critical series of exchanges was now, after much criticism and, frankly, embarrassment, finally available for reconciliation with the product, allowing examination and refutation of the IPCC's claim to "peer review."[119]

McLean suggests, "Perhaps the IPCC [was] afraid that the review process will be exposed to independent scrutiny and that questions will be asked about the veracity of the process and the claims of significant consensus by a large number of reviewers."[120] This seems likely, as the details of how many reviewers commented on how many sections and how those few comments were in great part disregarded are damning to the IPCC's supposed thoroughness and scientific clarity. They betray the universally reported notion that the IPCC represents the input, let alone the work, of thousands of scientists, all of whom the IPCC nonetheless associates with the conclusions.

Says Vincent Gray of the process, "Penetrating questions often ended without any answer. Comments on the IPCC drafts were rejected without explanation, and attempts to pursue the matter were frustrated indefinitely. Over the years...I have found increasing opposition by them to providing explanations, until I have been forced to the conclusion that for significant parts of the work of the IPCC, the data collection and scientific methods employed are unsound. Resistance to all efforts to try and discuss or rectify these problems has convinced me that normal scientific procedures are not only rejected by the IPCC, but that this practice is endemic, and was part of the organization from the very beginning."[121]

Gray's first-hand experience leads him to reach the same conclusion compelled by McLean's analysis. "The IPCC is fundamentally corrupt. The only 'reform' I could envisage would be its abolition."

In short, "Forget any illusion of hundreds of experts diligently poring over all chapters of the report and providing extensive feedback to the editing teams. The true picture is closer to 65 reviewers for any one chapter, with about half of those not commenting on any other chapter and one quarter commenting on just one other."[122] Of course, forgetting this illusion would mean forgetting about the larger illusion in whose service this and similar gambits are played.

ALARMISM WITH A PURPOSE, JUST NOT A REASON

When the IPCC released that November 2007 summary of prior summaries, the Associated Press reporter attending the Valencia event ably communicated the agenda, noting that the document "will be distributed to delegates at a crucial meeting in Indonesia next month that is intended to launch a political process on international cooperation to control global warming."[123] Indeed, the IPCC itself admits it "is designed to give impetus to the negotiations."

Aspiring to *give impetus* is certainly a different goal than to *give information*. Indeed, *giving impetus* is the stuff of advocacy groups rather than the stuff of scientists. But the IPCC is manifestly an ideological and agenda-driven organization.

On its face this is dangerous. For example, as noted by Philip Stott:

> What neither the IPCC, nor Mr. Ban, nor most media commentators seem to grasp is that the precautionary principle works both ways. Which is riskier, trying to follow the climate-change rhetoric of the IPCC and Green groups by warping world economics and politics to deal (impossibly) with climate change, or facing up to the economics and politics of the real world. Completely changing the world's economic and political basis for something that actually may not happen—and will most certainly not occur exactly as predicted—is for me a much, much riskier proposition, especially when one takes into account the fact that there will be benefits, as well as problems, from climate changes.[124]

Some IPCC authors admit, in the right company, to a commitment to political activism via their IPCC participation. Consider the experience of IPCC author Dr. John Christy:

> At an IPCC Lead Authors' meeting in New Zealand, I well remember a conversation over lunch with three Europeans, unknown to me but who served as authors on other chapters. I sat at their table because it was convenient. After introducing myself, I sat in silence as their discussion continued, which boiled down to this: 'We must write this report so strongly that it will convince the US to sign [sic] the Kyoto Protocol.' Politics, at least for a few of the Lead Authors, was very much part and parcel of the process.[125]

Christy understands the surprise such revelations may cause, but reminds us that "scientists are mere mortals. The tendency to succumb to group-think and the herd-instinct (now formally called the 'informational cascade') is perhaps as tempting among scientists as any group because we, by definition, must be the 'ones who know' (from the Latin *sciere*, to know)."[126] Other prominent scientists have publicly noted the IPCC's political nature.[127]

As already revealed in these pages, the IPCC process is staffed in great part by vested interests including pressure group activists. As Senator James Inhofe noted in a speech on the Senate floor specifically exposing the corruption of the IPCC process:

> [T]he UN allowed a Greenpeace activist to co-author a key economic report in 2007. Left unreported by most of the media was the fact that Bill Hare, an advisor to Greenpeace, was a lead co-author of a key economic report in the IPCC's 4th Assessment. Not surprisingly, the Greenpeace co-authored report predicted a gloomy future for our planet unless we follow the UN's policy prescriptions. The UN IPCC's own guidelines explicitly state that the scientific reports have to be "change[d]" to "ensure consistency with" the politically motivated Summary for Policymakers. In addition, the IPCC more closely resembles a political party's convention platform battle—not a scientific process. During an IPCC Summary for Policymakers process, political delegates and international bureaucrats squabble over the specific wording of a phrase or assertion.[128]

The greens candidly reveal the level and nature of their IPCC involvement. "'We would want to emphasize the urgency which comes from the science,' said Stephanie Tunmore of the Greenpeace environmental group ... 'I expect some scuffling over the final language,' especially over the urgency and the level of certainty of some predicted events, said Peter Altman, of the Washington-based lobby National Environmental Trust."[129] "The delegates slogged through line-by-line approval of the report on how the climate has changed and projecting future scenarios, from the extinction of frogs to the likelihood of more fierce floods and storms... 'We have made too little progress so far,' said Hans Verolme, of the World Wildlife Fund for Nature, or WWF, who is attending the sessions.... 'We want to make sure that what comes out in the end is crisp, well structured and understandable to the layman,' he said."[130] Increasingly, however, the real nature of the IPCC operation is becoming even more clear.

CONCLUSION

Heretics, Speak Out

THE GLOBAL WARMING ALARMIST INDUSTRY rests upon the frailest of arguments: computer modelers, their allies, and enablers warn us that their software shows we are doomed unless we adopt an agenda that, it turns out, the programmers and their cheerleaders generally desire in any event. Billions flow to this doomsday machine, which dines out on ever more implausible claims and attributions of whatever occurs as proof of their faith. It is an amazing story, one which I take great pleasure in exploring, and exposing.

One day, while being interviewed on a cable news show about my 2007 book, *The Politically Incorrect Guide to Global Warming and Environmentalism*, the host mentioned that I was coming out of Charlottesville. For more than two years prior to this, since relocating my family outside of Washington, I had been using the University of Virginia's television facilities without incident. The school holds itself out for the purpose and does well financially by it.

However, after that on-air revelation, the school suddenly refused request after request by the networks to rent its broadcast facility to shows seeking to interview me. I suspect that one phone call led to others expressing umbrage that the university—Mr. Jefferson's university, a public institution—would enable such incorrect speech. Regardless, in the event the school at first agreed they quickly caught their mistake and reversed course. With just one apparent lapse among a dozen requests, the answer continued to be *No*.

Unfortunately, U.Va. has cornered the local studio-for-hire market. Though I occasionally managed to make the two-hour roundtrip to another in Richmond, generally this meant the networks simply had to fill the airtime some other way. In short, using taxpayer resources, without explanation or apology, the school did its part to silence my voice.

I am confident that we will resolve this disturbing pattern now that I have put this project to bed. But that is only one forum and, as you now know, this is not an uncommon attitude on campus. And as I discovered writing this book, a school denying me access to its broadcast facilities was child's play compared to the depths to which so many now willingly sink, including calls for imprisonment, violence and even death for the supposed "crime"—though, in fact, *heresy*—of refusing to accept a dogma that stands on the weakest of premises.

These changing norms of behavior we are witnessing are in the cause of an ideological and political agenda threatening great cost to our individual and economic liberties. That doesn't seem to matter. It is clear that dissent can no longer be tolerated, and no one is above using their position—be it academic, governmental, political or otherwise—to stifle thought that frightens them or threatens to upset the gravy train.

As the United States prepares to inaugurate a president vocally in thrall to the global warming alarmist agenda, the question confronting us is what we are willing to do, in response, to fight back.

Notes

Chapter 1: Media on a Mission

1. "Shark 'kills swimming kangaroo'," BBC News, December 13, 2007, http://news.bbc.co.uk/2/hi/asia-pacific/7142453.stm.

2. Amy Kaleita and Gregory R. Forbes, "Environmental Alarmism in Context: Hysteria's History," Reason Foundation (September 2007), p. 16 (citations omitted) http://www.pacificresearch.org/docLib/20070920_Hysteria_History.pdf.

3. "Fashion warms to reality of climate change," *The Age* (Australia), October 7, 2007.

4. "Global warming: now it hits brothels," MetroUK, March 6, 2007, http://www.metro.co.uk/weird/article.html?in_article_id=39945&in_page_id=2.

5. "Climate change could be causing cougar attacks: expert," August 29, 2007, National Post, http://www.canada.com/nationalpost/news/story.html?id=c5e6120a-be10-4497-8f32-cd8585e5ca33&k=51234

6. "Africa: Link Between Crop Failure And Climate Change Often Missed and freezing," http://allafrica.com/stories/200807240806.html

7. "Penguin Chicks Frozen by Global Warming?" July 2, 2008, http://news.nationalgeographic.com/news/2008/07/080702-endangered-penguins.html

8. "Researchers find global warming may cause bread dough to 'rise nearly 20% less'," New Scientist, http://www.newscientist.com/blog/environment/2008/07/why-global-warming-is-bad-for-bread.html?DCMP=ILC-hmts&nsref=specrt14_bar, July 10, 2008.

9. "Climate change makes island kids bony, stunted," July 7, 2008 see http://newsbusters.org/blogs/terry-ann-rendon/2008/07/07/cnn-com-headline-climate-change-makes-island-kids-bony-stunted

10. "Blood Meant for Transfusions Can Get Contaminated Due to Global Warming," August 20, 2008, http://www.medindia.net/news/Blood-Meant-for-Transfusions-Can-Get-Contaminated-Due-to-Global-Warming-40825-1.htm.

11. "Rise in landslides linked to climate change," Monday, August 25, 2008 http://www.irishtimes.com/newspaper/ireland/2008/0825/1219449685569.html

12. CBS News, http://www.cbsnews.com/stories/2008/06/18/tech/main4191556.shtml.

13. http://blogs.discovermagazine.com/betterplanet/2008/06/17/rotten-tomatoes-caused-by-climate-change/

14. "Warmer temps, more kidney stones," *Time* Magazine, July 10, 2008.

15. "Tuatara," Catalyst March 25, 2004, http://www.abc.net.au/catalyst/stories/s1073835.htm

16. Baron Bodissary, "Does Global Warming Cause Rape Waves?" *Gates of Vienna* http://gatesofvienna.blogspot.com/2007/06/does-global-warming-cause-rape-waves.html read further

17. "Scientists fear Global Warming responsible for unprecedented camel deaths in North Africa," December 24, 2007, *San Francisco Sentinel*, http://www.sanfranciscosentinel.com/?p=8430

18. "Global warming will make Earth spin faster," April 7, 2007, New Scientist Environment, http://environment.newscientist.com/article/dn11555-global-warming-will-make-earth-spin-faster.html

19. Steven Milloy, "Global Warming Litigation Heating Up," FOXNews.com, October 9, 2003, http://www.foxnews.com/story/0,2933,99627,00.html

20. William Briggs, "Zombies no joke: global warming can cause anything," William M. Briggs Statistician blog, February 1, 2008, http://wmbriggs.com/blog/2008/02/01/zombies-no-joke-global-warming-can-cause-anything/.

21. "Pythons could squeeze into lower third of USA," *USA Today*, February 21, 2008.

22. Professor Philip Stott, "Today should visit LaBrea!" Global Warming Politics blog, February 28, 2008, http://web.mac.com/sinfonia1/iWeb/Global%20Warming%20Politics/A%20Hot%20Topic%20Blog/AAFB8068-EAB8-44ED-BB8E-C7296A77D01C.html citing a *Radio 2* (UK) interview by Jeremy Vine of weatherman John Ketley.

23. Emma Young, "Global warming poses deaf threat to tropical fish," New Scientist Environment, March 6, 2008, http://environment.newscientist.com/channel/earth/dn13417-global-warming-poses-deaf-threat-to-tropical-fish.html?feedId=online-news_rss20.

24. Curtis Brainard, "Where's the consensus, and where does it end?," *Columbia Journalism Review*, August 27, 2008.

25. Bill McIntyre, "Media campaign to silence global warming skeptics failing," *Canada Free Press*, January 18, 2008.

26. See, e.g., "Going Green: Can climate change make us sicker?" *Time* Magazine, April 4, 2008.

27. "Iwo Jima Veterans Blast Time's 'Special Environmental Issue' Cover," Business and Media Institute, April 19, 2008, http://www.businessandmedia.org/articles/2008/20080417171532.aspx, quoting *Time* managing editor Richard Stengel comments made to MSNBC.

28. "Oceans at Risk," *New York Times*, March 9, 2008

29. Credit goes to the *Seattle Post-Intelligencer* for noting this at the end of its coverage of the paper, if in a piece whose headline gives away their own willingness to see what they want to see, "Ocean dead zones off Oregon coast 'not normal,' scientists find," February 14, 2008.

30. "Birds, fleas - even elevated trees add to global warming," *Redlands (CA) Daily Facts*, November 16, 2007.

31. Hats off to the *Los Angeles Times* for allowing this opinion piece, which certainly went over well with its readership if it would instill mockery among most, "Killer cow emissions: Livestock are a leading source of greenhouse gases. Why isn't anyone raising a stink?" *Los Angeles Times*, October 15, 2007.

32. See, "Death and Death Rates Due to Extreme Weather Events: Global and U.S. Trends, 1900-2004," at http://members.cox.net/goklany/Extreme%20Events%20Note%20Hohenkammer.pdf.

33. See, e.g., "Cyclone Sidr would have killed 100,000 not long ago," http://www.alertnet.org/db/blogs/19216/2007/10/16-165438-1.htm.

34. See discussion of *Washington Post* hysteria on same, *infra*.

35. "Global warming could mean more heart problems, doctors warn," *International Herald Tribune*, September 5, 2007.

36. Respectively, these stories were debunked at "Virus now top suspect in mass bee deaths," September 6, 2007, *Columbus Dispatch* http://www.dispatch.com/live/content/local_news/stories/2007/09/06/bees.html; and http://www.ncbi.nlm.nih.gov/sites/entrez/, type in "cardiac temperature extremes," producing lots of scientific abstracts, and right on top [when checked, as of late September 2007] one from two scientists at Harvard Medical School, is a study with this conclusion: "Conclusions: we confirmed in a large sample of cities that both cold and hot temperatures increase the mortality risk."

37. Report, "U.S. Senate Report: Over 400 Prominent Scientists Disputed Man-Made Global Warming Claims in 2007," Senate Committee on Environment and Public Works (Minority), December 20, 2007, http://epw.senate.gov/public/index.cfm?FuseAction=Minority.Blogs&ContentRecord_id=f80a6386-802a-23ad-40c8-3c63dc2d02cb. One exception, of a sort, was how on September 14, 2007, the left-wing group Media Matters gave space to a collection of peer-reviewed research running counter the general hysteria over global warming, even some of which was authored by leading alarmists, for the purpose of claiming this proves the list as bogus.

38. The comparison was first made by Amy Menefee, "NYT Scoffs at 400+ Scientists, but Elevates 44 Southern Baptists," NewsBusters, March 11, 2008, http://newsbusters.org/blogs/amy-menefee/2008/03/11/nyt-scoffs-400-scientists-elevates-44-southern-baptists. The original article is Neela Banerjee, "Southern Baptists Back a Shift on Climate Change," *New York Times*, March 10, 2008.

39. "Global Warming Skeptics Insist Humans Not at Fault," *Washington Post*, March 4, 2008.

40. "Carbon Output Must Near Zero To Avert Danger, New Studies Say," *Washington Post*, March 10, 2008.

41. "Fogging up those old time forecasts," *Washington Post*, September 10, 2008.

42. "Skeptics seize on cold spell," *New York Times*, March 1, 2008.

43. "Global Temperatures to decrease," BBC, April 4, 2008.

44. Tim Worstall, "And here is the BBC News: your way!" Adam Smith Institute (London), April 8, 2008, http://www.adamsmith.org/blog/misc/and-here-is-the-bbc-news%3a-your-way!-200804081181/.

45. Daniel Cressey, "Heated row over cooling article," The Great Beyond (reposted at *Nature* Magazine), April 8, 2008, http://blogs.nature.com/ climatefeedback/2008/04/heated_row_over_cooling_articl.html.

46. See BBC guidelines at www.bbc.co.uk/blogs/theeditors/2006/10/sniffing_ out_edits.html.

47. Jennifer Marohasy, "The BBC changes news to accommodate activist," Jennifer Marohasy blog, April 7, 2008, http://www.jennifermarohasy.com/ blog/archives/002906.html. ·

48. Richard Black, "'No sun link' to climate change," BBC News, April, 2008 http://news.bbc.co.uk/2/hi/science/nature/7327393.stm (note, the currently available version is not the original) and is not to be confused with his piece of precisely the same title of July 10, 2007 at http://news.bbc.co.uk/2/hi/science/ nature/6290228.stm.

49. For a discussion of this episode, see Peter Risdon, "The BBC and Climate Change," John Freeborn blog, April 9, 2008, http://freebornjohn. blogspot.com/2008/04/bbc-and-climate-change.html.

50. "Media attacked for 'climate porn'," BBC, August 2, 2006 http://news. bbc.co.uk/2/hi/science/nature/5236482.stm.

51. "Storm porn," *The Star* (Toronto, CA), January 12, 2008.

52. See, e.g., "Senate Environment Chair Inhofe and Aide Take on AP/Borenstein, Brokaw, Revkin," http://www.environmentwriter.org/resources/ articles/0706_inhofe.htm.

53. See, e.g., "Alarm over dramatic weakening of Gulf Stream," December 1, 2005, *The Guardian* (UK).

54. Mike Hulme, "'Sexed-up' numbers should not always be accepted as science," *The Times* of London, March 8, 2008.

55. "US backs states' measures to cut emissions," September 13, 2007, *New York Times*.

56. California vs. General Motors, et al (ND CA), September 2007, http:// www.cand.uscourts.gov/cand/judges.nsf/61fffe74f99516d088256d480060b72d/6 1c396eab9121186882573590079 8cf7/$FILE/5755orderdism.pdf.

57. See, e.g., "NOAA Scientists Say Arctic Ice Is Melting Faster Than Expected," *Washington Post*, September 7, 2007.

58. See, e.g., "Record high Antarctic ice levels ignored by media," September 12, 2007, http://newsbusters.org/blogs/noel-sheppard/2007/09/12/record- antarctic-ice-levels-ignored-media. The University of Illinois Polar Research Group had also reported a new historic Southern hemispheric (SH) sea ice maximum breaking the previous maximum of 16.03 million sq. km at 16.26 million sq. km and representing an increase of about 1.4% above the previous SH ice area record high. Skeptics touted this and, within days, they claimed an undescribed "glitch"—relating apparently only to one of two hemispheres—had led to their own claim actually being false. Http://arctic.atmos.uiuc.edu/ cryosphere/; the glitch was then reversed, the researchers announced the maximum which announcement was, again, treated by the media as unwelcome or uninteresting (same cite, http://arctic.atmos.uiuc.edu/cryosphere/).

"UPDATE: Monday, October 1, 2007 - Record SH sea ice maximum and NH sea ice minimum").

59. "Escalating ice loss found in Antarctica," *Washington Post*, January 14, 2008, http://www.washingtonpost.com/wp-dyn/content/article/2008/01/13/AR2008011302753.html?nav=rss_email/components.

60. "Arctic meltdown, again," JunkScience, January 14, 2008, http://junkscience.com/blog/2008/01/14/antarctic-meltdown-again/.

61. "What's the Big Idea? Ice, Ice Baby (Circa 90 Million Years Ago)," *Washington Post*, January 13, 2008, http://www.washingtonpost.com/wp-dyn/content/article/2008/01/11/AR2008011101997_pf.html.

62. "Antarctic ice shelf did not just melt away," *Western Mail* (Wales), February 7, 2008, http://icwales.icnetwork.co.uk/news/wales-news/2008/02/07/antarctic-ice-shelf-did-not-just-melt-away-91466-20444895/.

63. "At the Poles, melting occurring at an alarming rate," *Washington Post*, October 22, 2007.

64. Grudd, H. 2008. Torneträsk tree-ring width and density AD 500–2004: a test of climatic sensitivity and a new 1500-year reconstruction of north Fennoscandian summers. Climate Dynamics, DOI 10.1007/s00382-007-0358-2, February 2008. See, e.g., "1,500 Years of Cooling in the Arctic," *World Climate Report*, February 4, 2008, http://www.worldclimatereport.com/index.php/2008/02/04/1500-years-of-cooling-in-the-arctic.

65. "Arctic Ocean Circulation Does An About-Face," *Science* Daily, November 14, 2007.

66. See NASA release at http://www.nasa.gov/vision/earth/lookingatearth/quikscat-20071001.html.

67. See, e.g., "Recent Rapid Decline in Sea Ice caused by Unusual Winds, says NASA," AccuWeather.com, October 2, 2007, http://global-warming.accuweather.com/2007/10/recent_rapid_decline_in_sea_ic.html.

68. See, e.g., Don Easterbrook, "Shifting of the PDO to Cool Mode Assures Global Cooling for the Next Three Decades," ICECAP.us, July 18, 2008, http://icecap.us/index.php/go/new-and-cool/shifting_of_the_pdo_to_cool_mode_assures_global_cooling_for_the_next_three_/.

69. See, e.g., "Disgraceful Global Warming Hysteria at NBC: 'Meltdown in Greenland'," September 19, 2007, http://newsbusters.org/blogs/noel-sheppard/2007/09/19/disgraceful-global-warming-hysteria-nbc-meltdown-greenland.

70. See video of September 17, 2007 NBC report, at http://video.msn.com/v/us/fv/msnbc/fv.htm??f= 00&g=78e48cf7-c2c5-478c-bb62-ce3d581014e6&p= source_nightly%20news&t=m5&rf= http://www.msnbc.msn.com/id/3032619/&fg= and critique of the bias at http://newsbusters.org/blogs/noel-sheppard/2007/09/19/disgraceful-global-warming-hysteria-nbc-meltdown-greenland.

71. Petr Chylek, M. McCabe, M. K. Dubey, and J. Dozier, "Remote sensing of Greenland ice sheet using multispectral near-infrared and visible radiances," Journal of Geophysical Research, Vol. 112, D24S20, doi:10.1029/2007JD008742, 2007, http://www.agu.org/pubs/crossref/2007/2007JD008742.shtml.

72. "Greenland thaw biggest in 50 years—Report," *Reuters*, January 15, 2008, http://in.reuters.com/article/worldNews/idINIndia-31415520080115?sp=true.

73. "Traversing the Arctic," Alaska Report.com November 4, 2007, http://alaskareport.com/news1007/do77856_traversing.htm.

74. See, e.g., "Shockwaves from melting icecaps are triggering earthquakes, say scientists," *Independent* (UK), September 8, 2007.

75. See, e.g., "Polar earthquakes are nothing new, and don't foretell catastrophe: We don't know yet whether melting icecaps play any role, but scare stories don't help, says Jose Rial," letter to The *Guardian* (UK), September 13, 2007, http://www.guardian.co.uk/commentisfree/2007/sep/13/climatechange.comment.

76. See, e.g., Tyndall Centre director Mike Hulme, "As activists organised by the group Stop Climate Chaos gather in London to demand action, one of Britain's top climate scientists says the language of chaos and catastrophe has got out of hand." "Chaotic world of climate truth," BBC News, November 4, 2006, http://news.bbc.co.uk/1/hi/sci/tech/6115644.stm.

77. See, e.g., the regional play given the opposing view, "Polar bear die-off unlikely: GN official," *Nunatsiaq News*, September 14, 2007, http://www.nunatsiaq.com/news/nunavut/70914_498.html.

78. See, e.g., Armstrong, et al., "Polar Bear Population Forecasts: A Public-Policy Forecasting Audit," Working Paper Version 20: 29 Nov., 2007, at http://forecastingprinciples.com/Public_Policy/PolBears.pdf; see also, "Last stand of our wild polar bears," Dr. Mitchell Taylor (Polar Bear Biologist, Department of the Environment, Government of Nunavut, Igloolik, Nunavut, Canada), May 1, 2006, http://meteo.lcd.lu/globalwarming/Taylor/last_stand_of_our_wild_polar_bears.html.

79. CAPE Project Members, 2006. Last interglacial Arctic warmth confirms polar amplification of climate change. *Quaternary Science Reviews*, 25, 1383-1400, reviewed by *World Climate Report*, "Arctic Lessons from the Last Interglacial (Polar bears survived)," February 5, 2007.

80. "Inhofe speech on polar bears and global warming," Senator James Inhofe, January 5, 2007, http://epw.senate.gov/public/index.cfm?FuseAction=PressRoom.Blogs&ContentRecord_id= f339c09a-802a-23ad-4202-611ef8047a6b.

81. See, e.g., Alister Doyle, "Polar bears drown amid Arctic thaw," *The Scotsman*, September 15, 2006.

82. "Yes, the water's warm…too warm," *Washington Post*, July 15, 2007, http://www.washingtonpost.com/wp-dyn/content/article/2007/07/13/AR2007071300531.html.

83. "Coral Reefs May Be Protected By Natural Ocean Thermostat," *Science Daily*, February 8, 2008.

84. See, e.g., Newsbusters' treatment, "ABC News publishes photo essay of US cities drowned by global warming," September 14, 2007, http://newsbusters.org/blogs/noel-sheppard/2007/09/14/abc-publishes-pictures-global-warming-drowned-american-cities.

85. See, e.g., G. Wöppelmann et al., "Geocentric sea-level trend estimates from GPS analyses at relevant tide gauges world-wide," *Global and Planetary Change*

57 (2007) 396–406, estimating the rate of world sea level rise to be 27% slower than the IPCC estimate.

86. See "Dissenters Are Left High And Dry In Bali," *Investor's Business Daily*, December 7, 2007.

87. See, e.g., "I have been the expert reviewer for the IPCC, both in 2000 and last year [NB: 2006, for 2007 Fourth Assessment Report]. The first time I read it, I was exceptionally surprised. First of all, it had 22 authors, but none of them— none—were sea-level specialists." Nils-Axel Mörner, Ph.D, "Claim That Sea Level Is Rising Is a Total Fraud: Interview with Dr. Nils-Axel Mörner." June 22, 2007 EIR Economics 33, http://www.mitosyfraudes.org/Calen7/MornerEng.html

88. Phil Rosenthal, "Reporting on global warming not clean, simple," *Chicago Tribune*, October 17, 2007.

89. From an internal Enron memo; see *PIG: GW*, discussion pp. 194–99,

90. This is true both directly and indirectly, as GE's products are marketed in part as ways to generate credits; see also, e.g., "GE unveils new 'green' card," CNNMoney.com, August 27, 2007, http://money.cnn.com/2007/07/25/magazines/fortune/ge_greencard.fortune/?postversion=2007072513.

91. Going Green http://www.nbc.com/Green/

92. See, e.g., Job Listing, "Seeking Vibrant Reporter/Host for Eco Beat," November 30, 2007, http://www.journalismjobs.com/Job_Listing.cfm?JobID=850633.

93. "Autumn 'one of driest on record'," BBC News, November 27, 2007, http://news.bbc.co.uk/2/hi/uk_news/7115258.stm.

94. "Vanity Fair Fails To Print Green Issue On Recycled Paper—Again," EcoRazzi, April 11, 2008, http://www.ecorazzi.com/2008/04/11/vanity-fair-fails-to-print-green-issue-on-recycled-paper-again/.

95. Mark Hertsgaard, "While Washington Slept," *Vanity Fair*, May 2006, 241.

96. Bob Carter, "There IS a problem with global warming…it stopped in 1998," *Telegraph* (London), September 4, 2006.

97. See, e.g., "Greenland thaw biggest in 50 years—Report," *Reuters*, January 15, 2008, http://in.reuters.com/article/worldNews/idINIndia-31415520080115?sp=true.

98. Amy Kaleita, Ph.D, Gregory R. Forbes, "Environmental Alarmism in Context: Hysteria's History," Reason Foundation (September 2007), 19 http://www.pacificresearch.org/docLib/20070920_Hysteria_History.pdf.

99. "Weather May Account for Reduced Honey Crop," *Washington Post*, September 10, 2007.

100. "Warming May Be Hurting Gray Whales' Recovery," *Washington Post*, September 11, 2007.

101. *San Francisco Chronicle*, June 28, 2006.

102. Sharon Begley, "The Truth about denial," *Newsweek*, August 13, 2007.

103. "The power and the story," *Time*, December 13, 1999.

104. See, e.g., http://www.exxonmobil.com/Corporate/community_contributions_report_environment.aspx.

105. Ron Kessler, "ACU's David Keene Says Press Favors McCain," *NewsMax.com*, February 3, 2008.

106. See *PIG: GW* 3–36.

107. Christopher Shea, "In the balance," *Boston Globe*, April 9, 2006.

108. Eleni Andreadis and Joe Smith, *British Journalism Review*, Vol. 18, No. 1, Feb. 2007.

109. SEJ website, "Vision and Mission," http://www.sej.org/about/index1.htm.

110. See, e.g., Joe D'Aleo, "Global Temperatures are Uncorrelated with Carbon Dioxide Trends This Last Decade," IceCap.us, Tuesday, November 27, 2007, http://icecap.us/index.php/go/joes-blog/global_temperatures_are_uncorrelated_with_carbon_dioxide_trends_this_last_d/.

111. "Talking Climate with The New York Times' Andrew Revkin," *University Communications*, University of Vermont, March 14, 2008.

112. SEJ's 18th Annual Conference, October 15-19, 2008, http://sej.org/confer/index1.htm.

113. "Majority Fact of the Day," Senate committee on Environment and Public Works, October 30, 2006, http://epw.senate.gov/fact.cfm?party=rep&id=265464.

114. Bill Blakemore, "'Schwarzenator' vs. Bush: Global Warming Debate Heats Up," ABCnews, August 30,2006, http://abcnews.go.com/US/print?id=2374968.

115. Bob Berwyn, "Global warming story hits critical mass," Summit Daily News, March 13, 2007 http://www.summitdaily.com/article/20070313/NEWS/103130045.

116. See, e.g., http://www.cbsnews.com/blogs/2006/03/22/publiceye/entry1431768.shtml.

117. Id.

118. Amy Kaleita, Ph.D, Gregory R. Forbes, "Environmental Alarmism in Context: Hysteria's History," Reason Foundation (September 2007), 17, presumably referring to Oppenheimer, CITE http://www.pacificresearch.org/docLib/20070920_Hysteria_History.pdf.

119. Found at http://www.sej.org/resource/index18.htm, January 2007.

120. "Global Warming Propaganda Factory," Christopher J. Alleva, *The American Thinker*, August 03, 2007,

121. "Study debunks 'global cooling' concern of '70s," *USA Today*, February 21, 2008, http://www.usatoday.com/tech/science/environment/2008-02-20-global-cooling_N.htm.

122. "*Fire and Ice: Journalists have warned of climate change for 100 years, but can't decide weather we face an ice age or warming,*" BMI Special Report, 2006, found at http://www.businessandmedia.org/specialreports/2006/fireandice/fireandice.asp.

123. *The Weather Conspiracy: The Coming of the New Ice Age* (New York: Ballantine, 1977), p. 71.

124. Dr. Fred Singer writes in an email, "In 1968 I organized a symposium on 'Global Effects of Environmental Pollution;' it was part of the Annual [meeting] of the AAAS and held in Dallas, TX. An expanded symposium volume was

published by Reidel (Doordrecht) in 1970. One of the main topics was Global Climate Change: Reid Bryson thought it would cool some more; Syukuro Manabe presented his initial climate model results and opted for greenhouse warming. The leading [government] climate expert, J. Murray Mitchell, backed both. A distinguished panel included oceanographers Roger Revelle and Athelstan Spilhaus. Quite an event. I learned a lot. [See also Eos, Vol 51, no. 5, May 1970]."

125. See, e.g., "Editorial bias and the prediction of climate disaster: The crisis of science communication," Paper presented by Benny Peiser at the conference Climate Change: Evaluating Appropriate Responses, Brussels, European Parliament, April 18, 2007, http://www.staff.livjm.ac.uk/spsbpeis/Editorial-bias.htm.

126. Roger Pielke Jr., "A Question for the Media," Prometheus blog, December 14, 2007,

127. See, e.g., Anthony Watts, "NOAA: Hurricane frequency and global warming NOT the cause of increased destruction," Watts up with that blog, February 21, 2008, http://wattsupwiththat.wordpress.com/ 2008/02/21/noaa-hurricane-frequency-and-global-warming-not-the-cause-of-increased-destruction/.

128. Henry Payne, "*Times*'s reporter on biased climate coverage," *National Review* Online's Planet Gore blog, December 17, 2007, http://planetgore.nationalreview.com/post/?q=YWVlOGJiNzgwY2RmNWYzYTEyMGUwMTg1MWE3YWJiNTk=.

129. Andrew Revkin, "Media Mania for a 'Front-Page Thought' on Climate," *New York Times'* Dot Earth blog, December 14, 2007, http://dotearth.blogs.nytimes.com/2007/12/14/the-mania-for-a-front-page-thought-on-climate/.

130. See note 128.

131. "Mammoth dung, prehistoric goo may speed warming," *Reuters*, September 16, 2007.

132. "Understanding global warming," WNYT Television, November 6, 2007, http://wnyt.com/article/stories/S248109.shtml?cat=300.

133. Bud Ward, "Climate Scientists, Reporters Swap Insights at Wilson Center Public Meeting," Environment Writer, August 2006.

134. Environment Writer, http://www.environmentwriter.org/resources/reports/November05_workshop.htm.

135. Lisa Stiffler, "Quibbling over a Hockey Stick While the Planet Burns," SeattlePI.com's "Dateline Earth" blog, July 20, 2006.

136. See, e.g., "Inhofe recycles unscientific attacks on global warming; NYT's Revkin gives him a pass," Climate Progress, December 21, 2007, http://climateprogress.org/2007/12/21/debunking-inhofe-report-over-400-prominent-scientists-disputed-man-made-global-warming-claims-in-2007-andy-revkin/.

137. For example, Andy actually fairly covered, on his NYT blog, Hansen's analogy of coal cars to the rail cars leading to the death camps, on his NYT blog at "Holocausts," http://dotearth.blogs.nytimes.com/2007/11/26/holocausts/, November 26, 2007. Revkin does often go to pains to note that the greens

complain about him, too (see, e.g., http://www.openmarket.org/2007/08/27/discouraging-data/#comments).

138. Andrew Revkin, "Global Meltdown," *AARP* magazine, July & August 2007.

139. Revkin, "Global Meltdown," gallery, AARPMagazine.org.

140. "Panel issue bleak report on climate change," *New York Times*, February 2, 2007.

141. Matt Batcheldor, "Speakers exhort crowd to act on Earth's behalf," *The Olympian*, October 2, 2007.

142. See, e.g., "NASA Revisions Create a Stir in The Blogosphere," *Washington Post*, August 14, 2007.

143. Sharon Begley, "The Truth about denial," *Newsweek*, August 13, 2007.

144. Patrick J. Michaels, "Meltdown: The predictable distortion of global warming by politicians, science and the media," Cato Institute, 2004, 69.

145. See, e.g., Marc Morano, "Newsweek's Climate Editorial Screed Violates Basic Standards of Journalism," Senate Committee on Environment and Public Works, Minority blog, August 5, 2007, http://epw.senate.gov/public/index.cfm?FuseAction=Minority.Blogs&ContentRecord_id=38d98c0a-802a-23ad-48ac-d9f7facb61a7.

146. Robert J. Samuelson, "Greenhouse simplicities," *Newsweek*, August 20, 2007.

147. See, e.g., "Newsweek Blames Midwest Floods on Global Warming," NewsBusters, http://newsbusters.org/blogs/noel-sheppard/2008/06/29/newsweek-blames-midwest-floods-global-warming.

148. Quoted from Bill Dawson, "How I did that story: Newsweek's 'Hoax' Cover Story Raises Ire of Deniers . . . and also Criticism from Within," The Yale Forum on Climate Change and the Media, October 1, 2007, at http://www.yaleclimatemediaforum.org/dept/0907_newsweek.htm.

149. John Coleman, "Comments About Global Warming," IceCap.US, Wednesday, November 07, 2007, http://icecap.us/index.php/go/joes-blog/comments_about_global_warming/.

150. Id.

151. "TWC CLIMATE STATEMENT," Ray Ban, EVP Meteorology Science & Strategy, Weather Channel, November 8, 2007, http://climate.weather.com/blog/9_14035.html, (emphasis added) (linking to http://www.weather.com/encyclopedia/global/index.html.

152. "Senator Inhofe & CNN Anchor in Heated Exchange over Global Warming Coverage," U.S. Senate Committee on Environment & Public Works, October 3, 2006, http://epw.senate.gov/public/index.cfm?FuseAction=PressRoom.PressReleases&ContentRecord_id =8A7668E8-DFD5-4BCB-BD3D-FE223DFE2CC3

153. Brad Wilmouth, "CNN's O'Brien Defends Gore Movie, Global Warming Debate Over," NewsBusters, October 15, 2007, http://newsbusters.org/blogs/brad-wilmouth/2007/10/15/cnns-obrien-defends-gore-movie-declares-global-warming-debate-over.

154. Brad Wilmouth, "CNN's O'Brien Talks to Gore Critic, Hints Doubters are 'In the Dark,'" NewsBusters, October 20, 2007, http://newsbusters.org/blogs/brad-wilmouth/2007/10/20/cnn-talks-gore-critic-suggests-doubters-are-dark.

155. See, e.g., "Senate Debates Global Warming, CNN Anchor Snoozes," NewsBusters.org, December 6, 2006, http://www.newsbusters.org/node/9500.

156. Carl Wunsch, "Gulf Stream safe if wind blows and Earth turns," Letters, *Nature*, Volume 428, Issue 6983, 601 (2004).

157. See, Paul Detrick, "CNN Predicts Possible 'Century of Fires' Due to Global Warming," Business and Media Institute, October 24, 2007, http://www.businessandmedia.org/articles/2007/20071024110403.aspx.

158. "Southern California Wildfires and Global Warming: No Connection," Center for Science and Public Policy, October 24, 2007, http://ff.org/index.php?option=com_content&task=view&id=393&Itemid=94.

159. See, e.g., Drudge Report, "CNN Memo: use fires to 'push' 'Planet in Peril' series; don't 'Irresponsibly' tie to global warming," October 18, 2007, http://www.drudgereport.com/flash6.htm (visited October 29, 2007).

160. See, "Latest Scientific Studies Refute Fears of Greenland Melt," U.S. Senate Committee on Environment and Public Works, Blog (Minority), July 30, 2007, http://epw.senate.gov/public/index.cfm?FuseAction= Minority.Blogs&ContentRecord_id=175B568A-802A-23AD-4C69-9BDD978FB3CD.

161. Petr Chylek, *et al.*, "Greenland warming of 1920-1930 and 1995-2005," Geophysical Research Letters, 33, L11707, June 13, 2006.

162. M.K. Taylor et al., 2001. Delineating Canadian and Greenland polar bear (Ursus maritimus) populations by cluster analysis of movements. Can. J. Zool. 79, 690–709.

163. See, e.g., "Blowing your own whistle," World Climate Report, October 28, 2004, http://www.worldclimatereport.com/index.php/2004/10/28/blowing-your-own-whistle/

164. December 21, 2006, International Herald Tribune, http://www.dandavidprize.org/pr/2007English_IHT211206.pdf

165. See: http://goliath.ecnext.com/coms2/gi_0199-6343558/Climate-scientist-sees-cover-up.html. "The Soros Threat to Democracy," *Investors Business Daily*, September 24, 2007, http://ibdeditorial.com/IBDArticles.aspx?id= 275526219598836. For update/response see "Excerpt: Hansen wrote: "I did not receive one thin dime from George Soros. Perhaps GAP [Government Accountability Project] did, but I would be surprised if they got $720,000 (that's a lot of Mercedes). Whatever amount they got, I do not see anything wrong with it. They are a non-profit organization. Seems like a great idea to have some good lawyers trying to protect free speech. By the way, in case anybody finds out that George Soros INTENDED to send me $720,000 but could not find my address, please let me know! We are pretty hard pressed here." To buttress his position, Hansen copied a letter sent by GAP and his counsel to NASA chief Michael Griffin asking for assurances he would "not be punished for exercising his rights under the First Amendment, Whistleblower

Protection Act (WPA), and the Anti-Gag Statute to share his internationally-renowned expertise on climate change." (Direct link to Hansen's response: http://www.columbia.edu/~jeh1/distro_Lawlessness_070927.pdf); also Noel Sheppard of Newsbusters.org http://newsbusters.org/blogs/noel-sheppard/2007/09/28/nasa-s-james-hansen-claims-he-s-being-swift-boated-critics".

166. See e.g., "Carbon Dioxide in Atmosphere Increasing," Associated Press, October 22, 2007, in the *San Francisco Chronicle*.

167. See Patrick Michaels, "Not so hot," *American Spectator*, December 27, 2007.

168. See, e.g., Seth Borenstein, "Scientists beg for climate action," Associated Press, December 6, 2007, http://ap.google.com/article/ALeqM5imWhKGmZBsBlyG5-14qU25zpSqhgD8TBDVFG0.

169. Report, "U.S. Senate Report: Over 400 Prominent Scientists Disputed Man-Made Global Warming Claims in 2007," Senate Committee on Environment and Public Works (Minority), December 20, 2007, http://epw.senate.gov/public/index.cfm?FuseAction=Minority.Blogs&ContentRecord_id=f80a6386-802a-23ad-40c8-3c63dc2d02cb.

170. Seth Borenstein, "Global warming critic for hire," LiveScience, July 27, 2006, http://www.livescience.com/environment/060727_global_critic.html.

171. Juliet Eilperin, "An Inconvenient Expert," *Outdoor* Magazine, October 2007.

172. See, e.g., Petition, signed by over 19,000, Oregon Institute for Science and Medicine, http://www.oism.org/pproject/s33p357.htm.

173. *Washington Post*, June 2006.

174. See Marlo Lewis, Ph.D., "A Skeptic's Guide to 'An Inconvenient Truth'," found in various short- and long-forms and video clips at http://www.cei.org/pages/ait_response.cfm.

175. Christopher Monckton of Brenchley, "35 Inconvenient Truths: The errors in Al Gore's movie," Science and Public Policy Institute, October 19, 2007, http://scienceandpublicpolicy.org/monckton/goreerrors.html.

176. Timothy Ball, PhD, "Gore wrong on warming," *Times Colonist* (Canada), Letters, October 2, 2007, http://www.canada.com/victoriatimescolonist/news/letters/story.html?id=568728ac-adb9-4703-9cd0-97d1bbd79345.

177. John Marchese, "Al Gore is a greenhouse gasbag: Penn professor Bob Giegengack has a few quibbles with the former VP on this whole global warming" *Philadelphia Magazine*, February 2007.

178. "AP Incorrectly Claims Scientists Praise Gore's Movie," U.S. Senate Committee on Environment & Public Works, June 27, 2006, http://epw.senate.gov/pressitem.cfm?id=257909&party=rep.

179. Seth Borenstein and Lisa Leff, "Gore: Award puts focus on global warming," *Boston Globe*, October 12, 2007.

Chapter 2: Fear and Loathing

1. See the 110th Congress's priority agenda at http://www.dailykos.com/story/2006/10/6/11034/1406.

2. Brendan O'Neill, "A climate of censorship", *Guardian* (UK), November 22, 2006.

3. See, e.g., "Blunt answers about risks of global warming", *Chicago Tribune*, August 3, 2008.

4. Discussion on Pielke Jr's Prometheus climate science blog, http:// sciencepolicy.colorado.edu/prometheus/archives/climate_change/001030so_what _happened_at_.html.

5. Brendan O'Neill, "A climate of censorship", *The Guardian*, November 23, 2006.

6. Marc. D. Davidson, "Parallels in reactionary argumentation in the US congressional debates on the abolition of slavery and the Kyoto Protocol", *Climatic Change*, Volume 86, Numbers 1–2, January, 2008, http://www. springerlink.com/content/q5021x4506k0r622/.

7. Joe Romm, "Media enable denier spin, part three: Please stop calling them 'skeptics'," *Grist* Magazine, March 2008, http://gristmill.grist.org/story/2008/3/ 10/16030/9906. Romm's Climate Progress blog actually falls under the auspices of the Center for American Progress (CAP) Action Fund, CAP's 501c4 arm, which raises legal questions given its incessant politicking.

8. Bonner Cohen, "The Green Wave: Environmentalism and its consequences," Capital Research Center, Washington, DC (2006).

9. Dr. Sallie Baliunas of the Harvard-Smithsonian Center for Astrophysics notes in her speeches 6,550 cases of witch-burnings in seven French and (now-) German provinces between 1580-1626, citing Johann Linden, Treves, ca. 1590, "Since everybody thought that the continuous crop failure was caused by witches from devilish hate, the whole country stood up for their eradication." *Source*: W. Behringer 1987, 1995; compare this with the approximately 2,000 who Dinesh D'Souza, citing Henry Kamen, claims fell prey to the Spanish Inquisition in his book *What's so great about Christianity* (Washington, D.C.: Regnery, 2007).

10. PoliticalCortex blog, December 24, 2007, http://www.political cortex.com/ story/2007/12/24/95158/283.

11. Marc Sheppard, "Global Warmists Exploit the Holocaust," *The American Thinker*, November 30, 2007.

12. Adam Wolfson, "Apocalypse Gore: The vice president's vision of our civilization 'in crisis'," *National Review*, March 8, 1999.

13. See R. Warren Anderson and Dan Gainor, "Fire and Ice," Business & Media Institute, May 17, 2006.

14. Al Gore, "An Ecological Kristalnacht. Listen," *New York Times*, March 19, 1989.

15. Mark Lynas, "Climate Denial Ads to Air on U.S. Television," MarkLynas.org, May 19, 2006, http://marklynas.org/2006/5/19/climate-denial-ads-to-air-on-us-national-television.

16. Marc Sheppard, "Global Warmists Exploit the Holocaust," *The American Thinker*, November 30, 2007.

17. Phoebe Sweet, "Sen. Reid accuses coal industry of using 'the old Hitler lie'," *Las Vegas Sun*, February 19, 2008.

18. See, e.g., Sallie Baliunas, "A climate alarmist takes on 'criminals against humanity'," book review of Gelbspan's *Boiling Point: How Politicians, Big Oil and Coal, Journalists and Activists Are Fueling the Climate Crisis—And What We Can Do to Avert the Disaster*, *Reason* Magazine, October 2005.

19. "Case Study; The Oregon Petition," http://www.ecosyn.us/adti/ Corrupt_Sallie_Baliunas.html.

20. Benny Avni, "Mayor compares threat of global warming to terrorism," *New York Sun*, February 12, 2008.

21. Marc Sheppard, "Global Warmists Exploit the Holocaust," *The American Thinker*, November 30, 2007.

22. Dennis Avery, "Skeptics shed needed light on truth," *Environment and Climate News*, November 2007.

23. See, e.g., "Newsweek mimics tobacco industry tactics," Science and Public Policy Institute, August 6, 2007, http://scienceandpublicpolicy.org/ press_ releases/newsweek_mimics_tobacco_industry_tactics.html.

24. John Atkinson, "Big Climate's Strange 'Science," *The Register* (UK), February 14, 2008,

25. See, e.g., Fred Lucas, "Al Gore's Carbon Empire: Cashing in on Climate Change," Capital Research Center, August 2008, http://www.capitalresearch.org/ pubs/pdf/v1217525953.pdf.

26. George Monbiot, "I'm all for putting more vehicles on our roads. As long as they're coaches," *Guardian* (UK) December 5, 2006.

27. http://pubs.giss.nasa.gov/docs/2006/2006_Hansen_supplement.pdf.

28. Roger Jr. Pielke, "The Future of Climate Policy Debates," Prometheus blog, December 5, 2006.

29. Stuart Blackman and Ben Pile, "Battle in Print: Climate science: truth you can wear on your hands," Battle of Ideas, October 2007, http://www. battleofideas.org.uk/index.php/site/battles/957/.

30. Sharon Jayson, "Psychologists determine what it means to think 'green'," *USA Today*, August 14, 2008.

31. "Climate Skeptics Reveal 'Horror Stories' of Scientific Suppression," Senate Environment Committee on Environment and Public Works blog (Minority), March 6, 2008, http://epw.senate.gov/public/index.cfm? FuseAction= Minority.Blogs&ContentRecord_id=865dbe39-802a-23ad-4949-ee9098538277.

32. Steven McIntyre, Comment, Climate Audit, October 18, 2006.

33. Report, "U.S. Senate Report: Over 400 Prominent Scientists Disputed Man-Made Global Warming Claims in 2007," Senate Committee on Environment and Public Works (Minority), December 20, 2007, http://epw. senate.gov/public/index.cfm?FuseAction=Minority.Blogs&ContentRecord_id=f8 0a6386-802a-23ad-40c8-3c63dc2d02cb.

34. Roger Pielke Sr., "TRMM (Tropical Rainfall Measuring Mission) Data Set Potential in Climate Controversy By Joanne Simpson, private citizen," February 27, 2008, http://climatesci.org/2008/02/27/trmm-tropical-rainfall-measuring- mission-data-set-potential-in-climate-controversy-by-joanne-simpson-private- citizen/.

35. Simpson, JoAnne, at Ibid.

36. Reginald E. Newell, Jane Hsiung, and Wu Zhongxiang, J. Hsiung, "Possible factors controlling global marine temperature variations over the past century," *Journal of Geophysical Research* July, 1990, Vol. 95 No. D8.

37. "Has the Globe Really Warmed?" Fort Freedom, http://www.fortfreedom. org/s47.htm

38. Available at http://web.archive.org/web/20070416212333/http:// blue.atmos.colostate.edu/publications/pdf/NR-143.pdf.

39. "The denial industry," excerpt from George Monbiot, Heat, How to Stop the Planet from Buring, in *Grist Magazine*, September 19, 2006, http://gristmill. grist.org/print/2006/9/19/11408/1106.

40. Chris de Freitas, "Don't blame me for the heat," *New Zealand Herald*, November 27, 2007.

41. "Outspoken ASU prof draws ire," *The Arizona Republic*, November 11, 2007.

42. Bob Cohen, "Scientific 'consensus' on global warming doesn't exist," *San Jose Mercury News*, March TK 5, 2007.

43. Mark Steyn, "What planet are the eco-cultists on?" *The Telegraph* (UK), June 12, 2005.

44. "Big chill a symptom of climate chaos," *Sydney Morning Herald*, September 1, 2008.

45. Lawrence Solomon, "Green hero slammed as climate heretic," *Financial Post* (CA), November 17, 2007.

46. David Bellamy, "What a load of poppycock!" *Daily Mail* (UK), July 9, 2004.

47. "Climate Change and the Threat of Litigation," American Justice Partnership and Southeastern Legal Foundation, January 31, 2008, http://www. legalreforminthenews.com/Reports/AJP-SLF_Global_ Warming_Litigation_1-31-07_Final.pdf p. 13.

48. Lawrence Solomon, "Green Hero Slammed as Climate Heretic," *Financial Post*, November 17, 2007.

49. Chris De Freitas, "Don't blame me for the heat," *New Zealand Herald*, November 27, 2007.

50. Robert M. Carter profile page, http://myprofile.cos.com/glrmc.

51. Discussion on Pielke Jr's Prometheus climate science blog, http:// sciencepolicy.colorado.edu/ prometheus/archives/climate_change/001030so_ what_happened_at_.html, citing Daniel P. Schrag, "On a Swift Boat to a warmer world," *Boston Globe*, December 16, 2007.

52. See, e.g., "Fact Check: Hillary Clinton Attacks Obama on Yucca But His Record of Opposition is Consistent and Clinton Has Taken Contributions from The Nuclear Industry," Barack Obama, January 17, 2008, http://factcheck. barackobama.com/factcheck/2008/01/17/fact_check_hillary_clinton_att.php.

53. See, e.g., "Alarmists decry donations of $10k as corrupting some individuals. How about $300k? I know you've heard of NETeller, the carbon trading company. They're mentioned here: http://www.timesonline.co.uk/article/

0,,748-2184360,00.html. I'm sure you know John Lefebvre founded NETeller, and that he's backing DeSmogBlog to the tune of said $300k. What might be the connection there?," post by Steve Hemphill, Prometheus blog, December 3, 2006, http://sciencepolicy. colorado.edu/prometheus/archives/climate_change/ 001004less_than_a_quarter_.html.

54. Doug Ward, "Teddy Bear Hippie is unlikely multimillionaire," *Vancouver Sun*, January 17, 2007.

55. "Modern witch hunts," Physics forums blog, http://www.physicsforums. com/showthread.php?t=145068&page=4.

56. See Christopher C. Horner, *The Politically Incorrect Guide to Global Warming and Environmenatlism* (Washington, D.C.: Regnery, 2007), 3-24, Amery quote 283.

57. Terence Corcoran, "Global Cooling Effect," *Financial Post*, September 16, 2006.

58. See also, Terrence Corcoran, "Who is James Hoggan?," *Financial Post* (CA), November 16, 2006.

59. Ibid.

60. See bio at http://www.whartoncostarica07.com/bio-s-eckhart.html.

61. Marlo Lewis, "Economic Climate Change," *American Spectator*, July 10, 2007.

62. The Phi Beta Kappa Society, http://staging.pbk.org/AM/Template. cfm?Section=About_PBK.

63. "Membership in Phi Beta Kappa," The Phi Beta Kappa Society, http:// staging.pbk.org/AM/Template.cfm?Section=Membership3&Template=/CM/HT MLDisplay. cfm&ContentID=1974.

64. Iain Murray, "A message from the President of the American Council on Renewable Energy," *National Review*'s Planet Gore, July 13, 2007.

65. See John McCaslin, "Inside the Beltway" ("Just 'jousting'"), *Washington Times*, July 20, 2007.

Chapter 3: The Establishment Attacks

1. "Global Warming Denier: Fraud or 'Realist'?" ABC News, March 23, 2008, video at http://www.abcnews.go.com/Technology/GlobalWarming/story?id= 4506059&page=1.

2. "Maurice F. Strong Is First Non-U.S. Citizen To Receive Public Welfare Medal, Academy's Highest Honor," Press Release, National Academy of Sciences, December 3, 2003, http://www8.nationalacademies.org/onpinews/ newsitem.aspx?RecordID=12032003.

3. Ralph Cicerone, Hearing before the House Committee on Energy and Commerce, 109th Congress, July 27, 2006.

4. Biography of Jane Loubchenco, http://www.motherjones.com/radio/2006/ 08/lubchenco_bio.html.

5. Richard Lindzen, "Climate Science: Is it currently designed to answer questions," August 2008 draft for proceedings of conference in San Mariono, CA.

6. "Report Provides Strategy for Transition to Sustainability; Actions Required Over Next Two Generations," Press Release, National Academy of Sciences, November 9, 1999, http://www8.nationalacademies.org/onpinews/newsitem. aspx?RecordID=9690.

7. There are many examples, but see, e.g., "The National Academies In Focus," National Academy of Sciences, Summer/Fall 2002, http:// infocusmagazine.org/portable/2.2.pdf.

8. Bruce Albets, "Harnessing Science for a More Rational World," speech presented to National Academy of Sciences at the Academy's 140th Annual Meeting, April 28, 2003, http://www.nasonline.org/site/DocServer/speech2003. pdf?docID=110.

9. Available at http://web.archive.org/web/20080114033513/http://www. princeton.edu/~step/people/oppenheimer.html.

10. John Tierney, "Global-Warming Payola," *New York Times*, March 6, 2008.

11. "As University of California physicist John Holdren has said, it is possible that carbon dioxide-induced famines could kill as many as a billion people before the year 2020." Paul Ehrlich, *The Machinery of Nature* (New York: Simon and Schuster, 1986), 274.

12. Robert Bradley, "False alarms and climate change," *Houston Chronicle*, March 29, 2008.

13. "Global Population and Environment," Sierra Club, April 27, 1995, http:// www.sierraclub.org/population/history.asp.

14. See, e.g., 1999 letter from Holdren and Peter Raven supporting the notion "that environmental research be made one of NSF's highest priorities and agree that funding should be substantially augmented" by $1 billion over five years, equal to about 20 percent of the then-current federal environmental R&D funding, http://www.ostp.gov/PCAST/00110.html.

15. Mark Shwartz, "Whole Earth Systems symposium celebrates climatologist Stephen Schneider," Stanford News Service, February 16, 2005, http://news-service.stanford.edu/news/2005/february16/heinz-021605.html.

16. Red Lodge Clearing House, http://www.redlodgeclearinghouse.org/ resources/fund_dyn.cfm?id=149.

17. CCB Standards, http://www.climate-standards.org/.

18. Climate Science Watch, http://www.climatesciencewatch.org/.

19. Biography available at http://web.archive.org/web/20070611023640/ http://iis-db.stanford.edu/evnts/4040/Attendees_Biographies_2.pdf

20. Bio available at http://web.archive.org/web/20070604205038/http://iis-db.stanford.edu/evnts/4040/Speaker_abstracts_4.pdf

21. "Communicating Climate Science to Decision-Makers, with Special Reference to the Policy Community," Elements of Change, Aspen Global Change Institute, 1998, 363-67, http://www.agci.org/publications/eoc98/AGCI%20EOC-98SIIpp356-402.pdf.

22. "Science Communications and the News Media Workshop," 1st Workshop in series, November 9-11, 2003, http://www.environmentwriter.org/resources/ reports/November03_workshop.htm.

23. Bud Ward, "Climate Scientists, Reporters Swap Insights at Wilson Center Public Meeting," Environment Writer, August 2006, http://www. environmentwriter.org/resources/articles/0706_wilsonctr.htm.

24. See, e.g., "Science Communications and the News Media," 2nd workshop in series, November 17-19, 2004, http://www.environmentwriter.org/resources/ reports/March04_workshop.htm, "Science Communications and the News Media," 3rd Workshop in series, November 8-10, 2004, http://www. environmentwriter.org/resources/reports/November04_workshop.htm, "Science Communications and the News Media," 4th Workshop in series, June 1-3, 2005, http://www.environmentwriter.org/resources/reports/June05_workshop.htm, and Bud Ward, "Climate Scientists, Reporters Swap Insights at Wilson Center Public Meeting," Environment Writer, August 2006, http://www.environmentwriter.org/ resources/articles/0706_wilsonctr.htm.

25. Naomi Oreskes, "Beyond the Ivory Tower: The Scientific Consensus on Climate Change," *Science*, http://www.sciencemag.org/cgi/content/full/306/ 5702/1686.

26. Nicholas Wade, *Science*, November 1979.

27. This occurred at a meeting of the NAS's National Climate Board standing committee according to a January 21, 1993, letter from former USDA official and botanist Albert Grable to Sherwood Idso.

28. See, e.g., Report of the 2006 IMAGE Advisory Board, Netherlands Environmental Assessment Agency (MNP), February 2007, http://www.mnp.nl/ bibliotheek/rapporten/500110003.pdf.

29. Potsdam Institute website: http://www.pik-potsdam.de/research/research-domains/earth-system-analysis/members/index_html.

30. *The Stern Review of the Economics of Climate Change* (Stern *et al.*, 2006). See report and documents that Stern finds relevant at http://www.hm-treasury.gov.uk/independent_reviews/stern_review_economics_climate_change/ste rnreview_index.cfm.

31. For a condensed discussion of Stern, see Lawrence Solomon, *The Deniers* (Minneapolis: Richard Vigilante Books, 2008) 23–29.

32. Thanks to Dennis Ambler for his research on Tyndall Centre and related relationships in the UK.

33. "About the Project," GLOGOV.org http://www.glogov.org/?pageid=2.

34. For more on this see Dennis Ambler, "Global Warming: The Social Construction of a Quasi-Reality?" *Energy & Environment*, Vol. 18 No. 6 2007.

35. See Hansen letter to James E. Rogers, March 25, 2008, available at http://gristmill.grist.org/story/2008/4/1/16055/76057.

36. Clipper Wind website: http://www.clipperwind.com/james_gp_dehlsen_ bm.html, viewed April 18, 2008.

37. Greenpeace Board of Directors, Greenpeace, Inc. http://www.greenpeace. org/raw/content/usa/press-center/reports4/greenpeace-board-of-directors.pdf.

38. About NRDC: Board of Trustees, Natural Resources Defense Council, http://www.nrdc.org/about/board.asp.

39. "A Disclaimer," RealClimate, February 14, 2005, http://www.realclimate. org/index.php?p=120.

40. "Overview," Environmental Media Services, ActivistCash.com, http://www.activistcash.com/organization_overview.cfm/oid/110.

41. Betsey Ensley, Web Editor and Program Coordinator (Past), Environmental Media Services (Past) http://www.zoominfo.com/Search/PersonDetail. aspx?PersonID=326603649.

42. Lubos Motl, "Bonus: Funding of RealClimate.org," The Reference Frame, April 7, 2008, http://motls.blogspot.com/2008/04/green-trolls-edit-wmo-bbc-reports.html.

43. See , e.g., Noel Sheppard, "NASA's Hansen Claims He's Being 'Swift-boated' by Critics," NewsBusters, September 28, 2007, http://www.newsbusters. org/blogs/noel-sheppard/2007/09/28/nasa-s-james-hansen-claims-he-s-being-swift-boated-critics.

44. Motl, "Bonus: Funding of RealClimate.org."

45. See discussion also at http://www.activistcash.com/organization_overview. cfm/oid/110.

46. See Christopher Horner, *The Politically Incorrect Guide™ to Global Warming and Environmentalism* (Washington, D.C.: Regnery Publishing, 2007), xv–xvi.

47 "Failure to tackle climate peril 'criminally irresponsible', IPCC told," *Agence France Press*, November 11, 2007.

48. "'Weapons stash' near Climate Camp: Police recover 'a stash of knives and weapons' from woodland near the Climate Camp in Kent," BBC News, August 5, 2008, http://news.bbc.co.uk/go/em/fr/-/nolpda/ukfs_news/hi/newsid_7542000/ 7542592.stm.

49. Iain Murray, "Eco-Censorship: The Effort to Thwart the Climate Change Debate," *The New Atlantis*, December 4, 2006.

50. See, e.g., "By any means necessary," *National Post* (CA), February 7, 2008.

51. Alexander Cockburn, "I am an intellectual blasphemer," *Spiked* Online, January 2008, http://www.spiked-online.com/index.php?/site/reviewofbooks_ article/4357.

52. "Perhaps there is a case for making climate change denial an offence. It is a crime against humanity, after all." See Margo Kingston, 'Himalayan lakes disaster,' *DailyBriefing*, November 21, 2005, quoted in "The Garden of Good and Evil," *The Age* (Australia), June 17, 2007.

53. "UK Bishop says skeptics of man-made global warming as 'guilty as' child sex abusers," *Birmingham Post* blog, May 31, 2008, http://www. birminghampost.net/news/west-midlands-news/2008/05/31/bishop-claims-environment-abusers-as-bad-as-sex-beast-fritzl-65233-21002385/.

54. "Vision for the future" *Sydney Morning Herald*, April 19, 2008.

55. Andrew Bolt, "Further scenes from the farce," *Herald-News* (Australia) blog, April 20, 2008, http://blogs .news.com.au/heraldsun/andrewbolt/index.php/ heraldsun/comments/further_scenes_from_the_farce/.

56. Paul Krugman, "Can the planet be saved?" *New York Times*, August 1, 2008.

57. "Is climate change 'human rights abuse'?" Reuters, November 13, 2007, http://blogs.reuters.com/environment/2007/11/13/is-climate-change-human-rights-abuse/.

58. See Roger Pielke Jr., "Misdefining 'climate change': consequences for science and action," *Environmental Science & Policy*, 8 (2005) 548–561, http://sciencepolicy.colorado.edu/admin/publication_files/resource-1841-2004.10.pdf.

59. David Deming, "Climatic warming in North America: analysis of borehole temperatures," *Science* 268: 1576–1577, 1995.

60. David Deming, 2005: "Global warming, the politicization of science, and Michael Crichton's 'State of Fear'," *Journal of Scientific Exploration*, 19: no.2.

61. C. Loehle, "A 2000-year global temperature reconstruction based on non-treering proxies," *Energy & Environment* 18 (7–8): 1049–1058], http://www.ncasi.org/publications/Detail.aspx?id=3025.

62. David Deming, 2005: "Global warming, the politicization of science, and Michael Crichton's 'State of Fear'," *Journal of Scientific Exploration*, 19: no.2.

63. Letter from attorney for Bob Stephenson to University of Oklahoma Provost Nancy Mergler, November 4, 2003, http://www.thefire.org/pdfs/7c373d7bd07dbf7497658df01e8431f1.pdf.

64. http://www.secinfo.com/dsvrp.835v.htm (see also PSEC Inc., formerly Potts-Stephenson Exploration Company, here he sells lots of shares of PSEC to ONEOK, in which he has interests); see also http://www.secinfo.com/dsvrp.835v.d.htm and Exhibit 2(a), Stock Purchase Agreement, http://sec.edgar-online.com/1997/04/28/00/0000950134-97-003248/Section2.asp.

65. Robert L. Bradley, "Corporate Social Responsibility and Energy: Lessons from Enron,", Lindenwood University Center for the Study of American Culture and Values, April 2008, http://www.politicalcapitalism.com/CSR/CSR-and-Energy.pdf.

66. "University of Oklahoma: Plot to Punish Professor for Political Beliefs, Whistleblowing," Foundation for Individual Rights in Education, http://www.thefire.org/index.php/case/658.html.

67. "University of Oklahoma Administration Plots to Punish Professor for Political Beliefs, Whistleblowing," Foundation for Individual Rights in Education, December 8, 2004, http://www.thefire.org/index.php/article/5076.html.

68. Richard Lindzen, "Climate of Fear," *Wall Street Journal*, April 12, 2006.

69. See, e.g., "Storm subsides between William Gray, CSU," *Houston Chronicle*, April 28, 2008, http://www.chron.com/disp/story.mpl/front/5736103.html.

70. "Associate State Climatologist Fired for Exposing Warming Myths," Environment News (Heartland Institute), June 2007, http://www.heartland.org/Article.cfm?artId=21207.

71. See, e.g., "Climate change claims a victim," *Capital Press*, March 2, 2007.

72. See, e.g., "Associate State Climatologist Fired for Exposing Warming Myths," Heartland Institute, June 2007 (emphasis added), http://www.heartland.org/Article.cfm?artId=21207.

73. Warren Cornwall, "UW study examines decline of snowpack," *Seattle Times*, August 6, 2008.

74. Michael Martinez, "Warming clouds national parks," *Chicago Tribune*, June 10, 2007.

75. Warren Cornwall, "How one number touched off big climate-change fight at UW," *Seattle Times*, March 15, 2007.

76. Editorial, "A muddle over climate jobs," *Albany Democrat Herald*, February 7, 2008.

77. Transcript, National Public Radio, May 31, 2007, http://www.npr.org/templates/story/story.php?storyId=10571499

78. Marc Kaufmann, "NASA Administrator questions need to fight global warming," *Washington Post*, June 1, 2007.

79. See, e.g., Michael Griffith, "DeSmogBlog," http://www.desmogblog.com/taxonomy/term/1744/0/feed.

80. Clayton Sandell and Bill Blakemore, "Scientists surprised by NASA chief's climate comments," ABC News, June 1, 2007, http://abcnews.go.com/Technology/story?id=3229696&page=1.

81. See, e.g., "NASA's Griffin regrets global warming remarks," *USA Today*, June 6, 2006.

82. "NASA chief: global warming treated 'almost as a religious issue'," Interview, SciGuy blog (Eric Berger), March 16, 2008, http://blogs.chron.com/sciguy/archives/2008/03/nasa_chief_glob.html.

83. Stuart Blackman and Ben Pile, "Battle in Print: Climate science: truth you can wear on your hands," Battle of Ideas, October 2007, http://www.battleofideas.org.uk/index.php/site/battles/957/.

84. "The Danish Committees on Scientific Dishonesty," Danish Agency for Science Technology and Innovation, July 12, 2006, http://fi.dk/site/english/councils-commissions-committees/the-danish-committees-on-scientific-dishonesty.

85. Bjorn Lomborg, *The Skeptical Environmentalist: Measuring the Real State of the World* (Cambridge and New York: Cambridge University Press, 2001).

86. James Glassman, "Why the Green Church of Environmentalism Has No Tolerance for Skeptics," *Capitalism*, March 17, 2002, http://www.capmag.com/article.asp?ID=1492.

87. For example, "*The Population Bomb* was sourced with 49 endnotes, only five of which were from peer-reviewed scientific journals. Of the 55 endnotes in *The Limits to Growth*, only three refer to peer-reviewed journals. More recently, in the Worldwatch Institute's State of the World 2002, the vast majority of endnotes are from newspapers, magazines, non-peer-reviewed books, government reports, and even activist pamphlets." See Ronald Bailey, "Green with Ideology: The hidden agenda behind the 'scientific' attacks on Bjørn Lomborg's controversial book, *The Skeptical Environmentalist*," *Reason*, May 2002.

88. See, for example, the reaction by Team Gore to the December 2007 list released by the Senate Environment Committee's Minority of over 400 scientists who challenged IPCC alarmism in 2007 alone. Team Gore's response announced

its own falsehood by claiming that "25 or 30" of the signatories had received funding from ExxonMobil. There was as much substance to this retort as there were names offered—none.

89. Bailey, "Green with Ideology."

90. Ibid.

91. Stuart Pimm and Jeff Harvey, "No Need to Worry about the Future," *Nature,* 414, 149–150 (November 8, 2001) | doi:10.1038/35102629.

92. Alison Abbott, "Ethics panel attacks environment book," *Nature* 421, 201 (January 16, 2003).

93. "More heat, less light on Lomborg," *Nature*, 421, 195 (January 16, 2003).

94. Jim Giles, "The man they love to hate," *Nature* 423, 216–218 (May 15, 2003).

95. Chris Thomas, "A sixth mass extinction?," *Nature* 450, 349 (November 15, 2007).

96. Daniel Cressey, "Noah's flood brought farming to Europe," *Nature* blog, November 19, 2007.

97. J. R. Minkel and Gary Stix, "Policy leader of the year," *Scientific American*, November 12, 2006.

98. "Misleading math about the earth: Science defends itself against The Skeptical Environmentalist," *Scientific American*, January 2002.

99. Lomborg responded at www.sciam.com/media/pdf/lomborgrebuttal.pdf (long version).

100. See, e.g., discussion at Mark Steyn, "The Enforcers," *National Review* Online's The Corner, December 22, 2007, http://corner.nationalreview.com/post/?q=YWU0NzliZWVkNTM2MzQ4ZmRhMjEyODE2ZTc5 YTBkN2U=.

101. Dennis Dutton, *Scientific American*, Letters, April 15, 2002.

102. You can find the original critique plus his rebuttal and counter-rebuttals at "Skepticism toward the Skeptical Environmentalist," *Scientific American*, April 15, 2002.

103. Quoted in "A reprieve for free speech," *The Economist*, December 18, 2003.

104. Charles Paul Freund, "Burn, Baby Bjørn, burn!" *Reason*, January 10, 2003.

105. "Lomborg celebrates ministry ruling," December 22, 2003, BBC, http://news.bbc.co.uk/2/hi/science/nature/3340305.stm.

106. Andrew Ferguson, "Skeptical Environmentalist Riles Other Kind," Bloomberg News, April 2, 2003, http://www.rff.org/rff/News/Coverage/2003/April/Skeptical-Environmentalist-Riles-Other-Kind-Andrew-Ferguson.cfm.

107. Jens Morten Hansen, "The Lomborg Case and the debate," Danish Research Agency, January 10, 2003, http://www.cambridge.org/uk/economics/lomborg/websites4.htm.

108. 2002 Annual Report of the Danish Committees on Scientific Dishonesty, p. 3, http://fi.dk/site/english/publications/2003/annual-report-2002-danish-committees-scientific-dishonesty/annual-report-2002-the-danish-committees-on-scientific-d.pdf.

109. 2005 Annual Report of the Danish Committees on Scientific Dishonesty, p. 27, http://fi.dk/site/english/publications/2006/annual-report-2005-danish-committees-scientific-dishonesty/annual-report-2005-the-danish-committees-on-scientific-d.pdf.

110. Cited at Bjorn Lomborg, Frequently Asked Questions, http://www.lomborg.com/faq/.

111. See 2005 Annual Report of the Danish Committees on Scientific Dishonesty, 27, http://fi.dk/site/english/publications/2006/annual-report-2005-danish-committees-scientific-dishonesty/annual-report-2005-the-danish-committees-on-scientific-d.pdf.

112. See press release at http://www.lomborg.com/dyn/files/basic_items/71-file/Press_release_UVVU_annullment_Dec_2003.pdf.

113. "A Critical Consideration of the Verdict of the Danish Committee on Scientific Dishonesty on the Book by Bjorn Lomborg 'The Skeptical Environmentalist'," Cambridge University Press 2001, April 4, 2003, http://www.lomborg.com/dyn/files/basic_items/75-file/CriticalConsideration.pdf.

114. Fred Pearce, "Climate change special: State of denial," *New Scientist*, November 4, 2006, http://environment.newscientist.com/channel/earth/mg19225765.000-climate-change-special-state-of-denial.html.

115. Gavin Schmidt, "The Physics of Climate Modeling," *Physics Today*, American Institute of Physics, January 2007.

116. Spencer Weart, "The Discovery of Global Warming," Septmeber 2008, http://www.aip.org/history/climate/links.htm.

117. Thomas C. Peterson et al., "The Myth of the 1970s Global Cooling Scientific Consensus," Bulletin of the American Meteorological Society, February 6, 2008, http://ams.allenpress.com/archive/1520-0477/preprint/2008/pdf/10.1175_2008BAMS2370.1.pdf.

118. For a contemporaneous article, see Mark P. McCarthy et al., "Assessing Bias and Uncertainty in the HadAT-Adjusted Radiosonde Climate Record," *Journal of Climate*, Vol. 21 No 4, February 2008, 817–32.

119. Joe D'Aleo, CCM, "Warmists in Frantic Effort to Save their Failing Theory," ICECAP blog, May 28, 2008, http://icecap.us/index.php/go/joes-blog/global_warmists_in_frantic_effort_to_save_their_failing_theory/.

120. David W. J. Thompson et al., "A large discontinuity in the mid-twentieth century in observed global-mean surface temperature," *Nature* 453, 646-49 (May 29, 2008) | doi:10.1038/nature06982; Received January 28, 2008; Accepted April 4, 2008.

121. "Climate change: is the US Congress bullying experts?" *Nature* 436, 7 (July 7, 2005) doi:10.1038/ 436007a; Published online July 6, 2005.

122. See discussion at "The Good Explanation—Apologies," Prometheus, June 13, 2005, http://sciencepolicy.colorado.edu/prometheus/archives/climate_change/000461the_good_explanation.html.

123. R.E. Davis et al., 2003. "Decadal changes in summer mortality in the U. S. cities," *International Journal of Biometeorology*, 47, 166–75.

124. Isabelle Chuine et al., "Historical phenology Grape ripening as a past climate indicator," 432, 289–290 (Nov 17, 2004), doi: 10.1038/432289a, abstract at http://www.nature.com/nature/journal/v432/n7015/abs/432289a.html.

125. John McLean, "Remarks about my report 'Grape harvest dates are poor indicators of summer warmth,' as well as about scientific publication generally," http://www.informath.org/apprise/a3200.htm, viewed March 13, 2008.

126. Steven McIntyre, "Nature blog withdraws invitation," ClimateAudit.org, May 15, 2007, http://www.climateaudit.org/?p=1578#comment-109605.

127. Benny Peiser, "Editorial bias and the prediction of climate disaster: the crisis of science communication," paper presented at the conference Climate Change: Evaluating Appropriate Responses. Brussels, European Parliament, April 18, 2007, AchGut blog, http://www.achgut.com/dadgdx/ index.php/dadgd/ article/editorial_bias_and_the_prediction_of_climate_disaster_the_crisis_of_ science/.

128. Christopher Shea, "In the balance: Is balanced journalism to blame for the lack of action on global warming?" *Boston Globe*, April 2006.

129. Editorial, "Nowhere to turn for Climate change deniers," New Scientist Environment, April 12, 2007, http://environment.newscientist.com/channel/earth/ mg19425993.000-editorial-nowhere-to-turn-for-climate-change-deniers.html.

130. See Benny Peiser, "Editorial bias and the prediction of climate disaster."

131. Leo Lewis, "Japan's Arctic methane hydrate haul raises environment fears," *The Times* (UK), April 14, 2008.

132. Stuart Blackman and Ben Pile, "Battle in Print: Climate science: truth you can wear on your hands," Battle of Ideas, October 2007, http://www. battleofideas.org.uk/index.php/site/battles/957/.

133. Willie Soon and Sallie Baliunas, "Proxy Climatic and Environmental Changes of the Past 1000 Years," *Climate Research*, January 31, 2003.

134. Transcript, Hearing of the Senate Committee on Environment and Public Works, July 29, 2003, http://frwebgate.access.gpo.gov/cgi-bin/getdoc.cgi? dbname=108_senate_hearings&docid=f:92381.wais.

135. S. Fred Singer, "Good science, bad font: Solving the problems of getting published," *Physics Today*, Letters, April 2006.

136. Dan Sorenson, "Sunspot cycle may be a 'dud'," Scripps Howard News Service, May 19, 2008, http://www.shns.com/shns/g_index2.cfm?action=detail& pk=SUNSPOTCYCLE-05-19-08.

137. "The Greenhouse Conspiracy," Channel 4 (UK), originally broadcast August 12, 1990; Michaels quote at approximately minute 42 of the version at http://video.google.com/videoplay?docid=-5949034802461518010; transcript available at http://fufor.twoday.net/stories/3428768/.

138. "360° with Anderson Cooper," CNN, November 8, 2007.

139. See, Richard North, "Sceptics: Cards on the table please!" BBC News, December 1, 2006, http://news.bbc.co.uk/1/hi/sci/tech/6196804.stm.

140. Richard Black, "Climate Science: Sceptical about bias," BBC News, November 14, 2007, http://news.bbc.co.uk/2/hi/science/nature/7092614.stm.

141. "Bias in Climate Change Research?" December 7, 2006, http:// timworstall.typepad.com/timworstall/2006/12/bias_in_climate.html.

142. "An Inconvenient Truth," December 7, 2006, See http://julesandjames. blogspot.com/2006/12/inconvenient-truth.html.

143. Ibid.

144. The paper is available at http://julesandjames.blogspot.com/2006/09/can-we-believe-in-high-climate.html.

145. See, e.g, "400 Prominent Scientists Dispute Global Warming—Bunk," DeSmogBlog, December 21, 2007, http://www.desmogblog.com/400-prominent-scientists-dispute-global-warming-bunk; for further outrage, see "Inhofe's latest windmill: more bogus climate skepticism," *Grist*, December 21, 2007, http:// gristmill.grist.org/story/2007/12/21/112933/48.

146. Richard North, "Sceptics: Cards on the table please!." 157. See, e.g., those included in S. Fred Singer et al., *Understanding Climate Change: The Report of the Nongovernmental International Panel on Climate Change*, (Chicago: The Heartland Institute, 2008.)

Chapter 4: Stifling Everyone's Speech

1. Fleming Rose and Bjorn Lomborg, "Will Al Gore Melt? If not, why did he chicken out on an interview?" *Wall Street Journal*, January 21, 2007.

2. David Adam, "Royal Society tells Exxon: stop funding climate change denial," *The Guardian* (UK), September 20, 2006.

3. "David Whitehouse on Royal Society Efforts to Censor," Prometheus blog, September 21, 2006, http:// sciencepolicy.colorado.edu/prometheus/archives/ the_honest_broker/000932david_whitehouse_on_.html.

4. "A guide to facts and fictions about climate change," Royal Society (UK), March 2005, http://royalsociety.org/downloaddoc.asp?id=1630.

5. Stuart Blackman and Ben Pile, "Battle in Print: Climate science: truth you can wear on your hands," Battle of Ideas, October 2007, http://www. battleofideas.org.uk/index.php/site/battles/957/.

6. Ibid.

7. David Adam, "Royal Society to Exxon: stop funding climate change denial," *The Guardian* (UK), September 20, 2006.

8. Letter by RS President Lord Rees to Rupert Wyndham, April 2007.

9. John Kay, "Science is the pursuit of the truth, not consensus," *Financial Times*, October 9, 2007.

10. Neil Collins, "Global warming generates hot air," *The Daily Telegraph*, May 16, 2005.

11. See, e.g., G8 Gleneagles Meeting official site, http://www.g8.gov.uk/servlet/ Front?pagename=OpenMarket/Xcelerate/ShowPage&c=Page&cid=1094235520 309

12. Press release, "Clear science demands prompt action on climate change say G8 science academics," June 7, 2005, http://www.royalsoc.ac.uk/news.asp?id= 3226

13. Sam Knight, "Anti-Bush gibe by Royal Society sparks climate change row," *Times Online* (UK), July 5, 2005, http://www.timesonline.co.uk/article/0,,22649-1681145,00.html

14. Policy Statement on Climate Variability and Change by the American Association of State Climatologists (AASC), November 2001, http://www.ncdc.noaa.gov/oa/aasc/aascclimatepolicy.pdf.

15. American Meteorological Society, http://www.ametsoc.org/sss/scienceservicesociety.html.

16. See "The February 2 2007 American Meteorological Society Statement on Climate Change," February 5, 2007.

17. "DRAFT AMS Statement on Climate Change," 20 October 2006, http://www.ametsoc.org/policy/draftstatements/climagechange7.pdf.

18. "AMS Statements in Process," American Meteorological Society, http://www.ametsoc.org/policy/draftstatements/index.html.

19. "Draft American Meteorological Society Statement on Climate Change," November 17, 2006.

20. "Several Science Errors (Or, At Best Cherrypicking) In the 2007 IPCC Statement For Policymakers," Climate Science blog, February 15, 2007, http://climatesci.org/2007/02/15/science-errors-or-at-best-cherrypicking-in-the-2007-ipcc-statement-for-policymakers/.

21. "The February 2, 2007 American Meteorological Society Statement on Climate Change," February 5, 2007, http://climatesci.colorado.edu/2007/02/05/the-february-2-2007-american-meterological-society-statement-on-climate-change/#comments; point #2 linked to Eric Swedlund, "3 UA climate science experts file brief in EPA suit," *Arizona Daily* Star, November 29, 2006.

22. "Climate Re-education Program," ClimateSkeptic.com, July 21, 2008, http://www.climate-skeptic.com/2008/07/climate-re-educ.html; abstract of the AMS article available at http://ams.allenpress.com/perlserv/?request=get-abstract&doi=10.1175%2F2007BAMS2432.1&ct=1.

23. Thomas C. Peterson, William C. Connolley, and John Fleck, "The Myth of the 1970s Global Cooling Scientific Consensus," Bulletin of the American Meteorological Society, April 2008.

24. Thomas Karl, National Climate Data Center, http://web.archive.org/web/20070814004717/http://www.jhu.edu/~climate/thomaska.htm

25. "Environmental Science Seminary Series Archives (ESSS)," American Meteorological Society, http://www.ametsoc.org/atmospolicy/environmentalsssarchives.html.

26. See James Hansen, "The shadow on American democracy," February 8, 2008, http://www.columbia.edu/~jeh1/mailings/20080125_AmericanShadow.pdf; see also discussion by Roger Pielke Jr., "Technocracy versus Democratic Control," Prometheus blog, February 11, 2008, http://sciencepolicy.colorado.edu/prometheus/archives/the_honest_broker/001342technocracy_versus_d.html.

27. "Congress 'still in denial' on global warming, NASA's Hansen says," *Environment & Energy Daily*, July 21, 2006.

28. Michael Asher, "Researcher: Basic Greenhouse Equations Totally Wrong," *DailyTech*, March 6, 2008.

29. Ferenc M. Miskolczi, "Greenhouse effect in semi-transparent planetary atmospheres," *Quarterly Journal of the Hungarian Meteorological Service,* Vol. 111, No. 1, January–March 2007.

30. Peter Foster, "The New Road to Serfdom," *Financial Post* (CA), March 12, 2008.

31. Testimony of Dr. Richard S. Lindzen, U.S. Senate Committee on Environment and Public Works, May 2, 2001.

32. In addition to the AMS and *USA Today* examples cited elsewhere, see the RealClimate gang's stab at this revisionism, http://www.realclimate.org/index. php/archives/2008/03/the-global-cooling-mole/#more-536.

33. John Kay, "Science is the pursuit of the truth, not consensus," *Financial Times,* October 9, 2007.

34. Robert M. Carter, "The Myth of Human-caused climate change," The AusIMM New Leaders' conference, Brisbane, Queensland, May 2-3 2007, 65, www.ICECAP.us/images/uploads/200705-03AusIMMcorrected.pdf.

35. Naomi Oreskes, "Beyond the Ivory Tower: The Scientific Consensus on Climate Change," *Science* Magazine, December 3, 2004: Vol. 306. no. 5702, 1686. For a more detailed discussion of the false claim that led to the continuing furor today over this claim, see Chris Horner, *The Politically Incorrect Guide™ to Global Warming and Environmentalism*(Washington: Regnery Publishing, 2007) 81-110.

36. Roger Pielke Jr., "On the value of 'consensus'," Prometheus blog, April 26, 2006, http://sciencepolicy.colorado.edu/prometheus/archives/climate_ change/ 000765on_the_value_of_con.html.

37. Rich Noyes, "ABC Touts Gore Some More; Lets RFK Rant About Exxon Conspiracy," NewsBusters.org, October 13, 2007, http://newsbusters.org/node/ 16337/print.

38. Dennis Bray and H. Von Storch, "The Perspectives of Climate Scientists on Global Climate Change," Institute for Coastal Research, GKSS-Forschungs- zentrum Geesthacht GmbH • Geesthacht • 2007, http://dvsun3.gkss.de/ BERICHTE/GKSS_Berichte_2007/GKSS_2007_11.pdf; see also Dennis Bray, "The not so clear consensus on climate change," at http://www.sepp.org/Archive/ NewSEPP/Bray.htm.

39. For example, on the regional level consider the poll of its membership by the Association of Professional Engineers, Geologists and Geophysicists of Alberta, Canada's oil patch, which found that 26 percent of respondents attributed warming to human activities, 27 percent blamed other, "natural" causes, and 45 percent blame a combination of human and natural influences. Sixty-eight percent disagreed with the claim that "the debate on the scientific causes of recent climate change is settled." "Causes of climate change varied: poll," *Edmonton Journal* (CA), March 7, 2008.

40. "First-Ever Survey of IPCC Scientists Undermines Alleged 'Consensus' on Global Warming; Poll Exposes Disagreement and Confusion Among United

Nations Scientists," News Release, http://prnewswire.com/cgi-bin/stories.
pl?ACCT=104&STORY=/www/story/11-08-2007/0004701174&EDATE=,
DemandDebate.com, November 8, 2007. Survey available at http://www.
DemandDebate.com/ipcc_survey.pdf.

41. Ibid.

42. Various caveats made it possible for research to be cited if not published or
in draft form by that date, but clearly this increased the likelihood that its
inclusion would be even less subject to the IPCC's touted, and debunked, claim
to stringent peer review. See, e.g., "IPCC Working Group I, Schedule for Fourth
Assessment Report," UN IPCC, http://ipcc-wg1.ucar.edu/wg1/docs/wg1_
timetable_2006-08-14.pdf.

43. "Environmental Reality," *Investor's Business Daily*, September 7, 2007.

44. Michael Asher, "Survey: Less Than Half of all Published Scientists Endorse
Global Warming Theory," DailyTech, August 29, 2007, http://www.
dailytech.com/Survey + Less + Than + Half + of + all + Published
+ Scientists + Endorse + Global + Warming + Theory/article8641.htm.

45. Richard Littlemore, "Schulte's analysis: Not published, not going to be,"
DeSmogBlog, September 20, 2007, http://www.desmogblog.com/schultes-
analysis-not-published-not-going-to-be.

46. Christopher Monckton, "Climate Sensitivity Reconsidered," American
Physical Society, July 17, 2008, http://www.aps.org/units/fps/newsletters/
200807/monckton.cfm.

47. Letter from Christopher Monckton to APS President Arthur Bienenstock,
July 19, 2008, http://scienceandpublicpolicy.org/images/stories/papers/
monckton/monkton_letter_pys.pdf.

48. Joe Romm, "American Physical Society stomps on Monckton
disinformation—thank you Climate Progress readers," ClimateProgress blog,
July 19, 2008, http://climateprogress.org/2008/07/19/american-physical-society-
stomps-on-monckton-disinformation-thank-you-climate-progress-readers/

49. "Global Warming 'Myth' Protest Tonight at HPL," 8 November 2007,
Undercurrents, http://hartfordimc.org/blog/2007/11/08/global-warming-myth-
protest-tonight-at-hpl/, and at http://www.thegreenvibration.com/blog, viewed
November 9, 2007.

50. Freeman Dyson, "The Question of Global Warming," *New York Review of
Books*, June 12, 2008.

51. Originally posted at http://www.earthtimes.org/articles/show/news_press_
release,176495.shtml, with the list subsequently posted at http://downloads.
heartland.org/21970.pdf.

52. "New Peer-Reviewed Scientific Studies Chill Global Warming Fears,"
Senate Committee on Environment and Public Works, Blog (Minority), August
20, 2007, http://epw.senate.gov/public/index.cfm?FuseAction=Minority.Blogs&
ContentRecord_id=84E9E44A-802A-23AD-493A-B35D0842FED8.

53. "Hume misrepresented study on the link between solar activity and global
warming," Media Matters, August 24, 2007, http://mediamatters.org/
items/200708240003.

54. Fred Pearce, "Is the U.S. headed for an environmental 9/11?" *The Telegraph* (UK), May 3, 2007.

55. Fred Pearce, "Global warming and cooling linked to the sunspot cycle," *New Scientist*, August 9, 2007.

56. "CEI Responds to Scientist's Criticism of Global Warming Ad Campaign," CEI press release, May 22, 2006, http://www.cei.org/gencon/003,05339.cfm.

57. As of this writing the video is available for on-line viewing via Google video at http://video.google.fr/videoplay?docid=-4123082535546754758, and its home page is http://www.channel4.com/science/microsites/G/great_global_warming_swindle/index.html.

58. See, e.g., http://www.chemlabs.bristol.ac.uk/outreach/resources/channel4_response.pdf.

59. Stuart Blackman and Ben Pile, "Battle in Print: Climate science: truth you can wear on your hands," Battle of Ideas, October 2007, http://www.battleofideas.org.uk/index.php/site/battles/957/.

60. OfCom's decision is available at the "OfCom Broadcast Bulletin," Issue 114, July 21, 2008, pp. 6-22, http://www.ofcom.org.uk/tv/obb/prog_cb/obb114/issue114.pdf. For a full treatment of the various complaints and issues see Steve McIntyre, "Ofcom Decision: A Humiliating Defeat for Bob Ward and the Myles Allen 37," ClimateAudit blog, July 21, 2008, http://www.climateaudit.org/?p=3328.

61. "Climate Swindle film: bruised egos, but no offence," *The Register*, July 21, 2008, http://www.theregister.co.uk/2008/07/21/ofcom_global_warming_swindle_adjudication/.

62. George Monbiot, "An Ongoing Swindle," *The Guardian* (UK), July 22, 2008.

63. http://ocean.mit.edu/~cwunsch/papersonline/responseto_channel4.htm, dated March 11, 2007.

64. Ben Goldacre and David Adam, "Climate scientist 'duped to deny global warming'," *The Guardian* (UK), March 11, 2007. It is not clear who the *Guardian* claims to be quoting in this headline as this quote does not come from Wunsch or apparently from anyone cited in the story. My personal experience with one of the story's authors, David Adam, suggests that he may be quoting himself.

65. S. Fred Singer, "The Week that Was," July 26, 2008.

66. Steve Connor, "The real global warming swindle," *The Independent* (London), March 14, 2007, http://findarticles.com/p/articles/mi_qn4158/is_20070314/ai_n18714753.

67. *An Inconvenient Truth*.

68. A.V. Fedorov, et al., "The Pliocene Paradox (Mechanisms for a Permanent El Niño)," *Science*, June 9, 2006: Vol. 312. no. 5779, 1485-1489, DOI: 10.1126/science.1122666.

69. Stephen McIntyre, "Gore Scientific 'Adviser' says that he has no 'responsibility' for AIT errors," Climate Audit, January 13, 2008, http://www.climateaudit.org/?p=2598.

70. John Marchese, "Al Gore is a greenhouse gasbag: Penn professor Bob Giegengack has a few quibbles with the former VP on this whole global warming thing," *Philadelphia Magazine*, February 2007.

71. Horner, *The Politically Incorrect Guide to Global Warming*, 95–100.

72. Noel Sheppard, "NYT Disgracefully Advances Global Warming Alarmism in an Obituary," February 12, 2008, http://newsbusters.org/blogs/noel-sheppard/2008/02/12/nyt-disgracefully-advances-global-warming-alarmism-obituary.

73. Elie Dolgin, "UW-Madison's Bryson was a pioneer in climate research," *Milwaukee Journal-Sentinel*, June 12, 2008.

74. Richard Lindzen, "Climate Science: Is it currently designed to answer questions?" August 2008 draft article for proceedings of conference in San Marino.

75. "Definition of 'Revise and Extend;" C-SPAN Congressinal Glossary," http://www.c-span.org/guide/congress/glossary/revise.htm.

76. Stephen Schneider and S.I. Rasool, "Atmospheric Carbon Dioxide and Aerosols—Effects of Large Increases on Global Climate," *Science*, Issue 173, 138–141.

77. John Daly, "Stephen Schneider: Greenhouse Superstar," http://www.john-daly.com/schneidr.htm.

78. Ibid.

79. J. Schell, "Our fragile Earth," *Discover* magazine, 45–48, October 1989; see also http://rpuchalsky.home.att.net/sci_env/sch_quote.html#quote.

80. "Climate Skeptics Say Debate Stifled," Associated Press, December 13, 2007, http://biz.yahoo.com/ap/071213/climate_naysayers.html?.v=1.

81. Gill Ereaut and Nat Segnit, "Warm Words: How are we telling the climate story and can we tell it better?" Institute for Public Policy Research, August 3, 2006, http://www.ippr.org.uk/publicationsandreports/publication.asp?id=485.

82. Susan Joy Hassol, "Improving How Scientists Communicate About Climate Change," *Eos*, Vol. 89, No. 11, March 11 2008, 106.

83. Ibid.

84. "Unified Synthesis Product: Global Climate Change in the United States," Climate Change Science Program, July 2008, http://www.climatescience.gov/Library/sap/usp/public-review-draft/usp-prd-all.pdf, Hassol bio at 167–168.

85. Daniel Lee Kleinman, Karen A. Could-Hansen, Christina Matta, and Jo Handelsman, "Controversies in Science & Technology Volume 2: From Climate to Chromosomes," 2007.

86. "Some 80 NGOs wrote to the National Geographic seeking to get the screening [of 'Mine your own business"] cancelled." "Irish film-makers attack environmentalists,"*The Sunday Times*, August 10, 2008.

87. This was provided, *inter alia*, in a presentation delivered by James Hansen to the Council on Environmental Quality (Washington, DC) on June 12, 2003. It is now available at James Hansen, "Can we defuse the global warming time bomb?" *Natural Science*, August 1, 2003, http://naturalscience.com/ns/articles/01-16/ns_jeh6.html.

88. David Roberts, "Al Revere: An interview with accidental movie star AI Gore," *Grist* Magazine, May 9, 2006, http://www.grist.org/news/maindish/2006/05/09/roberts/.

Chapter 5: Poisoning the Little Ones

1. See, e.g., Marilyn Elias, "'Green' bandwagon is getting a big push," *USA Today*, March 24, 2008.

2. "Growing up green: Youngsters are pressuring parents to make not-so-easy lifestyle changes to conserve the environment," Associated Press, April 19, 2008, http://www.gazette.com/articles/green_35451___article.html/growing_.html.

3. Lee Jones, "Turning children green with fear," *Spiked* Online, March 12, 2007, http://www.spiked-online.com/index.php?/site/article/2950/.

4. Sen. James Inhofe, "Inhofe slams DiCaprio and Laurie David for scaring kids in two-hour Senate speech debunking climate fears," Minority blog, United States Senate Committee on Environment and Public Works, October 26, 2007, http://epw.senate.gov/public/index.cfm?FuseAction=Minority.Blogs&ContentRecord_id=dddc4451-802a-23ad-4000-a9b55ed9489a&Issue_id=.

5. Jane Clee, "Youngsters get a lesson in climate change," 24Dash.com (UK), January 14, 2008, http://www.24dash.com/news/Communities/2008-01-14-Youngsters-get-a-lesson-in-climate-change

6. "Kids urged to become 'climate cops' to root out 'climate crimes'," EU Referendum blog, July 27, 2008, http://eureferendum.blogspot.com/2008/07/climate-nazis.html.

7. James Hansen, Letter to National Mining Association, November 21, 2007.

8. Beman Perry, "New plants put King Coal in the cross hairs in Iowa," *Des Moines Register*, November 7, 2007.

9. Andrew Revkin, "A Textbook Case of Downplaying Global Warming?" *New York Times* "Dot Earth" blog, April 10, 2008, http://dotearth.blogs.nytimes.com/2008/04/10/a-textbook-case-of-downplaying-global-warming/?ex=1208491200&en=c17df035aa975d7e&ei=5070&emc=eta1.

10. "A flood of new climate science seeps into classrooms very slowly," *E & E News Daily*, August 12, 2008.

11. See, e.g., "New UN Children's Book Promotes Global Warming Fears to Kids," NewsBusters, November 13, 2006, http://newsbusters.org/node/9058.

12. See, e.g., "What scorching weather!" European Commission, http://ec.europa.eu/environment/pubs/pdf/weather/en.pdf.

13. The 2008 Climate Change Lesson Plan Contest, https://www.teacherspayteachers.com/contest/

14. Amy DeMelia, "North Attleboro's students really going for the green," *Sun Chronicle* (Mass.), April 19, 2008.

15. "California Elementary School Teacher Encourages Political Activism by Middle School Students," *Environment News*, Heartland Institute, March 25, 2008.

16. See, e.g., Michael Chapman, "The greening of the classroom: Do kids learn junk environmentalism in schools?" *Investors Business Daily*, September 29, 1998, http://www.junkscience.com/sep98/learnjun.htm.

17. Sen. James Inhofe, "Inhofe slams DiCaprio and Laurie David for scaring kids in two-hour Senate speech debunking climate fears," Minority blog, United States Senate Committee on Environment and Public Works, October 26, 2007, http://epw.senate.gov/public/index.cfm?FuseAction=Minority.Blogs&Content Record_id=dddc4451-802a-23ad-4000-a9b55ed9489a&Issue_id=.

18. Stuart Dimmock v. Secretary of State for Education and Skills (now Secretary of State for Children, Schools and Families), Case No.: CO/3615/2007, October 10, 2007, http://www.globalwarming.org/files/Dimmock.pdf.

19. See, e.g., "*Waverly Insider* 12-27-06," Waverly (IA) Public Library, http://city.waverlyia.com/docs/Waverly%20Insider%2012-27-06new.pdf.

20. See, e.g., "Children particularly at risk from global warming: report," Agence France-Presse, Oct. 29, 2007, http://newsinfo.inquirer.net/breakingnews/world/view_article.php?article_id=97562.

21. Marilyn Elias, "Global warming may hit kids harder, pediatrics group says," *USA Today*, October 29, 2007.

22. Jen Kelly, "Baby tax needed to save planet, claims expert," News.com.au (Australia), December 10, 2007, http://www.news.com.au/story/0,23599,22896334-2,00.html.

23. "Planet in Peril," CNN.com/World, http://www.cnn.com/SPECIALS/2007/planet.in.peril/studentnews.html.

24. http://www.nick.com/biggreenhelp/

25. See, e.g., Press Release, "Kids Speak Out to Grownups About Saving the Planet as Nick News With Linda Ellerbee Presents A Global Warning From the Kids of the World," November 27, 2007, http://news.yahoo.com/s/usnw/20071127/pl_usnw/kids_speak_out_to_grownups_about_saving_ the_planet_as_nick_news_with_linda_ellerbee_presents_a_global_warning_from_the_kids_of_.

26. Anthony Watts, "TV Network Tells Kids How Long Their Carbon Footprint Should Allow Them to Live," Watts Up With That? http://wattsupwiththat.wordpress.com/2008/05/31/tv-network-tells-kids-when-their-carbon-footprint-says-they-should-die/. Read more about global warming propaganda campaign aimed at children On the U.S. Senate Environment Committee's website (minority page) at http://epw.senate.gov/public/index.cfm?FuseAction=Minority.Blogs&ContentRecord_id=DDDC4451-802A-23AD-4000-A9B55ED9489A.

27. "Leonardo DiCaprio talks to USA WEEKEND," *USA Weekend*, September 20, 2007.

28. "DiCaprio sheds light on '11th Hour'," *The Hollywood Reporter*, May 20, 2007.

29. Sen. James Inhofe, "Inhofe slams DiCaprio and Laurie David for scaring kids in two-hour Senate speech debunking climate fears," Minority blog, United States Senate Committee on Environment and Public Works, October 26, 2007,

http://epw.senate.gov/public/index.cfm?FuseAction=Minority.Blogs&Content Record_id=dddc4451-802a-23ad-4000-a9b55ed9489a&Issue_id=.

30. "Disney's Miley Cyrus Sings 'Global Warming Anthem'," July 28, 2008 http://aftermathnews.wordpress.com/2008/07/28/disneys-teen-siren-miley-cyrus-sings-%e2%80%9cglobal-warming-anthem%e2%80%9d/.

31. Dominic Tocci, "The North Pole is Melting," Atom, http://www.atomfilms.com/film/north_pole_melting.jsp.

32. Cody Calamaio, "Environmentalists: make it 'Hallowgreen'," DailyWildcat.com (University of Arizona), October 29, 2007, http://media.wildcat.arizona.edu/media/storage/paper997/news/2007/10/29/News/Environmentalists.Make.It.hallowgreen-3062232.shtml.

33. Jennifer Harper, "Green activists chime in on holiday do's and don'ts," *Washington Times*, November 21, 2007.

34. Lee Jones, "The Grinch who stole Christmas cards," *Spiked* Online, November 19, 2007, http://www.spiked-online.com/index.php?/site/printable/4097/.

35. Id.

36. Gil Hoffman, "Green Hanukkah campaign draws ire," *Jerusalem Post*, December 4, 2007.

37. Id., citing Lee Jones, "Turning children green with fear," *Spiked* Online, March 12, 2007, http://www.spiked-online.com/index.php?/site/article/2950/.

38. Allegra Goodman, "The dark dreams of global warming," *Boston Globe*, September 8, 2008.

39. Id.; see also Lee Jones, "The Grinch who stole Christmas cards," *Spiked* Online, November 19, 2007, http://www.spiked-online.com/index.php?/site/printable/4097/.

40. Staff writers, "Save the world: buy UHT milk," News.com.AU, October 15, 2007, http://www.news.com.au/story/0,23599,22588489-13762,00.html.

41. "More Stuff about Climate Change," http://www.4million.org.nz/climatechange/stuff/index.php.

42. See, e.g., School Stuff, http://www.4million.org.nz/climatechange/understanding/schoolstuff/index.php and http://www.4million.org.nz/climatechange/understanding/schoolstuff/playitcool/index.php.

43. "Climate Change," http://www.4million.org.nz/climatechange/understanding/schoolstuff/climate-change-1.pdf.

44. The EPA Climate Change Kids Site, http://www.epa.gov/climatechange/kids/ and "So What's the Big Deal?" http://www.epa.gov/ climatechange/kids/bigdeal.html.

45. National Center for Atmospheric Research, Earth Observing Laboratories, "How Much Do You Spew?" http://www.eol.ucar.edu/ apol/activity8.pdf.

46. University Corporation for Atmospheric Research, "About Us," http://www.ucar.edu/org/about-us.shtml.

47. "Most terrifying video you'll ever see," http://www.youtube.com/watch?v=bDsIFspVzfI.

48. Cindy Long, "Global Warming 101," National Education Association, http://www.nea.org/neatodayextra/willsteger.html.

49. See, e.g., "Environmental Education Materials: Guidelines for Excellence: KEY CHARACTERISTIC #4 ACTION ORIENTATION," http://naaee.org/npeee/materials_guidelines/chap4.pdf.

50. Id. Ch. 1, http://naaee.org/npeee/materials_guidelines/chap1.pdf.

51. Kevin Sweeney, "Truth and Consequences: Teaching Global Warming Doesn't Have to Spell 'Doom'," Edutopia, http://www.edutopia.org/global-warming-fear.

52. The website directs readers EElink, http://eelink.net/pages/Climate+Change.

53. Available through http://www.naaee.org/conference.

54. National Environmental Education Foundation, http://www.neefusa.org/.

55. NEEF U.S.A. Press release, "The Weather Channel Joins with the National Environmental Education Foundation to Launch Dynami Environmental Education Progream in U.S. High Schools," http://www.neefusa.org/about/NEEF_TWC_Partnership.htm.

56. Alan Fischer, "Students show off their talents at science fair," *Tucson Citizen*, March 18, 2008, http://www.tucsoncitizen.com/daily/frontpage/79938.php.

57. Michael Morton, "Breaking the ice on climate change," *MetroWest Daily News*, March 2, 2008.

58. See, e.g., Olivia Girard, "A Writing Environment," *Berkshire Eagle* (Mass.), April 8, 2008; Joyce Kelly, "Kids Launch green initiative," *Milford Daily News* (Conn.), April 3, 2008. Susan Greene, "Dark night lights a fire in kids," *Denver Post*, April 1, 2008.

59. Tammy Marashlian, "Meadows students dominate in philosophy slam," Santa Clarita Valley *Signal*, June 24, 2008, http://www.the-signal.com/news/archive/2525/.

60. See, e.g., Alan Quist, "The Fed's Cure for 'Nature Deficit Disorder' in Our Kids," Alan Quist, EdAction, July 15, 2008, discussing H.R.3036 (S.1981), 110th Congress, http://www.edaction.org/2008/071508-NDDa.htm.

61. Id.

62. *20/20*, ABC News, October 19, 2007.

63. Joe Wolfcale, "Elementary school students join fight against global warming," *Marin Independent Journal*, November 7, 2007.

64. See, e.g., Karen Voyles, "Focus the Nation gets kids involved," *Gainesville Sun* (Fla.), February 2, 2008, http://www.gainesville.com/article/20080202/NEWS/802020320/1002/NEWS.

65. Dialectics for Kids, "What The Heck is Dialectics?" http://home.igc.org/~venceremos/whatheck.htm.

66. "Elementary school students join fight against global warming," *Marin Independent Journal*.

67. "A Fundamental Scientific Error in 'global warming' Book for Children," Science and Public Policy Institute, September 13, 2007, http://scienceandpublicpolicy.org/other/childrensbookerror.html.

68. See, e.g., H. Fischer et al., 1999, "Ice Core Records of Atmospheric CO2 Around the Last Three Glacial Terminations," *Science*, v. 283, p.1712ñ1714.

69. "The lags of CO2 with respect to Antarctic temperature over glacial terminations V to VII are 800, 1600, and 2,800 years, respectively, which are consistent with earlier observations during the last four cycles." Siegenthaler, Urs, et al, 2005, "Stable Carbon Cycle-Climate Relationship During the Late Pleistocene," *Science*, v. 310, p. 1313-1317

70. Laurie David, "The Children's Book That Has Global Warming Deniers Up in Arms," *Huffington Post*, September 19, 2007, http://www.huffingtonpost. com/laurie-david/the-childrens-book-that-_b_64998.html.

71. Press release, "Inconvenient Truth Producer to Speak at Green Schools Summit," November 21, 2007, http://www.prweb.com/releases/ 2007/11/ prweb570735.htm.

72. Eric M. Jackson, "Scholastic author: manipulate kids on global warming to influence parents," ConservativePublisher.com, August 3, 2007, http:// conservativepublisher.blogspot.com/2007/08/scholastic-author-manipulate-kids-on.html.

73. See, e.g., *Publisher Weekly's* online discussion of the objections to David's asserted agenda, serially noting that critics are conservative while her radical alarmism receives no such qualifier (at their "Children's Bookshelf" forum, found at http://www.publishersweekly.com/enewsletter/ CA6482956/2788. html?q=laurie+1 david).

74. Nathalie op de Beeck, "A Green call to arms," *Publisher's Weekly*, August 2, 2007, http://www.publishersweekly.com/index.asp?layout=articlePrint& articleID=CA6464654

75. Ellen Gamerman, "Inconvenient Youths," *Wall Street Journal*, September 29, 2007.

76. "*Inconvenient Truth* Producer Targets Children," Environment & Climate News, October 1, 2007, http://www.heartland.org/Article.cfm?artId= 21991.

77. Sonja Bolle, "For Earth's sake," *Los Angeles Times*, September 23, 2007, http://www.latimes.com/features/printedition/books/la-bkw-wordplay23sep 23,1,5196152.story?ctrack=1&cset=true

78. "Alaska Teachers Indoctrinated with Misleading Global Warming Materials," *Energy and Environment News*, The Heartland Institute, October 2007, http://www.heartland.org/Article.cfm?artId=21991.

79. James M. Taylor, "Alaska Teachers Indoctrinated with Misleading Global Warming Materials," *Environment & Climate News*, October 1, 2007, The Heartland Institute, http://www.heartland.org/Article.cfm?artId=21983.

80. Id.

81. Id.

82. See, e.g., Chylek, et al., "Greenland warming of 1920-1930 and 1995-2005," *Geophysical Research Letters*, 33, L11707, 13 June 2006, doi:10.1029/2006GL026510, http://www.agu.org/pubs/crossref/2006/ 2006GL026510.shtml.

83. See, e.g., "Greenland's glaciers have been shrinking for 100 years: study," *Space Daily*, August 21, 2006.

84. For a compendium of related research see "Latest Scientific Studies Refute Fears of Greenland Melt," July 30, 2007, Senate Environment and Public Works Committee, Minority, http://epw.senate.gov/public/ index.cfm?FuseAction= Minority.Blogs&ContentRecord_id=175B568A-802A-23AD-4C69-9BDD978FB3CD.

85. Contained in an emailed announcement from the UNFCCC, December 11, 2007.

86. Ellen Gamerman, "Inconvenient Youths," *Wall Street Journal*, September 29, 2007.

87. Center for American Progress, "Global Boiling," The Progress Report, June 12, 2008, http://pr.thinkprogress.org/2008/06/pr20080612

88. See, e.g., "Eskimo Teen Blubbers about Global Warming," Sweetness & Light, November 6, 2007, http://sweetness-light.com/archive/cheryl-lockwood-testimony-see-it-and-weep.

89. Andrew Bolt, "Doomed to a fatal delusion over climate change," *Herald Sun*, July 9, 2008.

90. Editorial, "Readin', writin' and warmin'," *Investor's Business Daily*, February 19, 2008.

Chapter 6: Big Government

1. Peter Foster, "The New Road to Serfdom," *Financial Post* (Canada), March 12, 2008.

2. Ibid.

3. Portugese environment scientist Professor Delgado Domingos, "Q&A with prof. Delgado Domingos," *European Tribune*, January 28, 2008.

4. Lord Giddens in the United Kingdom Parliament, March 1, 2005 column 150, transcript available at http://www.publications.parliament.uk/pa/ld200405/ldhansrd/vo050301/text/50301-12.htm.

5. Rebecca Tuhus-Dubrow, "Brother, can you spare a carbon credit?" *Boston Globe*, February 24, 2008.

6. "PM warns stores over carrier bags," BBC News, February 29, 2008.

7. "Britons fear the carbon cops are coming," *Reuters*, 25 June 2008, http://uk.reuters.com/article/topNews/idUKL2459239920080624?feedType=RSS&feedName=topNews.

8. Brendan O'Neill, "Greens are the enemies of liberty: Environmentalists want to curb our freedom far more than the government's anti-terrorist laws ever will," *The Guardian*, July 15, 2008.

9. Mark Steyn, "People who don't need people," National Review Online's *The Corner*, November 7, 2007, http://corner.nationalreview.com.

10. "Submission to the Garnaut Enquiry into Global Warming," Carbon Sense Coalition (Australia), February 17, 2008, http://carbon-sense.com/wp-content/uploads/2008/01/garnaut-submission.pdf.

11. Alan Murray, "Next President needs to uncap debate on cost of emissions curbs," *Wall Street Journal*, March 17, 2008.

12. See, e.g., "Dominic Lawson, "This is a Government which doesn't really believe in the threat of climate change," *Independent* (UK), March 14, 2008.

13. See, e.g., John Vidal, "Government figures hide scale of CO2 emissions, says report," *The Guardian* (UK), March 17, 2008, and "Carry on polluting," *The Guardian* (UK), March 17, 2008.

14. Klaus says this serially. See, e.g., "Freedom, not climate, is under threat," *Reuters*, December 11, 2007, http://www.planetark.com/dailynewsstory.cfm/newsid/45904/story.htm.

15. "Illarionov Likens Kyoto to Gosplan," *Moscow Times*, February 20, 2004.

16. UK Green candidate for the European Parliament Rupert Read, "Is there still a role for the State?" February 18, 2008, http://rupertsread.blogspot.com/2008/02/is-there-still-role-for-state.html.

17. FOE "climate justice campaigner Emma Brindal quoted at http://www.climatenetwork.org/bali-blog/ngo-bustle-in-bali, a link which was no longer active as of early 2008 after Marc Morano brought attention to it at "Global Carbon Tax Urged at UN Climate Conference," Senate EPW Minority blog, December 13, 2007, http://epw.senate.gov/public/index.cfm?FuseAction=Minority.Blogs&ContentRecord_id =D5C3C93F-802A-23AD-4F29-FE59494B48A6.

18. Meanwhile, the headline to the story revealing such absurd lack of measure tried to tone things down, Joseph Coleman, "UN Suggests Bali Targets Too Ambitious," Associated Press, December 13, 2007.

19. Simon Caldwell, "The Pope condemns the climate change prophets of doom," *The Daily Mail* (London), December 13, 2007.

20. "Address by His Excellency Mr. Maumoon Abdul Gayoom, President of the Republic of Maldives, at the Opening of the Joint High-level Segment of the 13th Session of the Conference of the Parties of the UNFCCC and the 3rd Session of the Meeting of the Parties to the Kyoto Protocol," Nusa Dua, Bali, 12 December 2007, available at http://www.presidencymaldives.gov.mv.

21. "A plan to 'save the planet' but is anyone willing to pay the price?" *Local Transport Today*, December 6–19, 2007.

22. David Shearman and Joseph Wayne Smith, *The Climate Change Challenge and the Failure of Democracy*, (Praeger, 2007).

23. Nigel Purvis, "Paving the Way for U.S. Climate Leadership: The Case for Executive Agreements and Climate Protection Authority," Resources for the Future, April 2008, http://www.cleanair-coolplanet.org/documents/Purvis_RFF.pdf.

24. See e.g., "Imbalance of Powers," *Investor's Business Daily*, April 10, 2008.

25. Larry Elliot, "Can a dose of recession solve climate change?" *The Guardian*, August 25, 2008.

26. Elisabeth Rosenthal, "Can polyester save the world?" *New York Times*, January 25, 2007.

27. Vaclav Klaus, *Blue Planet in Green Shackles* (Washington: Competitive Enterprise Institute, 2008), 5–6.

28. See, e.g., Bryan Walsh, "Going Green: Can climate change make us sicker?" *Time* Magazine, April 4, 2008.

29. See, e.g., "At Man's expense," *Investor's Business Daily*, December 27, 2007.

30. Donald J. Boudreaux, "Global-warming skepticism," Letter to the Editor, *Boston Globe*, February 15, 2008.

31. Keynote Foreign Policy Speech, Prime Minister Gordon Brown, Kennedy Memorial Lecture, April 18, 2008, http://usvisit.pm.gov.uk/2008/04/18/keynote-foreign-policy-speech/.

32. Claudia Kade, "Merkel backs climate deal based on population," *Reuters*, Aug 31, 2007.

33. Erik Kirschbaum, "Czech leader raises new doubts on climate change," *Reuters*, November 11, 2007, http://www.reuters.com/article/latestCrisis/idUSL11213678.

34. Klaus, *Blue Planet in Green Shackles*, 7.

35. Ibid., 14. Citing Janet Biehl, *Ecology and Modernization of Fascism in the German Ultra-Right*, in *Ecofascism: Lessons from the German Experience,* ed. Janet Biehl and Peter Staudenmaier, (Oakland, CA: AK Press, 1995), 22.

36. Ibid., 14. Citing Paul R. Ehrlich and Richard L. Harriman, *How To Be a Survivor: A Plan to Save Spaceship Earth* (London: Ballantine Books, 1971).

37. George Monbiot, "Green Lifeline," *The Guardian* (UK), July 1, 2008.

38. *Calgary Herald*, December 14, 1998.

39. Simon Cox, "EU 'wasting' cash on lobby groups," BBC News, December 7, 2007.

40. "Klimaekspert anklaget for lobbyarbejde for staten," *Berlingske Tidende*, December 15, 2007.

41. "Green tax a state cash cow: The tax minister admits that CO2 levy is solely in place to fill state treasury," *The Copenhagen Post*, January 15, 2007.

42. David Evans, "Why I bet against global warming," August 5, 2008, http://www.lavoisier.com.au/articles/greenhouse-science/climate-change/evansd2007-12.php.

43. Senator Bob Dutton, "Business development is the key to fixing California's budget woes," *Highland News* (Canada), June 6, 2008.

44. See, e.g., "Global Carbon Tax Urged at UN Climate Conference," Senate Committee on Environment and Public Works blog (Minority), December 13, 2007, http://epw.senate.gov/public/index.cfm?Fuse Action=Minority.Blogs&ContentRecord_id=d5c3c93f-802a-23ad-4f29-fe59494b48a6&Issue_id=.

45. See compilation of McKitrick articles on his "T3 Tax" at http://ross.mckitrick.googlepages.com/#t3tax.

46. Ron Bailey, "Do the Rich Owe the Poor Climate Change Reparations?" *Reason* Magazine, December 11, 2007.

47. Ibid.

48. Ibid.

49. "How about an atmospheric trust to slow global warming?" *Seattle Post-Intelligencer*, July 23, 2008.

50. "Rich nations must pay more for climate change aid," Agence France Presse, November 10, 2007.

51. "China: Rich 'culprits' on Climate Change," Associated Press, February 16, 2008.

52. "Brazilian president says rich countries do not follow Kyoto Protocol," *Xinhua News*, February 22, 2008.

53. "Brazil urges rich to fund environment reform," *Reuters*, February 22, 2008, http://uk.reuters.com/article/oilRpt/idUKN2145533820080222.

54. "Bolivian President to UN: To save planet 'we have a duty to put an end to the capitalist system,'" BBC News, April 21, 2008, http://news.bbc.co.uk/2/hi/americas/7359880.stm.

55. Dr. Gideon Polya, "Bali Exposes US, Canada And Australian Climate Racism, Climate Terrorism, Climate Criminals And Climate Genocide," Countercurrents.org, December 18, 2007, http://www.countercurrents.org/polya181207.htm.

56. Phoebe Sweet, "Sen. Reid accuses coal industry of using 'the old Hitler lie," *Las Vegas Sun*, February 19, 2008.

57. Cecelia M. Vega, "Mayor's aide gets $160,000 a year," *San Francisco Chronicle*, February 20, 2008.

58. See, e.g., "California AG Puts Climate Skeptics on Trial," JunkScience.com, August 1, 2006, http://www.junkscience.com/Skeptics_on_trial.htm.

59. "Govt rushing emissions scheme: Turnbull," *The West* (Australia), July 18, 2008.

60. "A Briefing Report on Climate Change and the Threat of Litigation," American Justice Partnership and Southeastern Legal Foundation, January 31, 2008, http://www.legalreforminthenews.com/Reports/AJP-SLF_Global_Warming_Litigation_1-31-07_Final.pdf, 14.

61. Mark Steyn, "Children? Not if you love the planet," *Orange County Register*, December 14, 2007.

62. Ibid.

63. Jen Kelly, "Baby tax needed to save planet, claims expert," News.com.au (Australia), December 10, 2007, http://www.news.com.au/story/0,23599,22896334-2,00.html.

64. See, e.g., "'Tax Parents for Children's Carbon Emissions'," CNSNews.com, December 10, 2007.

65. See, e.g., Mark Steyn, "Season to be wary," *Washington Times*, December 17, 2007.

66. Andrew Bolt, "Handy ideas to make us green and mouldy," *Herald Sun* (Australia), December 19, 2007.

67. Ross McKitrick CEI paper/Kaya Identity

68. "Roger Pielke Jr., "Carbon emissions success stories," February 15, 2008, Prometheus blog, http://sciencepolicy.colorado.edu/prometheus/archives/climate_change/001345carbon_emissions_suc.html.

69. "Kids 'risk' to climate," *Mirror*, November 13, 2007.

70. Ibid.

71. See, e.g., Alister Doyle, "Poor nations brake greenhouse gas rise: U.N. draft," *Reuters*, May 2, 2007.

72. Alister Doyle, "China says one-child policy helps protect climate," August 30, 2007, Reuters.

73. Ibid.

74. Al Gore, *Earth in the Balance: Ecology and the Human Spirit* (Bel Air, CA: Plume, 1993), 308.

75. Chris Horner quoting Myron Ebell, "Chairman Mao, environmentalist," *National Review* Online's Planet Gore blog, May 2, 2007, http://planetgore. nationalreview.com/post/?q=MGZkODJhNWFhYjVlOT kzYTE3YTZiOTczYTc0ZDQ4OGU=.

76. John Feeney, "Humanity is the greatest challenge," BBC.com, November 7, 2007, http://news.bbc.co.uk/1/hi/sci/tech/7078857.stm.

77. "Rockefeller and Snowe Demand that Exxon Mobil End Funding of Campaign that Denies Climate Change," Press Release, Senator Olympia Snowe, October 30, 2006, http://snowe.senate.gov/public/index.cfm?FuseAction= PressRoom.PressReleases&ContentRecord_id=9ACBA744-802A-23AD-47BE-2683985C724E.

78. See, e.g., Press Release, "ExxonMobil Plans $100 Million Investment in Stanford University's Global Climate and Energy Project," November 20, 2002, http://www.csrwire.com/PressRelease.php?id=1411.

79. Marlo Lewis, "The Snowe-Rockefeller Road to Kyoto," *American Spectator*, November 3, 2006.

80. Review & Outlook, "Global Warming Gag Order," *Wall Street Journal*, December 4, 2006.

81. Liberal-Democrat Shadow Secretary Chris Huhne, House of Commons Debate, October 12, 2006.

82. They apparently engaged the Nashville bureaucracy to block the launch of a hot air balloon intended to draw attention to Gore's lavish lifestyle and hypocrisy. Press release, "BREAKING: Gore Allies Attempting to Ground Our Hot Air Tour in Nashville," Americans for Prosperity, June 20, 2008, http://www.americansforprosperity.org/index.php?id=5916.

83. Letter from Kelvin Thomson, September 27, 2006, http://jennifermarohasy. com/data/Kelvin%20Thomson_against%20freedom.pdf.

84. See discussion, Christopher C. Horner, *PIG to Global Warming* (Washington, D.C.: Regnery, 2007), 128–131.

85. See discussion, *PIG to Global Warming*, 95–103.

86. For example, a recent poll found that 74 percent of the British respondents "agreed that so-called 'green' taxation on polluting cars and flights were a 'con'"; David Smith and Jonathan Oliver, "Support for Labour hits 25-year low," *The Sunday Times* (London), March 16, 2008. These results were affirmed

by later polling. Colin Brown, "Majority of Britons opposed to green taxation, not as gullible as its politicians and media," *The Independent*, May 2, 2008.

87. Jeffrey M. Jones, "Polluted Drinking Water Was No. 1 Concern Before AP Report: Global warming way down the list," Gallup, Inc., Princeton, N.J., March 12, 2008.

88. The above Gallup figures are supported by a contemporaneous poll by University of Missouri professor David Konisky, "Public attitudes on the environment," Institute of Public Policy, University of Missouri, March, 2008, http://truman.missouri.edu/uploads/Publications/4-2008%20Public%20Attitudes%20on%20the%20Environment.pdf.

89. "Monkeying with the Message," *Plenty* Magazine, March 18, 2008.

90. Paul M. Kellstedt, Sammy Zahran, and Arnold Vedlitz, "Personal Efficacy, the Information Environment, and Attitudes Toward Global Warming and Climate Change in the United States," *Risk Analysis,* Vol. 28, No. 1, 2008.

91. PBS *Frontline*, special airing, April 24, 2007.

92. Transcript, Hot Politics, http://www.pbs.org/wgbh/pages/frontline/hotpolitics/etc/script.html

93. Stayton Bonner, "Leaves of Gold," *Texas Observer*, November 30, 2007.

94. *Massachusetts v. EPA*, 127 S. Ct. 1438 (2007).

95. Holman Jenkins, "The Science of Gore's Nobel" *Wall Street Journal*, December 5, 2007.

96. Review & Outlook, "A Glorious Mess," *Wall Street Journal*, April 12, 2008.

97. Edwin Meese, Todd Gaziano, and Ben Lieberman, "Memorandum to Interested Parties Re: Possible EPA Regulation of Carbon Dioxide Emissions," Heritage Foundation, December 13, 2007.

98. Iain Murray, "Re: Divorce Story," *National Review Online's* The Corner, December 4, 2007, http:// corner.nationalreview.com/.

99. Editorial, "Globaloney," *Washington Times*, November 11, 2007.

100. See, e.g., "Analysis of The Lieberman-Warner Climate Security Act (S. 2191) Using The National Energy Modeling System (NEMS)," Report for the American Council for Capital Formation and the National Association of Manufacturers Analysis Conducted by Science Applications International Corporation (SAIC), March 13, 2008, http://www.accf.org/pdf/NAM/fullstudy031208.pdf.

101. "Cost Estimate for S. 2191, America's Climate Security Act of 2007, with an amendment," Congressional Budget Office, April 10, 2008, http://www.cbo.gov/ftpdocs/91xx/doc9121/s2191_EPW_Amendment.pdf.

102. See "EPA Says Carbon Caps Won't Harm Economy Much," *Wall Street Journal*, March 17, 2008.

103. See, e.g., Steven Hayward, "The United States and the Environment: Laggard or Leader?" Environmental Policy Outlook (American Enterprise Institute, Washington, DC), February 21, 2008.

104. "The Big Secret: Climate Bills Result in No Meaningful Impact on Global Temperature," 20 November 2007, World Climate Report, http://www. worldclimatereport.com/index.php/2007/11/20/the-big-secret-climate-bills-result-in-no-meaningful-impact-on-global-temperature/.

105. Pat Michaels, "The Big Secret: Climate Bills Result in No Meaningful Impact on Global Temperature," World Climate Report, November 20, 2007, http://www.worldclimatereport.com/index.php/2007/11/20/ the-big-secret-climate-bills-result-in-no-meaningful-impact-on-global-temperature/.

106. Steven Mufson, "Europe's problems color U.S. plans to curb carbon gases," *Washington Post*, April 9, 2007.

107. Hoffert et al, "Advanced Technology Paths to Global Climate Stability: Energy for a Greenhouse Planet," *Science*, November 1, 2002, Vol. 298. no. 5595, 981—987 DOI: 10.1126/science.1072357.

108. Juliet Eilpren, "Climate is a risky issue for Democrats: Candidates back costly proposals," *Washington Post*, November 6, 2007.

109. "Obama pledges to cut global warming pollution," *Baltimore Sun*, February 11, 2008.

110. "John Stossel Exposes Global Warming Myths," NewsMax, October 17, 2007, http://www.newsmax. com/insidecover/global_warming/2007/10/ 17/41855.html; segment aired October 20, 2007.

111. Brendan O'Neill, "A climate of censorship," *The Guardian*, November 23, 2006.

112. http://www.euportal.cz/Articles/1852-global-warming-hysteria-or-freedom-and-prosperity-.aspx.

Chapter 7: Stupid Science Tricks

1. Note: When quoting alarmist and rationalist alike, at the suggestion of one reviewer of my manuscript I have taken the liberty to correct obvious typographical errors, so as to not belabor the text with "[sic]", limiting the use to egregious errors, matters of dispute or distinctions in customary spellings.

2. "Drilling into a climate hotspot," BBC News, April 4, 2008, http://news. bbc.co.uk/2/hi/science/nature/7326011.stm.

3.Roger Pielke Jr. "Teats on a Bull," Prometheus science blog, May 8, 2008, http://sciencepolicy.colorado.edu/prometheus/archives/climate_change/ 001420teats_on_a_bull.html.

4. Roger Pielke, Jr. "Global Cooling Consistent With Global Warming," Prometheus science blog, April 30, 2008, http://sciencepolicy.colorado.edu/ prometheus/archives/climate_change/001413global_cooling_consi.html.

5. Models are wrong on Antarctic warming: AGU & National Center for Atmospheric Research, AGU Release No. 08-17; "Climate Models Overheat Antarctica," 7 May 2008, http://news.yahoo.com/s/livescience/20080507/ sc_ livescience/coldwaterthrownonantarcticwarmingpredictions;_ylt=Ajf9979PST5R BDjgUP5IUoEPLBIF. A. J. Monaghan, D. H. Bromwich, and D. P. Schneider (2008), "Twentieth-century Antarctic air temperature and snowfall simulations

by IPCC climate models," Geophysical Research Letters, 35, L07502, doi:10.1029/2007GL032630.

6. Frank J. Wentz, Lucrezia Ricciardulli, Kyle Hilburn, and Carl Mears, "How Much More Rain Will Global Warming Bring?" Science Express Reports, May 31, 2007.

7. "Destruction Of Greenhouse Gases Over Tropical Atlantic May Ease Global Warming," Science Daily, June 26, 2008.

8. "Bangladesh gaining land, not losing: scientists," Agence France-Press, July 30, 2008.

9. J.K. Willis, D. P. Chambers, R.S. Nerem, "Assessing the globally averaged sea level budget on seasonal to interannual timescales," Journal of Geophysical Research 113(c6): C06015, June 14, 2008.

10. "North Pole Notes," Real Climate, June 27, 2008, Http://www. realclimate.org/index.php/archives/2008/06/north-pole-notes/#comment-91087. The MODID satellites provide near real-time visible/actual photos of the Arctic Ocean from space. See satellite photo at: http://rapidfire.sci.gsfc.nasa.gov/ realtime/single.php?2008181/crefl1_143.A2008181053500-2008181053959. 4km.jpg (last viewed June 29, 2008). Http://rapidfire.sci.gsfc.nasa.gov/realtime/ single.php?2008181/crefl1_143.A2008181021500-2008181021959.4km.jpg.

11. World Climate Report's Chip Knappenberger also comments on the described phenomenon on a Colorado State University science blog, at: http:// climatesci.colorado.edu/2007/06/14/snow-cover-trends-in-south-america/feed/.

12. "The Mystery of Global Warming's Missing Heat," National Public Radio, March 2, 2008, http://www.npr.org/templates/story/story.php?storyId=88520025.

13. United Nations Framework Convention on Climate Change, at: www.UNFCCC.int.

14. Summary and Index available at: http://www.acia.uaf.edu/.

15. See discussion in Christopher Horner, The Politically Incorrect Guide to Global Warming and Environmentalism (Regnery, 2007), 144ñ45.

16. See, e.g., D'Aleo, Joe, "Global Temperatures are Uncorrelated with Carbon Dioxide Trends This Last Decade," IceCap.us, November 27, 2007, http://icecap.us/index.php/go/joes-blog/global_temperatures_are_uncorrelated_ with_carbon_dioxide_trends_this_last_d/.

17. See, e.g., "The road from climate science to climate advocacy," New York Times DotEarth blog, January 9, 2008, http://dotearth.blogs.nytimes. com/2008/ 01/09/the-road-from-climate-science-to-climate-advocacy/?hp.

18. Daniel B. Botkin, "Science and soothsayingk," International Herald Tribune, December 29, 2007.

19. "Global Warming - A Chilling Possibility," FirstScience.com (citing a NASA report available at: http://www.iamamerica.com/media/Chilling_ Possibility.pdf), January 6, 2001, http://www.firstscience.com/home/articles/ earth/global-warming-a-chilling-possibility_1252.html.

20. Holman Jenkins, "The Science of Gore's Nobel" Wall Street Journal, December 5, 2007.

21. "Global Warming," http://en.wikipedia.org/wiki/Global_warming, "West Antarctic Ice Sheet," http://en.wikipedia.org/wiki/West_Antarctic_ Ice_Sheet, "Climate Change Science Program," http://en.wikipedia.org/wiki/Climate_ Change_Science_Program.

22. See, e.g., Lawrence Solomon, "Wikipedia's zealots," *Financial Post* (CA), April 12, 2008, http://www.nationalpost.com/todays_paper/story.html?id= 440268.

23. Pielke, R. A., Sr., et al. (2007), Unresolved issues with the assessment of multidecadal global land surface temperature trends, *J. Geophysical Research Letters* 112, D24S08, doi:10.1029/2006JD008229, 8, http://climatesci. colorado.edu/publications/pdf/R-321.pdf.

24. James Watts, "NOAA/NCDC throws a roadblock my way," June 30, 2007, http://www.norcalblogs.com/watts/2007/06/noaa_throws_a_ roadblock_my_ way.html

25. James Watts, "NOAA and NCDC restore data access," July 7, 2007, http://www.norcalblogs.com/watts/2007/07/noaa_and_ncdc_restore_data_acc. html

26. Pielke's blog post, "NOAA Cover Up Of US Historical Climate Network Surface Station Photographs," http://climatesci.colorado.edu/2007/06/29/ noaa-cover-up-of-us-historical-climate-network-surface-station-photographs/.

27. Anthony Watts of SurfaceStations.org has been conducting experiments revealing the impact of this switch. See comment re: same on Climate audit at http://www.climateaudit.org/?p=1702#comment-114585, at "The Stevenson Screen Paint Test," http://www.norcalblogs.com/watts/2007/07/ (July 14, 2007), and data at http://www.surfacestations.org/downloads/paint_test1.zip (zip file), about which Watts says "These are all comma demilited text files, suitable for import into R or Excel. This is three weeks worth of data."

28. Chart courtesy of Joe D'Aleo Power Point, Center for Science and Public Policy, slide 12 at www.ff.org/centers/csspp/docs/20070316_daleo.ppt.

29. Goddard Institute for Space Studies, http://www.giss.nasa.gov/, visited September 18, 2007.

30. James Hansen, "Global Warming, Playing Dice, and Berenstain Bears," NASA Science Briefs, January 2000, http://www.giss.nasa.gov/research/ briefs/hansen_08/.

31. Stephen McIntyre, "Should NASA climate accountants adhere to GAAP?," Climate Audit blog, September 17, 2007, http://www.climateaudit. org/?p=2077.

32. Pat Michaels, "Our climate numbers are a big old mess," *Wall Street Journal*, April 18, 2008.

33. Ibid.

34. Anthony Watts, "How not to measure temperature part 25," WattsUpWithThat blog, July 26, 2007, http://www.norcalblogs.com/watts/2007/ 07/how_not_to_measure_temperature_23.html.

35. Steve McIntyre, "Does Hanson's Error 'Matter'?" Climate Audit, August 11, 2007, see http://www.climateaudit.org/?p=1885.

36. For the "jump" at this station see http://www.norcalblogs.com/watts/images/Detroit_lakes_GISSplot.jpg.

37. See McIntyre post of August 6, 2007, "Quantifying the Hansen Y2K error," at http://www.climateaudit.org/?p=1868.

38. See the distribution at http://www.climateaudit.org/wp-content/uploads/2007/08/hansen40.gif.

39. Mark Steyn, "Warm-mongers and cheeseburger imperialists," *Orange County Register*, August 12, 2007.

40. Steve McIntyre, " A New Leadership at the U.S. Open," Climate Audit, August 8, 2007, see http://www.climateaudit.org/?p=1880.

41. Joe D'Aleo, "Accurate Climate Change Assessment—An Impossible Task?" Science and Public Policy Institute, September 2007, http://scienceandpublicpolicy.org/images/stories/papers/originals/accurate climatechange/accclimatechange.pdf.

42. See, e.g., Gunter, Lorne, "Global warming? Look at the numbers," *National Post* (CA), August 13, 2007.

43. See, J.R. Christy and R.W. Spencer, 2005: Correcting temperature data sets, *Science*, 310, 972.

44. Ibid.

45. Steve McIntyre, "The September 2007 Bear Market in NASA Temperature 'Pasts'," Climate Audit, September 13, 2007, http://www.climateaudit.org/?p=2049.

46. Comment on Steve McIntyre, "A New Leadership at the U.S. Open," Climate Audit, August 8, 2007, http://www.climateaudit.org/?p=1880#comment-138046.

47. Roger Pielke, Jr., "James Hansen on One Year's Temperature," Prometheus blog, January 14, 2008, http://sciencepolicy.colorado.edu/prometheus/archives/prediction_and_forecasting/index.html#001322.

48. James Hansen, "GISS 2007 Temperature Analysis," January 2008, http://www.columbia.edu/%7Ejeh1/mailings/20080114_GISTEMP.pdf.

49. Ibid.

50. Iain Murray, "Discouraging Data," Open Market, August 27, 2007, http://www.openmarket.org/2007/08/27/discouraging-data/.

51. Rob Gutro, "2005 Warmest Year in Over a Century," NASA, http://www.nasa.gov/vision/earth/environment/2005_warmest.html.

52. 2005 GISS Surface Temperatures Analysis, Goddard Institute for Space Studies, http://data.giss.nasa.gov/gistemp/2005/.

53. Leslie McCarthy, "2006 Was Earth's Fifth Warmest Year," February 8, 2007, http://www.nasa.gov/centers/goddard/news/topstory/2006/ 2006_warm.html.

54. Rob Gutro, "Earth Gets a Warm Feeling All Over," NASA, February 8, 2005, http://www.nasa.gov/vision/earth/lookingatearth/earth_warm.html.

55. 2003 GISS Surface Temperature Analysis, http://data.giss.nasa.gov/gistemp/2003/.

56. 2002 GISS Surface Temperature Analysis, http://data.giss.nasa.gov/gistemp/2002/.

57. Roger Pielke, Jr., "James Hansen on One Year's Temperature," Prometheus blog, January 14, 2008, http://sciencepolicy.colorado.edu/ prometheus/archives/prediction_and_forecasting/index.html#001322.

58. Hansen lapsed right back into his practice of focusing on individual years, at "GISS 2007 Temperature Analysis," January 2008, http://www.columbia.edu/%7Ejeh1/mailings/20080114_GISTEMP.pdf.

59. Hansen et al 2001, http://pubs.giss.nasa.gov/abstracts/2001/ Hansen_etal. html.

60. Steve McIntyre, "Hansen and the 'Destruction of Creation,'" Climate Audit, August 20, 2007, http://www.climateaudit.org/?p=1946.

61. John Goetz, "The Accidental Tourist," May 20, 2008, Climate Audit blog, http://www.climateaudit.org/?p=3094.

62. Dr. Fred Singer, "A Climate of Deception," *The Week That Was* Update, Science and Environment Policy Project, August 2, 2008.

63. "The Soros threat to democracy," *Investors Business Daily*, September 24, 2007.

64. See, e.g., Roger Pielke, Jr., "Updated IPCC Forecasts vs. Observations," Prometheus, January 26, 2008, http://sciencepolicy.colorado.edu/prometheus/archives/climate_change/001335updated_ipcc_forecas.html.

65. Ibid.

66. Ibid.

67. See E. Friis-Christensen and K. Lassen, "Length of the solar cycle: An indicator of solar activity closely associated with climate," *Science* 254: 698-700, 2000. Reply to "Solar cycle lengths and climate: A reference revisited" by P. Laut and J. Gundermann. *Journal of Geophysical Research* 105: 27,493-27,495; Mann, M.E., Bradley, R.S. and Hughes, M.K. 1998. "Global-scale temperature patterns and climate forcing over the past six centuries," *Nature* 392: 779-787; M. E. Mann, R. S. Bradley, and M. K. Hughes, "Northern Hemisphere temperatures during the past millennium: Inferences, uncertainties, and limitations," *Geophysical Research Letters* 26: 759-762. H. Svensmark, "Influence of cosmic rays on Earth's climate," *Physical Review Letters* 22: 5027-5030. H. Svensmark, and E. Friis-Christensen, "Variation of cosmic ray flux and global cloud coverage - A missing link in solar-climate relationships," *Journal of Atmospheric and Solar-Terrestrial Physics* 59: 1225-1232. See also, "Solar wind warming up Earth," September 28, 2007, RIA Novosti, http://en.rian.ru/analysis/20070928/81541029.html; see also, I. Habibullo Abdussamatov, "About the long-term coordinated variations of the activity, radius, total irradiance of the Sun and the Earth's climate," *Multi-Wavelength Investigations of Solar Activity, Proceedings IAU Symposium No. 223, 2004*, International Astronomical Union DOI: 10.1017/S1743921304006775, http://journals.cambridge.org/ production/action/cjoGetFulltext?fulltextid=288609; see also, F. Boberg & H. Lundstedt, "Solar Wind Variations Related to Fluctuations of the North Atlantic Oscillation," Geophysial Research Letters, VOL. 29, NO. 15, 1718,

10.1029/2002GL014903, 2002: 2) D. R. Palamara and E. A. Bryant, Geomagnetic activity forcing of the Northern Annular Mode via the stratosphere, Annales Geophysicae (2004) 22: 725–731).

68. Warwick Hughes, "Exactly where Lockwood and Fröhlich are wrong," August 11, 2007, http://www.warwickhughes.com/blog/?p=131#comments.

69. See Ilya G. Usoskin and Gennady A. Kovaltsov, "Cosmic rays and climate of the Earth: possible connection," (viewed as corrected proof in early March 2008, before publication in Comptes Rendus Geoscience) at http://cc.oulu.fi/~usoskin/personal/CRAS2A_2712.pdf.

70. Thanks to Joe D'Aleo for this summary.

71. T. R. Oke, "City size and the urban heat island," Atmospheric Environment, 7 769-779.

72. Hoyt, D., "Urban Heat Islands and Land Use Changes," http://www.warwickhughes.com/hoyt/uhi.htm.

73. Hinkel, et al, "The Urban Heat Island in Winter at Barrow, Alaska," Int. J. Climatol. 23: 1889–1905 (2003), http://www.geography.uc.edu/~kenhinke/uhi/HinkelEA-IJOC-03.pdf.

74. Testimony of Dr. John Christy, United States Senate Commerce, Science and Transportation Committee, November 14, 2007, http://commerce.senate.gov/public/_files/ChristyJR_CST_071114_written.pdf.

75. See "Terminating Warming? A Look at California," World Climate Report, November 28, 2007, http://www.worldclimatereport.com/index.php/2007/11/28/terminating-warming-a-look-at-california. S. LaDochy, R. Medina, and W. Patzert, "Recent California climate variability: spatial and temporal patterns in temperature trends," Climate Research, 33, 159–169.

76. Http://www.informath.org/WCWF07a.pdf. The two papers are Jones P.D., Groisman P.Y., Coughlan M., Plummer N., Wang W.-C., Karl T.R. (1990), "Assessment of urbanization effects in time series of surface air temperature over land," Nature, 347: 169–172, and Wang W.-C., Zeng Z., Karl T.R. (1990), "Urban heat islands in China," Geophysical Research Letters, 17: 2377–2380.

77. Douglas J. Keenan, "The Fraud Allegation Against Some Climatic Research of Wei-Chyung Wang," Energy & Environment, Vol. 18, No. 7 + 8, 2007, 985-995, http://www.informath.org/pubs/EnE07a.pdf.

78. Douglas J. Keenan, remarks, http://www.informath.org/apprise/a5620.htm

79. Ibid.

80. As of March 2008 this issue was still under inquiry by Wang's employer, see http://www.informath.org/apprise/a5620.htm, viewed March 13, 2008. See also McLean's inquiry into Chuine, et al., discussed elsewhere.

81. "Ad Hoc Committee Report on the 'Hockey Stick' Global Climate Reconstruction," for the Chairmen of the U.S. House Committee on Energy and Commerce and of the Subcommittee on Oversight and Investigations, Edward J. Wegman, David W. Scott, and Yasmin H. Said, National Academies of Sciences, available at http://www.climateaudit.org/pdf/others/07142006_Wegman_Report.pdf.

82. Jones P.D., Groisman P.Y., Coughlan M., Plummer N., Wang W.-C., Karl T.R. (1990), "Assessment of urbanization effects in time series of surface air temperature over land," *Nature*, 347: 169–172.

83. "Assessment of Urban Versus Rural In Situ Surface Temperatures in the Contiguous United States: No Difference Found," http://www.ncdc.noaa.gov/oa/climate/research/population/article2abstract.pdf.

84. Stephen McIntyre, "Trends in Peterson 2003," Climate Audit, August 4, 2007, http://www.climateaudit.org/?p=1859.

85. Ibid., comparing Peterson sites that are home to Major League Sports Franchises with a Rural Network.

86. Parker D.E. (2006), "A demonstration that large-scale warming is not urban," *Journal of Climate*, 19: 2882–2895. [This is one of the main works cited by the IPCC [2007] to support the conclusion that urbanization effects on temperature measurements are insignificant. The work has been strongly criticized; the only response from Parker of which I am aware is blogged here (http://www.climateaudit.org/?p=1813).] from Keenan, Notes.

87. Ren G.Y., Chu Z.Y., Chen Z.H., Ren Y.Y. (2007), "Implications of temporal change in urban heat island intensity observed at Beijing and Wuhan stations," *Geophysical Research Letters*, 34. doi: 10.1029/2006GL027927. [This argues that a large part of the observed warming in China is due to urbanization effects on measurement.]

88. Keenan Notes http://www.informath.org/apprise/a5620.htm; see also extensive comment and reference by Roger A. Pielke Sr. at http://www.climateaudit.org/?p=1813#comment-119394, and also He J.F., Liu J.Y., Zhuang D.F., Zhang W., Liu M.L. (2007), "Assessing the effect of land use/land cover change on the change of urban heat island intensity," *Theoretical and Applied Climatology*. doi: 10.1007/s00704-006-0273-1. http://www.springerlink.com/content/1434-4483/.

89. Lubos Motl, "RSS MSU: November 2007 was the coldest month since January 2000," Reference Frame blog, December 6, 2007, http://motls.blogspot.com/2007/12/rss-msu-november-2007-was-coldest-month.html; citing McKitrick, R. and Michaels, P., "Quantifying the influence of anthropogenic surface processes and inhomogeneities on gridded global climate data," Journal of Geophysical Research, Vol. 112, D24S09, doi:10.1029/2007JD008465, 2007, available at: http://www.uoguelph.ca/~rmckitri/research/jgr07/M&M.JGRDec07.pdf.

90. Keenan, "The Fraud allegation against some climatic research of Wei-Chung Wang," *Energy & Environment* · Vol. 18, No. 7 + 8, 2007, at 986.

Chapter 8: The Intergovernmental Panel on Climate Change

1. About the IPCC at www.IPCC.ch. See, e.g., http://www.ipcc.ch/about/about.htm.

2. IPCC AR4 WGI, Chapter 10, Global Climate Projections, p. 805, http://ipcc-wg1.ucar.edu/wg1/Report/AR4WG1_Print_Ch10.pdf.

3. See, e.g., "Dissenters are left high and dry in Bali," *Investor's Business Daily*, December 7, 2007.

4. Dr. Philip Stott, "Hunting the Climate Change Snark," Global Warming Politics blog, November 18, 2007, http://web.mac.com/sinfonia1/iWeb/ Global%20Warming%20Politics/A%20Hot%20Topic%20Blog/ CA1422FB-B3E5-4D06-B828-422738E3E832.html.

5. Ibid.

6. Secretary-General Ban Ki-moon, Address to the Intergovernmental Panel on Climate Change (IPCC) upon the release of its fourth assessment synthesis report, November 17, 2007, http://www.un.org/apps/news/infocus/sgspeeches/ statments_full.asp?statID=151.

7. "Skeptics Denied Press Credentials at UN Climate Meeting in Bali," NewsBusters.org, December 4, 2007, http://newsbusters.org/blogs/noel-sheppard/2007/12/04/skeptics-denied-press-credentials-un-climate-meeting-bali.

8. "Skeptical Scientists Kicked Off UN Press Schedule in Bali ... Again," News Release, December 13, 2007, http://www.breitbart.com/article.php?id=prnw.20071213.DC09846&show_article=1.

9. "World leaders discuss risks of rising temperatures," *The Hindu*, December 12, 2007.

10. "UN Admits to Long-term Alarmism over AIDS Epidemic," Daily Tech, November 20, 2007, http://www.dailytech.com/UN + Admits + to + Longterm + Alarmism + over + AIDS + Epidemic/article9725.htm

11. "UN to cut estimate of AIDS epidemic," *Washington Post*, November 20, 2007.

12. See, "Panel questions IPCC analysis: scientists find discrepancies in global warming," published in Eco-Logic, August 1992, 8. http://www.sepp.org/ Archive/controv/ipcccont/Item01.htm.

13. Frederick Seitz, "A Major Deception on Global Warming," *Wall Street Journal*, June 12, 1996, http://www.sepp.org/Archive/controv/ipcccont/Item05.htm.

14. "Letters to the Editor: No Deception in Global Warming Report," *Wall Street Journal*, June 25, 1996.

15. Ibid.

16. Ibid.

17. For a discussion of the meaning and impact of the changes, see Singer's "Letter to *Science*: Changes in the Climate Change Report," July 3, 1996, at http://www.sepp.org/Archive/controv/ipcccont/Item07.htm.

18. The Summary and the subsequently produced underlying work purportedly being summarized are available at http://ipcc-wg1.ucar.edu/wg1/wg1-report.html.

19. Intergovernmental Panel on Climate Change Fourth Assessment Report Climate Change 2007: Synthesis Report, Summary for Policymakers, 2007, http://www.ipcc.ch/pdf/assessment-report/ar4/syr/ar4_syr_spm.pdf.

20. Steven F. Hayward, Kenneth P. Green, and Joel Schwartz, "Politics Posing as Science: A Preliminary Assessment of the IPCC's Latest Climate Change

Report," American Enterprise Institute for Public Policy Research, Number 4, December 2007, http://www.joelschwartz.com/pdfs/Schwartz_IPCC_SR_analysis_120407.pdf.

21. John McLean, "The IPCC's dubious evidence for a human influence on climate," 1, first published at www.IceCap.us, October 2007, http://mclean.ch/climate/IPCC_evidence.pdf.

22. John McLean, "Peer review? What peer review? Failures of scrutiny in the UN's Fourth Assessment Report," Science and Public Policy Institute, September 2007, http://scienceandpublicpolicy.org/images/stories/papers/originals/mclean/mclean_IPCC_review_final_9-5-07.pdf.

23. Melanie Phillips, "Dirty work at the green crossroads," February 8, 2007, http://www.melaniephillips.com/diary/?p=1457.

24. "Uganda: Climate Change Increases Early Marriages - Report," *New Vision* (Uganda) as posted on AllAfrica.com, November 13, 2007, http://allafrica.com/stories/200711140057.html.

25. See, e.g., Ray Evans, "The Kyoto Protocol's statistical fallacies," Quadrant, May 1, 2003, quoting Pachauri on February 20, 2003 as saying in response to a question about skeptical scientists "About 300 years ago, a Flat Earth Society was founded by those who did not believe the world was round. That society still exists; it probably has about a dozen members."

26. Letters from Castles and Henderson to Pachauri, at http://downloads.heartland.org/11865.pdf.

27. See, e.g., IPCC Chair Trots out Hitler," http://www.globalwarming.org/node/595.

28. "IPCC Press Information on AR4 and Emissions Scenarios," Intergovernmental Panel on Climate Change, December 8, 2003, http://www.ipcc.ch/pdf/press-releases/pr-08december2003.pdf.

29. For discussion see, e.g., *The Economist* Magazine's "Hot Potato: Projecting greenhouse-gas emissions," February 13, 2003 and "Hot Potato Revisited: The IPCC and its critics," November 6, 2003.

30. Hoffert et al, "Advanced Technology Paths to Global Climate Stability: Energy for a Greenhouse Planet," *Science*, November 1, 2002, Vol. 298. no. 5595, 981–987 DOI: 10.1126/science.1072357.

31. "Dr. Alan Greenspan Speaks at CERAWeek 2008 on Recession, Credit Markets, Oil Prices, Nuclear Power, Cap & Trade," Cambridge Energy Research Associates, February 17, 2008, http://www.cera.com/aspx/cda/public1/news/pressReleases/pressReleaseDetails.aspx?CID=9290.

32. "Al Gore tipped to win Nobel," *The Times* (UK), October 7, 2007.

33. Then-European Union Commissioner for the Environment Margot Wallstrom said, "This is about international relations, this is about economy about trying to create a level playing field for big businesses throughout the world. You have to understand what is at stake and that is why it is serious," quoted by *The Independent* (London), March 19, 2002.

34. See, e.g., "Libya joins UN Security Council after leaving US terrorist list," *Times* of India, October 17, 2007.

35. See, e.g., "Annan slams Bush on global warming," BBC News, May 21, 2001, http://news.bbc.co.uk/1/hi/sci/tech/1341421.stm, and "Global warming is as serious as WMD," NewsBusters, November 15, 2006 http://www.newsbusters.org/node/9100.

36. "UN official warns of ignoring warming," Associated Press, November 12, 2007, http://news. yahoo.com/s/ap/20071112/ap_on_sc/ climate_change_conference;_ylt=AlPdBBJS8jlu_fFfBuQpslqs0NU.

37. "U.N. official says it's 'completely immoral' to doubt global warming fears," United Press International, May 10, 2007, http://www.upi.com/International_Intelligence/Analysis/2007/05/10/analysis_un_calls_climate_debate_over/6480/.

38. "Climate Change Behind Darfur's Killing: UN's Ban," Agence France Presse, June 16, 2005.

39. "Plants fighting back against African desert areas," Reuters, September 19, 2002, http://www.planetark.org/dailynewsstory.cfm/ newsid/17813/story. htm

40. Secretary-General Ban Ki-moon, Address to the Intergovernmental Panel on Climate Change (IPCC) upon the release of its fourth assessment synthesis report, November 17, 2007, http://www.un.org/apps/news/infocus/sgspeeches/statments_full.asp?statID=151.

41. See e.g., "Negotiators complete key document for policymakers on climate change," Associated Press, November 18, 2007, http://www.pr-inside.com/negotiators-complete-key-document-for-r305695.htm.

42. "Panel: Earth is rapidly getting warmer," Associated Press, November 17, 2007, http://apnews.myway.com/article/20071117/D8SVD6JG0.html.

43. Terry Corcoran, "Battle of the Nobel Climate Horror Disaster Movies," *National Post* (CA), November 20, 2007.

44. Steven F. Hayward, "Cooler Heads Prevail," National Review, October 22, 2007, available at http://www.aei.org/publications/pubID.26938, filter.all/pub_detail.asp.

45. Terry Corcoran, "Battle of the Nobel Climate Horror Disaster Movies," *National Post* (CA), November 20, 2007.

46. Wesley Pruden, "Need a legacy? Al's got a hot one," *Washington Times*, November 27, 2007.

47. John S. Jones and William T. Smith, "Warming not Man-made," *Washington Times*, November 25, 2007.

48. See, e.g., "Global warming: Earth cooled 0.05°C in the last 10 years," December 6, 2007, http://denerding.blogspot.com/2007/12/global-warming-earth-cooled-005c-in.html.

49. See, Letter from scientists to Ban Ki-moon, Secretary General of the United Nations, at e.g., "Don't fight, adapt," *National Post* (CA), December 12, 2007, http://www.nationalpost.com/news/story.html?id=164002.

50. See, IPCC, 2007: Summary for Policymakers. In: *Climate Change 2007: The Physical Science Basis. Contribution of Working Group I to the Fourth Assessment Report of the Intergovernmental Panel on Climate Change*, S. Solomon, D. Qin, M. Manning, Z. Chen, M. Marquis, K.B. Averyt, M.Tignor

and H.L. Miller, eds. (Cambridge: Cambridge University Press, 2007). Also available at http://ipcc-wg1.ucar.edu/wg1/Report/AR4WG1_Print_SPM.pdf.

51. This analysis is according to the review by researcher John McLean, at "Peer Review, What Peer Review?," Science and Public Policy Institute, September 6, 2007, http://scienceandpublicpolicy.org/sppi_originals/ peerreview. html. See also Marshall Institute Policy Outlook, "Working Group (WG) I's Contribution to the IPCC's Fourth Assessment Report (AR4): A Critique," George C. Marshall Institute, March 2007, 3, http://www.marshall.org/pdf/ materials/515.pdf.

52. John McLean, "Peer review? What peer review? Failures of scrutiny in the UN's Fourth Assessment Report," Science and Public Policy Institute, September 2007, http://scienceandpublicpolicy.org/images/stories/papers/originals/mclean/ mclean_IPCC_review_final_9-5-07.pdf, 24.

53. See letter from scientists to Ban Ki-moon, Secretary General of the United Nations, at e.g., "Don't fight, adapt," *National Post* (CA), December 12, 2007.

54. Andrew Dessler, "Inhofe's latest windmill: More bogus skepticism," *Grist Magazine*, December 21, 2007, http://gristmill.grist.org/story/2007/12/21/ 112933/48.

55. Dr. Sivan Kartha, Biography, Stockholm Environment Institute, Cf. Ibid. with http://www.sei.se/index.php?page=staffbiog&staffid=B6.

56. Dr. Tariq Banuri, Biography, Stockholm Environment Institute, See http:// www.sei.se/index.php?page=staffbiog&staffid=A1.

57. See, e.g., "Members of Gore's Nobel Prize-winning panel address global climate change," *Tufts Daily*, November 29, 2007.

58. As an aside, note that CP's head honcho, the gentleman wondering about the relevance of non-climatologists is Joe Romm. His Wikipedia entry, to which CAP's website refers readers, touts his expertise in, e.g., "energy efficiency, green energy technologies and green transportation technologies," but not climatology, and that "Romm's book on global warming, Hell and High Water, published in December 2006, claims that humans have a window of opportunity of only about a decade to head off the most catastrophic effects of global warming and calls upon Americans to demand government action to require the use of emission-cutting technologies that are available now. Romm was interviewed on Fox News about the book, the new IPCC Fourth Assessment Report on climate change, and global warming politics and solutions." (citations omitted) So, he's an activist, and one qualified to comment on the IPCC even if he had no idea who is involved. But others aren't.

59. "Inhofe recycles unscientific attacks on global warming; NYT's Revkin gives him a pass," Climate Progress, December 21, 2007, http://climateprogress. org/2007/12/21/debunking-inhofe-report-over-400-prominent-scientists- disputed-man-made-global-warming-claims-in-2007-andy-revkin/.

60. That only "climatologists" may opine was demanded by, e.g., *Grist Magazine's* Dave "Nuremburg-style trials," Roberts on Fox News Channel's "Hannity and Colmes" program, opposite me, on December 21, 2007. It was

also on spectacular display in DeSmogBlog's response, "400 Prominent Scientists Dispute Global Warming - Bunk," December 21, 2007, http://www.desmogblog. com/400-prominent-scientists-dispute-global-warming-bunk, which also mischaracterized the beliefs of cited skeptics, such as Eigil Friis-Christensen.

61. "The State of Climate Change Science 2007," Hearing Charter, Committee on Science and Technology U.S. House of Representatives, February 8, 2007, http://democrats.science.house.gov/Media/File/ Commdocs/hearings/2007/full/ 08feb/hearing_charter.pdf.

62. Andrew Dessler, "The 'Inhofe 400': Busting the 'consensus busters'," *Grist* Magazine, December 27, 2007, http://gristmill.grist.org/story/2007/12/26/1971/ 6517.

63. See, e.g., Lead Author Bert Metz, http://www.technewsworld.com/story/ 60306.html.

64. See, e.g., Howard University professor Joshua Halpern, who anonymously writes his nasty, name-calling blog under the pseudonym Eli Rabbett.

65. Walter Gibbs and Sarah Lyall, "Gore Shares Peace Prize for Climate Change Work," *The New York Times*, October 13, 2007.

66. Alexander G. Hibbins, "Gore, Scientist Share Nobel Peace Prize," *USA Today*, October 12, 2007, http://www.usatoday.com/tech/science/2007-10-12-1979965791_x.htm (called a "climatologist" in photo caption).

67. "Al Gore tipped to win Nobel," *The Times* (UK), October 7, 2007.

68. Charles J. Hanley, "UN: US States, cities can impact climate," Boston.com, December 7, 2007, See, e.g., http://www.boston.com/news/world/asia/articles/ 2007/12/07/un_us_states_cities_can_impact_ climate, in which the *Boston Globe* also incorrectly calls him a "climatologist."

69. Dr. R.K. Pachauri, Biography, US Climate Change Science Program, See, e.g., http://www.climatescience.gov/Library/bios/pachauri.htm and http://en. wikipedia.org/wiki/Rajendra_K._Pachauri.

70. "Remember those 400 'Scientists' Against Global Warming? Turns out it's a very sketchy list including a lot of economists," Crooks and Liars blog, December 24, 2007, http://www.crooksandliars.com/2007/12/24/dont-believe-inhofes-hype/.

71. "Physician heal thyself," Climate Resistance, December 28, 2007, http://www.climate-resistance.org/2007/12/physician-heal-thyself.html.

72. See, e.g., "Climate Talk's Cancellation Splits a Town," *New York Times*, January 17, 2008.

73. Rami Zurayk, "Senate skeptics," Land and People blog, December 27, 2007, http://landandpeople.blogspot.com/2007/12/senate-skeptics.html, page viewed December 28, 2007; Zurayk's relevant information is found at http://www.ncb.gov.jo/content/memberDetail.php?memberID=118.

74. Brendan O'Neill, "Apocalypse my arse," *Spiked* Online, March 9, 2007, http://www.spiked-online.com/index.php?/site/article/2948/.

75. See, e.g,, "Further reports announced by climate-change panel," 16 April 2008 | Nature | doi:10.1038/452796b, http://www.nature.com/news/2008/

080416/full/452796b.html, and "IPCC Tunes Up for Its Next Report Aiming for Better, Timely Results," Science 18 April 2008: Vol. 320. no. 5874, p. 300, DOI: 10.1126/science.320.5874.300, http://www.sciencemag.org/cgi/content/full/320/5874/300.

76. "Survey of IPCC Climate Experts," DemandDebate.com, November 8, 2007, See http://www.DemandDebate.com/ipcc_survey.pdf.

77. Hansen, et al., "Climate forcings in the Industrial era," Proceedings of the National Academy of Science, Vol. 95, 12753, 1998.

78. John Christy, "Viewpoint," BBC, November 14, 2007, http://news.bbc.co.uk/2/hi/science/nature/7081331.stm.

79. William M. Briggs, "Statistics' dirtiest secret," Statistician blog, February 18, 2008, http://wmbriggs.com/blog/2008/02/18/statistics-dirtiest-secret/, (emphases in original).

80. United Nations Intergovernmental Panel on Climate Change, Third Assessment Report, 2001b, 37.

81. Middlebury.net/op-ed/global-warming-01.html.

82. Roy W. Spencer, "Hey, Nobel Prize winners, answer me this," Science and Public Policy Institute, March 15, 2008, http://scienceandpublicpolicy.org/images/stories/papers/commentaries/nobel_winners_answer_me.pdf.

83. Steven McIntyre, "Kiehl (2007) on Tuning GCMs," Climate Audit, December 1, 2007, http://www.climateaudit.org/?p=2475#more-2475, citing Kiehl, J. T. (2007), Twentieth century climate model response and climate sensitivity, Geophys. Res. Lett., 34, L22710, doi:10.1029/2007GL031383.

84. Kesten C. Green and J. Scott Armstrong, "Global Warming: Forecasts by Scientists Versus Scienfitic Forecasts," Reprinted from Energy & Environment, vol. 18, no. 7 & 8, 2007, http://www.forecastingprinciples.com/Public_Policy/WarmAudit31.pdf.

85. "The Climate Bet" post of February 14, 2008, http://theclimatebet.com/2008/02/14/gore-proposes-new-condition-on-climate-forecasting-challenge-armstrong-accepts-and-awaits-a-reply/, viewed September 29, 2008.

86. See, e.g., "Dissenters are left high and dry in Bali," Investor's Business Daily, December 7, 2007, http://www.investors.com/editorial/editorialcontent.asp?secid=1501&status=article&id=281923042847901.

87. Lawrence Solomon, "Bitten by the IPCC," National Post, March 23, 2007, http://www.nationalpost.com/news/story.html?id=0ea8dc23-ad1a-440f-a8dd-1e3ff42df34f&p=1.

88. Roger Pielke Sr., "The 2007 IPCC Assessment Process - Its Obvious Conflict of Interest," September 1, 2007, http://climatesci.colorado.edu/2007/09/01/the-2007-ipcc-assessment-process-its-obvious-conflict-of-interest.

89. For discussion, see Horner, The Politically Incorrect Guide to Global Warming and Environmentalism, 119–131.

90. IPCC Fourth Assessment Report, Working Group I, "The Physical Science Basis," Chapter 6 "Paleoclimate," 466–474, http://www.ipcc.ch/pdf/assessment-report/ar4/wg1/ar4-wg1-chapter6.pdf.

91. See respectively, "Ad Hoc Committee Report on the 'Hockey Stick' Global Climate Reconstruction," for the Chairmen of the U.S. House Committee on Energy and Commerce and of the Subcommittee on Oversight and Investigations, Edward J. Wegman, David W. Scott, and Yasmin H. Said, National Academies of Sciences (Wegman Report), http://www.climateaudit. org/pdf/others/07142006_ Wegman_Report.pdf, and "Surface temperature reconstructions for the past 2,000 years" ("North Report"), Committee on Surface Temperature Reconstructions for the Last 2,000 Years," Board on Atmospheric Sciences and Climate, Division on Earth and Life Studies, National Research Council of the National Academies, (Washington: National Academies Press, 2006), http://books.nap.edu/openbook.php?isbn=0309102251.

92. See e.g., Testimony of Edward Wegman, United States House of Representatives, Committee on Energy and Commerce, July 27, 2006, 3, http:// republicans.energycommerce.house.gov/108/hearings/07272006Hearing2001/ Wegman.pdf.

93. Wegman, et al, 48.

94. See e.g., Testimony of Edward Wegman, United States House of Representatives, Committee on Energy and Commerce, July 27, 2006, 2–3, http://republicans.energycommerce.house.gov/108/hearings/07272006Hearing20 01/Wegman.pdf.

95. Wegman et al. 4–5.

96. Ibid., 28.

97. Ibid.

98. "Ad Hoc Committee Report on the 'Hockey Stick' Global Climate Reconstruction," Wegman, et al. (2006), 5, http://www.climateaudit.org/pdf/ others/07142006_Wegman_Report.pdf

99. As this book went to publication, Mann and colleagues had just released an effort to rehabilitate the Hockey Stick and all that its defrocking wrought. Thanks to more open access, statisticians and others immediately exposed it for, among other things, having cherry-picked 11 percent of the relevant data with an apparent bias toward those providing positive results. See, e.g., discussion at ClimateAudit.org and NoConsensus.wordpress.com blogs which published focused analyses.

100. See also William Briggs, "Statisticians global warming plea: don't forget about us!" January 17th, 2008, http://wmbriggs.com/blog/2008/01/17/ statisticians-global-warming-plea-dont-forget-about-us/.

101. Christopher Landsea, "Open letter to the Community," January 17, 2005, http://www.tsaugust.org/Landsea_Letter.htm.

102. Ibid.

103. Hans LaBohm, "Klimakatastrophenzweifel—eine Einführung," NOVO, January/February 2007, http://www.novo-magazin.de/86/novo8624.htm.

104. IPCC home page, http://www.ipcc.ch/, viewed on October 9, 2007.

105. Various caveats made it possible for research to be cited if not published or in draft form by that date, but clearly this increased the likelihood that its inclusion would be even less subject to the IPCC's touted, and debunked, claim

to stringent peer review. See, e.g., "IPCC Working Group I, Schedule for Fourth Assessment Report," UN IPCC, http://ipcc-wg1.ucar.edu/wg1/docs/wg1_timetable_2006-08-14.pdf.

106. Roy W. Spencer, William D. Braswell, John R. Christy, and Justin Hnilo, "Cloud and radiation budget changes associated with tropical intraseasonal oscillations," *Geophysical Research Letters*, Vol. 34, L15707, doi:10.1029/2007GL029698, 2007, http://www.agu.org/pubs/crossref/2007/2007GL029698.shtml. It appears also that leading alarmists support this, see, e.g., Kevin Trenberth's comments at "The mystery of global warming's missing heat," http://www.npr.org/templates/story/story.php?storyId=88520025.

107. See, e.g., Anastasios A. Tsonis, Kyle Swanson, and Sergey Kravtsov: Atmospheric Sciences Group, Department of Mathematical Sciences, University of Wisconsin-Milwaukee, Milwaukee, Wisconsin, U.S.A. See August 2, 2007 *Science Daily*—"Synchronized Chaos: Mechanisms For Major Climate Shifts," discussed at http://www.sciencedaily.com/releases/2007/08/070801175711.htm.

108. See, e.g., Svensmark et al., "Reply to Lockwood and Fröhlich—The persistent role of the Sun in climate forcing," Danish National Space Center, DNSC-Scientific report 3/2007 (PDF) at http://www.spacecenter.dk/publications/scientific-report-series/Scient_No._3.pdf/view; see also other studies and scientists confirmed the solar-climate link at http://scienceandpublicpolicy.org/sppi_reprint_series/a_critique _on_the_lockwood_ frochlich_paper_in_the_royal_society_proceedings.html, http://www.globalwarminghysteria.com/blog/2007/7/17/no-sun-link-study-debunked-again.html, and http://scienceandpublicpolicy.org/sppi_originals/the_unruly_sunne_cannot_be_ruled_out_as_a_cause_of_recent_climate_variation.html.

109. Charles D. Camp and Ka Kit Tung: Department of Applied Mathematics, University of Washington, Seattle, Washington, *Geophysical Research Letters* (GRL) paper 10.1029/2007GL030207, 2007, discussed at http://www.sciencedaily.com/releases/2007/08/070801174450.htm; as discussed elsewhere in these pages, although one of the co-authors protests this study being cited in opposition to alarmism, in reality the paper is an important contribution affirming the solar-climate link.

110. Letter to the editor, *The Hill* (Ottawa, Canada), May 28, 2007, at http://www.hilltimes.com/html/cover_index.php?display=story&full_path=/2007/may/28/letter4/&c=1; See also related letters by Tim Ball and Tom Harris at the same URL.

111. Lawrence Solomon, "Bitten by the IPCC," *National Post* (Canada), March 23, 2007.

112. John McLean, "Peer review? What peer review? Failures of scrutiny in the UN's Fourth Assessment Report," Science and Public Policy Institute, September 2007, http://scienceandpublicpolicy.org/images/stories/papers/originals/mclean/mclean_IPCC_review_final_9-5-07.pdf, page 4.

113. Ibid.

114. Ibid., 7 (emphasis in original).

115. Ibid.

116. John McLean, "An Analysis of the Review of the IPCC 4AR WG I Report," October 2007, 12, http://mclean.ch/climate/IPCC_review_updated_analysis.pdf.

117. John McLean, "Peer review? What peer review? Failures of scrutiny in the UN's Fourth Assessment Report," Science and Public Policy Institute, September 2007, 8, http://scienceandpublicpolicy.org/images/stories/papers/originals/mclean/mclean_IPCC_review_final_9-5-07.pdf.

118. Ibid.

119. See e.g., "Climate Science Anything but 'Clear', Mr. Baird: UN Climate Agency's implication that 2,500 scientist reviewers agree with its report is a deception," Media Release, Natural Resources Stewardship Project, November 19, 2007, http://www.nrsp.com/releases/release-07.11.19.html. JunkScience.com posted the draft scientific reports, revealing the truth to all who claim to be genuinely concerned, at http://www.junkscience.com/ draft_AR4/.

120. Ibid., 4.

121. Lawrence Solomon, "Bitten by the IPCC," National Post (CA), March 23, 2007.

122. John McLean, "An Analysis of the Review of the IPCC 4AR WG I Report," October 2007, 6, http://mclean.ch/climate/IPCC_review_updated_analysis.pdf.

123. See e.g., "Negotiators complete key document for policymakers on climate change," Associated Press, November 18, 2007, http://www.pr-inside.com/negotiators-complete-key-document-for-r305695.htm.

124. Philip Stott, "Reality, Rhetoric and Risk," Global Warming Politics, November 17, 2007, http://web.mac.com/sinfonia1/iWeb/Global%20Warming%20Politics/A%20Hot%20Topic%20Blog/2C451496-B754-4C7D-A378-9A5FED7BE27F.html.

125. John Christy, "Viewpoint," BBC, November 14, 2007, http://news.bbc.co.uk/2/hi/science/nature/7081331.stm.

126. Ibid.

127. See, e.g., Roger Pielke Jr., "Whose political agenda is reflected in the IPCC Working Group 1, Scientists or Politicians?" Prometheus blog, March 26, 2007 http://sciencepolicy.colorado.edu/prometheus/archives/ author_pielke_jr_r/index.html#001148, and Syun-Ichi Akasofu, "On the fundamental defect in the IPCC's approach to global warming research," http://climatesci.colorado.edu/2007/06/15/on-the-fundamental-defect-in-the-ipcc%e2%80%99s-approach-to-global-warming-research-by-syun-ichi-akasofu/.

128. Sen. James Inhofe floor speech, October 26, 2007, see press release, "Inhofe Debunks So-Called 'Consensus' On Global Warming," http://epw.senate.gov/public/index.cfm?FuseAction=Minority.Blogs&ContentRecord_id=595F6F41-802A-23AD-4BC4-B364B623ADA3.

129. "Delegates debate urgency of climate change in key policy report," Associated Press, April 4, 2007, http://www.iht.com/articles/ap/2007/04/04/europe/EU-GEN-Belgium-Climate-Report.php.

130. Ibid.

Index